Dylan —
Here's wishing you
many joyous meals
of your own
creation.

Love, Dad

BIRTHDAY '04

Vegetables Every Day

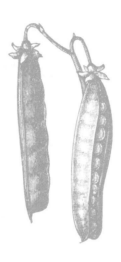

ALSO BY JACK BISHOP

Pasta e Verdura

Vegetables Every Day

THE DEFINITIVE GUIDE TO BUYING AND COOKING TODAY'S PRODUCE, WITH MORE THAN 350 RECIPES

Jack Bishop

HarperCollins*Publishers*

HarperCollins books may be purchased for educational, business, or sales promotional use. For information, please write: Special Markets Department, HarperCollins Publishers Inc., 10 East 53rd Street, New York, NY 10022.

FIRST EDITION

Printed on acid-free paper

Library of Congress Cataloging-in-Publication Data
Bishop, Jack.
   Vegetables every day : the definitive guide to buying and
   cooking today's produce, with more than 350 recipes/
   Jack Bishop.
      p. cm.
   ISBN 0-06-019221-6 (hardcover)
   1. Cookery (Vegetables)   2. Vegetables.   I. Title.
   TX801.B58 2001
   641.6'5—dc21   00-040823

01 02 03 04 05 ❖/RRD 10 9 8 7 6 5 4 3 2

To Rose and Eve

Eat your vegetables, please.

Contents

Acknowledgments

MY AGENT, ANGELA MILLER, HAS BEEN A TRUE FRIEND AND AD-VISER FOR ALMOST A DECADE. Much of my success and good fortune is due to her unflagging efforts on my behalf.

Thank you to my editor, Susan Friedland, for recognizing the potential in my original proposal and then helping me realize my vision in this book. I appreciate the efforts of the Harper-Collins team, including Vanessa Stich, Estelle Laurence, Sue Llewellyn, Betty Lew, and Roni Axelrod.

My colleagues at *Cook's Illustrated* have been my food family for many years. Thanks to Barbara Bourassa, Chris Kimball, Amy Klee, Kay Rentschler, Adam Ried, Doc Willoughby, Anne Yamanaka, and Dawn Yanagihara.

My friend Nice Polido spent hundreds of hours in the kitchen cooking with me through many long days of recipe testing. I appreciate her good food sense and good humor.

Thanks to the staff at the Green Thumb in Water Mill, New York, for specially picking veg-etables from their marvelous organic farm so I could test recipes.

My in-house tasters include my wife, Lauren Chattman, our daughters, Rose and Eve, and their baby-sitter, Yvette Willock. Thanks to all of them for many fun hours of tasting and critiquing recipes.

Introduction

VEGETABLES ARE THE HEART OF ALL MEALS IN MY HOME. THEY ARE WHAT CONNECT ME AND my family to the season and to our neighbors. In October, we eat the brilliant white cauliflower pulled from local fields. In January, it's turnip greens and potatoes. By May, local asparagus is in season, and the summer brings a bumper crop of tomatoes, zucchini, and corn.

Perhaps I love vegetables so much because I never know exactly what I'm going to get. In this mechanized age, where chicken tastes the same 365 days of the year and where shoppers in places as far-flung as Italy, the Dominican Republic, Japan, and the United States can all buy the same brand of pasta, vegetables refuse to be standardized.

Plant scientists, geneticists, and some farmers have tried to produce a tomato that looks and tastes the same 365 days of the year. I am thankful that they have failed. Vegetables remain untamed.

I go to my farmstand several times a week and never know what I'm going to find. This week's eggplant may look and taste quite different from the eggplant I bought last week at the same stand.

Each vegetable at the market tells its own story. There are so many choices and factors that influence its appearance and flavor. The farmer has numerous seed options—everything from heirloom varieties to modern hybrids bred for all kinds of reasons. The time of year that the plant was grown, the soil, the amount and frequency of the rainfall, how and when the vegetable was picked—these factors all affect us every time we shop for sweet potatoes or green beans. Of course, how the vegetable has been handled during shipping and at the market is also of critical importance.

Because of all these variables, the same vegetable tastes a bit different each time it is prepared. This tremendous variation in quality may be one reason why many modern cooks have gotten themselves into a rut when it comes to vegetable cookery. Most cooks I know prepare the same half dozen vegetables over and over again. They cook what they know and strive for consistency—a goal that always proves elusive. They are afraid of taking a chance.

This is a shame since vegetable selection has never been better in this country. The average American supermarket now carries almost 400 kinds of vegetables and fruits during the course of the year. At any given time, most supermarkets have at least 50 vegetables in the produce aisle.

This tremendous selection is the result of several factors. Many dedicated small farmers have made a commitment to vegetables or varieties that were in danger of falling out of fashion. My favorite local farm grows everything from burdock to sorrel as well as ten kinds of chiles and six kinds of heirloom tomatoes, all on just eighty acres.

Recent waves of immigration from Asia and Latin America have transformed the produce aisle in most of America. Even though the immigrant population in my area is relatively low, my local supermarket regularly stocks jicama and chayote as well as bok choy and daikon radishes.

In addition to this wide selection of vegetables (the best-ever in history), modern cooks have access to more flavoring ideas and cuisines than ever before. Thirty years ago my mother (as well as most American mothers) prepared asparagus the same way—it was steamed and sauced with butter, lemon, or hollandaise. That's how you cooked asparagus.

Today, my mother is just as likely to roast asparagus with rosemary and garlic, Italian style, or dress spears with a Thai peanut sauce. We have the world and its flavors at our fingertips.

While I find these choices and possibilities invigorating, I know many cooks are overwhelmed. I have written this book to help guide you through the process of buying and cooking all the vegetables you are likely to see at supermarkets and farmers' markets, as well as some of the more versatile and popular vegetables you will see at ethnic markets.

Throughout the book, I have developed recipes with accessibility in mind. I have kept the techniques simple and the ingredient lists short. Flavors are interesting and varied but I have not been a slave to tradition. I taken the best ideas from Thai, Mexican, Caribbean, Japanese, Italian, Chinese, French, and Indian cuisines and used them to create simple, sensible recipes for modern American cooks.

You know vegetables are good for you. You don't need medical studies to tell you what is obvious. What I have attempted to do in this book is to make vegetables approachable, easy, and interesting. You want to eat vegetables every day. You want to eat vegetables that are simple to prepare yet delicious. I hope this book can help.

How to Use This Book

The book is organized alphabetically by vegetable or category of vegetables. Some entries refer to a single vegetable (such as asparagus), while others refer to a category of vegetables (such as winter squash and pumpkin) that can be prepared and cooked in pretty much the same fashion.

After a brief introduction that explains the general shopping and cooking issues and lists any major varieties you need to know about, each entry is divided into the following sections:

OTHER COMMON NAMES: These are the vegetable names you may see when shopping, especially at ethnic markets.

AVAILABILITY: Many vegetables are now available 12 months of the year. I have indicated the traditional season where appropriate.

SELECTION: Good vegetable cookery begins with good shopping. Each entry describes how the vegetable should look when fresh. I have also listed some signs that indicate when a vegetable is over the hill. In many cases, I find that size is an important consideration (smaller is usually, but not always, better) and have offered my recommendations where appropriate.

STORAGE: Most vegetables will do best in a loosely sealed plastic bag in the vegetable crisper drawer. Don't seal the bag completely; you don't want to trap moisture and thus hasten softening. Leave the top of the bag open or poke a few holes in a bag that is sealed.

When storing leafy greens, you may want to blot up some of the excess moisture when you get home. Many markets mist vegetables to keep them fresh-looking. However, all that moisture can cause rot to develop. If your spinach or let-tuce is swimming in water when you get home, take it out of the bag, blot it dry, and then drop it into a dry bag.

Many root vegetables do best in a cool pantry, away from the sunlight. You can store many of these vegetables in the refrigerator, but they will not last as long.

BASIC PREPARATION: All preparation begins with washing. In the case of most vegetables, a quick rinse under cool, running water is fine. Root vegetables should be scrubbed with a small vegetable brush with bristles that are firm but not sharp.

Leafy greens require a somewhat more complicated washing regimen since tiny bits of sand tend to cling to leaves. I place leafy greens in a large bowl of cold water and swish them around in the water with my hands to loosen any dirt. Lift the greens out of the water and rub your hand along the bottom of the bowl. If you see or feel any grit, dump out the water, rinse the bowl, add fresh water, and then return the greens for another round of swishing. Keep repeating this process until the water and bowl are clean.

Once washed, leafy greens should be gently shaken to remove excess water. If the greens are destined for the salad bowl, they should be thoroughly dried in a salad spinner and then on paper towels.

In addition to a salad spinner, there are a couple of other pieces of equipment you will use over and over again when preparing vegetables. A paring knife is essential for peeling many root vegetables. A chef's knife is better for most chopping, mincing, or slicing tasks.

The other "must-have" tool when preparing vegetables is a peeler. If you have an old-fashioned metal peeler with a dull blade that swivels, throw it out. A couple of years ago I bought a super-sharp peeler with a comfortable black plastic handle. The Oxo Good Grips peeler is sharp enough to skin a tomato and sturdy enough to make quick work of a knobby root vegetable or hard squash. I consider it indispensable.

BEST COOKING METHODS: Each entry lists the cooking methods that deliver the best results with that particular vegetable. However, just because a cooking method isn't listed doesn't mean you can't prepare a vegetable that way. Think of this list as my favorite or recommended cooking methods.

I find it helpful to think of cooking methods as either moist heat or dry heat. Moist-heat cooking methods will preserve color and cause the texture to soften. Moist-heat cooking methods can wash away some flavor, especially if the cooking time is prolonged. Often, vegetables are cooked by moist heat to soften their texture and then they are cooked by dry heat for flavor and crispness.

Dry-heat cooking methods drive off moisture (all vegetables have a high percentage of water) and cause browning, which builds flavor. As a result, vegetables cooked by dry heat are crisper and generally more flavorful than vegetables cooked by moist heat.

Boiling, poaching, and steaming are all moist-heat cooking methods. *Boiling* involves cooking food directly in boiling liquid, usually water. *Poaching* is much the same, except that the heat is

very low or turned off and the cover is placed on the pot. This method is more gentle than boiling since the water is not agitated. *Steaming* is different from boiling and poaching because the food is cooked above the water, not in it. As a result, the flavor and texture of the vegetable are better preserved.

Many cooks, myself included, use the term *blanching* when referring to vegetable cookery. Blanching is the same thing as boiling but implies that the food has been cooked very briefly (and not completely) in order to set the color and soften the texture. Many green vegetables are blanched, drained, and then sautéed.

Dry-heat cooking methods including grilling, broiling, roasting, sautéing (or stir-frying), or frying (both pan-frying and deep-frying).

Grilling and *broiling* are very similar. Foods are usually lightly coated with oil to prevent sticking and encourage browning. With grilling, the heat source comes from below; with broiling, the heat comes from above. Grill heat is usually more intense and causes more browning and better evaporation of moisture than broiling. For this reason, grilling is my preference in most recipes, although the broiler is a fine second choice in almost every instance. Timing will be different in the broiler, but if you follow the visual clues given in grilled vegetable recipes you will have no trouble adapting them for the broiler.

If you own a gas grill, you may opt (as I often do) to light the grill simply to cook a vegetable or two. If you grill over charcoal, recipes that call for grilling a vegetable make sense only when lighting a fire to cook fish, poultry, or meat. Purists rightly argue that charcoal gives fish, poultry, and meat a better flavor and crust than gas. However, since vegetables spend so little time on the grill, the differences between gas and charcoal are minimal.

Roasting occurs in the oven, usually at temperatures of 400 degrees or higher. Foods are usually coated with oil to promote browning and they are cooked on a rimmed baking sheet. Roasted foods should be turned at least once to promote even browning. Because foods that are roasted usually cook for quite a long time (up to an hour), they shed a tremendous amount of moisture and shrink in volume as they cook.

Sautéing and *stir-frying* are two words that describe the same technique. In each case, food is cooked in a light film of hot fat in a pan on top of the stove. Usually the food is cut small (or is thin) so that it will cook through quickly. Make sure to use the right size pan (foods piled up in a small skillet will steam rather than sauté) and to use enough heat. If the heat is too low, you won't get as much browning and the food won't taste as good.

Frying involves cooking food that is partially or completely submerged in hot oil. When sautéing or stir-frying, you measure the cooking oil by the tablespoon. When frying, you measure oil by the cup. *Pan-frying* occurs in a large skillet in a shallow depth of oil, usually between ⅛ and ½ inch. *Deep-frying* involves more oil, at least an inch and perhaps 2 inches of oil measured into a deep pot.

Make sure to use the proper size pot when deep-frying. When food is added to hot oil, the oil can rise dramatically. If the pot is too small, the oil can rise right out of the pot and onto your stove, causing a very dangerous situation.

Always fry in small batches so that the temperature of the oil does not drop precipitously. If the oil is not hot enough, the food will taste greasy. When deep-frying, you will need a candy/deep-frying thermometer. Clip this thermometer (which should register temperatures up to 400 degrees) onto the side of the pot before you start. When pan-frying, there's not enough oil to use a thermometer. Look for visual clues (the oil will shimmer when it is hot, but not smoke) or try adding a small cube of bread to make sure that it sizzles immediately on contact with the oil.

Braising offers a combination of dry and moist heat. The most common kind of braising starts with sautéing to brown a vegetable lightly. A little liquid is added to the pan, the pan is covered, and the vegetable cooks (by steam heat) until tender. In some cases, a little fat and liquid may be added at the outset, the vegetable is cooked in a covered pan until tender, and then the cover is removed and the vegetable is cooked until the liquid evaporates and the vegetable browns in the remaining fat.

Either way, braising offers many of the benefits of both moist and dry heat. Vegetables cooked this way are tender but flavorful. The key to successful braising is a pan (usually a sauté pan with straight sides) that has a tight-fitting lid.

OTHER RECIPES: Most entries end with a list of other recipes that may be of interest. Recipes have been listed for several reasons. If the vegetable being discussed in a particular chapter plays a major supporting role in a dish elsewhere in the book, that dish will be listed. For instance, a recipe for roasted carrots and onions that appears in the carrots chapter, will be cross-referenced in the onion chapter. However, I have not listed every recipe in the book that calls for a particular vegetable. For instance, dishes that include a minced onion or two are generally not cross-referenced in the onion chapter because the onion plays a rather insignificant role in these dishes.

I have also mentioned recipes that could be prepared with the vegetable being discussed. For example, most spinach recipes can be made with chard. The chard listing will alert you to this fact.

Notes About Some Important Ingredients

I have been fairly specific in recipes about the kinds of ingredients I want you to use. Vegetable dishes are usually quite simple and succeed only when the highest-quality seasonings are used. Here are a couple of general points to keep in mind.

OILS: When I want to add flavor, I usually opt for extra-virgin olive oil. (Don't bother with lesser grades of olive oil.) For an Asian dish, I usually choose roasted peanut oil (this kind of peanut oil is not highly refined and actually smells and tastes like peanuts). Loriva peanut oil (available in many supermarkets and natural food stores) is your best bet. I also use toasted (or dark) sesame oil for flavor. This oil has a very strong flavor and must be used in small amounts, generally as a seasoning rather than as a cooking fat. Walnut oil is too strong-tasting for cooking but makes an excellent addition to a salad dressing.

There are occasions when I don't want flavor from cooking oil. For instance, an Indian dish made with curry, ginger, and garlic may taste a bit odd with olive oil, or another of the flavorful oils. In these cases, I chose canola or one of the other neutral-tasting (or flavorless) oils. You can substitute as you like in these recipes—using canola, vegetable, corn, safflower, or refined peanut oil—since flavor is not an issue.

For frying, I generally prefer refined peanut oil because it has such a high smoke point. Vegetable oil is fine here, as are the other tasteless oils.

SALT AND PEPPER: Salt and pepper are used in the vast majority of recipes in this book. I use kosher salt in my kitchen. I like its clean flavor (many table salts have chemical additives) and the large crystals, which are easy to pick up between my thumb and forefinger. I keep a ramekin filled with salt near the stove. As for pepper, I grind my own black peppercorns as needed. Keep a grinder right next to the salt.

I recommend that you season at several points in the cooking process. If blanching or boiling a vegetable, I usually salt the water. I often add salt and pepper with other ingredients when braising or stewing, taste the dish when it is done, and adjust the seasonings, adding more salt and pepper as needed. Try not to wait until the very end of the cooking process to add salt and pepper. (Sometimes this cannot be helped.) Food that is seasoned as it cooks has a chance to absorb the salt and pepper and it's not just the surface that is well seasoned.

HERBS: I rarely use dried herbs. Their texture is powdery and not appropriate in most quick-cooking vegetable dishes. Fresh herbs are far superior, adding their bright flavor to countless recipes in this book. If a recipe calls for fresh basil, it's better to use fresh parsley, cilantro, or mint instead than to use dried basil.

When making substitutions, keep in mind the intensity of the herb that is called for in a recipe and the herb you are using. Leafy, soft herbs like basil, parsley, mint, chives, and cilantro are used in much greater amounts than drier, more potent herbs such as sage, rosemary, oregano, and thyme.

PARMESAN CHEESE: Parmesan adds a buttery, nutty finish to many vegetable dishes. Use the real thing, Parmigiano-Reggiano from Italy. Buy hunks with the rind still attached and look for the words Parmigiano-Reggiano stenciled on the rind. Yes, this cheese can be expensive (expect to pay as much as $12 to $14 a pound), but you generally use so little. Don't skimp here and try to use lesser grades of Parmesan (from the United States or elsewhere) or, God forbid, grated cheese from a jar.

TOMATOES: Canned tomatoes are another staple ingredient used in countless dishes. For convenience, I use Muir Glen Diced Tomatoes, which are nothing more than diced organic California tomatoes packed with some tomato juice and salt. These tomatoes are recipe-ready (no need to chop whole tomatoes) and delicious.

STOCKS: I use chicken and vegetable stock in many recipes in this book. I prefer homemade stock but use store-bought broth if you like. I find that Swanson's or Campbell's low-sodium chicken broth is the best. It has a decent chicken flavor and is not overwhelmed by salt, as are many other brands.

Among vegetable broths, stick with something from your natural food stores. I like Pacific Foods Organic Vegetable Broth, which comes in a bright yellow aseptic carton. Unlike many canned broths that are too sweet (one brand is orange from so many carrots), Pacific Foods Organic Vegetable Broth is savory, and no single vegetable dominates.

Vegetables Every Day

Artichokes

Fresh artichokes require a lot of effort on the part of the cook, and they are not really an "everyday" vegetable. However, if you have the 20 minutes it takes to clean a few artichokes, you will be rewarded with meaty texture and complex flavor that only fresh artichokes can deliver.

There are two ways to think about cooking an artichoke. Moist heat (steaming or braising) makes the flesh especially creamy and tender. Dry heat (grilling, roasting, or sautéing) crisps the edges of the leaves and makes them crunchy and delicious. I prefer the latter cooking methods, but both have their merits.

AVAILABILITY: Spring is the traditional season for artichokes, although you may see them through the summer and a second California crop comes to market in the early fall.

SELECTION: When shopping, remember that an artichoke is a flower bud. A tightly closed, heavy artichoke is fresher than one that has opened up and feels light. Try bending back an outer leaf. If it snaps off, the artichoke is fresh. Leaves on older artichokes are more pliable and will bend all the way back. The color should be green, with no brown or yellow spots.

Artichokes vary in size from golf balls to softballs. Avoid really large artichokes—they can be woody. Medium artichokes (about 8 ounces each) offer the best combination of quality and ease of preparation. Smaller artichokes may require less cooking time but can be tedious to clean.

I always buy artichokes with the stems attached. Once peeled, the stem is delicious, almost as good as the heart.

STORAGE: Artichokes will keep for several days in a loosely sealed plastic bag in the refrigerator.

BASIC PREPARATION: There are two possible modes of attack. You can trim away all inedible portions (as I have done in all but the last recipe in this chapter) so that what reaches the table can be eaten easily. Although a lot of work for the cook, this method is my preference. Besides making the dining experience easier and less messy, I find that you have more cooking options when artichokes have been trimmed.

The other school of thought is to remove the inedible portions that are easily trimmed (such as the pointed tips of the leaves) but not to bother with the hard-to-reach fuzzy choke. The whole artichokes are steamed and each person must separate the edible from the inedible at the table with their teeth and a knife and fork. (See the steamed artichoke recipe on page 7.) Artichokes prepared this way are usually boiled or steamed (I prefer steaming, which washes away less flavor) and then served with mayonnaise or vinaigrette.

No matter how you are preparing artichokes, they will turn gray as soon as they are cut. Although you can't prevent all discoloration, rubbing the cut surfaces on the artichoke with a lemon half as you work will help retain some of the bright green color. Squeeze the other lemon half into a bowl of cold water and drop the trimmed artichokes in this acidulated water to prevent further discoloration as you prepare subsequent artichokes and other ingredients.

BEST COOKING METHODS: Braising, grilling, or steaming. Thinly sliced artichokes can be roasted or sautéed.

Crisp Pan-Fried Artichoke Slices with Garlic

If you slice trimmed artichokes thin enough, they will become crisp and crunchy when sautéed in olive oil. The keys here are to use a large skillet (so the artichokes aren't piled too high) and to cook them over medium heat. (At higher heat, the artichokes will brown before they really soften.) Artichokes cooked this way are delicious on their own (I sometimes serve this as a snack while everyone stands around the kitchen watching me prepare dinner) or as a side dish with chicken or fish.

SERVES 4 AS A SIDE DISH

- 1 lemon, halved
- 4 medium artichokes (about 2 pounds total weight)
- ⅓ cup extra-virgin olive oil
- 2 large garlic cloves, peeled
  Salt
  Freshly ground black pepper

1. Squeeze half of the lemon into a large bowl of cold water; add the lemon half to the bowl. Use the other lemon half to rub over cut surfaces as you prepare the artichokes. Working with one artichoke at a time, bend back and snap off the tough outer leaves. Remove several layers until you reach the leaves that are mostly pale green or yellow except for the tips. Cut off the dark green pointed tips. Trim the end of the stem with a paring knife. With a vegetable peeler, shave the outer layer of the stem. Use a paring knife or the peeler to remove any dark green leaf bases that surround the top of the stem. Cut the artichoke in half through the stem end. Use a grapefruit knife or small spoon to loosen and remove the spiky inner leaves and the fuzzy choke. Rinse the artichoke under cold running water to flush out any remaining hairs, then drop it into the bowl of water. Repeat this process with the remaining artichokes.

2. Work with one artichoke half at a time; remove it from the water and cut it lengthwise into very thin strips. Put the strips back into the bowl with the lemon and water. Repeat until all the artichokes have been sliced very thin.

3. Place the oil and garlic in a large skillet. Drain the artichokes and add them to the pan. Turn the heat to medium and cook, stirring often, until the artichokes turn crisp and are lightly browned, about 10 minutes. Remove and discard the garlic cloves. Season with the salt and pepper to taste and serve immediately.

Grilled Artichokes, Two Ways

There are two ways to grill an artichoke. If the artichoke is fresh, you may simply trim away the inedible portions and cut the artichoke in half, brush it with olive oil, and cook it over a medium-low grill fire until tender. *The leaves will crisp, char slightly, and open like a flower. The flavor is intense and smoky. The other option is to blanch the trimmed artichoke halves for 5 minutes, then grill them. The texture is silkier and moister, not crunchy as with the first method, and the flavor is less smoky since they are done so much more quickly. Personally, I prefer the first method, but it won't work with tougher, woodier artichokes, so you may want to try blanching if you are in doubt about the quality of your artichokes.*

SERVES 4 AS A SIDE DISH

1 lemon, halved
4 medium artichokes (about 2 pounds total weight)
2 tablespoons extra-virgin olive oil
Salt

1. Light the grill.
2. Squeeze half the lemon into a large bowl of cold water and then add the lemon half to the bowl. Use the other lemon half to rub over cut surfaces as you prepare the artichokes. Working with one artichoke at a time, bend back and snap off the tough outer leaves. Remove several layers until you reach the leaves that are mostly pale green or yellow except for the tips. Cut off the dark green pointed tips. Trim the end of the stem with a paring knife; with a vegetable peeler, shave the outer layer from the stem. Use a paring knife or the peeler to remove any dark green leaf bases that surround the top of the stem. Cut the artichoke in half through the stem end. Use a grapefruit knife or small spoon to loosen and remove the spiky inner leaves and the fuzzy choke.

Rinse the artichoke under cold running water to flush out any remaining hairs and then drop it into the bowl of water. Repeat this process with the remaining artichokes. Proceed to either step 3 or step 4, depending on grilling method chosen.

3. Drain the artichokes and brush them with the oil. Sprinkle generously with the salt. Grill over a medium-low fire, turning several times, until the outer leaves have charred slightly, about 20 minutes. Serve hot or warm.
4. Alternately, bring several quarts of water to a boil in a large saucepan. Drain the artichokes and add them to the boiling water along with salt to taste. Cook until almost tender, about 5 minutes. Drain well and place in a bowl. Add the oil and salt to taste and toss well. Grill over a medium fire, turning once, until lightly streaked with grill marks, about 7 minutes. Serve hot or warm.

Roasted Artichokes and New Potatoes

Although the potatoes form the bulk of this dish, the artichokes are the star here. Thin strips of trimmed artichokes are blanched and then added to a pan of roasting potatoes. The artichokes crisp and become frizzled. The relatively bland potatoes are the perfect foil for the rich-tasting roasted artichokes.

SERVES 4 AS A SIDE DISH

4 tablespoons extra-virgin olive oil, plus extra for the roasting pan

2 medium garlic cloves, minced

1 pound new potatoes, scrubbed and halved (quartered if large)
Salt

1 lemon, halved

3 medium artichokes (about 1½ pounds total weight)

1. Preheat the oven to 425 degrees.

2. Combine 2 tablespoons oil and the garlic in a small bowl and set aside. Place the potatoes in a greased roasting pan. Drizzle the remaining 2 tablespoons oil over the potatoes and stir to coat evenly. Sprinkle with salt to taste.

3. Roast the potatoes in the preheated oven for 30 minutes.

4. Meanwhile, bring several quarts of salted water to a boil in a large saucepan. Squeeze half of the lemon into a large bowl of cold water and then add the lemon half to the bowl. Use the other lemon half to rub over cut surfaces as you prepare the artichokes. Working with one artichoke at a time, bend back and snap off the tough outer leaves. Remove several layers until you reach the leaves that are mostly pale green or yellow except for the tips. Cut off the dark green pointed tips. Trim the end of the stem with a paring knife and then use a vegetable peeler to peel the outer layer from the stem. Use a paring knife or the peeler to remove any dark green leaf bases that surround the top of the stem. Cut the artichoke in half through the stem end. Use a grapefruit knife or small spoon to loosen and remove the spiky inner leaves and the fuzzy choke. Rinse the artichoke under cold running water to flush out any remaining hairs and then drop it into the bowl of water. Repeat this process with the remaining artichokes.

5. When the water comes to a boil, cut the cleaned artichoke halves lengthwise into thin strips. Immediately add the artichoke pieces to the boiling water and cook until almost tender, about 5 minutes. Drain and set aside.

6. Once the potatoes have roasted for 30 minutes, add the blanched artichoke strips to the roasting pan and stir to combine with the potatoes. Continue roasting for 10 minutes. Drizzle the garlic-oil mixture over the potatoes and artichokes and continue roasting until the potatoes are golden brown and the artichokes are lightly crisped, about 5 minutes. Adjust the seasonings and serve immediately.

Browned Baby Artichokes and Mushrooms with Garlic

"Baby" artichokes are not younger than regular artichokes; they just grow smaller on the same plant as larger specimens. Small artichokes can be browned in a hot skillet so the cut leaves are crisp. Don't try this recipe with large artichokes; they will be tough and woody.

SERVES 4 AS A SIDE DISH

1 lemon, halved

7 small artichokes (about ¾ pound total weight)

2 tablespoons extra-virgin olive oil

¼ cup chicken or vegetable stock or water

10 ounces white button mushrooms, wiped clean and halved (quartered if large)

3 medium garlic cloves, minced

Salt

Freshly ground black pepper

1. Squeeze half of the lemon into a large bowl of cold water; add the lemon half to the bowl. Use the other lemon half to rub over cut surfaces as you prepare the artichokes. Working with one artichoke at a time, bend back and snap off several layers of leaves, until you reach leaves that are mostly yellow or pale green. With a paring knife, trim any dark green material from around the base of the artichoke. Cut off ½ inch or so from the top of the artichoke and then cut the artichoke in half through the base. Use a grapefruit knife or paring knife to scrape out the fuzzy choke. Drop the cleaned artichoke halves into the bowl of lemon water. Repeat this process with the remaining artichokes.

2. Heat the oil in a large sauté pan over medium heat. Drain the artichokes and blot dry with paper towels. Place the artichoke halves, cut side down, in the pan. Cook until the artichokes have soaked up some of the oil, about 2 minutes. Add the stock and cover the pan. Simmer until the liquid in the pan has evaporated and the artichokes are frying in the oil (you should hear them sizzling), about 5 minutes. Remove the cover and continue

to cook until the bottoms of the artichokes are lightly browned, 1 to 2 minutes.

3. Add the mushrooms, garlic, and salt and pepper to taste to the pan. Cook, stirring occasionally, until the mushrooms are nicely browned and the artichokes are completely tender, 8 to 10 minutes. Adjust the seasonings and serve immediately.

Artichokes Braised with Onion and Thyme

Cleaned artichoke quarters absorb the flavors of the stock as they soften slowly in a covered pan. Try to use homemade stock—you can taste the difference in this dish. Serve with poached fish or chicken. I also like this dish as a main course for two, especially when served over a mound of mashed potatoes.

SERVES 4 AS SIDE DISH

1 medium lemon, halved

4 medium artichokes (about 2 pounds total weight)

2 tablespoons extra-virgin olive oil

1 medium onion, minced

1 cup chicken or vegetable stock

Salt

2 teaspoons minced fresh thyme leaves

1. Squeeze half the lemon into a large bowl of cold water and add that half to the bowl. Use the

other lemon half to rub over cut surfaces as you prepare the artichokes.

2. Working with one artichoke at a time, bend back and snap off the tough outer leaves. Remove several layers until you reach the leaves that are mostly pale green or yellow except for the tips. Cut off the dark green pointed tips. Trim the end of the stem with a paring knife; with a vegetable peeler shave the outer layer from the stem. Use a paring knife or the peeler to remove any dark green leaf bases that surround the top of the stem. Quarter the artichoke lengthwise, leaving a part of the stem attached to each piece. Slide a small, sharp knife under the fuzzy choke and cut toward the leaf tips to remove the choke. Slide the cleaned quarters into the bowl of cold water and start working on the next artichoke. When done, set the artichokes aside.

3. Heat the oil in a large sauté pan. Add the onion and sauté over medium heat until golden, about 5 minutes. Drain the artichokes and add them to the pan. Stir to coat the artichokes with the oil.

4. Add the stock to the pan and bring the liquid to a boil. Reduce the heat to a moderate simmer and cover the pan. Simmer, turning the artichokes occasionally, until they are quite tender, 25 to 30 minutes. There should be a few tablespoons of liquid still left in the pan. Stir in salt to taste and the thyme. Serve immediately.

Steamed Artichokes with Garlic Mayonnaise

This is the classic artichoke recipe. The preparation time here is minimal, but diners must do some work since most of the inedible portions of the artichoke have not been trimmed away by the cook. To eat a steamed artichoke, pull off one leaf at a time and slide it through your teeth to extract the meaty portion of the bottom of each leaf. For added flavor, I like to dip the bottom of each leaf in some garlicky homemade mayonnaise before putting it in my mouth. If you are averse to eating dishes made with raw eggs, you may substitute a lemon vinaigrette instead. Steamed artichokes are delicious served warm or chilled.

SERVES 4 AS A FIRST COURSE

1 lemon, halved
4 medium artichokes (about 2 pounds total weight)
⅞ cup Garlic Mayonnaise (page 8)

1. Squeeze half of the lemon into a large bowl of cold water and then add that half to the bowl. Use the other lemon half to rub over cut surfaces as you prepare the artichokes. Working with one artichoke at a time, cut off the top 1 inch or so of the leaves. With a pair of scissors, snip away any thorny ends of the leaves that remain. Peel the stem and drop the artichoke in the bowl of water. Repeat this process with the other artichokes.

2. Fit a wide saucepan with a steamer basket and add enough water to reach ½ inch below the

basket. Cover the pan and bring the water to a boil. Place the prepared artichokes, stem side up, in the steamer basket, cover the pot, and steam until the outer leaves can be easily pulled from the artichokes, about 30 minutes. Check the pot occasionally to make sure there is enough water, adding more if necessary.

3. Remove the artichokes from the steamer basket. Let cool for 15 minutes or so until just warm or chill in the refrigerator for several hours, removing the artichokes about 30 minutes before serving. Serve with garlic mayonnaise.

GARLIC MAYONNAISE

Aioli, or garlic mayonnaise, is the perfect way to enliven steamed or boiled vegetables. This mayonnaise is thick and eggy like all homemade mayo but has a strong garlic flavor that helps cut the richness of the sauce. Making mayonnaise in a food processor or blender is foolproof and also minces the garlic into extremely fine pieces. As for the oil, a blend of canola or another mild oil and extra-virgin olive oil tastes right to my palate. Mayonnaise made with just olive oil can be very harsh-tasting.

MAKES ABOUT ⅞ CUP

1 large egg
3 medium garlic cloves, peeled

½ teaspoon salt
⅜ cup canola or other tasteless oil
⅜ cup extra-virgin olive oil

1. Place the egg, garlic, and ½ teaspoon salt in a food processor or blender. Process until the mixture is smooth.
2. Combine the oils in a measuring cup. With the motor running, slowly add the oils until the mayonnaise thickens. (It should take a minute or two to add all the oil.)
3. Scrape the mayonnaise into an airtight container and adjust the seasonings. (The mayonnaise may be refrigerated for 1 day.)

Arugula

This peppery, leafy green is mainly used in salads. it has become ubiquitous in the past decade, no doubt because it's so delicious. Some arugula can be just mildly peppery; other bunches are downright spicy. The only way to find out is to taste some.

When arugula is mild (as is usually the case with bunches purchased in the supermarket), it makes a fine salad on its own. If you want to tame its spicy bite, try combining it with such milder greens as baby spinach or leaf lettuce.

OTHER COMMON NAMES: Rocket, roquette, and rucola.

AVAILABILITY: Year-round in most markets.

SELECTION: These leaves should be crisp and dark green with stems and roots still attached. Avoid bunches of arugula with yellow or slimy leaves. Arugula goes bad very quickly so only buy bunches that look extremely fresh.

STORAGE: Arugula should be used as soon as possible, preferably within a day or two of its purchase. Refrigerate unwashed arugula in a loosely sealed bag (you want moisture to be able to evaporate). If the arugula seems damp (as is often the case if it has been misted at the supermarket), blot it dry with paper towels when you get home and then put it into a dry bag. Wrapping the roots in a damp paper towel may keep arugula fresh and healthy-looking for an extra day or two, but don't count on it.

BASIC PREPARATION: Arugula bruises easily, so wait until just before serving to handle it. Arugula stems are generally tough and should be snapped off by hand. Wash arugula leaves in a bowl of cold water, changing the water several times, until clean and then dry in a salad spinner. Blot dry any remaining moisture with paper towels.

I usually keep the leaves whole (they aren't very big), but you may tear them by hand if you prefer.

BEST COOKING METHODS: You can't really cook arugula—it's too delicate to handle like other leafy greens. However, it can be added to hot foods and allowed to wilt on contact. Shower some chopped arugula over a cheese pizza as soon as it comes out of the oven. Or, stir some chopped arugula into risotto or soup just before serving.

OTHER RECIPES WITH ARUGULA: Arugula, Endive, and Radicchio Salad with Balsamic Vinaigrette (page 202)

Simplest Arugula and Tomato Salad

Arugula and tomatoes complement each other extremely well. The sweetness and acidity of the tomatoes temper the bite of the arugula. This simple salad can be embellished in numerous ways. Try adding some olives, capers, sliced red onions, diced hard-boiled egg, or even some garlicky croutons (page 132).

Note that this salad is not dressed with vinaigrette. As is often the custom in Italy, vinegar is drizzled over the salad, then oil, and everything is tossed until well coated. (I have used two vinegars here for added complexity.) Dressing a salad this way lets the flavor of the vinegar stand out. This salad could also be dressed with sherry vinegar or all red wine vinegar.

SERVES 4 AS A FIRST COURSE OR AFTER THE MAIN COURSE

- 4 cups stemmed arugula leaves, washed and thoroughly dried
- 2 medium ripe tomatoes (about 1 pound), cored and cut into thin wedges
  Salt
  Freshly ground black pepper
- 1 teaspoon balsamic vinegar
- 1 teaspoon red wine vinegar
- 2 tablespoons extra-virgin olive oil

1. Place the arugula and tomatoes in a large bowl. Sprinkle with salt and pepper to taste. Drizzle the vinegars and then the oil over the salad and toss. Adjust the seasonings and serve immediately.

Arugula Salad with Aged Goat Cheese and Walnuts

Use a crumbly aged goat cheese (with an edible rind) if you can. Its firmer, drier texture works better than fresh goat cheese, which can be sticky. Walnut oil has a rich flavor that works well in the dressing for this salad. However, since walnut oil is so potent, it is best to combine it with olive oil. If you don't have walnut oil, use two tablespoons of extra-virgin olive oil in the dressing.

SERVES 4 AS A FIRST COURSE OR AFTER THE MAIN COURSE

- 2 tablespoons lemon juice
- 1 tablespoon walnut oil
- 1 tablespoon extra-virgin olive oil
  Salt
  Freshly ground black pepper
- 6 cups stemmed arugula leaves, washed and thoroughly dried
- ½ cup walnuts, toasted in a dry skillet until fragrant, cooled, and chopped
- 2 ounces aged goat cheese, crumbled (about ½ cup)

1. Whisk the lemon juice and oils together in a small bowl until the dressing is smooth. Whisk in salt and pepper to taste.
2. Place the arugula and walnuts in a large bowl. Drizzle the dressing over the salad and toss to

coat. Sprinkle the cheese over the salad, toss once, and serve immediately.

Warm Arugula Salad with Pancetta, Figs, and Blue Cheese

When I really want a first course salad that will wow guests, this is what I serve. The warm lemony dressing wilts the arugula slightly. The combination of fresh, ripe figs, crisp pancetta, and soft blue cheese is unbeatable. Use a creamy, mild blue cheese, such as Saga blue or a dolce Gorgonzola. Pungent, crumbly Roquefort can overwhelm the other ingredients in this salad.

SERVES 4 AS A FIRST COURSE

2 ounces pancetta, chopped
2 tablespoons extra-virgin olive oil
1 medium shallot, minced
2 tablespoons lemon juice
    Freshly ground black pepper
6 cups stemmed arugula leaves, washed and thoroughly dried
8 ripe figs, hard stems discarded, quartered through the stem end
2 ounces mild blue cheese, crumbled (about ½ cup)

1. Place the pancetta and oil in a medium skillet. Turn the heat to medium and cook until the pancetta is very crisp, 5 to 6 minutes. Use a slotted spoon to transfer the pancetta to a plate lined with paper towels.

2. Add the shallot to the fat in the skillet and cook until softened, 2 to 3 minutes. Stir in the lemon juice and pepper to taste and remove the pan from the heat.

3. Place the arugula in a large bowl. Drizzle the warm dressing over the salad and toss gently. Adjust the seasonings. Add the pancetta, figs, and blue cheese and toss gently. Serve immediately.

Arugula and Mango Salad with Toasted Pumpkin Seeds

This dish comes from the Yucatán, where the dressing is made with juice from sour oranges. A combination of sweet orange juice and red wine vinegar delivers similar results. Pumpkin seeds are toasted like any other seeds or nuts—in a dry skillet until fragrant. With pumpkin seeds, you have an additional clue as to when they have been toasted long enough—they will start to pop. If you can't find pumpkin seeds, toast pine nuts instead.

SERVES 4 AS A FIRST COURSE OR
AFTER THE MAIN COURSE

2 tablespoons orange juice
1 teaspoon red wine vinegar
    Salt
    Freshly ground black pepper

2 tablespoons extra-virgin olive oil

6 cups stemmed arugula leaves, washed and thoroughly dried

2 medium mangoes, peeled, pitted, and sliced thin

¼ cup raw hulled green pumpkin seeds, toasted in a dry skillet until fragrant

1. Whisk the orange juice, vinegar, and salt and pepper to taste together in a small bowl. Whisk in the oil until the dressing is smooth. Adjust the seasonings.

2. Place the arugula, mangoes, and toasted pumpkin seeds in a large bowl. Drizzle the dressing over salad and toss to combine. Serve immediately.

Fusilli with Arugula and Tomato Sauce

This is one of my favorite ways to "cook" with arugula. Damp, chopped arugula is tossed with cooked, drained pasta and tomato sauce just until it wilts. I like to pair arugula with other strong flavors, so I add anchovies, olives, and capers to the tomato sauce. However, this technique works with almost any basic tomato sauce.

SERVES 4 AS A MAIN COURSE

2 tablespoons extra-virgin olive oil

2 medium garlic cloves, minced

3 anchovy fillets, minced
Two 14.5-ounce cans diced tomatoes

8 large black olives, such as Kalamatas, pitted and chopped

1 tablespoon drained capers
Salt

1 pound fusilli

3 cups stemmed arugula leaves, washed, shaken to remove excess water, and chopped

1. Bring 4 quarts of water to a boil in a large pot for cooking the pasta.

2. Heat the oil, garlic, and anchovies in a large saucepan over medium heat. Sauté until the garlic is fragrant but not brown, about 2 minutes. Add the tomatoes, olives, and capers and simmer until the sauce thickens a bit, about 10 minutes. Add salt (sparingly) to taste.

3. Meanwhile, add the pasta and salt to taste to the boiling water. Cook until al dente. Drain the pasta and return it to the cooking pot. Add the sauce and arugula and stir until the arugula wilts, about 30 seconds. Serve immediately.

Asparagus

Ease of preparation is certainly part of the attraction when buying asparagus. Three dozen spears are ready to be cooked in 3 minutes and they can be on the table in 10 minutes. Once reserved for special occasions (because of their price and seasonal availability), asparagus have become a standard vegetable in many American homes. Since everyone in my family likes asparagus, we have it at least once a week, most every week of the year.

My mother (as did most women of her generation) steamed or boiled asparagus. Although I still blanch asparagus and dress them with vinaigrette, I generally cook asparagus by dry heat to intensify their flavor and crisp up their exterior. This means grilling, roasting, or sautéing.

AVAILABILITY: There was a time (not long ago) when cooks waited patiently for early spring and the first asparagus crop. In recent years, asparagus has become a year-round staple in most markets.

SELECTION: The biggest issue is size. Some chefs tout "jumbo" asparagus on menus. However, spears larger than the pinkie on an average adult hand are stringy and must be peeled. Since I find this a bother (as I suspect most home cooks do), I stick with thin or medium asparagus, which don't require any peeling.

Buy stalks that are firm and have tightly closed, compact buds. Examine the ends of the spears and make sure they don't look woody or overly dried out. Try to get spears that are all the same thickness so that they will cook at the same rate.

STORAGE: Asparagus will keep in a loosely sealed plastic bag in the refrigerator for several days. If the spears are moist when you get home from the market, blot them dry with a paper towel and put them into a dry bag.

BASIC PREPARATION: No tools needed. Simply hold the end of the spear in one hand, grasp the upper portion of the spear in your other hand, and snap. The asparagus will naturally break just where the spear becomes tough and woody.

BEST COOKING METHODS: Boiling, grilling, roasting, sautéing, and steaming.

OTHER RECIPES WITH ASPARAGUS: Spring Vegetable Ragout with Fava Beans (page 156)

Roasted Asparagus with Olive Oil and Salt

This is my favorite way to cook asparagus year-round. Roasting concentrates the flavor of the asparagus and there's no need to fuss with a steamer. Use the best-quality oil and kosher or coarse sea salt.

SERVES 4 AS A SIDE DISH

1½ pounds thin asparagus, tough ends snapped off
2 tablespoons extra-virgin olive oil
Salt

1. Preheat the oven to 450 degrees.
2. Place the asparagus on a large baking sheet. Drizzle the oil over them and toss gently with your hands to coat each spear from end to end. Spread the spears out in a single layer over the baking sheet.
3. Roast in the preheated oven, shaking the pan once or twice to turn the spears, until the asparagus are lightly browned, 12 to 15 minutes.
4. Transfer the asparagus to a serving platter. Sprinkle with the salt and serve hot, warm, or at room temperature.

VARIATION: ROASTED ASPARAGUS WITH ROSEMARY AND GARLIC

Asparagus works well with strong flavors like rosemary and garlic. Other herbs (thyme is a good choice) and aromatics (such as shallots) may be used in the same fashion.

Add 2 medium garlic cloves, minced, and 1 teaspoon minced fresh rosemary leaves to the oil, then coat the asparagus with this mixture.

Roasted Asparagus with Peanut Sauce

The strong flavor of roasted asparagus is the perfect foil for this Asian peanut sauce. Soy sauce is typically added to Chinese peanut sauces, while fish sauce is a common ingredient in Thai peanut sauces. Use either, depending on the desired effect. Make sure to use a natural peanut butter, not one loaded with sweeteners.

SERVES 4 AS A FIRST COURSE OR SIDE DISH

1½ pounds thin asparagus, tough ends snapped off
2 tablespoons roasted peanut oil
2 medium garlic cloves, minced
2 tablespoons smooth peanut butter
1½ teaspoons soy sauce or fish sauce
1½ teaspoons lemon juice
¼ teaspoon hot red pepper flakes
2 to 3 tablespoons water

1. Preheat the oven to 450 degrees. Place the asparagus on a large baking sheet.
2. Combine the oil and garlic in a small bowl. Drizzle the oil mixture over the asparagus and toss gently with your hands to coat each spear

from end to end. Spread the spears out in a single layer over the baking sheet.

3. Roast the asparagus in the preheated oven, shaking the pan once or twice to turn the spears, until they are lightly browned, 12 to 15 minutes.

4. Meanwhile, combine the peanut butter, soy sauce, lemon juice, and pepper flakes in a small bowl. Use a rubber spatula to work the ingredients together until well combined. Add as much water as necessary until the consistency is thin enough to pour smoothly. Adjust the seasonings.

5. Transfer the roasted asparagus to a large platter. Drizzle the peanut sauce over the spears and serve immediately.

Roasted Asparagus Salad with Blood Orange Vinaigrette

Blood oranges have purplish-red flesh and a musky, slightly sweet, slightly sour flavor. The juice makes an excellent vinaigrette for roasted asparagus and shallots. The dressing dyes the roasted shallots a pretty pink color and gives this simple dish plenty of flavor. If you can't find blood oranges (this Mediterranean native is now being grown in California and is sometimes labeled a moro orange), use the juice from a sweet orange supplemented by a teaspoon of red wine vinegar for some kick. The flavor is not the same, but it is still delicious.

SERVES 4 AS A FIRST COURSE

1¼ pounds thin asparagus, tough ends snapped off

4 large shallots, peeled and sliced crosswise very thin

3 tablespoons extra-virgin olive oil
Salt

2 tablespoons blood orange juice
Freshly ground black pepper

1. Preheat the oven to 450 degrees. Place the asparagus and shallots on a large baking sheet.

2. Drizzle 1 tablespoon of the oil over the asparagus and shallots. Toss gently with your hands to coat the vegetables lightly with the oil. Spread the vegetables out in a single layer over the baking sheet and sprinkle with salt to taste.

3. Roast the vegetables in the preheated oven, shaking the pan once or twice to turn them, until the asparagus and shallots are lightly browned, 12 to 15 minutes.

4. While the vegetables are roasting, whisk together the blood orange juice, salt, and pepper in a small bowl. Whisk in the remaining 2 tablespoons oil until the dressing is smooth.

5. Transfer the roasted vegetables to a serving platter. Drizzle the dressing over them and set them aside for at least 15 minutes to allow the vegetables to soak up the flavors of the dressing. Serve warm or at room temperature. (The vegetables can marinate for up to 1 hour.)

Grilled Asparagus

This is the easiest and perhaps the best way to cook asparagus. Grilling makes them especially crisp, almost as if they had been fried. A little charring is a good thing here, but don't overdo it. Blackened asparagus will taste ashy. Use the best olive oil possible and try kosher salt (the larger crystals are better here). I find the flavor of grilled asparagus is so delicious that I don't bother with seasonings beyond salt and oil.

SERVES 4 AS A SIDE DISH

1½ pounds thin or medium asparagus, tough
    ends snapped off
2 tablespoons extra-virgin olive oil
    Salt

1. Light the grill. Place the asparagus on a large rimmed baking sheet. Drizzle the oil over the asparagus and toss with your hands to coat evenly. Sprinkle with salt to taste.
2. Transfer the asparagus from the baking sheet to the grill. Grill over a medium fire, turning once, until the spears are crisp and lightly charred, about 8 minutes. Serve immediately.

Pan-Browned Asparagus with Butter

This unusual method for cooking asparagus relies on the steam trapped in a covered pan. Where does the steam come from? From the butter and the liquid in the asparagus. There's not much moisture here, so keep the heat at medium and make sure the asparagus are in a single layer in the pan. Once the asparagus are almost tender, remove the cover and sauté until the spears are nicely browned. Don't try this recipe with thick asparagus, which may remain woody in the center if cooked this way.

SERVES 4 AS A SIDE DISH

2 tablespoons unsalted butter
1½ pounds thin or medium asparagus, tough
    ends snapped off
    Salt
    Freshly ground black pepper

1. Melt the butter in a large skillet set over medium heat. Place the asparagus in the skillet in a single layer. Season with salt to taste. Cover and cook until they are crisp-tender, 5 to 7 minutes, depending on the thickness of the asparagus.
2. Remove the cover, raise the heat to medium-high, and cook the asparagus, shaking the pan occasionally to turn them, until lightly browned, about 4 minutes.
3. Use a slotted spoon to transfer the asparagus to a serving platter. Season with pepper to taste. Adjust the seasonings and serve immediately.

Stir-Fried Asparagus and Basil with Spicy Orange Sauce

Instead of parboiling, the asparagus is stir-fried, tossed with a liquid sauce, and then covered so that it steams. Keep small basil leaves whole but tear larger leaves into several pieces. This stir-fry is fairly hot and best served over a generous portion of steamed white rice.

SERVES 4 AS A SIDE DISH

⅓ cup orange juice
1½ tablespoons soy sauce
½ teaspoon hot red pepper flakes, or more to taste
1½ pounds asparagus
4 teaspoons roasted peanut oil
2 medium garlic cloves, minced
1 tablespoon minced fresh gingerroot
½ cup packed fresh basil leaves

1. Combine the orange juice, soy sauce, and hot red pepper flakes in a small bowl and set aside.
2. Snap off the tough ends of the asparagus. If the asparagus are thin, cut them on the diagonal into 2-inch pieces. If the asparagus are average or thicker, cut the spears in half lengthwise and then on the diagonal into 2-inch pieces.
3. Heat 1 tablespoon of the oil in a large nonstick skillet set over high heat. When the oil is shimmering but not smoking, add the asparagus and stir-fry for 2 minutes. Push the asparagus to the sides of the pan and place the garlic and ginger in the center. Drizzle the remaining 1 teaspoon oil over the garlic and ginger. Cook until fragrant, about 20 seconds. Add the orange juice mixture, toss to coat well, and cover. Cook until the asparagus are tender, 2 to 3 minutes, depending on the thickness of the spears.
4. Remove the cover and add the basil. Stir-fry until the sauce has reduced to a thick glaze, about 30 seconds. Serve immediately.

Chinese Egg Noodles with Spicy Asparagus Sauce

Chinese egg noodles are a more traditional choice, but you can use fresh fettuccine if you like. Dried pasta won't absorb the sauce quite as well but works in a pinch.

SERVES 4 AS A MAIN COURSE

12 ounces fresh Chinese egg noodles
Salt
1 teaspoon roasted peanut oil or toasted sesame oil
1 recipe Stir-Fried Asparagus and Basil with Spicy Orange Sauce (above)
½ cup chicken or vegetable stock

1. Bring 4 quarts of water to a boil in large pot. Add the noodles and salt to taste and cook until

al dente. Drain and toss with the oil. Set aside for up to 1 hour.

2. When the asparagus are done, add the noodles and stock to the skillet. Toss to coat and cook just until the noodles are hot, 1 to 2 minutes. Adjust the seasonings and serve immediately.

Asparagus with Lemon-Mustard Vinaigrette

This is a classic recipe. Asparagus works well with the straightforward flavors of lemon and mustard. Traditionally, asparagus for this recipe are tied in a bundle and steamed. This method always seemed a bit fussy to me. I find that asparagus come out just fine when boiled as long as you keep the cooking time to a minimum and make sure to blot the spears dry before dressing them. If you like, this dish can be served at room temperature or chilled.

SERVES 4 AS A FIRST COURSE

2 tablespoons lemon juice
1 teaspoon Dijon mustard
Salt
Freshly ground black pepper
¼ cup extra-virgin olive oil
1½ pounds medium asparagus, tough ends snapped off

1. Bring several quarts of water to a boil in a large saucepan.

2. While waiting for the water to boil, whisk the lemon juice, mustard, and salt and pepper to taste in a small bowl. Whisk in the oil until the dressing is smooth.

3. Add the asparagus and salt to taste to the boiling water. Cook until the spears are tender but not limp, about 4 minutes. Drain the asparagus and refresh in a bowl of ice water. Drain again and blot dry with paper towels.

4. Arrange the asparagus in a single layer on a large platter. (The asparagus can be covered with plastic wrap and refrigerated for several hours.) Rewhisk the dressing and drizzle it over the asparagus. Serve immediately.

VARIATION: ASPARAGUS WITH LEMON-GINGER VINAIGRETTE

This Asian variation requires very finely minced ginger. You can do this by hand, sprinkling the ginger with salt to help break it down as you chop it with a knife. (Just make sure to omit the salt in the dressing.) However, a garlic press works more quickly and efficiently.

Replace the mustard with 1 tablespoon very finely minced fresh gingerroot.

Asparagus Frittata

*Asparagus has a real affinity for eggs. Keep the fla-
vors uncomplicated here—a little scallion (or onion),
a little minced fresh herb, and some grated Parmesan—so you can really taste the asparagus. An excellent use for thicker asparagus.*

SERVES 2 TO 4 AS A LIGHT MAIN COURSE

- 1 pound asparagus, tough ends snapped off
  Salt
- 6 large eggs
- ½ cup grated Parmesan cheese
- 1 tablespoon minced fresh parsley leaves
  Freshly ground black pepper
- 2 tablespoons extra-virgin olive oil
- 3 medium scallions, white and light green
  parts, sliced thin

1. Bring several quarts of water to a boil in a
medium saucepan.

2. Slice the asparagus in half lengthwise and
roughly chop. Add the asparagus and salt to taste
to the boiling water and cook until the asparagus
begins to soften, about 1 minute. Drain the
asparagus and set it aside.

3. Use a fork to lightly beat the eggs, cheese,
parsley, and salt and pepper to taste in a medium
bowl; set aside.

4. Adjust the oven rack to the top position and
preheat the broiler.

5. Heat the oil in a 10-inch nonstick skillet with
an ovenproof handle. Swirl the hot oil to coat the
bottom of the pan evenly. Add the scallions and
sauté over medium heat until softened, about 2
minutes. Add the asparagus and cook for 30 seconds. Add the egg mixture and stir gently with a
fork to incorporate the vegetables. Cook over
medium-low heat, occasionally sliding a spatula
around the edges of the pan to loosen the frittata
as it sets. Continue cooking until the frittata is
set on the bottom and still loose on top, about 8
minutes.

6. Place the pan directly under the broiler and
cook just until the top is golden brown and set,
1 to 2 minutes. Do not let the frittata burn.
Slide the frittata onto a large platter. Cut it into
wedges and serve. (The frittata may be cooled to
room temperature and then cut and served.)

Avocado

Like the tomato, the avocado is a fruit that we treat like a vegetable since it is not sweet. It is commonly used in dips, salsas, salads, and cold soups. Avocados are rich in fat (although it is unsaturated fat, like that found in olives) and unctuous, almost buttery. A small portion generally satisfies.

The key thing to remember when using avocados is that ripeness is paramount. An underripe avocado will be hard and bland. Only when fully ripe does the avocado achieve its unique texture and flavor.

AVAILABILITY: Year-round, although best in the spring and summer.

SELECTION: There are many varieties of avocado but only two appear in most American markets. Fuerte avocados have thin, bright green, smooth skin. They are large, often the size of a mango. Haas avocados are smaller (about the size of a small pear) and have pebbly, brownish-black skin. The flesh inside a Haas avocado is creamier and richer-tasting. The Fuerte can taste a bit watery and fibrous by comparison.

STORAGE: Avocados should not be refrigerated. Keep them on the counter. If they are rock-hard, they will ripen over the course of several days. Once they yield to gentle pressure, avocados are ripe and should be used. To hasten ripening, place the avocados in a sealed paper bag with some bananas.

BASIC PREPARATION: The skin and large pit must be removed. I find it best to attack the pit, then deal with the tough peel. Cut around the ends of the avocado with a sharp knife. With your hands, twist to separate the halves. Carefully stick the blade of a chef's knife into the pit and then wiggle to free it from the flesh. Working over a garbage pail, knock the pit off the knife with a wooden spoon.

At this point, you have two halves of avocado flesh surrounded by tough skin. You could try peeling the skin away with your fingers. This almost works with a Haas avocado, although you will mash the flesh in places, especially if the avocado is dead-on ripe. I find it easier to slide a rubber spatula between the skin and flesh to pop out the flesh in one piece. This method is quicker and ensures that the flesh does not become mangled so it can be cut it into long slices if you like.

Avocado turns brown very quickly, so use the flesh as soon as it is freed from the skin. All avocado recipes contain some acid (usually citrus juices) to keep the flesh green.

BEST COOKING METHODS: Don't cook avocados. They can be used in soups but are added once the ingredients have cooled to room temperature, usually in the blender.

Basic Guacamole

This is the simplest and most delicious guacamole recipe. You can get more adventurous and add other ingredients, but the classic combination still tastes best. Onion is the most common choice in Mexican recipes. However, I prefer the slightly sweeter, milder flavor of shallot.

SERVES 4 AS AN APPETIZER, WITH CHIPS

1 tablespoon minced shallot or onion
1 small garlic clove, minced
1 small jalapeño chile, stemmed, seeded, and minced
2 tablespoons minced fresh cilantro leaves
2 medium ripe Haas avocados
1 tablespoon lime juice
Salt

1. Place the shallot, garlic, chile, and cilantro in a medium bowl. Cut around the ends of the avocados and twist to separate the halves. Remove the pit and discard. Slide a rubber spatula between the skin and flesh to pop out the flesh. Add the flesh to the bowl with the seasonings.
2. Sprinkle the lime juice over the avocado and seasonings. Mash with a large fork until the mixture forms a chunky puree. (Guacamole should not be smooth). Add salt to taste and serve immediately. (You can refrigerate the guacamole for several hours, if you press a piece of plastic wrap directly onto the surface of the guacamole; otherwise the avocado will discolor. Bring guacamole to room temperature before serving.)

VARIATION: GUACAMOLE WITH TOMATOES

For many people, guacamole must have tomatoes.

Stir 1 small ripe tomato, cored and diced small, into the finished guacamole.

Avocado, Orange, and Radish Salad with Lime-Chile Dressing

This Mexican salad is especially refreshing on a hot summer day. If you like, substitute pink grapefruits for the oranges. Serve as a side dish with grilled fish or as a first course.

SERVES 4 AS A FIRST COURSE OR SIDE DISH

2 medium seedless oranges
2 medium ripe Haas avocados
4 medium radishes, cut into very thin rounds
1 tablespoon lime juice
1 teaspoon chili powder
3 tablespoons extra-virgin olive oil
Salt

1. Trim thick slices from the ends of the oranges so they can sit flat on a work surface. Slice downward around the oranges to remove the peel and white pith. Slice the peeled fruit crosswise into ¼-inch-thick circles.
2. Cut around the ends of the avocados and twist to separate the halves. Remove the pit and dis-

card. Slide a rubber spatula between the skin and flesh to pop out the flesh. Cut the halves lengthwise into ¼-inch-thick slices.

3. Arrange the avocado and orange slices on a platter. Sprinkle the radish rounds over the avocado and orange.

4. Whisk the lime juice and chili powder together in a small bowl. Whisk in the oil until the dressing is smooth. Add salt to taste.

5. Drizzle the dressing over the salad (don't toss) and serve immediately.

Shrimp and Avocado Salad with Grapefruit Dressing

Avocado halves filled with seafood salad are a cliché. While some clichés are delicious, I find that not enough seafood can fit into the hole left by the pit, so the avocado overwhelms everything and the dish is exceedingly rich. This version—with shrimp salad spooned over slices of tomato and avocado—works far better. Serve with bread to sop up the extra dressing.

SERVES 4 AS A LIGHT MAIN COURSE

- 2 tablespoons extra-virgin olive oil
- 2 medium garlic cloves, minced
- ½ cup grapefruit juice
- 1 tablespoon minced fresh mint leaves
  Salt

Freshly ground black pepper
- 1¼ pounds shelled cooked shrimp
- 1 tablespoon drained capers
- 2 medium ripe Haas avocados
- 4 medium ripe tomatoes, cored and sliced crosswise into thin rounds

1. Heat the oil in a small skillet. Add the garlic and sauté over medium heat until golden, about 1 minute. Add the grapefruit juice and simmer until the sauce has thickened considerably, 2 to 3 minutes. Stir in the mint leaves and salt and pepper to taste. Toss the warm dressing with the shrimp and capers and set aside. (The shrimp salad may be refrigerated for up to 6 hours.)

2. Cut around the ends of the avocados and twist to separate the halves. Remove the pit and discard. Slide a rubber spatula between the skin and flesh to pop out the flesh. Cut the halves lengthwise into ¼-inch-thick slices.

3. Arrange slices of the avocado and tomato on four serving plates. Spoon some shrimp salad over the avocado and tomato and serve immediately.

Chilled Avocado-Tomatillo Soup

Roasted tomatillos, garlic, and chile give this soup a wonderful flavor and help thicken the texture without using any cream, which would make the soup too rich. In addition, I find that avocados need tart, sour, and savory flavors, like those in this recipe, not half-

and-half or cream. This soup is still rich, so serve it in small portions as a first course.

SERVES 6 AS A FIRST COURSE

1¼ pounds tomatillos, husked and rinsed
4 medium garlic cloves, peeled
1 large jalapeño chile, stemmed, halved, and seeded
1 tablespoon extra-virgin olive oil
1 tablespoon lime juice, plus more if needed
3 medium ripe Haas avocados
2 to 2½ cups chicken or vegetable stock
Salt
6 tablespoons sour cream or plain yogurt
1 large tomato, cored, seeded, and diced fine

1. Preheat the oven to 450 degrees.

2. Place the tomatillos, garlic, and chile on a rimmed baking sheet. Drizzle with the oil and toss until evenly coated. Roast until nicely browned and quite soft, about 20 minutes. Cool to room temperature.

3. Place the roasted vegetables and any juices they have exuded in a blender. Add the lime juice and puree until smooth.

4. Cut around the ends of the avocados and twist to separate the halves. Remove the pit and discard. Slide a rubber spatula between the skin and flesh to pop out the flesh.

5. Add the avocados and 2 cups stock to the blender and pulse until fairly smooth. Add more stock as needed until the soup is perfectly smooth and has a thick, but pourable consistency. Transfer the soup to a container and stir in salt to taste. Cover and refrigerate until well chilled, at least 2 hours and up to 8 hours.

6. When ready to serve, taste the soup and adjust the seasonings, adding more lime juice or salt as needed. Ladle the soup into six bowls. Float a dollop of sour cream in the center of each bowl and sprinkle with a little tomato. Serve immediately.

Beets

People who say they don't like beets usually change their minds after eating beets at my home. Invariably, these people grew up eating canned beets. If they have tried to make beets at home, they probably steamed them and were overwhelmed by the mess and underwhelmed by the flavor.

I feel strongly that roasting is the best all-purpose method for preparing beets. Roasting concentrates the flavor of the beets and makes the texture firmer and creamier. Steamed beets taste watery and washed out by comparison.

When roasting beets, there's almost no preparation. Just lop off the greens and any dangling rootlets, wash the beets, and wrap them in foil. They are now ready for the oven. If you handle beets this way, they can be peeled after cooking, when the peels rub off with almost no effort.

Once the beets have been roasted, they are usually dressed and served as a warm or room temperature salad. They can be also diced and quickly sautéed.

Although roasting is the best way to handle beets in most instances, I sometimes peel and shred them for a quick raw salad. Beets turned into a slaw are crunchy and refreshing. The other option is to mix shredded beets with shredded potatoes and then sauté the vegetables to make a crisp, savory cake.

AVAILABILITY: Summer and fall are the best time for beets, although they show up year-round in many markets.

SELECTION: As with any root vegetable that is sometimes sold with the greens still attached, I recommend buying beets this way. Beets trimmed of their greens may be fine, but you don't know how old they are. If the greens are attached, you can be assured that the beets were recently dug since the greens have a limited shelf life. An added bonus of buying beets with greens attached is of course the greens, which are closely related to chard and can be cooked like chard or spinach.

Really large beets can be woody and tough. Beets that weigh about 4 ounces each (when trimmed of their greens) are perfect. Beets in the same bunch can vary greatly in size. This can cause problems for the cook—one beet will be tender after 45 minutes of roasting, while another is still tough. Try to choose beets that are roughly the same size (an ounce or two difference in size won't matter) so they will cook at the same rate.

Although the standard beet is a purplish-red color, farmers' markets sell some other varieties. Chioggia beets have bright red skin with alternating bands of white and red flesh. Golden beets are pale yellow and less sweet than the standard variety.

STORAGE: Beets with greens attached will keep in a loosely sealed plastic bag for several days in the refrigerator. If you remove the greens, you can prolong the shelf life of the roots by at least a week or two.

BASIC PREPARATION: Trim the stems about an inch or so above the point where they meet the bulbous root. Use a paring knife to cut away any thin, dangling roots. The skin can be removed with a vegetable peeler (a messy job, so don't wear anything you value) or you can wait until after the beets have been roasted and rub off the skin with paper towels.

BEST COOKING METHODS: Roasting is less messy than steaming, the other traditional choice. Beets can also be grated for use in raw salads or sautéed vegetable cakes.

OTHER RECIPES WITH BEETS: If you have some nice-looking beet greens, cook them as you would chard (page 101) or spinach (page 307).

Roasted Beet Salad with Sherry Vinegar

Sharp, flavorful sherry vinegar tames some of the sweetness of the beets. This dish is especially good at room temperature as part of a summer meal.

SERVES 4 AS A SIDE DISH OR APPETIZER

4 medium beets (about 1 pound without greens)
1 tablespoon sherry vinegar
2 tablespoons extra-virgin olive oil
Salt
Freshly ground black pepper

1. Preheat the oven to 400 degrees.
2. Trim all but the last inch or so of the stems from the beets. Wash the beets well and trim any dangling roots. Wrap the beets in aluminum foil. Place the beets in the oven and roast until a metal skewer glides easily through them, 1 to 1¼ hours.
3. Remove the beets from the oven, open up the foil, and cool slightly. Discard the foil. Use paper towels to hold the warm beets and rub them gently to slip off their skins. Slice the beets into ¼-inch-thick rounds.
4. Arrange the warm beet slices on a platter. Drizzle the vinegar, then the oil over the beets. Sprinkle with salt and pepper to taste and serve warm or at room temperature.

Roasted Beet Salad with Lemon and Olives

Salty olives and bright-tasting lemon juice are good foils for beets. Although you could serve this salad as a side dish with a Mediterranean meal, I generally put it out as part of an antipasto spread of marinated vegetables.

SERVES 4 AS AN APPETIZER OR SIDE DISH

4 medium beets (about 1 pound without greens)
1 tablespoon lemon juice
Salt
Freshly ground black pepper
2 tablespoons extra-virgin olive oil
12 large Kalamata olives, pitted and chopped
2 tablespoons minced fresh parsley leaves

1. Preheat the oven to 400 degrees.
2. Trim all but the last inch or so of the stems from the beets. Wash the beets well and trim any dangling roots. Wrap the beets in aluminum foil. Place the beets in the oven and roast until a metal skewer glides easily through them, 1 to 1¼ hours.
3. Remove the beets from the oven, open up the foil, and cool slightly. Discard the foil. Use paper towels to hold the warm beets and rub them gently to slip off their skins. Slice the beets into ¼-inch-thick rounds.
4. Arrange the warm beet slices on a platter. Whisk the lemon juice and salt and pepper to

taste together in a small bowl. Whisk in the oil. Drizzle the dressing over the beets. Sprinkle the olives and parsley over the beets and serve immediately or at room temperature.

Roasted Beet Salad with Walnuts and Goat Cheese

Warm roasted beets are sliced and served over a bed of beet greens. A light balsamic vinaigrette is drizzled over the roasted beets and greens. Toasted walnuts and crumbled goat cheese round out this rich salad of contrasting flavors and textures. If you can't find beets with healthy-looking greens attached, use red chard in place of the beet greens. A bit more work than other beet salads, but much more complex-tasting.

SERVES 4 AS A FIRST COURSE

4 medium beets (about 1 pound without greens), plus 4 cups packed beet greens

4 tablespoons extra-virgin olive oil

2 medium shallots, sliced thin
Salt
Freshly ground black pepper

2 teaspoons balsamic vinegar

2 teaspoons red wine vinegar

½ cup walnuts, toasted in a dry skillet until fragrant

2 ounces goat cheese, crumbled (about ½ cup)

1. Preheat the oven to 400 degrees.

2. Trim all but the last inch or so of the stems from the beets. Wash the beets well and trim any dangling roots. Wrap the beets in aluminum foil. Place the beets in the oven and roast until a metal skewer glides easily through them, 1 to 1¼ hours.

3. While the beets are roasting, wash and shake dry the beet greens. Tear any large leaves in half.

4. Heat 1 tablespoon oil in a medium skillet. Add the shallots and sauté over medium heat until golden brown and crisp, about 5 minutes. Add the damp beet greens and sauté until wilted, about 2 minutes. Season with salt and pepper to taste and cool to room temperature.

5. Place the vinegars and salt and pepper to taste in a small bowl. Whisk in the remaining 3 tablespoons oil until the dressing is smooth. Set the dressing aside.

6. When the beets are tender, remove them from the oven, open up the foil, and cool slightly. Discard the foil. Use paper towels to hold the warm beets and rub them gently to slip off their skins. Slice the beets into ¼-inch-thick rounds.

7. Divide the beet greens among four individual salad plates. Arrange the beet slices over the greens and drizzle with the dressing. Garnish the salad with toasted walnuts and cheese. Serve immediately.

Sautéed Beets with Butter and Orange Juice

In this recipe, the beets are roasted, peeled, cut into cubes, and then quickly sautéed. The small amount of lemon juice helps balance the flavors and prevents this dish from becoming too sweet. Excellent with fish or chicken.

SERVES 4 AS A SIDE DISH

4 medium beets (about 1 pound without greens)
1 tablespoon unsalted butter
¼ cup orange juice
1 tablespoon lemon juice
Salt
Freshly ground black pepper

1. Preheat the oven to 400 degrees.
2. Trim all but the last inch or so of the stems from the beets. Wash the beets well and trim any dangling roots. Wrap the beets in aluminum foil. Place the beets in the oven and roast until a metal skewer glides easily through them, 1 to 1¼ hours.
3. Remove the beets from the oven, open up the foil, and cool slightly. Discard the foil. Use paper towels to hold the warm beets and rub them gently to slip off their skins. Cut the beets into ½-inch cubes.
4. Melt the butter in a large skillet. Add the beets and cook, stirring often, over medium-high heat just until the beets are lightly coated with butter,

about 1 minute. Add the orange and lemon juices and cook just until the liquid reduces and thickens to a glaze, about 2 minutes. Season with salt and pepper to taste and serve immediately.

Crisp Beet and Potato Cake

Shredded beets don't seem nearly so sweet when they are paired with shredded potatoes to make a crisp savory cake. This vegetable cake is moister and creamier than one made with just potatoes (see page 269). I serve this cake with roast chicken or pork.

SERVES 4 AS A SIDE DISH

1 pound russet potatoes
1½ teaspoons salt
4 medium beets (about 1 pound without greens)
¼ cup snipped fresh chives
2 tablespoons unsalted butter

1. Peel the potatoes. Using the shredding disk on the food processor or the large holes on a box grater, cut the potatoes into thin shreds. Toss the potatoes with the salt.
2. Trim the stems and any dangling roots from the beets. Remove the skins from the beets with a vegetable peeler. Shred the beets in a food processor (much less messy) or with a box grater. Mix the beets with the potatoes. Add the chives and mix well.

3. Heat 1 tablespoon of the butter in a 10-inch nonstick skillet. When the foam subsides, distribute the shredded beets and potatoes evenly in the pan. Use a spatula to press down on the mixture to form a compact circle. Cook over medium heat, occasionally pressing down on the beets and potatoes with a spatula, until the underside is crisp and nicely browned, 10 to 12 minutes.

4. Slide the pancake onto a large plate. Invert the pancake onto a second large plate. Add the remaining tablespoon of butter to the pan and heat briefly. Slide the pancake, browned side up, back into the pan. Cook until the second side is nicely browned, 8 to 10 minutes. Slide the pancake onto a large plate, cut it into wedges, and serve immediately.

Grated Beet Salad

This is the quickest, simplest way to enjoy the flavor of beets. Use the freshest beets in this recipe, and avoid any large specimens that may be woody. Raw beets are not as sweet as cooked beets, but they still benefit from aggressive flavors. Here, lemon juice, mustard, and a little garlic balance and enhance the flavor of the beets. To contain the mess, shred the beets in a food processor. I usually serve this salad at a summer meal with other cool vegetable salads.

**SERVES 4 TO 6 AS AN ANTIPASTO
OR SIDE DISH**

4 medium beets (about 1 pound without greens)

2 tablespoons lemon juice
1 tablespoon Dijon mustard
1 medium garlic clove, minced
  Salt
  Freshly ground black pepper
2 tablespoons extra-virgin olive oil
2 teaspoons minced fresh tarragon or parsley leaves

1. Trim the stems and any dangling roots from the beets. Remove the skins from the beets with a vegetable peeler. Using the shredding disk on the food processor or the large holes on a box grater, shred the beets. Transfer them to a medium serving bowl.

2. Whisk the lemon juice, mustard, garlic, and salt and pepper to taste together in a small bowl. Whisk in the oil. Whisk in the tarragon and adjust the seasonings.

3. Drizzle the dressing over the shredded beets. Toss to coat the beets with the dressing. Serve immediately.

Bok Choy

This Chinese cabbage has become a familiar item in many American supermarkets as well as farmers' markets and Asian groceries. with its ivory stalks and dark green, crinkly leaves, bok choy is always easy to spot.

Although bok choy is often treated like a leafy green (chard is the closest culinary equivalent), the flavor reminds us that it is a cabbage after all. The white stems have a strong cabbage flavor and intriguing texture that goes from crisp (like celery) to creamy and rich. The leaves are a bit tougher than spinach or chard but turn tender when cooked for several minutes. The flavor is earthy and robust, not hot or peppery.

OTHER COMMON NAMES: Bai cai, bok choi, pak choi, and Chinese cabbage.

AVAILABILITY: Year-round. A staple in Asian markets, although commonly sold in many supermarkets.

SELECTION: Look for heads of bok choy with bright green, crisp leaves. There should not be any yellowing or signs of decay in the leaves. As for the stalks, they should be bright white. Tiny brown spots are a sign that the bok choy is past its prime.

Most supermarkets carry full-size heads of bok choy that weigh about 2 pounds. If you shop at an Asian market, you will see baby bok choy (just a few ounces each) as well as Shanghai bok choy (the stalks are a lovely pale green color, not white). Baby bok choy must be handled somewhat differently (see the recipe on page 36), but full-sized Shanghai bok choy can prepared like regular bok choy.

STORAGE: Bok choy should be refrigerated in a loosely sealed plastic bag. It should keep for several days.

BASIC PREPARATION: Unlike many leafy greens, you can cook and enjoy both the fleshy stalks and leafy greens. However, since the stalks will take longer to cook, they must be given a head start. This affects how you prepare bok choy.

Start by pulling off the individual leaves of the cabbage and washing them in a bowl of cold water. Use a chef's knife to separate the leafy greens from the white stems. The bottom inch or two of the stems is usually pretty thick and tough, so I cut it off and save it for composting. I slice the stems crosswise into thin strips.

I then turn my attention to the leaves. I stack them up like other large leafy greens (such as chard) and slice them crosswise into thin strips. If the strips seem particularly long, I might turn my knife 90 degrees and chop the pile of greens once or twice in the other direction.

BEST COOKING METHODS: Braising and stir-frying. Always add the white stalks first since they require more cooking time than the tender greens.

OTHER RECIPES WITH BOK CHOY: Soba Noodles with Spicy Broccoli Rabe (page 53)

Braised Bok Choy with Plenty of Garlic

This recipe produces a side dish that captures the essence of bok choy with minimal distractions. Braising highlights the creamy nature of bok choy and garlic is a natural complement to the earthy flavor of this Chinese cabbage. Serve this saucy side dish with meat (such as pork) or fish (use the bok choy as a bed for roasted cod or snapper) that benefits from the addition of some "gravy."

SERVES 4 AS A SIDE DISH

1 large head bok choy (about 2 pounds)
2 tablespoons roasted peanut oil
6 medium garlic cloves, sliced thin
1 cup chicken or vegetable stock
Salt
Freshly ground black pepper

1. Separate the leafy green portions of the bok choy from the white stalks. Discard the tough bottom portion from each stalk. Cut the stalks crosswise into thin strips. (You should have about 5 cups.) Cut the leaves crosswise into thin strips. (You should have about 7 cups.) Set the stalks and leaves aside separately.
2. Heat the oil in a large nonstick skillet over high heat until almost smoking. Add the bok choy stalks and stir-fry until slightly softened, about 2 minutes. Add the garlic and stir-fry until lightly colored, about 2 minutes.
3. Add the bok choy greens, stock, and salt and pepper to taste to the pan. Stir to combine the ingredients. Cover, reduce the heat, and simmer, stirring once or twice, until the bok choy is very tender, about 10 minutes. Remove the cover, raise the heat, and simmer briskly until the excess liquid has evaporated, 3 to 4 minutes. (The bok choy should be moist but not soupy.) Adjust the seasonings. Serve immediately.

Stir-Fried Bok Choy with Ginger and Hoisin Sauce

The rich, slightly bitter flavor of bok choy takes well to the sweetness of hoisin sauce. This stir-fry is extremely simple.

SERVES 4 AS A SIDE DISH

⅓ cup chicken or vegetable stock
2 tablespoons hoisin sauce
1 tablespoon rice vinegar
1 large head bok choy (about 2 pounds)
2 tablespoons roasted peanut oil
2 tablespoons minced fresh gingerroot
Salt
Freshly ground black pepper

1. Combine the stock, hoisin sauce, and vinegar in a small bowl and set the mixture aside.
2. Separate the leafy green portions of the bok choy from the white stalks. Discard the tough bottom portion from each stalk. Cut the stalks crosswise into thin strips. (You should have about

5 cups.) Cut the leaves crosswise into thin strips. (You should have about 7 cups.) Set the stalks and leaves aside separately.

3. Heat the oil in a large nonstick skillet over medium-high heat until almost smoking. Add the bok choy stalks and stir-fry until slightly softened, about 2 minutes. Add the ginger and stir to combine. Continue cooking until the stalks start to brown, about 2 minutes.

4. Add the bok choy leaves and the hoisin mixture to the pan. Cover and cook until the stalks are tender and the leaves have wilted, about 2 minutes. Uncover and stir-fry until the sauce thickens a bit, about 30 seconds. Season with salt and pepper to taste. Serve immediately.

Sesame-Glazed Baby Bok Choy

Small baby bok choy (about 3 to 4 ounces each) can be halved through the bulb and then cooked as is. The contrast between the fleshy, creamy white bulb and the tender leaves is delicious. Sear baby bok choy until lightly browned and then glaze it with a soy, sesame, and rice vinegar mixture. Serve this quick and elegant vegetable with any Asian meal. It is especially good with meat. Baby Shanghai bok choy, which has pale green stalks, can be cooked this way, too.

SERVES 4 AS A SIDE DISH

1½ tablespoons rice vinegar
1½ tablespoons soy sauce
2 teaspoons toasted sesame oil
½ teaspoon sugar
1 tablespoon sesame seeds
2 tablespoons roasted peanut oil
4 baby bok choy (about 1 pound total weight), halved lengthwise through the bulb end
3 medium garlic cloves, minced
1 tablespoon minced fresh gingerroot
2 medium scallions, sliced thin

1. Combine the vinegar, soy sauce, sesame oil, and sugar in a small bowl and set this mixture aside.

2. Toast the sesame seeds in a large nonstick skillet set over medium heat until golden, about 3 minutes. Transfer the toasted seeds to a small bowl.

3. Return the empty skillet to the stove and raise the heat to high. Add 1½ tablespoons of the peanut oil and heat briefly. Place the bok choy, cut side down, in the skillet in a single layer. Sauté until lightly browned, about 2 minutes. Turn the bok choy pieces and continue cooking for 1 minute. Transfer the bok choy to a platter.

4. Heat the remaining ½ tablespoon peanut oil in the empty skillet. Add the garlic, ginger, and scallions and stir-fry until fragrant, about 30 seconds. Add the vinegar mixture and simmer just until thickened, about 30 seconds.

5. Return the bok choy, cut side down, to the skillet and cook for 15 seconds. Turn and cook another 15 seconds. Sprinkle the toasted sesame seeds over the bok choy and transfer to a serving platter. Serve immediately.

Boniato

I n most of the world, a sweet potato is not bright orange. it has white or pale yellow flesh and an intriguing nutty flavor that reminds many cooks (myself included) of chestnuts. While orange sweet potatoes are creamy and moist, white or yellow sweet potatoes are dry and fluffy, more like russet potatoes in texture.

This tropical sweet potato goes by hundreds of names, although the terms *boniato* and *batata* are the most common in this country. Boniatos look a bit like our sweet potatoes but they are generally round and the skin is tinted pink or light purple and blotched.

Of all the tropical tubers, this one probably has the most appeal to American cooks. It is light and fluffy so it can be baked like a potato or sweet potato (most other tropical tubers are much too dry and starchy to handle like this).

Most tropical tubers are bland, best used as a foil for potent seasonings. Boniato has a delicious flavor of its own, so don't load up on the garlic and chiles here.

OTHER COMMON NAMES: Batata, camote, Cuban sweet potato, and Puerto Rican yam.

AVAILABILITY: Year-round, mostly in Latino markets.

SELECTION: When shopping, try to buy smooth, round boniato if possible. Gnarly, knobby boniatos are difficult to peel, and there will be a lot of waste. Boniatos should be rock hard.

STORAGE: Boniatos should be kept at cool room temperature. They will go soft fairly quickly and should be used as soon as possible.

BASIC PREPARATION: If baking a boniato, simply scrub the skin with a brush to remove all the caked-on mud.

If preparing it by some other method (boiling or frying), you will need to remove the skin, which I find tough and not very appetizing. Use a paring knife to peel around this knobby tuber and remove a good bit of the flesh right beneath the skin, which tends to be bruised. When you are done, the boniato should be ivory-colored or pale yellow (depending on the variety) and free of blemishes. Peeled boniato discolors very quickly, so drop chunks into a bowl of cold water as you work.

BEST COOKING METHODS: Baking, boiling, and frying. Also delicious in stews.

OTHER RECIPES WITH BONIATOS: Boniatos can be peeled, cut into thin strips, and used in place of sweet potatoes to make fries (see page 317). I especially like to sprinkle ground cumin or grated nutmeg (both are traditional in the Caribbean) over the fries, along with a good deal of salt.

Baked Boniatos with Lime and Hot Sauce

This is the easiest way to enjoy the fluffy light texture and rich chestnut flavor of boniatos. The skins become hard and brittle in the oven and should not be eaten.

SERVES 4 AS A SIDE DISH

4 medium boniatos (about 2½ pounds), scrubbed
Salt
Lime wedges
Hot sauce, optional

1. Preheat the oven to 425 degrees.
2. Line a rimmed baking sheet with foil. Place the boniatos on the baking sheet. Bake until the boniatos are tender when pierced with a skewer, about 1¼ hours. (Boniato skin becomes very tough when baked so don't let this fool you when testing them for doneness. Once a skewer glides easily through the flesh, the boniatos are done.)
3. Slit open the boniatos lengthwise and push on the sides to loosen the flesh. Sprinkle with salt to taste. Serve immediately, with the lime wedges and hot sauce passed at the table.

Mashed Boniatos

This is a delicious and unusual vegetable puree. The color is a not bright white like potatoes (it's more like off-white) and the texture is a tad fibrous, but not objectionably so. However, the flavor is fantastic. A little butter highlights the nutty flavor of the boniato. Serve with meat or poultry, preferably with a main course that has some gravy or sauce to moisten the puree.

SERVES 4 TO 6 AS A SIDE DISH

2 pounds boniatos
Salt
2 tablespoons unsalted butter, softened

1. Fill a large saucepan with several quarts of cold water. Working with one boniato at a time, use a paring knife to remove the skin and about ¼ inch of the flesh right beneath the skin. You want to remove all brown or discolored portions. Cut the peeled boniato into 1½-inch chunks and quickly drop the chunks into the saucepan with the water. (Boniato discolors rapidly, so don't omit this step.)
2. When all the boniatos are in the pan, add a generous amount of salt. Turn the heat to high and bring the liquid to a boil. Reduce the heat and simmer until the boniato chunks are very tender, about 15 minutes. Drain. (It's fine if the boniato looks a bit watery. It will dry out as you mash it.)
3. Return the boniatos to the empty saucepan set over low heat. Add the butter and use a potato masher to turn the boniatos into a smooth puree.

Beat in salt to taste with a wooden spoon. Serve immediately.

Broiled Boniato with Rum–Brown Sugar Sauce and Rosemary

This unusual dish is one of those culinary inventions that just seemed to happen in the kitchen one day. In the Caribbean, boniato chunks are often boiled and then tossed with a brown sugar–rum sauce. I find that dish a bit sweet and too mushy. I decided to run the sauced boniatos under the broiler to crisp them up. The rosemary adds an herbaceous flavor that helps cut some of the sweetness. While under the broiler, the boniatos absorb all the sauce and become fluffy and lightly crisped. Serve with pork roast or chicken.

SERVES 4 AS A SIDE DISH

> 2 pounds boniatos
> Salt
> 2 tablespoons unsalted butter
> 2 tablespoons brown sugar
> 2 tablespoons rum
> 1 teaspoon minced fresh rosemary leaves

1. Fill a large saucepan with several quarts of cold water. Working with one boniato at a time, use a paring knife to remove the skin and about ¼ inch of the flesh right beneath the skin. You want to remove all brown or discolored portions. Cut the peeled boniato into 1-inch chunks and quickly drop the chunks into the saucepan with the water. (Boniato discolors rapidly, so don't omit this step.)

2. When all the boniatos are in the pan, add a generous amount of salt. Turn the heat to high and bring the liquid to a boil. Reduce the heat and simmer until the boniato chunks are tender but still holding their shape (they should not be falling apart), about 10 minutes.

3. While the boniatos are cooking, adjust the oven rack to the second-highest position and preheat the broiler. (The rack should be about 5 inches from the heat source.) Combine the butter, brown sugar, rum, and a pinch of salt in a small saucepan. Bring to a boil and simmer until the mixture thickens slightly, about 2 minutes. Remove pan from heat and set aside.

4. When the boniatos are tender, drain them well and transfer them to a 13 by 9-inch baking dish. Drizzle the rum–brown sugar sauce over the boniatos and sprinkle with the rosemary. Toss gently to coat evenly.

5. Place the baking dish under the broiler. Broil until the top is lightly browned in spots, 6 to 8 minutes. (Watch carefully, the boniatos will burn quickly.) Serve immediately.

Broccoli

Broccoli is one of the most popular vegetables in this country. The appeal of this green vegetable is clear. Broccoli is available year-round and generally holds up well both in supermarkets and at home in the refrigerator. Even in the most mediocre produce department, the broccoli generally looks pretty good. In addition, broccoli is rich in nutrients and can be prepared in minutes to accompany meat, chicken, or fish.

The challenge for many cooks is figuring out how to flavor broccoli. While it is possible (and certainly delicious) to follow the Italian model and simply drizzle the finest extra-virgin olive oil over cooked broccoli (a sprinkling of coarse salt helps as well), this preparation can become a bit boring, especially if you eat broccoli a lot.

Like all brassicas (a family that includes cabbage and Brussels sprouts), broccoli has a strong flavor. I find that equally strong seasonings, such as chiles, ginger, garlic, citrus juices, and spices, are a must. A delicate herb vinaigrette is fine with asparagus, but broccoli calls out for stronger-tasting ingredients.

In recent years, the familiar green bunch of broccoli has been joined by some other varieties. Some heads look like regular broccoli but are tinged purple. These can be cooked much like broccoli. Pale green broccoflower is shaped like cauliflower but tastes more like broccoli and can be cooked just like broccoli. Tiny broccolini resemble miniaturized broccoli spears and are tender enough to sauté without precooking.

Do not overcook any kind of broccoli. The longer you simmer the broccoli, the more vitamins will be lost to the cooking water. In addition to losing nutrition and texture, broccoli that is cooked too long develops an unpleasant sulfurous odor.

AVAILABILITY: Year-round, although the traditional season for broccoli is fall through spring.

SELECTION: Choose broccoli with tightly closed florets that are dark green or purplish-green. If the florets are soft or open, the broccoli is past its prime. If you want to cook the stems, make sure they aren't extremely wide, a sign that they may be woody.

STORAGE: Broccoli should be refrigerated in a loosely sealed plastic bag. It will remain fresh for several days, if not a week, as long as excess moisture doesn't cause decay.

BASIC PREPARATION: Rinse the broccoli and separate the stalks from the florets where they meet with a sharp knife. Cut off the woody ends of the stalks. Use a paring knife to trim away ⅛ inch of the outer peel from the stalks. (You want to reveal the pale green flesh beneath the skin.) Cut the peeled stalks in half lengthwise and then into bite-sized pieces. If necessary, separate the florets with a paring knife into smaller sections. Try to cut the florets in such as way as to keep the tender green tops from crumbling.

BEST COOKING METHODS: Stalks are best boiled, while florets become mushy when boiled and should be steamed. (See below for information on cooking the stalks and florets in one pot.) Once cooked, broccoli can be dressed with vinaigrette or sautéed. Broccoli can also be braised or stir-fried.

Broccolini are tender enough to sauté without precooking. Broccoflower should be steamed to protect the delicate florets from becoming soggy.

Steamed/Boiled Broccoli

Thick stalks need to be boiled in order to cook through. However, tender florets can become mushy when cooked this way; they respond better to the gentle heat of steaming. The method outlined in this recipe allows the stalks and florets to cook perfectly in the same pan. The peeled and sliced stalks cook in simmering water while the florets are set over the stalks in a basket, where they steam. A pasta pot with steamer insert is ideal for this job; however, any deep, wide pot along with a lid and a collapsible steamer basket will work fine. Steamed/boiled broccoli can be seasoned with almost any kind of dressing. See the ideas that follow.

MAKES ENOUGH BROCCOLI FOR ONE OF THE FOLLOWING RECIPES

1 large bunch broccoli (about 1½ pounds)
Salt

1. Rinse the broccoli and separate the stalks from the florets where they meet. Cut off the woody ends of the stalks. Use a paring knife to trim away ⅛ inch of the outer peel from the stalks. Cut the peeled stalks in half lengthwise and then into bite-sized pieces. If necessary, separate the florets into smaller sections. Arrange the florets in a steamer insert or basket.
2. Bring about 1 inch of water to a boil in a deep, wide pot. Add the stalks and salt to taste to the simmering water. Carefully lower the basket with the florets into the pot, making sure it rests above water. Cover and simmer until the broccoli is just tender, 4 to 5 minutes. Drain well and season as in the following recipes.

Broccoli with Extra-Virgin Olive Oil and Garlic

The simplest way to season steamed/boiled broccoli, and the best when serving broccoli with other strongly flavored foods and/or sauces.

SERVES 4 AS A SIDE DISH

1 recipe Steamed/Boiled Broccoli
2 tablespoons extra-virgin olive oil
1 small garlic clove, minced fine
Salt

While the broccoli is cooking, combine the oil, garlic, and salt to taste in a small bowl. Drain the broccoli well and gently toss it with the garlic oil. Adjust the seasonings. Serve immediately.

Broccoli with Spicy Balsamic Dressing and Black Olives

Use good-quality olives such as Kalamatas in this simple Italian recipe with olive oil, balsamic and red wine vinegars, garlic, and hot red pepper flakes.

SERVES 4 AS A SIDE DISH

1 recipe Steamed/Boiled Broccoli (above)
2 teaspoons balsamic vinegar

2 teaspoons red wine vinegar

1 small garlic clove, minced

½ teaspoon hot red pepper flakes, or to taste

4 tablespoons extra-virgin olive oil
   Salt

12 large black olives, such as Kalamatas, pitted and quartered

1. While the broccoli is cooking, whisk the vinegars, garlic, and hot red pepper flakes together in a small bowl. Whisk in the oil until the dressing is smooth. Add salt (sparingly) to taste.

2. Drain the broccoli well and gently toss it with the dressing and olives. Adjust the seasonings. Serve immediately or at room temperature.

Broccoli with Orange-Ginger Dressing

A slightly sweet Asian dressing gives plain broccoli a tremendous boost in flavor. Toasted walnuts add crunch.

SERVES 4 AS A SIDE DISH

1 recipe Steamed/Boiled Broccoli (page 43)

1 tablespoon roasted peanut oil

1 tablespoon soy sauce

1 tablespoon honey

1 tablespoon grated orange zest

3 tablespoons orange juice

1 small garlic clove, peeled
   One 1-inch piece peeled fresh gingerroot
   Salt

2 medium scallions, white and green parts, sliced thin

⅔ cup walnuts, toasted in a dry skillet until fragrant, cooled, and chopped

1. While the broccoli is cooking, process the oil, soy sauce, honey, orange zest, orange juice, garlic, and ginger in a food processor, scraping down the sides of the bowl as needed, until smooth. Add salt to taste.

2. Drain the broccoli well and gently toss it with the dressing, scallions, and walnuts. Adjust the seasonings. Serve immediately or at room temperature.

Broccoli with Lime-Cumin Dressing

Residual heat from the broccoli tames the raw red onions or shallots in this Caribbean-inspired dressing. Add as much, or as little, hot sauce as desired.

SERVES 4 AS A SIDE DISH

1 recipe Steamed/Boiled Broccoli (page 43)

1 teaspoon grated lime zest

1 tablespoon lime juice

½ teaspoon ground cumin
   Salt
   Hot sauce, such as Tabasco

3 tablespoons extra-virgin olive oil

¼ cup minced red onion or shallots

1. While the broccoli is cooking, whisk the lime zest, lime juice, cumin, salt, and hot sauce to taste

together in a small bowl. Whisk in the oil until the dressing is smooth. Stir in the onion.

2. Drain the broccoli well and gently toss it with the dressing. Adjust the seasonings. Serve immediately or at room temperature.

Slow-Cooked Broccoli with Garlic and Anchovies

This Italian recipe breaks most of the standard practices for cooking broccoli. Instead of trying to preserve the crisp texture of the stalks and florets, in this recipe the broccoli is braised until it almost falls apart. Because the broccoli is cooked with the seasonings for so long, it really takes on the flavor of the garlic and anchovies. Every bite is heady and delicious.

SERVES 4 AS A SIDE DISH

1 large bunch broccoli (about 1½ pounds)
3 tablespoons extra-virgin olive oil
3 large garlic cloves, sliced thin
3 medium anchovies, minced
⅔ cup water
   Salt
   Freshly ground black pepper

1. Rinse the broccoli and separate the stalks from the florets where they meet. Cut off the woody ends of the stalks. Use a paring knife to trim away ⅛ inch of the outer peel from the stalks.

Cut the peeled stalks in half lengthwise and then into bite-sized pieces. If necessary, separate the florets into smaller sections.

2. Heat the oil, garlic, and anchovies in a large sauté pan over medium heat. Cook until the garlic turns golden, about 4 minutes. Add the broccoli and stir to coat well with the oil. Stir-cook for 1 minute.

3. Add the water and salt and pepper to taste, cover, and simmer, stirring once or twice, until the broccoli is tender, about 10 minutes. Uncover and cook until any remaining water in the pan evaporates. Adjust the seasonings and serve immediately.

Sesame Stir-Fried Broccoli

Many cooks dread the two-step cooking process outlined in most recipes for stir-fried broccoli. It seems antithetical to quick cooking to blanch or steam the vegetable and then to stir-fry it. I have found that broccoli (as well as other green vegetables) can be stir-fried without precooking. This process is a bit unusual, but it works. Stir-fry the broccoli briefly in hot oil, add the aromatics (garlic, ginger, etc.), then add a fairly liquid sauce. Quickly throw a cover over the pan and let it simmer away. The steam from the liquid cooks the broccoli through and the liquid reduces to become a sauce for the broccoli. This technique cooks florets beautifully but doesn't work as well when the stalks are added.

SERVES 4 AS A SIDE DISH

½ cup chicken or vegetable stock
1 tablespoon toasted sesame oil
1 tablespoon soy sauce
1 tablespoon sesame seeds
1 tablespoon plus 1 teaspoon roasted peanut
   oil
1 large bunch broccoli (about 1½ pounds),
   stalks discarded and florets cut into bite-
   sized pieces
2 medium garlic cloves, minced
1 tablespoon minced fresh gingerroot

1. Combine the stock, sesame oil, and soy sauce in a small bowl. Set this mixture aside.

2. Place the sesame seeds in a large nonstick skillet set over medium heat. Toast the seeds, shaking the pan occasionally to turn them, until lightly browned, about 3 minutes. Transfer the seeds to a small bowl.

3. Raise the heat to high and briefly heat 1 tablespoon of the oil in the empty skillet until shimmering. Add the broccoli and stir-fry until well coated with oil, about 30 seconds.

4. Clear a space in the center of the pan and add the garlic and ginger. Drizzle the remaining 1 teaspoon of oil over the garlic and ginger and cook until fragrant, about 30 seconds. Stir the garlic and ginger into the broccoli.

5. Add the chicken stock mixture to the pan, cover, reduce the heat to medium, and cook until the broccoli is tender, about 2 minutes. If necessary, briefly simmer, uncovered, to reduce the sauce to just a tablespoon or two. Stir in the sesame seeds and serve immediately.

Stir-Fried Broccoli with Fermented Black Bean and Orange Sauce

If you have access to salted fermented black beans, you must add them to your list of staples. Whenever I am in Chinatown, I buy a bag and stick it in the freezer. The salty, robust flavor of fermented black beans works especially well with broccoli.

SERVES 4 AS A SIDE DISH

½ cup orange juice
1 tablespoon soy sauce
1 tablespoon plus 1 teaspoon roasted peanut
   oil
1 large bunch broccoli (about 1½ pounds),
   stalks discarded and florets cut into bite-
   sized pieces
2 tablespoons fermented black beans
2 large garlic cloves, sliced thin
1 tablespoon minced fresh gingerroot

1. Combine the orange juice and soy sauce in a small bowl and set the mixture aside.

2. Heat 1 tablespoon of the oil in a large nonstick skillet until shimmering. Add the broccoli and stir-fry over high heat until well coated with oil, about 30 seconds.

3. Clear a space in the center of the pan and add the beans, garlic, and ginger. Drizzle the remaining 1 teaspoon oil over the aromatics and cook

until fragrant, about 1 minute. Stir the aromatics into the broccoli.

4. Add the orange-soy mixture to the pan, cover, reduce the heat to medium, and cook until the broccoli is tender, about 2 minutes. If necessary, briefly simmer, uncovered, to reduce the sauce to a glaze. Serve immediately.

Stir-Fried Broccoli and Mushrooms with Oyster Sauce

A Chinese restaurant classic. Oyster sauce has a rich, almost meaty flavor that works especially well with the broccoli and mushrooms. If you like Chinese food with some sweetness, try this recipe with hoisin sauce in place of the oyster sauce and omit the sugar.

SERVES 4 AS A SIDE DISH

¼ cup chicken or vegetable stock or water

2 tablespoons sherry or rice wine

2 tablespoons oyster sauce

1 tablespoon soy sauce

1 teaspoon toasted sesame oil

½ teaspoon sugar

2 tablespoons plus 1 teaspoon roasted peanut oil

8 ounces shiitake or other mushrooms, sliced thick (discard stems first if using shiitakes)

1 large bunch broccoli (about 1½ pounds), stalks discarded and florets cut into bite-sized pieces

3 medium garlic cloves, minced

1 tablespoon minced fresh gingerroot

1. Combine the stock, sherry, oyster sauce, soy sauce, sesame oil, and sugar in a small bowl and set the sauce aside.

2. Heat 1 tablespoon of the oil in a large nonstick skillet until shimmering. Add the mushrooms and stir-fry over high heat until golden brown, about 2 minutes. Transfer the mushrooms to a bowl.

3. Heat another tablespoon of oil in the empty skillet. Add the broccoli and stir-fry over high heat until well coated with oil, about 30 seconds.

4. Clear a space in the center of the pan and add the garlic and ginger. Drizzle the remaining 1 teaspoon oil over the aromatics and cook until fragrant, about 1 minute. Stir the aromatics into the broccoli.

5. Return the mushrooms to the pan. Add the sauce, cover, reduce the heat to medium, and cook until the broccoli is tender, about 2 minutes. If necessary, briefly simmer, uncovered, to reduce the sauce to a glaze. Serve immediately.

Broccolini with Garlic and Olive Oil

This diminutive form of broccoli, which is sometimes called baby broccoli, has started showing up in many supermarkets. Unlike regular broccoli, the stalks are quite tender and can be eaten without peeling. (I do find that the end of each stalk dries out and should be trimmed, as if cutting away the end of a mushroom stem.) Broccolini will cook through without blanching. Simply toss the trimmed pieces in some garlicky oil, add a little stock, cover, and simmer until tender.

SERVES 4 AS A SIDE DISH

2 tablespoons extra-virgin olive oil
2 medium garlic cloves, minced

10 ounces broccolini, thin slice trimmed from
each stem end
½ cup chicken or vegetable stock
Salt

1. Heat the oil and garlic in a large sauté pan over medium heat until the garlic is golden, about 2 minutes. Add the broccolini and toss to coat evenly with the oil and garlic.

2. Add the stock and salt to taste, cover, and simmer until the broccolini is tender and the liquid in the pan has been absorbed, about 6 minutes. (If the broccolini is tender but some liquid remains in the pan, simmer, uncovered, for a minute or two to evaporate liquid.) Adjust the seasonings and serve immediately.

Broccoli Rabe

This nonheading variety of broccoli (the flowers grow amid the leaves, and not in one large head) offers contrasting textures and tastes. Although the toughest portions of the stems are discarded, you can eat the thinner stems, the leaves, and the flowers. The flavor ranges from mild (almost like broccoli) to downright peppery. The leaves and flowers tend to be hotter than the stalks. There is also tremendous variation in the overall heat level in a crop depending on the growing conditions.

Broccoli rabe may be a member of the broccoli family, but in the kitchen we handle it like bitter leafy greens. I generally blanch it in boiling water to set the color and get the stems crisp-tender. The broccoli rabe is then drained and cooked again, usually in hot oil with seasonings. Make sure to drain the broccoli rabe well after it is blanched. If left too wet, the broccoli rabe will cause the hot oil to sizzle excessively.

OTHER COMMON NAMES: Broccoletti di rape, broccoli raab, and rapini.

AVAILABILITY: Year-round.

SELECTION: Look for broccoli rabe with stalks no thicker than a pencil (less waste this way) and healthy-looking leaves. The leaves should be green and crisp and the flower buds tightly closed.

STORAGE: Broccoli rabe will keep in the refrigerator for several days in a loosely sealed plastic bag.

BASIC PREPARATION: The lower portion of the stems is too tough to cook with the rest of the broccoli rabe, so discard it. Cut off the stems just below the point where they start to branch out and the leaves begin. You will still have plenty of crunchy (but thinner) stalks mixed in with the leaves. Rinse the broccoli rabe well and proceed with cooking.

BEST COOKING METHODS: Blanching then sautéing. Can also be chopped fine for sauces, stir-fried over high heat, and then simmered with liquid in a covered pan (in effect, braised).

Spicy Broccoli Rabe with Garlic

A southern Italian classic. For a very spicy dish, increase the hot red pepper flakes to 1 teaspoon.

SERVES 4 AS A SIDE DISH

1¼ pounds broccoli rabe
   Salt
 2 tablespoons extra-virgin olive oil
 4 medium garlic cloves, sliced thin
 ½ teaspoon hot red pepper flakes

1. Bring several quarts of water to a boil in a large pot.
2. Trim the thick, tough stems from the broccoli rabe just below where the stems branch or the leaves start.
3. Add the broccoli rabe and salt to taste to the boiling water. Cook until the broccoli rabe is tender, about 2 minutes. Drain well and set aside.
4. Heat the oil in a medium skillet over medium heat. Add the garlic and cook until golden, 2 to 3 minutes. Add the hot red pepper flakes and cook for 30 seconds to release their oils.
5. Add the broccoli rabe and cook, stirring constantly, until heated through, 1 to 2 minutes. Adjust the seasonings. Serve immediately.

VARIATION: ORECCHIETTE WITH SPICY BROCCOLI RABE

Another Italian classic. Use small shells or penne if you can't find ear-shaped orecchiette.

SERVES 4 AS A MAIN COURSE

1. Prepare the broccoli rabe, chopping it after it has been cooked in step 3. Proceed as directed, increasing the oil in step 4 to ¼ cup. Finish cooking broccoli rabe as directed in step 5.
2. While preparing the broccoli rabe, bring 4 quarts of water to a boil in a large pot. Add 1 pound orecchiette and salt to taste and cook until al dente. Reserve ¾ cup cooking water and drain the pasta. Toss the pasta with the broccoli rabe, adding as much of the reserved cooking water as necessary to moisten the pasta.

Broccoli Rabe with Red Bell Pepper, Olives, and Garlic

The condiments in this recipe—sweet bell pepper, salty olives, and savory garlic—complement the mildly bitter flavor of broccoli rabe.

SERVES 4 AS A SIDE DISH

1¼ pounds broccoli rabe
   Salt
 2 tablespoons extra-virgin olive oil
 ½ medium red bell pepper, cored, seeded, halved crosswise, and sliced thin
 2 medium garlic cloves, minced
 8 large black olives, such as Kalamatas, pitted and sliced

1. Bring several quarts of water to a boil.
2. Trim the thick, tough stems from the broccoli rabe just below where the stems branch.
3. Add the broccoli rabe and salt to taste to the boiling water. Cook until the broccoli rabe is tender, about 2 minutes. Drain well and set aside.
4. Heat the oil in a medium skillet over medium heat. Add the bell pepper and sauté, stirring occasionally, until slightly softened, about 3 minutes. Add the garlic and cook until fragrant, about 30 seconds.
5. Add the broccoli rabe and olives and cook, stirring constantly, until heated through, 1 to 2 minutes. Adjust the seasonings. Serve immediately.

Broccoli Rabe with Sun-Dried Tomatoes and Pine Nuts

This dish is colorful and quick to prepare.

SERVES 4 AS A SIDE DISH

1¼ pounds broccoli rabe
   Salt
 2 tablespoons extra-virgin olive oil
 2 medium garlic cloves, sliced thin
 2 tablespoons pine nuts
 8 sun-dried tomatoes packed in oil, drained and sliced thin
 ½ teaspoon hot red pepper flakes

1. Bring several quarts of water to a boil.
2. Trim the thick, tough stems from the broccoli rabe just below where the stems branch or the leaves start.
3. Add the broccoli rabe and salt to taste to the boiling water. Simmer until the broccoli rabe is tender, about 2 minutes. Drain well and set aside.
4. Heat the oil in a medium skillet over medium heat. Add the garlic and pine nuts and cook until golden, 2 to 3 minutes.
5. Add the broccoli rabe, sun-dried tomatoes, and hot red pepper flakes and cook, stirring constantly, until heated through, 1 to 2 minutes. Adjust the seasonings. Serve immediately.

Soba Noodles with Spicy Broccoli Rabe

The hearty flavor of buckwheat noodles is a good foil for the pungent flavors of garlic, hot red pepper flakes, and leafy greens. Although this recipe calls for broccoli rabe, it works equally well with kale or bok choy as long as you adjust the cooking time for the greens as necessary. Depending on how much of the stem is attached, you will need between 1 and 1½ pounds of greens to yield the necessary 8 cups when chopped.

SERVES 4 AS A MAIN COURSE

12 ounces soba noodles
 1 medium bunch broccoli rabe (about 1¼ pounds)

1 tablespoon roasted peanut oil
1 tablespoon toasted sesame oil
4 medium garlic cloves, minced
1 teaspoon hot red pepper flakes, or to taste
¼ cup mirin (Japanese sweet rice wine) or sherry
2 tablespoons soy sauce

1. Bring 4 quarts of water to a boil in a large pot. Add the soba noodles and cook until al dente, 4 to 5 minutes. Drain and rinse under warm, running water to remove excess starch. Set the noodles aside.

2. Trim the thick, tough stems from the broccoli rabe just below where the stems branch or the leaves start. Chop the broccoli rabe.

3. Heat the oils in a large nonstick skillet. When the oils are quite hot, add the garlic and hot red pepper flakes and stir-fry until fragrant, about 20 seconds. Add the broccoli rabe and cook, stirring to coat with the oil, about 30 seconds. Add the mirin and ½ cup water, cover, and cook until the greens are tender, 3 to 4 minutes.

4. Uncover the pan and add the soba noodles and soy sauce. Stir-fry, tossing to combine ingredients, until the noodles are hot, about 1 minute. Serve immediately.

Brussels Sprouts

Brussels sprouts look like tiny, perfectly round cabbages. as their appearance and flavor suggest, they are closely related to green cabbages. Unlike cabbages, however, they grow on a tall, heavy stalk.

Many people object to Brussels sprouts because of their aggressive flavor. However, if Brussels sprouts are grown and cooked properly, they are sweet and nutty. So what makes some sprouts delicious?

They are sweetest if harvested after the first frost of the season. Late fall and winter are the best time to buy Brussels sprouts, especially if they have been grown in an area that experiences cold weather.

Second, I find that Brussels sprouts are much better when they are harvested small. Large sprouts, bigger than golf balls, are bitter and often woody in the center. Stick with smaller sprouts and you will be rewarded.

Of course, the cook has a role in making great Brussels sprout dishes. Don't overcook Brussels sprouts—they suffer from the same chemical reaction that makes overcooked broccoli taste objectionable. Properly cooked sprouts are crisp-tender, not mushy or soft.

AVAILABILITY: Fall and winter.

SELECTION: Look for small Brussels sprouts (they should be smaller than a Ping-Pong ball) that are dark green and crisp. Wilted or yellow leaves are a sign that the sprouts are past their prime. The sprouts should be tightly closed as well.

You may be able to find sprouts still on the stalk at farmers' markets. Store them on the stalk and then cut them off when you are ready to cook the sprouts.

STORAGE: Brussels sprouts should be refrigerated in a loosely sealed plastic bag. They will remain fresh for several days, if not a week.

BASIC PREPARATION: The outer leaves on each Brussels sprout can be dry, so I usually peel off a layer or two of leaves. Trim a thin slice from the stem end of each sprout. (This too is often dry.)

BEST COOKING METHODS: Blanching (and then sautéing) or braising.

Shredded Brussels Sprouts with Balsamic Vinegar and Pine Nuts

Brussels sprouts are blanched until almost tender and then sautéed until lightly browned. This two-step cooking process reduces their strong "cabbage" flavor and actually makes them taste sweet.

SERVES 4 TO 6 AS A SIDE DISH

1 pound small Brussels sprouts
Salt
¼ cup pine nuts
3 tablespoons extra-virgin olive oil
1 medium onion, chopped fine
2 medium garlic cloves, minced
2 tablespoons balsamic vinegar

1. Bring several quarts of water to a boil in a medium saucepan.
2. Meanwhile, trim and discard a layer or two of loose outer leaves from each Brussels sprout. Trim a thin slice from the stem end of each sprout. Add the trimmed sprouts and salt to taste to the boiling water. Cook until the sprouts are almost tender, about 4 minutes. Drain and cool. Cut the sprouts crosswise (not through the stem end) into thin strips.
3. Place the nuts in a large skillet over medium heat. Toast, shaking the pan occasionally to turn the nuts, until they are golden brown and fra-

grant, about 3 minutes. Transfer the nuts to a small plate.
4. Briefly heat the oil in the empty skillet. Add the onion and sauté over medium heat until golden, about 5 minutes. Add the garlic and cook until fragrant, about 1 minute. Add the Brussels sprouts and salt to taste. Cook, stirring occasionally, until the sprouts have browned slightly, 5 to 7 minutes. Add the vinegar and cook just until the liquid evaporates, about 1 minute. Stir in the nuts and adjust the seasonings. Serve immediately.

VARIATION: SHREDDED BRUSSELS SPROUTS WITH ORANGE JUICE AND PECANS

These flavors work well with a Thanksgiving meal.

Replace the pine nuts with an equal amount of pecans. Add 1 teaspoon grated orange zest with the garlic. Replace the vinegar with ¼ cup orange juice.

Brussels Sprouts with Bacon

This is a staple on many holiday tables. Bacon will entice even the pickiest eater who says he or she doesn't like Brussels sprouts. Use a couple of slices of diced pancetta if you prefer.

SERVES 4 AS A SIDE DISH

1 pound small Brussels sprouts
Salt
4 strips bacon (about 3 ounces), diced
Freshly ground black pepper

1. Bring several quarts of water to a boil in a medium saucepan

2. Meanwhile, trim and discard a layer or two of loose outer leaves from each Brussels sprout. Trim a thin slice from the stem end of each sprout. Add the trimmed sprouts and salt to taste to the boiling water. Cook until the sprouts are tender, about 6 minutes. Drain well. (The sprouts are best finished off right away, but they can be set aside for up to an hour or two.)

3. Fry the bacon in a large skillet over medium heat until crisp, about 5 minutes. Spoon off all but the sheerest film of fat. Add the Brussels sprouts and pepper to taste to the pan. Cook, stirring to coat the sprouts with bacon fat, until heated through, 1 to 2 minutes. Adjust the seasonings and serve immediately.

Braised Brussels Sprouts with Mustard Cream Sauce

This recipe intensifies the flavor of Brussels sprouts and is designed for people who really like this small cabbage—and will surprise and encourage those who don't. Here, the sprouts are braised, without blanching first, in a little cream and stock. They actually absorb all the cream and thus become especially rich and a bit sweet. A swirl of mustard gives the Brussels sprouts added flavor and an attractive sheen.

SERVES 4 AS A SIDE DISH

1 pound small Brussels sprouts
1 tablespoon unsalted butter
2 medium shallots, minced
¼ cup heavy cream
¼ cup chicken or vegetable stock
Salt
1 tablespoon Dijon mustard
1 tablespoon minced fresh parsley leaves
Freshly ground black pepper

1. Trim and discard a layer or two of loose outer leaves from each Brussels sprout. Trim a thin slice from the stem end of each sprout. Set the trimmed Brussels sprouts aside.

2. Melt the butter in a large sauté pan. Add the shallots and sauté over medium heat until softened, about 3 minutes. Add the Brussels sprouts, cream, stock, and salt to taste. Cover and simmer until the sprouts are tender, about 10 minutes.

3. Remove the cover and stir in the mustard, parsley, and pepper to taste. Adjust the seasonings. Serve immediately.

Burdock

Wild burdock is a bothersome weed that chokes out other plants in many gardens. In contrast, cultivated burdock is a delicacy in Japan, prized for its unusual flavor and texture.

This slender beige root can grow to be three or four feet long and doesn't really resemble any other root vegetable. Burdock is related to carrots and parsnips and, like these more common root vegetables, it has a pleasant sweet flavor. However, while carrots and parsnips can be achingly sweet and fairly one-dimensional in flavor, burdock has a robust, meaty quality. Burdock is also much chewier and more fibrous than other common root vegetables. Carrots and parsnips will become mushy if overcooked; there's little danger of overcooking sturdy burdock.

Because of its texture, I find it best to braise burdock. Boiling washes away too much of its flavor, but dry-heat cooking methods, such as roasting, don't soften this curious root properly. When cut fairly small and braised with some flavorful liquid in a covered pot, burdock can be delicious and relatively easy to prepare.

OTHER COMMON NAMES: Gobo.

AVAILABILITY: Fall through spring, mostly in natural food stores, Japanese markets, and occasionally at farmers' markets.

SELECTION: Because burdock is fibrous, it's important to choose thin roots (no thicker than an inch and preferably thinner) that are not too tough. Make sure the roots are quite firm. Although the ends may bend, the roots should not be flaccid or soft.

STORAGE: Wrap burdock roots in damp paper towels and then in plastic and refrigerate them for a day or two at most. Burdock becomes soft rather quickly. Do not cut burdock before you are ready to prepare it. Super-long roots can be gently bent to fit inside the vegetable crisper drawer.

BASIC PREPARATION: Most Japanese cookbooks say not to peel burdock because the peel and the layer of flesh right beneath it are so flavorful. Although skeptical about this advice, I have cooked peeled and unpeeled pieces from the same root and can report that the difference in flavor is quite significant. With the peel on, burdock tastes sweeter and more robust. And since the skin is so thin, unpeeled burdock is only slightly chewier than peeled burdock. When possible, I recommend that you skip peeling and scrub the root vigorously under cold, running water to remove any soil.

Of course, if you have purchased burdock that is particularly gnarled or dirty, you will need to peel it. Just go lightly, removing as little flesh as possible with the skin.

The other main issue to consider is discoloration. Burdock will brown, much like an apple, when cut. As you cut burdock to the desired size, place the pieces in a bowl of cold water. (Some sources suggest adding some lemon juice or vinegar but I have found no benefit to adding either.) Soaking in the cold water also helps loosen any remaining granules of dirt that your scrub brush may have missed.

BEST COOKING METHOD: Braising.

Braised Burdock and Carrots, Japanese Style

This dish can be served hot as a side dish with beef or chicken, or cooled to room temperature and served as a light salad before the meal. It's important to cut the burdock and carrots into very thin pieces so they will cook through quickly.

SERVES 4 AS A SIDE DISH OR SALAD

6 ounces burdock

3 small carrots (about 6 ounces)

2 tablespoons sake

1½ tablespoons soy sauce

1 tablespoon honey

2 tablespoons water

1 tablespoon sesame seeds

2 teaspoons canola or other tasteless oil

2 teaspoons toasted sesame oil

1. Scrub the burdock well. If the roots are too dirty to clean properly, peel them. Cut the burdock into 2-inch lengths. Cut each length in half lengthwise. Lay each half cut side down on a cutting board and cut lengthwise into very thin slivers. Place the burdock in a bowl of cold water as soon as the pieces have been cut. Repeat this process with the remaining burdock chunks. Peel and cut the carrots the same way but do not place them in the cold water.

2. Combine the sake, soy sauce, honey, and water in a small bowl and set the mixture aside.

3. Set a large skillet over medium heat. Add the sesame seeds and toast, shaking the pan occasionally to turn the seeds, until golden brown, about 3 minutes. Scrape the toasted seeds onto a plate. Set the skillet aside briefly.

4. Drain and pat dry the burdock pieces. Put the skillet back over medium-high heat. Add the canola and sesame oils and heat until shimmering. Add the burdock and carrots and sauté until the pieces start to brown a bit, about 4 minutes.

5. Add the sake mixture to the skillet. Cover and reduce the heat to medium-low. Simmer just until the vegetables are tender and have absorbed all the liquid, about 8 minutes. Sprinkle with the toasted sesame seeds and serve immediately.

Braised Burdock with Dried Shiitake Mushrooms

Dried shiitake mushrooms bring a tremendous amount of flavor to this dish. They also provide a pleasing textural contrast to the burdock. The mushrooms are chewy and slippery; the burdock chewy and a tad fibrous. The combination is quite good. Serve this hearty side dish with meat or chicken. Depending on its age and thickness, burdock will absorb liquid at different rates. The directions in step 5 will help you compensate for burdock that cooks a little faster or slower than usual.

SERVES 4 AS A SIDE DISH

1 ounce dried shiitake mushrooms

¼ cup mirin (Japanese sweet rice wine)

2 tablespoons soy sauce

¾ pound burdock

2 tablespoons canola or other tasteless oil

1 medium onion, chopped

¼ teaspoon hot red pepper flakes

1. Place the dried mushrooms in a small bowl and cover with 2 cups of hot tap water. Set aside to soak until softened, about 20 minutes. Remove the mushrooms with a fork from their soaking liquid, reserving the liquid, and transfer them to a cutting board. Slice the mushrooms, discarding any portions that are still hard (there may be some small bits of stem that are still very hard). Set the mushrooms aside.

2. Strain the soaking liquid through a sieve lined with a coffee filter or paper towel and into a small bowl. Stir in the mirin and soy sauce and set the mushroom stock aside.

3. While the mushrooms are soaking, scrub the burdock well. If the roots are too dirty to clean properly, peel them. Slice the burdock on the bias into ½-inch chunks. Place the burdock in a bowl of cold water as soon as the pieces have been cut.

4. Heat the oil in a medium sauté pan. Add the onion and sauté over medium heat until golden, about 4 minutes. Add the sliced shiitake mushrooms and cook, stirring often, to bring out their flavor, about 1 minute. Drain the burdock (do not bother to blot dry) and add to the pan along with the hot red pepper flakes. Stir-cook for 1 minute.

5. Add the mushroom stock, reduce the heat to medium-low, cover, and simmer until the burdock is crisp-tender and all the liquid in the pan has evaporated, about 20 minutes. If the pan is dry but the burdock is not tender enough, add a little water, cover, and continue cooking. If, on the other hand, the burdock is tender but there's still liquid left in the pan, remove the cover and simmer for a minute or two to evaporate the excess liquid. Adjust the seasonings, adding more soy sauce or hot red pepper flakes if desired. Serve immediately.

Cabbage

There are dozens of cabbages grown around the world. This chapter focuses on four cabbages commonly available in American markets—red, Savoy, green, and napa. (Bok choy and tiny Brussels sprouts are so distinct that I have discussed each in its own chapter.)

Red cabbage is the sweetest of the cabbages. I find it tastes best when paired with vinegar. Use it in salads for crunch or braise it in a covered pan until tender. Red cabbage dyes everything it touches purple.

Although standard green cabbage (also called Dutch head cabbage) is fine in many recipes, I prefer Savoy cabbage in almost every instance. Regular green cabbage has light green, smooth leaves. Savoy cabbage has dark green, crinkly leaves. The real difference is the flavor. Green cabbage is bland and crunchy, which makes it ideal for coleslaw. Savoy cabbage has a sweeter, nuttier flavor that becomes more pronounced when the cabbage is cooked.

Napa cabbage (sometimes called Chinese, Peking, Tientsin, or nappa cabbage) has a crisp, refreshing texture and a mild, slightly sweet flavor. The base of the stalks is milky white and the ruffled leaves are the palest green. I find it best raw in salads. (When I want to cook with a Chinese cabbage, I use more flavorful and sturdier bok choy. However, if you want to cook napa cabbage, use it in any of the bok choy recipes on pages 35 through 36, reducing the cooking time slightly.)

AVAILABILITY: Year-round, although you will have best selection and highest quality from late summer through the winter.

SELECTION: Cabbage should look crisp and fresh. A couple of dry outer leaves are fine but the head should be tightly closed. (The leaves on Savoy and napa cabbage will open up a bit more.)

Red and green cabbages are long keepers, with Savoy following quickly behind. Many markets simply remove outer leaves as the cabbage dries out. If the color of the cabbage looks washed out, the darker outer leaves have probably been removed and the cabbage is fairly old. Stick with brightly colored cabbages.

Napa cabbage is much more perishable. Avoid napa cabbage with leaves that are limp or show any signs of decay. The crisp white stalks may be covered with tiny dark spots, which are normal and should be ignored.

STORAGE: All cabbages can be refrigerated in a loosely sealed plastic bag for several days. With the exception of napa cabbage (its open, looser leaves tend to wilt faster), most cabbages will hold for a week, or even longer, in the refrigerator.

BASIC PREPARATION: Red, green, and Savoy cabbages are all prepared in the same fashion. Tough or dry outer leaves are peeled off and discarded. The cabbage is then cut through the stem end into four pieces. With a knife, cut out the hard, white piece of the core that is attached to the base of each cabbage quarter. Flip the cabbage over on a flat side and then slice crosswise to cut the cabbage into thin strips.

Napa cabbage is long and narrow, not round like the other cabbages. If cut into quarters, the resulting strips of cabbage are quite small. I prefer to cut the cabbage in half through the stem end once the tough outer leaves have been removed. The hard piece of the core is removed from each half, which is then turned over and sliced crosswise into thin strips.

BEST COOKING METHODS: Blanching and then sautéing, boiling (in soups), or braising. Cabbages can be sliced thin and used raw in salads; they are often salted after they are sliced to make the cabbage tender.

Braised Red Cabbage with Onions

Make sure to use a large, wide pot for this recipe so that the cabbage has room to cook down. This sweet, tender cabbage dish is a natural with pork or with roasted chicken.

SERVES 6 TO 8 AS A SIDE DISH

1 medium head red cabbage (about 2 pounds)

3 tablespoons extra-virgin olive oil

2 medium onions, halved and sliced thin

2 medium garlic cloves, minced

Salt

Freshly ground black pepper

¾ cup chicken or vegetable stock

¼ cup minced fresh parsley leaves

2 tablespoons balsamic vinegar

1. Remove any tough or dry outer leaves from the head of cabbage. Quarter the cabbage through the stem end. Cut out and discard the hard piece of the core at the base of each quarter. Slice the cabbage crosswise into thin strips. (You should have about 10 cups.)

2. Heat the oil in a large casserole or Dutch oven. Add the onions and cook over medium heat until golden, about 8 minutes. Add the garlic and cook until fragrant, about 1 minute.

3. Stir in the cabbage and sprinkle with salt and pepper to taste. Cover and cook, stirring several times, until the cabbage has partially wilted, about 5 minutes.

4. Add the stock, cover, and continue cooking until the cabbage is tender, about 10 minutes. Uncover and simmer until any liquid in the pan evaporates, 2 to 3 minutes. Stir in the parsley and vinegar and adjust the seasonings. Serve immediately.

VARIATION: BRAISED RED CABBAGE WITH PORT AND WALNUTS

More festive, perfect for a holiday meal.

Reduce the amount of stock to ½ cup and add ¼ cup port with the stock. Omit the vinegar and stir in ½ cup walnuts, toasted and chopped, with the parsley.

Warm Red Cabbage Salad with Bacon and Goat Cheese

An excellent first course before a winter meal, especially for the holidays. Thick-cut bacon, with its chewy texture, makes a real difference here.

SERVES 6 AS A FIRST COURSE

1 small head red cabbage (about 1½ pounds)

6 ounces thick-cut bacon, chopped

2 tablespoons extra-virgin olive oil

2 medium shallots, minced

3 tablespoons sherry vinegar
Salt
Freshly ground black pepper
4 ounces goat cheese, crumbled (about 1
cup)

1. Remove any tough or dry outer leaves from the head of cabbage. Quarter the cabbage through the stem end. Cut out and discard the hard piece of the core at the base of each quarter. Slice the cabbage crosswise into thin strips. (You should have about 8 cups.) Place the cabbage in a large bowl and set it aside.

2. Cook the bacon in a medium skillet over medium heat until very crisp, 8 to 10 minutes. Use a slotted spoon to transfer the bacon to a platter lined with paper towels. Drain off all but 1 tablespoon of the bacon fat.

3. Add the oil to the bacon fat left in the pan and heat briefly. Add the shallots and sauté over medium heat until softened, about 2 minutes. Whisk in the vinegar and salt and pepper to taste. Simmer for 30 seconds to combine the flavors.

4. Pour the dressing over the cabbage and toss to combine. Add the bacon and goat cheese and toss several times. Divide the salad among individual plates and serve immediately.

Browned Savoy Cabbage with Pancetta and Onions

Crinkly Savoy cabbage is especially popular in Italy, where it is often cooked with pancetta (Italian bacon) and onion. Unlike American bacon, pancetta is unsmoked and is never cured with sugar. You may use American bacon with slightly different results. Make sure to really brown the cabbage well. It's fine if it starts to stick to the pot a bit. When the stock is added, it will deglaze the pan, freeing any stuck bits of cabbage or onion.

SERVES 6 AS A SIDE DISH

1 medium head Savoy cabbage (about
2½ pounds)
Salt
2 tablespoons extra-virgin olive oil
2 ounces thinly sliced pancetta, cut into
½-inch dice
2 medium onions, chopped
1¼ cups chicken or vegetable stock
Freshly ground black pepper

1. Bring 4 quarts of water to a boil in a large pot.

2. Remove any tough or dry outer leaves from the head of cabbage. Quarter the cabbage through the stem end. Cut out and discard the hard piece of the core at the base of each quarter. Slice the cabbage crosswise into thin strips. (You should have about 12 cups.) Add the cabbage and salt to

taste to the boiling water. Cook until the cabbage is tender, about 5 minutes. Drain and set the cabbage aside.

3. Heat the oil, pancetta, and onions in a large casserole or Dutch oven over medium heat. Cook until the pancetta is crisp and the onion begins to brown, about 6 minutes. Stir in the cabbage and cook, stirring occasionally, until wilted and lightly browned, about 12 minutes.

4. Add the stock and bring the liquid to a boil. Cook just until the liquid in the pot evaporates, 3 to 5 minutes. Add salt and pepper to taste and serve immediately.

Savoy Cabbage Soup with Jumbo Parmesan Croutons

Cabbage makes an especially hearty soup. Add an oversized crouton covered with Parmesan cheese and you have dinner. You may want to serve the soup with a fork and knife to cut up the crouton. This soup is better with mild, nutty-tasting Savoy cabbage, but still good with green cabbage.

SERVES 6 AS A MAIN COURSE

1 small head Savoy cabbage (about
  2 pounds)
4 tablespoons extra-virgin olive oil
2 medium onions, chopped fine
3 medium garlic cloves, minced

7 cups chicken or vegetable stock
  Salt
  Freshly ground black pepper
6 slices country white bread (each 3 to 4
  inches across and ¾ inch thick)
6 tablespoons grated Parmesan cheese, plus
  extra for the table

1. Remove any tough or dry outer leaves from the head of cabbage. Quarter the cabbage through the stem end. Cut out and discard the hard piece of the core at the base of each quarter. Slice the cabbage crosswise into thin strips. (You should have about 10 cups.)

2. Heat 2 tablespoons of the oil in a large casserole or Dutch oven. Add the onions and sauté over medium heat until golden, about 6 minutes. Add the garlic and continue cooking until fragrant, about 1 minute.

3. Add the cabbage to the pot and stir to coat with the oil. Cook until slightly wilted, about 5 minutes. Add the stock and salt and pepper to taste. Bring to a boil, reduce the heat to medium-low, cover, and simmer until the cabbage is tender, about 1 hour. Adjust the seasonings.

4. When the soup is almost ready, preheat the broiler. Brush the remaining 2 tablespoons of oil over both sides of the bread slices. Place the bread on a baking sheet and broil until crisp on the first side. Remove the baking sheet from the oven, turn the bread slices, and sprinkle the cheese over the untoasted side of the bread slices. Return the baking sheet to the broiler and broil until the bread is crisp on the second side and the cheese has melted. Watch carefully to make sure the croutons do not burn.

5. Ladle the soup into individual bowls. Float one crouton, cheese side up, in each bowl. Serve immediately, passing more grated cheese at the table.

Slow-Cooked Cabbage with Apples and Juniper

An unusual but delicious Central European dish. The apple falls apart during the cooking process, leaving behind its sweet flavor but no texture. Juniper berries (sold in the spice aisle of many supermarkets) have a resinous, woodsy flavor that works well with the cabbage and apples. If you can't find juniper berries, use a cinnamon stick instead. This recipe can also be made with Savoy cabbage. Serve with pork roasts or chops or chicken.

SERVES 6 TO 8 AS A SIDE DISH

1 medium head green cabbage (about 2 pounds)
2 tablespoons unsalted butter
2 medium McIntosh apples, peeled, cored, and chopped
1 medium onion, chopped
1 teaspoon juniper berries
¾ cup apple cider
1 tablespoon cider vinegar
Salt
Freshly ground black pepper

1. Remove any tough or dry outer leaves from the head of cabbage. Quarter the cabbage through the stem end. Cut out and discard the hard piece of the core at the base of each quarter. Slice the cabbage crosswise into thin strips. (You should have about 10 cups.)

2. Melt the butter in a large casserole or Dutch oven. Add the apples and onion and sauté over medium heat until golden, about 7 minutes. Add the juniper berries and stir-cook until fragrant, about 30 seconds.

3. Add the cabbage, stirring to coat with the fat in the pan. Add the cider, reduce the heat, cover, and cook, stirring occasionally, until the cabbage is tender, about 35 minutes.

4. Stir in the vinegar and salt and pepper to taste. Simmer, uncovered, just until any excess liquid in the pot evaporates, 1 to 2 minutes. Serve immediately. (The juniper berries are edible, but just barely so. Pick out as many berries as you can before serving and then suggest that everyone fish out the remaining berries as they eat the cabbage.)

Creamy Coleslaw

My friend and colleague Pam Anderson showed me the benefits of salting cabbage for coleslaw. The liquid in the cabbage drains so the dressing doesn't become watery, even if the coleslaw is kept in the refrigerator for a day or two. I like to kick up the flavor in my coleslaw dressing with some Dijon mustard and tarragon.

½ large head green cabbage (about
    1¼ pounds)
1 large carrot, peeled and shredded on the
    large holes of a box grater
2 teaspoons kosher salt
½ cup mayonnaise
2 tablespoons rice vinegar
1 tablespoon Dijon mustard
1 tablespoon minced fresh tarragon leaves
    Freshly ground black pepper

1. Remove any tough or dry outer leaves from the cabbage half. Cut the cabbage in half through the stem end. Cut out and discard the hard piece of the core at the base of both pieces of cabbage. Slice the cabbage crosswise into the thinnest strips possible. (You should have about 6 cups.)
2. Toss the cabbage, carrot, and salt in a large strainer or colander set over a bowl. Let stand until the cabbage wilts, about 1½ hours. Thoroughly rinse under cold running water and then pat completely dry with paper towels. Place the dried cabbage and carrot in a large bowl.
3. Whisk together the mayonnaise, vinegar, mustard, tarragon, and pepper to taste in a small bowl. Pour the dressing over the cabbage and carrot and toss to coat evenly. Adjust the seasonings. Serve immediately or better still refrigerate for at least several hours (and up to several days) and serve chilled.

Salted and Pressed Cabbage with Asian Flavors

Salting and pressing cabbage yields a tender, highly seasoned salad that is best served as an accompaniment to a meal. The Szechwan peppercorns add a mildly peppery, floral note that is delicious and slightly exotic. Make the effort to find this item. Many supermarkets and gourmet stores stock it, as do Asian food shops.

SERVES 4 TO 6 AS A SIDE DISH

½ large head green cabbage (about 1¼
    pounds)
2 tablespoons rice vinegar
2 tablespoons soy sauce
1 teaspoon toasted sesame oil
1 tablespoon Szechwan peppercorns, toasted
    in a dry skillet until fragrant

1. Remove any tough or dry outer leaves from the cabbage half. Cut the cabbage in half through the stem end. Cut out and discard the hard piece of the core at the base of both pieces of cabbage. Slice the cabbage crosswise into the thinnest strips possible. (You should have about 6 cups.)
2. Combine the cabbage, vinegar, soy sauce, oil, and peppercorns in a large bowl.
3. Fill a gallon-sized zipper-lock plastic bag with cold water. Place the bag on top of the cabbage and let stand for 1 hour. Remove the weight, toss

gently, and weight again until the cabbage has wilted, about 1 hour more. Discard the weight. Serve as is or refrigerate for up to several days.

Kimchi

Kimchi is the fiery, garlicky condiment served with many Korean meals. It works well with fish, chicken, or meat. I especially like to serve kimchi with grilled flank steak or pork chops.

SERVES 8 OR MORE AS A CONDIMENT

1 large head napa cabbage (about 2 pounds)
1 tablespoon kosher salt
2 tablespoons fish sauce
2 tablespoons soy sauce
1 tablespoon sugar
4 medium garlic cloves, minced
1 tablespoon minced fresh gingerroot
2 teaspoons hot red pepper flakes, or more to taste
⅓ cup thinly sliced scallion greens

1. Remove any tough or dry outer leaves from the head of cabbage. Cut the cabbage in half through the stem end. Cut out and discard the hard core at the base of each half. Slice the cabbage cross-wise into thin strips. (You should have about 10 cups.)

2. Place the cabbage in a colander. Sprinkle the salt over the cabbage and toss to coat evenly. Set aside, stirring occasionally, until wilted, about 1 hour. Rinse the cabbage thoroughly to remove all traces of salt. Blot dry with paper towels.

3. While the cabbage is being salted, combine the fish sauce, soy sauce, sugar, garlic, ginger, and hot red pepper flakes in a bowl. Stir occasionally to help the sugar dissolve.

4. Toss the cabbage with the dressing and the scallions. Serve immediately or refrigerate up to 3 days. (The flavors actually intensify and improve as the cabbage marinates.)

Napa Cabbage Salad with Southeast Asian Flavors

This flavorful slaw makes an excellent accompaniment to pork or seafood. The flavors are bright and crisp.

SERVES 6 TO 8 AS A SIDE DISH

- 1 medium napa cabbage (about 1½ pounds)
- 2 medium carrots, peeled and shredded on the large holes of a box grater
- 12 large fresh basil leaves, cut into thin strips
- 12 large fresh mint leaves, cut into thin strips
- 2 tablespoons minced fresh cilantro leaves
- 2 tablespoons lime juice
- 1½ tablespoons fish sauce
- 1 small Thai red chile, stemmed, seeded, and minced
- 1 teaspoon sugar
- 2 tablespoons roasted peanut oil
- ¼ cup roasted peanuts, roughly chopped

1. Remove any tough or dry outer leaves from the head of cabbage. Cut the cabbage in half through the stem end. Cut out and discard the hard core at the base of each half. Slice the cabbage crosswise into thin strips. (You should have about 8 cups.)

2. Place the cabbage, carrots, and herbs in a large bowl.

3. Whisk the lime juice, fish sauce, chile, and sugar together in a small bowl. Stir occasionally to help the sugar to dissolve, about 10 minutes. Whisk in the oil. Pour the dressing over the salad and toss to combine. Add the peanuts, toss, and serve immediately.

Calabaza

Calabaza is the most popular hard-skinned squash grown in the Caribbean. It is actually a member of the pumpkin family. (On the English-speaking islands, it is known as West Indian pumpkin.) Calabaza is too delicious to carve for Halloween.

While most American pumpkin varieties cook up stringy and bland (why do you think canned pumpkin is so popular?), calabaza has a lovely smooth flesh that cooks up moist but not mushy. The texture is firm and not fibrous, and the flavor is rich and a bit sweet.

It can be hard to recognize calabaza from the outside. The skin can be tan like a butternut squash, green, or yellowish. The skin is sometimes solid, sometimes speckled, and sometimes striped. It's a lot easier to recognize calabaza from the inside. The flesh is a brilliant orange color—similar to butternut squash, only brighter.

Calabaza is usually sold in large wedges (most markets cut a whole pumpkin into four to six pieces), so you can identify it by the flesh rather than the skin. Calabaza is related to winter squash (see page 350) and can be prepared in much the same fashion as butternut squash, which has a similarly firm, smooth-grained flesh. The recipes that follow have been designed to showcase the fine texture of calabaza and I have mostly relied on Caribbean flavorings.

OTHER COMMON NAMES: Cuban squash, giraumon, and West Indian pumpkin.

AVAILABILITY: Year-round, mostly in markets that cater to Latino shoppers.

SELECTION: Even if you can find one, you probably won't want to buy a whole cal-abaza. It weighs as much as 10 pounds and is just too much food. Luckily, most markets cut the calabaza into wedges and wrap them in plastic. Besides being more convenient than buying a whole pumpkin, this way you can see the flesh. It should be bright orange, firm, and creamy-looking. If the flesh is pithy, dry, or soft, the calabaza is past its prime.

STORAGE: Once sliced, calabaza will soften fairly quickly. Put slices wrapped in plastic in the refrigerator when you get home from the market, and use them within a few days.

BASIC PREPARATION: Use a large dinner spoon to scrape the seeds and stringy fibers from the calabaza and discard. At this point, I usually wash and pat dry the calabaza with paper towels.

If roasting slices of calabaza, leave the skin on. Simply cut the pumpkin into wedges or slices that are manageable on a dinner plate. A 2-pound chunk of calabaza should be cut into about eight pieces.

If braising or steaming calabaza, it's necessary to peel the thin skin. Cut the calabaza into pieces a little smaller than your hand. With a vegetable peeler, remove the skin. You will need to go over the same spot two or three times in order to remove any white or green flesh right under the skin. (The process is similar to peeling a butternut squash.) Once peeled, cut the bright-orange calabaza flesh into cubes.

BEST COOKING METHODS: Baking, braising, or steaming.

OTHER RECIPES WITH CALABAZA: Calabaza can be used in any recipe that calls for butternut squash.

Baked Calabaza Slices with Orange-Molasses Glaze

This recipe takes less than 10 minutes to get into the oven and highlights the dense, creamy flesh of West Indian pumpkin. Serve with pork or chicken.

SERVES 4 TO 6 AS A SIDE DISH

2 pounds calabaza
2 tablespoons unsalted butter
2 tablespoons orange juice
2 tablespoons molasses
½ teaspoon ground allspice
½ teaspoon salt

1. Preheat the oven to 375 degrees. Line a rimmed baking sheet with foil.
2. Use a spoon to scrape the seeds and stringy fibers from the calabaza slices and discard. Cut the calabaza into wedges about 1 inch wide. Cut any long wedges in half. (You want to produce pieces that are a reasonable size for individual servings and won't look silly on a dinner plate.) Place the calabaza slices, skin side down, on the baking sheet.
3. Combine the butter, orange juice, molasses, allspice, and salt in a small saucepan over medium heat. Stir just until the butter melts and the ingredients are combined.
4. Brush half the orange-molasses glaze over the fleshy side of the calabaza wedges. Bake for 30 minutes. Brush the remaining glaze over the calabaza and continue baking until tender, about 30 minutes. Adjust the seasonings. Serve immediately.

Braised Calabaza with West Indian Flavors

The key to this recipe is low heat. You want the calabaza to steam in its own juices until tender. If the heat is too high, the calabaza will scorch.

SERVES 6 AS A SIDE DISH

2 pounds calabaza
2 tablespoons extra-virgin olive oil
1 medium onion, diced
1 medium red bell pepper, stemmed, seeded, and diced
2 medium garlic cloves, minced
2 teaspoons curry powder
   Salt
2 tablespoons minced fresh cilantro leaves

1. Use a spoon to scrape the seeds and stringy fibers from the calabaza and discard. Cut the calabaza into pieces small enough to hold in your hand. With a vegetable peeler, remove the skin. (You will need to go over the same spot two or three times in order to reveal the orange flesh.) Cut the calabaza flesh into 1-inch cubes.
2. Heat the oil in a large sauté pan. Add the onion and pepper and sauté over medium heat

until softened, about 5 minutes. Stir in the garlic and curry powder and cook until fragrant, about 30 seconds. Add the calabaza and salt to taste and stir to coat with the spices.

3. Cover the pan and reduce the heat to medium-low. Cook, stirring occasionally, until the calabaza is tender but still firm, about 25 minutes. (If the calabaza is sticking or scorching, lower the heat.) Add the cilantro and adjust the seasonings. Serve immediately.

Steamed Calabaza Salad with Sour Orange-Chile Vinaigrette

I serve this salad at room temperature with summer meals from the grill. As the calabaza cools, it slowly absorbs the flavors of the dressing. It's fine if some dressing remains at the bottom of the bowl at serving time—spoon the juices over grilled chicken, red snapper, pork chops, or steaks. For an authentic Caribbean dish, use an incendiary Scotch bonnet or habanero chile. If you like your food milder, use a jalapeño.

SERVES 6 AS A SIDE DISH

2 pounds calabaza
¼ cup orange juice
1 tablespoon lime juice

1 medium garlic clove, minced
1 medium fresh chile, stemmed, seeded, and minced
  Salt
2 tablespoons canola or other tasteless oil
1 medium red bell pepper, cored, seeded, and diced small

1. Use a spoon to scrape the seeds and stringy fibers from the calabaza and discard. Cut the calabaza into pieces a little smaller than your hand. With a vegetable peeler, remove the skin. (You will need to go over the same spot two or three times in order to reveal the orange flesh.) Cut the calabaza flesh into 1-inch cubes.

2. Fit a wide saucepan with a steamer basket and add enough water so that it comes to within ½ inch of the basket. Cover the pan and bring the water to a boil. Place the calabaza in the basket, cover, and steam until the calabaza is tender but still holds its shape, about 12 minutes.

3. While the calabaza is cooking, whisk the juices, garlic, chile, and salt together in a small bowl. Whisk in the oil until the dressing is smooth.

4. Drain any excess water from the steamer basket. Transfer the cooked calabaza to a large bowl. Add the red bell pepper to the bowl. Drizzle the dressing over the calabaza and pepper and toss gently to combine. Let cool for at least 30 minutes, tossing occasionally. Adjust the seasonings and serve warm or at room temperature.

Cardoon

To the uninitiated (and that includes 99.9 percent of the American public), cardoons look like celery gone mad. Ridged stalks grow in a tightly closed head that can measure 2 feet from end to end. At the top is a flourish of dark leaves. The long stalks are what we eat.

Despite the resemblance to celery, cardoon is a thistle and is closely related to artichokes. One taste and you will understand the connection. A cardoon has the same complex, slightly bitter, and herbaceous flavor as the artichoke. The texture is dense and meaty, almost like an artichoke heart.

Raw cardoon is usually quite bitter, almost inedible. It is also extremely crisp, almost hard. This vegetable needs to be boiled in order to soften the texture and wash away the bitter elements so you can taste (and chew) the cardoon. Depending on their size and age, cardoon stalks need 10 to 30 minutes of boiling to soften.

As with artichokes, cardoons require some tedious preparation, which can be done before or after boiling the stalks. Long strings (like those found in celery) are embedded on the ridged side of the stalk. Although you can attempt to peel the stalks before cooking, the curved shape of the crisp stalk and its deep ridges make this very challenging. I usually end up breaking the stalk in half as I press the vegetable peeler down too hard.

I prefer to cut cardoon stalks into smaller pieces (about 3 inches long is fine) and then boil the pieces until they are tender. The cardoon pieces are drained, cooled, and then peeled. At this point, they are pliable and are far less likely to snap in half when peeled.

The skin helps retain the vegetable's flavor while still permitting the bitter compounds to leech out.

Once the cardoon pieces have been boiled and peeled, they are ready to be cooked again (sautéed, fried, roasted) with seasonings. Keep it simple; you want to taste the cardoon.

OTHER COMMON NAMES: Cardi

AVAILABILITY: This hard-to-find vegetable is available from spring through the fall, although its appearance is limited to farmers' markets and is totally unreliable and usually unexpected.

SELECTION: Cardoons are sold two ways—as individual stalks and in a bunch, like celery. I much prefer to buy cardoons in a bunch, which is actually the heart of the plant that has been harvested intact. Individual stalks often come from the outer layers of the plant and can be tough. In addition, they dry out more quickly than whole heads.

Whole cardoon heads usually come with their green leaves attached. If they look fresh, you know the cardoon stalks will be crisp. If you can, break open a stalk. As the plant dries out, the inside of the stalk can become hollow and spongy. If you don't see a firm, meaty interior, move on.

STORAGE: Cardoons will keep loosely wrapped in a plastic bag in the refrigerator for several days.

BASIC PREPARATION: Complicated enough to merit its own recipe—see Boiled Cardoons (page 77). Cooking not only softens cardoons but helps loosen the pesky strings.

BEST COOKING METHODS: Braising, pan-frying, roasting, and sautéing—all after the cardoons have been boiled until tender.

Boiled Cardoons

If you have never cooked cardoons, they look intimidating. You want to keep only the inner stalks. Even these thinner stalks have tough, thick bottom portions that will need to be trimmed. A typical 3-pound head yields a pound or so of edible vegetable.

MAKES ENOUGH CARDOONS FOR ONE
OF THE FOLLOWING RECIPES

1 lemon, halved
1 medium head cardoon (about 3 pounds)
Salt

1. Squeeze half the lemon into a large bowl of cold water and add the lemon half to the bowl. Use the other lemon half to rub over cut surfaces as you prepare the cardoon to prevent the pieces from discoloring.
2. Remove and discard the tough, outer stalks. Separate the remaining portion into individual stalks. Use a sharp knife to slice along the edges of the stalks to remove the leaves. Once the leaves and any tiny thistles have been removed, cut the stalks into 3-inch lengths, making sure to discard any brown or thick portions of the stalks. (With the exception of the innermost stalks, this means discarding several inches from the bottom of each stalk.) As you work, place the pieces in the bowl of cold water.
3. Bring several quarts of water to a boil in a large pot. Add the lemon half used to rub the cardoons and a generous amount of salt to the boiling water. Add the cardoons and simmer until tender, at least 15 minutes and as long as 30 minutes depending on the size and freshness of the cardoons. (Remove a piece and test to see if it is tender when pricked with a fork.) Drain the cardoons and set aside until cool.
4. Use a vegetable peeler to remove the stringy fibers on the ridged side of each piece. Set the cardoons aside. (They can be covered and kept at room temperature for several hours.)

Sautéed Cardoons with Olive Oil and Herbs

This is the simplest way to cook cardoons. The flavorings are plain here, so the focus remains squarely on the unusual flavor of the cardoons. Serve this dish with fish or chicken.

SERVES 4 AS A SIDE DISH

2 tablespoons extra-virgin olive oil
1 recipe Boiled Cardoons (above), blotted
   dry with paper towels
1 tablespoon minced fresh parsley, basil, or
   tarragon leaves
   Salt
   Freshly ground black pepper

Heat the oil in a large skillet. Add the cardoons and sauté over medium heat until lightly browned, 8 to 10 minutes. Stir in the herb and season with salt and pepper to taste. Serve immediately.

Stewed Cardoons with Tomatoes, Garlic, and Anchovies

Cardoons have enough flavor to stand up to potent ingredients like garlic and anchovies. Serve with fish, especially red snapper or cod.

SERVES 4 AS A SIDE DISH

2 tablespoons extra-virgin olive oil
2 medium garlic cloves, minced
3 anchovy fillets, minced
2 medium tomatoes, cored, peeled, seeded, and diced
   Salt
   Freshly ground black pepper
1 recipe Boiled Cardoons (page 77)
1 tablespoon minced fresh parsley leaves

1. Heat the oil, garlic, and anchovies in a medium sauté pan over medium heat. Cook until the garlic is golden, about 2 minutes. Add the tomatoes and salt and pepper to taste. Cover and cook just until the tomatoes soften, about 3 minutes.

2. Add the cardoons, cover, and cook until the flavors have blended, about 10 minutes. Stir in the parsley and adjust the seasonings. Serve immediately.

Pan-Fried Cardoons

My favorite way to prepare cardoons. I serve these crunchy morsels with drinks as a snack.

SERVES 4 AS AN APPETIZER

1 cup flour
   Salt
   Freshly ground black pepper
1 recipe Boiled Cardoons (page 77), blotted dry with paper towels
   About 1 cup extra-virgin olive oil for frying
   Lemon wedges

1. Place the flour and salt and pepper to taste in a paper bag. Add the cardoons and shake to coat. Drop the cardoons into a strainer and shake gently to remove the excess flour.

2. Heat ¼ inch of oil in a large skillet. When the oil is quite hot and shimmering, add as many cardoon pieces as will fit in a single layer. Fry, turning once, until golden brown and crisp, 3 to 4 minutes.

3. Use a slotted spoon to transfer the cardoons to a platter lined with paper towels. Season with salt to taste. Serve immediately with the lemon wedges. Repeat the process with the remaining cardoon pieces.

Cardoon Gratin with Butter and Parmesan

This rich preparation is best suited to a late fall meal, perhaps with a roast. In the oven the cardoon pieces will become golden brown and a bit crunchy around the edges.

SERVES 4 TO 6 AS A SIDE DISH

1 recipe Boiled Cardoons (page 77)
1 tablespoon unsalted butter, diced, plus more for the baking dish
½ cup grated Parmesan cheese

1. Preheat the oven to 400 degrees. Place the cardoons in a buttered 13 by 9-inch baking dish. Dot the cardoons with butter and sprinkle with the cheese.

2. Bake until the cardoon pieces are lightly browned, about 20 minutes. Serve immediately.

Carrots

Other than beets (which are used to make granulated sugar), carrots have more natural sugar than any other vegetable. Their sweetness is a good backdrop for many flavors, especially rich, warm spices like ginger, curry, and nutmeg. Getting carrots to taste good is fairly easy. The trick is cooking them to the proper texture. Undercooked carrots taste like rabbit food, and overcooked carrots resemble baby mush. The relatively long cooking times and the natural variability among carrots (there's a big difference between a carrot that's as thick as an adult pinkie and one as thick as a thumb) mean that tasting often as carrots cook is essential.

AVAILABILITY: Year-round.

SELECTION: Look for small to medium carrots (no more than six per pound) when shopping. Large carrots may seem more convenient (less peeling and chopping) but they usually contain tough, wooden cores that are tasteless. Larger carrots also tend to be less sweet since many of the natural sugars have been converted to starches during the long growing process.

Carrots should be firm (never flexible) and the ends should be smooth, not cracked or desiccated. White rootlets are a sign of age. Fresh-looking greens that are crisp and green are a sign that the carrots have been recently dug (trim the greens when you get home to make storage easier), but the quality of bagged carrots is usually quite good. Just peek through the bag and make sure that the carrots do not exhibit any signs (outlined above) that they have been warehoused for weeks. A deep orange color indicates the presence of more vitamin A, but I have not found any relationship between color and flavor.

Peeled baby carrots are sold in many markets. I find they are a bit bland and can dry out, so I prefer to peel carrots myself. However, peeled baby carrots are fine in stews, where there is plenty of moisture, and they look so nice.

STORAGE: If you buy carrots with the greens still attached, twist them off and discard them at the store or as soon as you get home. The greens will quickly become damp and can cause the carrots to rot prematurely. Stored in the crisper drawer of the refrigerator, carrots should stay firm and fresh for a week or more.

BASIC PREPARATION: Nothing more than a quick trim from either end and then peeling off the tough outer skin. A vegetable peeler makes quick work of the skin, although you can scrape the skin off with a knife in a pinch. When slicing carrots, cut them on the diagonal so that the pieces are fairly large. Although thickness determines cooking time, wider ovals make a better presentation.

BEST COOKING METHODS: Boiling, braising, roasting, and sautéing. Also used raw in salads, especially when grated.

OTHER RECIPES WITH CARROTS:
Spring Vegetable Ragout with Fava Beans (page 156)
Jicama and Carrot Salad with Ginger-Sesame Vinaigrette (page 183)
Hearty Mushroom Stew (page 216)
Maple-Braised Turnips and Carrots (page 343)
Shredded Zucchini and Carrot with Garlic and Herbs (page 370)

Boiled Carrots with North African Spices

This cooking method softens the carrots quickly but still permits them to retain a good bit of their shape and texture. Pour the spiced dressing over the carrots when they are hot for maximum flavor absorption. This dish (and the variations) is excellent with roast chicken.

SERVES 4 AS A SIDE DISH

6 medium carrots (about 1 pound), peeled and cut into ½-inch dice
Salt
1 tablespoon lemon juice
2 tablespoons extra-virgin olive oil
½ teaspoon sweet paprika
½ teaspoon ground cumin
½ teaspoon ground cinnamon
2 tablespoons minced fresh parsley leaves

1. Bring several quarts of water to a boil in a large saucepan. Add the carrots and salt to taste. Reduce the heat to a simmer and cook until the carrots are tender but not mushy, 8 to 10 minutes. Drain the carrots and place them in a serving bowl.
2. While the carrots are cooking, whisk the lemon juice and oil together in a small bowl. Whisk in the spices and salt to taste.
3. Pour the dressing over the hot carrots. Sprinkle with the parsley and toss to coat the carrots with the dressing. Adjust the seasonings. Serve hot or better still at room temperature so that the dressing is completely absorbed. (The carrots can be refrigerated for several days. Bring to room temperature before serving.)

VARIATIONS: CARROTS WITH INDIAN SPICES

Cook carrots as directed in step 1 but omit remaining ingredients. Meanwhile, whisk 1 tablespoon lime juice and 2 tablespoons extra-virgin olive oil together in a small bowl. Whisk in ½ teaspoon each ground ginger and ground cardamom. Toss carrots with dressing and 2 tablespoons minced fresh cilantro or mint leaves.

CARROTS WITH ASIAN SPICES

Five-spice powder (sometimes called Chinese five-spice powder) is an aromatic blend of star anise, cloves, cinnamon, fennel seed, and Szechwan peppercorns. It is available in many supermarkets in the spice section.

Cook carrots as directed in step 1 but omit remaining ingredients. Meanwhile, whisk 1 tablespoon rice vinegar and 2 tablespoons roasted peanut oil together in a small bowl. Whisk in 1 teaspoon five-spice powder. Toss carrots with dressing, 2 tablespoons minced fresh cilantro, and 1 tablespoon toasted sesame seeds.

Roasted Carrots and Turnips

Roasting brings out all the sweetness in carrots. In fact, roasted carrots are so sweet they need to be balanced with a vegetable that is peppery or slightly bitter, such as turnips. The key to roasting two or more vegetables together is making sure the pieces are all cut to roughly the same thickness. Serve with roast pork or fish.

SERVES 4 TO 6 AS A SIDE DISH

6 medium carrots (about 1 pound)
6 medium turnips (about 1 pound)
3 tablespoons extra-virgin olive oil
Salt

1. Preheat the oven to 400 degrees.
2. Peel and cut the carrots in half lengthwise. Cut the carrots into 2-inch lengths.
3. Use a paring knife or heavy-duty vegetable peeler to remove the tough outer skin from the turnips. Cut the turnips into ½-inch-thick circles.
4. Place the carrots and turnips in a roasting pan large enough to hold them in a single layer. Drizzle with the oil and sprinkle with salt to taste. Toss to evenly coat the vegetables.
5. Roast, turning several times, until the vegetables are tender and lightly browned, about 45 minutes. Serve immediately or cool slightly and serve warm.

Maple-Glazed Carrots

Braising carrots in a flavorful liquid has a number of advantages. First, as the carrots soften they will absorb the flavors of the cooking liquid. Second, once the carrots are almost tender, the pan can be uncovered and the cooking liquid will reduce to a thick glaze, especially if maple syrup or honey is part of the recipe. Many similar traditional recipes call for chicken stock. I prefer to use water and let the flavors of the carrots—as well as the butter, shallots, and maple syrup—come through more clearly.

SERVES 4 AS A SIDE DISH

1 tablespoon butter
2 medium shallots, minced
6 medium carrots (about 1 pound), peeled and cut on the diagonal into ½-inch-thick ovals
½ cup water
2 tablespoons maple syrup
Pinch ground nutmeg
Salt
1 tablespoon minced fresh parsley leaves

1. Melt the butter in a medium skillet. Add the shallots and sauté over medium heat until golden, about 4 minutes. Add the carrots, water, maple syrup, nutmeg, and salt to taste. Cover and cook for 10 minutes.
2. Remove the cover and simmer briskly until the carrots are tender but not mushy and the liquid in the pan has thickened and coats the carrots nicely, 3 to 4 minutes. Remove the pan from the

heat, stir in the parsley, adjust the seasonings, and serve immediately.

VARIATIONS: BRAISED CARROTS
WITH MUSTARD-MAPLE GLAZE

Mustard tames the sweetness of glazed carrots.

After uncovering the pan, stir in 1 tablespoon Dijon mustard.

BRAISED CARROTS WITH ORANGE-HONEY GLAZE

You will need two oranges to yield the zest and juice needed for this variation.

Replace the water with orange juice and 1 tea-spoon grated orange zest. Replace the maple syrup with honey. For a Middle Eastern flavor, garnish with ¼ cup chopped roasted pistachios (salted nuts are fine) just before serving.

Bistro Carrot Salad

This simple grated salad is a standard in French homes and restaurants. A little minced tarragon works especially well with the sweetness of the carrots, but parsley is fine. Serve this salad as is or spooned over some tender leafy lettuces.

SERVES 4 AS A FIRST COURSE OR SIDE DISH

1 tablespoon lemon juice
2 tablespoons extra-virgin olive oil

Salt
Freshly ground black pepper
4 medium carrots (about ¾ pound), peeled
1 tablespoon minced fresh tarragon or pars-ley leaves

1. Whisk the lemon juice and oil together in a large bowl. Stir in salt and pepper to taste.
2. Grate the carrots using the shredding disk of a food processor or the large holes on a box grater. Stir the carrots into the vinaigrette. Stir in the tarragon and serve immediately.

Caramelized Carrots with Bacon

Although carrots are quite hard and usually cooked with moist heat or roasted, it's possible to sauté them if sliced quite thin. The carrots brown and become crisp when cooked this way in bacon fat. This rich dish is appropriate for holiday meals when luxury is a must.

SERVES 4 AS A SIDE DISH

3 slices bacon, cut crosswise into ½-inch strips
6 medium carrots (about 1 pound), peeled and cut on the diagonal into ¼-inch-thick ovals
1 tablespoon minced fresh parsley leaves
Freshly ground black pepper
Salt

1. Cook the bacon in a medium skillet over medium heat until crisp and the fat has been rendered, about 5 minutes. Use a slotted spoon to transfer the bacon to a plate. Set the bacon aside.

2. Add the carrot slices to the bacon drippings in the pan. Sauté, stirring often, until the carrots are tender and nicely browned, about 10 minutes.

3. Remove the pan from the heat. Sprinkle the bacon and parsley over the carrots. Add a generous grinding of black pepper and toss to combine. Taste and add salt if needed. Serve immediately.

Curried Carrot Soup

Most pureed carrot soups are loaded down with cream. For a stronger carrot flavor, I prefer to cook the carrots in either chicken or vegetable stock and then enrich the soup with a little whole milk while pureeing it. I find the blender is the best tool for pureeing soups since hot liquids often leak out of food processors.

SERVES 4 AS A FIRST COURSE

2 tablespoons canola or other tasteless oil

1 medium leek, white and light green parts only, sliced thin

2 tablespoons dry sherry or white wine

9 medium carrots (about 1½ pounds), peeled and cut into 1-inch chunks

2 cups chicken or vegetable stock

1 teaspoon curry powder
  Salt

1¼ to 1½ cups whole milk

2 teaspoons minced fresh cilantro leaves

1. Heat the oil in a medium pot. Add the leek and sauté over medium heat until starting to brown, about 5 minutes. Add the sherry and carrots and stir-cook for 30 seconds.

2. Add the stock, curry powder, and salt to taste to the pot. Bring the mixture to a boil. Reduce the heat to a moderate simmer, cover, and cook until the carrots are tender, about 20 minutes.

3. Use a ladle to transfer the carrot mixture to a blender. Add 1¼ cups milk and blend until very smooth.

4. Return the soup to a clean pot and reheat briefly. Do not let the soup boil. If desired, stir in an additional ¼ cup milk to thin the consistency. Adjust the seasonings. (The soup can be refrigerated for 3 days and reheated just before serving.) Ladle the soup into individual bowls. Garnish with the cilantro and serve immediately.

Cauliflower

Cauliflower is the mildest-tasting member of the brassica family, which includes broccoli, kale, and cabbage. Cauliflower has a sweet, almost nutty flavor because the tender curdlike florets are shielded from the sun by the plant's leaves as they grow. The absence of sunlight means that the curds stay milky white and delicate-tasting.

Many cooks think broccoli and cauliflower are interchangeable. However, I find that they cook and taste quite different. Cauliflower florets are much firmer than broccoli florets. I often braise cauliflower—it is sautéed in a little oil until lightly colored and then cooked with some liquid in a covered pan. Cauliflower soaks up flavors when braised, but remains firm. In contrast, broccoli prepared this way becomes soft and almost loses its shape.

I find broccoli so potent-tasting that I generally stick with equally strong seasonings. The milder flavor of cauliflower makes it possible to season it with a wider variety of flavors. Cauliflower works well with chiles and ginger as well as with butter and toasted nuts.

AVAILABILITY: Year-round, although traditionally the season is fall and winter.

SELECTION: Cauliflower should be milky white without black spots or discoloration. The florets should be firm and crisp. The leaves should be green and not limp.

STORAGE: Cauliflower should be refrigerated in its cellophane wrapping or in a dry plastic bag. It will keep for several days, if not longer.

BASIC PREPARATION: Start by laying the head of cauliflower on its side and cutting off as much as you can of the thick stalk on its underside. You will need a heavy chef's knife to cut through the stalk. Any leaves should come off when you cut the stalk.

Once the stalk has been cut, turn the cauliflower upside down (with the florets facing away from you) and use a paring knife to cut around the thick, white core. Make a circular incision around the core, cutting fairly close to the florets (leave about ½ inch of the stem attached to the florets). When you have completed making a circle around the core, it should lift right out. What's left is florets with little stems attached. Simply cut the florets apart, or break them apart by hand. Wash the florets and they are ready to be cooked.

BEST COOKING METHODS: Braising or steaming (and then sautéed or dressed with vinaigrette).

Braised Cauliflower with Curry and Yogurt

Sautéing the cauliflower before braising intensifies its naturally mild, sweet flavor. Yogurt is the braising medium here. It mellows the flavors of the curry and makes the cauliflower especially rich-tasting.

SERVES 4 AS A SIDE DISH

1½ tablespoons extra-virgin olive oil
1 medium head cauliflower (about 2 pounds), trimmed, cored, and cut into florets
1 medium onion, halved and sliced thin
1 teaspoon curry powder
¼ cup plain yogurt mixed with ¼ cup water
2 tablespoons minced fresh cilantro leaves
  Salt
  Freshly ground black pepper

1. Heat the oil in a large skillet or sauté pan set over medium heat. Add the cauliflower and onion and cook, stirring occasionally, until the florets are lightly browned, about 7 minutes. Stir in the curry powder and continue cooking until fragrant, about 1 minute.

2. Add the thinned yogurt, cover the pan, and reduce the heat to medium-low. Simmer until the florets are tender but still hold their shape, about 6 minutes. Stir in the cilantro and season with salt and pepper to taste. If necessary, simmer, uncovered, to evaporate any remaining liquid in the pan. Serve immediately.

Braised Cauliflower with Asian Flavors

Hoisin sauce glazes cauliflower with a rich fermented black bean flavor. Rice vinegar helps cuts the sweetness of the hoisin, and soy sauce adds another layer of flavor.

SERVES 4 AS A SIDE DISH

2 tablespoons hoisin sauce
1 tablespoon soy sauce
1 tablespoon rice vinegar
¼ cup water
1½ tablespoons roasted peanut oil
1 medium head cauliflower (about 2 pounds), trimmed, cored, and cut into florets
2 medium garlic cloves, minced
1 tablespoon minced fresh gingerroot
2 medium scallions, sliced thin
  Salt
  Freshly ground black pepper

1. Combine the hoisin sauce, soy sauce, vinegar, and water in a small bowl and set the mixture aside.

2. Heat the oil in a large skillet or sauté pan set over medium heat. Add the cauliflower and cook, stirring occasionally, until the florets are lightly browned, about 7 minutes. Add the garlic, ginger, and scallions and continue cooking until fragrant, about 30 seconds.

3. Add the reserved hoisin mixture, cover the pan, and reduce the heat to medium-low. Simmer until the florets are tender but still hold their shape, about 6 minutes. Season with salt and pepper to taste. If necessary, simmer, uncovered, to evaporate any remaining liquid in the pan. Serve immediately.

Sicilian-Style Braised Cauliflower with Tomatoes and Raisins

Chopped canned tomatoes are the braising medium in this recipe. Use canned tomatoes packed in juice and chop three or four tomatoes to make almost a cup. Add a few tablespoons of juice to reach the 1 cup needed here. The juice is essential because it provides the steam that will finish cooking the cauliflower and also cushions the cauliflower against scorching.

SERVES 4 AS A SIDE DISH

1½ tablespoons extra-virgin olive oil
  1 medium head cauliflower (about 2 pounds), trimmed, cored, and cut into florets
  1 medium onion, halved and sliced thin
  3 medium garlic cloves, minced
  3 tablespoons raisins
  1 cup chopped canned tomatoes with some of their liquid
  2 tablespoons minced fresh basil leaves

Salt
Freshly ground black pepper

1. Heat the oil in a large skillet or sauté pan set over medium heat. Add the cauliflower and onion and cook, stirring occasionally, until the florets are lightly browned, about 7 minutes. Add the garlic and raisins and cook until the garlic is fragrant, about 1 minute.

2. Add the tomatoes, cover the pan, and reduce the heat to medium-low. Simmer until the florets are tender but still hold their shape, about 6 minutes. Stir in the basil and season with salt and pepper to taste. If necessary, simmer, uncovered, to evaporate any remaining liquid in the pan. Serve immediately.

Steamed Cauliflower with Salsa Verde

Salsa verde is a piquant Italian sauce usually served with boiled meats. Made with parsley, capers, anchovies, and olives, it adds plenty of flavor to cauliflower. Unlike pesto, this thick sauce should not be perfectly smooth, so mince the ingredients on a cutting board and then stir them together rather than making the sauce in a food processor.

SERVES 4 AS A SIDE DISH

¼ cup minced fresh parsley leaves
  1 tablespoon drained capers, minced
  8 medium green olives, pitted and minced

2 anchovy fillets, minced
1 tablespoon lemon juice
3 tablespoons extra-virgin olive oil
  Salt
  Freshly ground black pepper
1 medium head cauliflower (about 2 pounds), trimmed, cored, and cut into florets

1. Combine the parsley, capers, olives, anchovies, and lemon juice in a small bowl. Stir in the oil and season with salt (sparingly) and pepper to taste.

2. Meanwhile, place a steamer basket inside a wide, deep saucepan. Fill the pan with enough water to reach just below the bottom of the steamer basket. Turn the heat to high and bring the water to a boil. Add the cauliflower to the basket, cover the pan, and steam until the cauliflower is tender but not mushy, about 6 minutes.

3. Transfer the cauliflower to a serving bowl. Scrape the salsa verde over the cauliflower and toss to coat. Serve hot, warm, or at room temperature.

Steamed Cauliflower with Buttered Walnuts and Parsley

Steamed cauliflower gets flavor from a quick toss in a skillet with toasted walnuts and butter. The walnuts are toasted in butter to make them especially rich; the

butter browns a bit, adding further character to this dish.

SERVES 4 AS A SIDE DISH

1 medium head cauliflower (about 2 pounds), trimmed, cored, and cut into florets
2 tablespoons unsalted butter
¼ cup chopped walnuts
2 tablespoons minced fresh parsley leaves
  Salt
  Freshly ground black pepper

1. Place a steamer basket inside a wide, deep saucepan. Fill the pan with enough water to reach just below the bottom of the steamer basket. Turn the heat to high and bring the water to a boil. Add the cauliflower to the basket, cover the pan, and steam until the cauliflower is tender but not mushy, about 6 minutes. Set the cauliflower aside.

2. Heat the butter in a large skillet. Add the nuts and cook over medium heat, stirring often, until the nuts are fragrant and the butter turns a medium brown color, about 2 minutes. (Do not let the butter burn.) Add the cauliflower and cook, stirring often, until heated through, 1 to 2 minutes. Add the parsley and season with salt and pepper to taste. Serve immediately.

Stir-Fried Cauliflower and Spinach with Red Curry Sauce

This Thai-style curry sauce soaks into the cauliflower to give it a rich, spicy flavor. Look for Thai red curry paste with other Thai products in your supermarket. It's usually sold near the coconut milk and rice noodles. If you can't find red curry paste, use 2 teaspoons of curry powder combined with cayenne pepper to taste. Note that 1 teaspoon of red curry paste will make this dish hot. Two teaspoons and the stir-fry will be fiery. Either way, serve this stir-fry with plenty of steamed rice to cushion the heat.

SERVES 4 AS A MAIN COURSE

RED CURRY SAUCE

½ cup coconut milk

2 tablespoons soy sauce

2 tablespoons minced fresh cilantro or basil leaves

1 to 2 teaspoons Thai red curry paste

2 tablespoons roasted peanut oil

1 medium head cauliflower (about 2 pounds), trimmed, cored, and cut into florets

1 medium onion, chopped

1 pound spinach, preferably flat-leaf, stems removed unless they are very thin, washed, shaken dry to remove excess water, and chopped (about 6 cups, tightly packed)

Salt

1. Combine the coconut milk, soy sauce, cilantro, and curry paste in a small bowl and set it aside.

2. Heat 1½ tablespoons of the oil in large non-stick skillet over medium-high heat until almost smoking. Add the cauliflower and stir-fry until lightly browned, about 4 minutes.

3. Push the cauliflower to the sides of the pan and place the onion in the center. Drizzle the remaining ½ tablespoon of oil over the onion. Cook until the onion is lightly browned, about 1 minute. Add the red curry sauce, toss to coat well, and cover. Cook until the cauliflower is almost tender, about 3 minutes.

4. Remove the cover and add the spinach to the pan. Cover and cook, stirring once, briefly, until the spinach has wilted, 2 to 3 minutes. Adjust the seasonings, adding salt if necessary. Serve immediately.

Celery

Anyone who cooks much has a bunch of celery in the vegetable crisper drawer, but few cooks set out to make a dish with celery. It is used as an aromatic (with onions and carrots) in many stocks, soups, and sauces. Sometimes we slice it for salads. Most of all, we eat celery sticks raw with dip.

However, celery is surprisingly versatile, as the recipes that follow demonstrate. As a salad ingredient it can take center stage. Its crisp, mild, lightly sweet flavor is refreshing.

Perhaps more surprising is how celery tastes when cooked. It becomes dense and meaty, almost like cooked fennel. The flavor is sweet and more herbaceous. Because celery is so commonly available (even in the dead of winter), it makes sense to learn how to prepare this underappreciated vegetable.

AVAILABILITY: Year-round.

SELECTION: If possible, buy celery with the dark green leaves attached. As always, healthy leaves are a sign that the celery has been recently harvested and well treated during shipping. Examine the outer stalks and make sure you don't see any browning, especially at the tips.

STORAGE: Celery will keep in the refrigerator in a loosely sealed plastic bag for at least a week, and possibly much longer.

BASIC PREPARATION: Start by separating the head of celery into individual stalks. If the celery is a bit past its prime, you might need to discard a few outer stalks. However, in most cases, there should be edible material on even the outer stalks. Wash and dry the stalks.

Use a knife to trim and discard any tough portions from the bottom and top of each celery stalk. If cooking celery, I always peel the outside of the stalks to remove the stringy fibers. Run a vegetable peeler over the ridged side of the stalk and the strings will quickly be removed. I often peel celery for use in salads, although this is optional. After peeling, the celery is ready to be sliced.

Don't automatically discard the dark green leaves at the top of the celery bunch. If you like, mince the celery leaves and use them as a flavorful garnish. They taste like parsley, only stronger and more vegetal.

BEST COOKING METHODS: Braising. Also used raw in salads.

Braised Celery with Butter, Shallots, and Parsley

This simple dish really lets the sweet, aromatic flavor of the celery shine through. Serve braised celery with white-fleshed fish, such as flounder, or chicken. If you have a lot of celery leaves, use just a little parsley; if not, use the full 2 tablespoons.

SERVES 4 AS SIDE DISH

1 pound celery, with leaves
2 tablespoons unsalted butter
2 medium shallots, minced
1 cup chicken or vegetable stock
1 to 2 tablespoons minced fresh parsley
     leaves (see Headnote)
Salt
Freshly ground black pepper

1. Mince the celery leaves and set them aside. Trim and discard any tough portions from the bottom and top of each celery stalk. Peel the outside of the stalks to remove the stringy fibers. Cut the stalks into 2-inch lengths. (You should have about 4 cups.)

2. Melt the butter in a large sauté pan. When the foaming subsides, add the shallots and sauté over medium heat until golden, about 3 minutes. Add the celery and cook, turning once, until slightly softened, about 4 minutes.

3. Add the stock, bring to a boil, reduce the heat, cover the pan, and simmer, turning once, until the celery is tender, about 20 minutes.

4. Remove the cover, raise the heat, and simmer briskly until the liquid in the pan reduces to a glaze, 2 to 3 minutes. Stir in the celery leaves, parsley, and salt and pepper to taste. Serve immediately.

Braised Celery with Tomatoes, Capers, and Olives

In this recipe, the celery is braised with Italian seasonings. The dish is more aggressive, ideal with pork chops and strong-flavored fish, such as red snapper.

SERVES 4 AS A SIDE DISH

1 pound celery, with leaves
2 tablespoons extra-virgin olive oil
1 medium onion, minced
1 cup canned diced tomatoes, drained
1 tablespoon drained capers
8 large black olives, such as Kalamatas,
     pitted and chopped
2 tablespoons minced fresh basil leaves
     Salt
     Freshly ground black pepper

1. Mince the celery leaves and set them aside. Trim and discard any tough portions from the

bottom and top of each celery stalk. Peel the outside of the stalks to remove the stringy fibers. Cut the stalks into 2-inch lengths. (You should have about 4 cups.)

2. Heat the oil in a large sauté pan. Add the onion and sauté over medium heat until softened, about 3 minutes. Add the celery and cook, turning once, until slightly softened, about 4 minutes.

3. Add the tomatoes, bring to a boil, reduce the heat, cover the pan, and simmer, turning once, until the celery is tender, about 20 minutes.

4. Stir in the capers and olives. Raise the heat and boil briskly, uncovered, until the juices from the tomatoes thicken, 2 to 3 minutes. Stir in the celery leaves, basil, and salt and pepper to taste. Serve immediately.

Waldorf Salad (Celery, Apple, and Walnut Salad)

This classic American dish has become a cliché, but only because it has been so abused by thoughtless cooks. Don't add grapes, orange segments, or marshmallows—they make this salad cloying and take the focus off the clear, crisp flavors of celery, apple, and walnuts. Toasting the walnuts is essential. As for the herb, I prefer the anise flavor of tarragon, but parsley is fine. Serve as you would potato salad, as an accompaniment to sandwiches. As with all mayonnaise-based salads, Waldorf salad is rich and a little goes a long way.

6 medium celery stalks, with leaves
1 medium Granny Smith apple, peeled, cored, and cut into ½-inch dice
1 tablespoon lemon juice
½ cup mayonnaise
2 teaspoons minced fresh tarragon or parsley leaves
½ cup walnuts, toasted in a dry skillet until fragrant, cooled, and chopped
Salt
Freshly ground black pepper

1. Mince the celery leaves and set them aside. Trim and discard any tough portions from the bottom and top of each celery stalk. Peel the outside of the stalks to remove the stringy fibers. Slice the celery crosswise into thin pieces.

2. Combine the celery, apple, lemon juice, mayonnaise, tarragon, and walnuts in a medium bowl. Add salt and pepper to taste. Serve immediately, or better yet chill for about 1 hour and then serve. (Salad can be refrigerated overnight.)

Celery Heart Salad with Pears and Parmesan

This Italian recipe will make even the most doubtful person a celery fan. I serve this salad after a heavy meal as a palate cleanser. It's also delicious as a plated first course before a winter meal. Make sure the pears are ripe but still firm enough to slice thinly. Use red-skinned pears for a particularly attractive salad. Use only the most tender, white celery stalks from the heart.

SERVES 4 TO 6 AS A FIRST COURSE OR AFTER THE MAIN COURSE

3 cups thinly sliced celery heart, cut on the bias no more than ⅛ inch thick

2 medium ripe pears, halved, cored, and sliced lengthwise ⅛ inch thick

2 tablespoons lemon juice

2 tablespoons extra-virgin olive oil
Salt
Freshly ground black pepper

1 large piece Parmigiano-Reggiano (you will use about 1 ounce)

1. Toss the celery, pears, lemon juice, oil, and salt and pepper to taste together in a medium bowl. Transfer the salad to a wide, shallow serving platter.

2. Run a vegetable peeler across the piece of cheese, letting the thin shavings shower down over the salad. Serve immediately.

Celery Root

Celery root is a variety of celery that is cultivated for its gnarly, bulbous root rather than its stems. Although celery root is one of the least-promising-looking vegetables in the market, remove the thick brown skin and you will uncover creamy, dense, white flesh.

You can cook celery root much like parsnips or turnips and use it in purees, soups, or stews. However, it is neither sweet like parsnips nor peppery like turnips. Celery root tastes like celery with perhaps a dash of parsley. I generally use celery root in raw salads (to appreciate its full flavor) or combine it with potatoes to make a lovely vegetable puree.

OTHER COMMON NAMES: Celeriac, knob celery.

AVAILABILITY: Late summer through winter, although best in the late fall and winter.

SELECTION: Mammoth celery roots tend to be pithy or tough. Choose relatively smooth roots (about a pound or so is fine) that feel heavy for their size, a sure sign that the flesh is dense and creamy.

Occasionally you may see celery root with the stalks still attached at farmers' markets. If the stalks look good, you can be assured that the root was freshly dug.

STORAGE: Celery root has excellent keeping properties. Before the advent of air-shipping, many rural cooks stored celery root in cool cellars for several months. In a loosely sealed plastic bag in the refrigerator, expect celery root to remain firm and fresh for at least a week or two, if not longer.

BASIC PREPARATION: If you have ever peeled a whole orange or grapefruit for salad with a knife, then you know how to peel celery root. Start by cutting a thin slice from either end of the celery root. Place the root cut side down on a cutting board and cut around the root with a paring knife to remove the skin (and the layer of flesh right beneath it) as if removing the peel and pith from an orange to expose the flesh.

Once peeled the celery root will appear creamy white and can be sliced, diced, or shredded as desired.

Celery root will quickly discolor once it has been cut. For salad, make sure to toss the shredded celery root with an acidic dressing as soon as it comes out of the food processor. If boiling, get the chunks into the cooking water quickly so they will not oxidize.

BEST COOKING METHODS: Boiling. Can also be shredded very thin and used raw in slaw-like salads.

Celery Root and Apple Salad with Creamy Mustard Dressing

This classic bistro salad is called rémoulade *in France. It makes a nice starter to a meal or it can be served as a side dish, like any slaw, with chicken, fish, or pork.* Rémoulade *also makes a good accompaniment to sandwiches.*

SERVES 6 AS A LIGHT FIRST
COURSE OR SIDE DISH

2 tablespoons lemon juice
1 tablespoon Dijon mustard
3 tablespoons extra-virgin olive oil
2 tablespoons plain yogurt
1 tablespoon minced fresh parsley leaves or
   1½ teaspoons minced fresh tarragon leaves
   Salt
   Freshly ground black pepper
1 medium celery root (about 1 pound)
1 medium Granny Smith apple

1. Whisk the lemon juice and mustard together in a small bowl. Whisk in the oil until the dressing is smooth. Whisk in the yogurt and parsley. Add salt and pepper to taste.

2. Cut a thin slice from either end of the celery root. Place the celery root on a cutting board and cut around the root with a paring knife to remove the skin as if removing the peel and pith from an orange to expose the flesh. Cut the peeled celery root into chunks that will fit in the feed tube of a food processor. Quarter and core the apple. (Do not peel.)

3. Shred the celery root and apple in a food processor fitted with the shredding disk. Place the shredded celery and apple in a large bowl and toss with the dressing. Adjust the seasonings. Serve immediately or refrigerate up to 2 hours and serve chilled.

Mashed Celery Root and Potatoes

Celery root turns mashed potatoes a light tan color and gives them a sweet, slightly vegetal flavor. This chunky puree is especially good with a roast and flavorful pan sauce. Don't try using all celery root in this recipe. It makes a watery puree and is much improved by the starchy potatoes.

1 medium celery root (about 1 pound)
2 medium russet potatoes (about 1 pound),
  peeled and cut into 1-inch chunks
  Salt
2 tablespoons unsalted butter, softened
¼ cup milk, warmed

1. Cut a thin slice from either end of the celery root. Place the celery root on a cutting board and cut around the root with a paring knife to remove the skin as if removing the peel and pith from an orange to expose the flesh. Cut the peeled celery root into 1-inch chunks.

2. Place the celery root and potatoes in a large saucepan and add enough water to cover by about 2 inches. Add a generous amount of salt and bring the water to a boil. Cook until the celery root and potatoes are tender, about 15 minutes. Drain the celery root and potatoes well.

3. Return the vegetables to the empty saucepan set over the warm burner. Add the butter and use a potato masher to turn the vegetables into fine bits. Stir in the milk and add salt to taste. Serve immediately.

Chard

C hard is really two vegetables in one—the dark green, ruffled leaves and the white or colored stems. The greens can be cooked pretty much any way that spinach is. They are a tad more fibrous (so they cook down less and are chewier) and have a slightly stronger, earthier flavor, but otherwise chard and spinach are similar.

The thick, fleshy stems are usually cooked on their own. They are a bit tough, so they are first blanched and then usually baked, often with butter, cheese, or white sauce.

Until recently, we generally saw only two varieties of chard in this country—one with white stems and veins running through the leaves and another with red stems and veins. Farmers' markets now offer chard with pink, orange, and yellow stems and veins. As far as I can tell, the colored varieties are slightly sweeter than white chard, but only marginally so. Use them all interchangeably.

Chard is closely related to beets. Red chard is a dead ringer for beet greens—the only real difference is the larger size and ruffled appearance of the chard leaves.

OTHER COMMON NAMES: Swiss chard.

AVAILABILITY: Year-round, although chard is most abundant from summer through early winter.

SELECTION: Chard should be a deep green color (never yellow or brown) with crisp leaves and stems. Avoid bunches with ragged-looking leaves, or leaves with lots of rips and holes. In addition, the stems should be firm and brightly colored (even when white), not bruised or covered with brown spots. Chard should smell fresh and earthy, not musty or sour.

STORAGE: Chard can be refrigerated in a dry, open plastic bag for a couple of days. Moisture will hasten its decline, so if the bag is full of water when you get home from the market, blot the chard dry and place it in a new bag.

BASIC PREPARATION: Most chard recipes are designed for either the leaves or stems; even those that call for both the leaves and stems, usually call for cooking the stems longer. Therefore, the first step is to separate the leaves from the thick stems. I find it easiest to do this machete style with a chef's knife. Hold each leaf by the stem end with the leaf pointing down. Slash on either side of the stem to cut away the leafy green portion.

I usually separate the leaves from the stems in a sink over a bowl of cold water. Like all greens, chard can be gritty and needs a thorough washing in successive bowls of cold water. The stems, which look a bit like celery stalks, should be rinsed to wash away any dirt. Trim any blemished portions of the stems before cooking them.

BEST COOKING METHODS: Blanching and then baking for the stems; boiling or braising for the leaves.

OTHER RECIPES WITH CHARD:
Roasted Beet Salad with Walnuts and Goat Cheese (page 30)
Stewed Rutabaga with Chard and Garlic (page 291)
Chard can be used in any recipe that calls for cooked spinach, but chard leaves are tougher than spinach and don't work well raw in salads.

Chilled Chard with Lemon

This dish offers chard at its purest and simplest. The leaves are cooked in a covered pot in their own juices, chilled, and served as a salad with a touch of lemon and olive oil. Perfect on a hot summer day.

SERVES 4 AS A FIRST COURSE OR
AFTER THE MAIN COURSE

2 pounds chard, stems and thick ribs discarded; leaves washed, shaken to remove excess water, and chopped roughly (about 10 packed cups)
Salt
4 teaspoons lemon juice
4 teaspoons extra-virgin olive oil
Ground black pepper

1. Place the damp chard in a large stockpot, sprinkling with salt to taste as you add the leaves. Turn the heat to medium, cover, and cook, stirring occasionally, until wilted, about 10 minutes. Remove the cover and simmer until any water in the pot evaporates. Transfer the chard to a colander set over a bowl and allow to cool for 30 minutes. Discard any liquid in the bowl. Transfer the drained chard to an airtight container and refrigerate until well chilled.
2. Divide the chard among four small plates. Drizzle 1 teaspoon lemon juice, then 1 teaspoon oil over each serving. Grind some fresh pepper over each plate and serve immediately.

Slow-Cooked Chard

Both the stems and leaves are used in this dish where the chard is cooked down until dense and creamy. Thanks to Deborah Madison, who first showed me that chard is delicious when cooked for a long time. I serve this earthy, puree-like chard with a bowl of rice for lunch or a light dinner. The chard is quite rich so a little is filling. I prefer to use red chard here—the color is more attractive—but white chard is just as delicious.

SERVES 4 AS A LIGHT MAIN COURSE,
6 AS A SIDE DISH

2 pounds chard, washed and shaken to remove excess water
3 tablespoons extra-virgin olive oil
1 medium onion, minced
2 medium garlic cloves, minced
¼ cup chicken or vegetable stock
Salt
Freshly ground black pepper

1. Remove the thick stems and ribs from the chard and cut into ¼-inch dice. Slice the leaves crosswise into ½-inch-wide strips. Set the prepared stems and leaves aside separately.
2. Heat the oil in a large casserole or Dutch oven over medium heat. Add the onion and sauté until golden, about 5 minutes. Add the garlic and cook until fragrant, about 1 minute. Stir in the chard stems until well coated with oil. Add the stock and salt and pepper to taste, cover, and reduce the heat to medium-low. Cook, stirring occasionally,

until the chard stems are starting to lose their shape, about 30 minutes.

3. Raise the heat to medium, stir in the chard leaves, cover the pan, and cook, stirring occasionally, until the leaves have wilted and are quite tender, 12 to 15 minutes. Adjust the seasonings and serve immediately. (The chard can also be refrigerated in an airtight container and then reheated—a microwave is best here—just before serving.)

Garlicky Chard

If desired, you may use spinach or beet greens in place of the chard. Serve over pureed white beans, rice, or polenta as a vegetarian main course for three or four, or use as an accompaniment to meat, poultry, or fish.

SERVES 4 TO 6 AS A SIDE DISH

2 tablespoons extra-virgin olive oil
2 medium onions, halved and sliced thin
4 medium garlic cloves, minced
2½ pounds chard, stems and thick ribs discarded, leaves washed, shaken to remove excess water, and chopped roughly (about 12 packed cups)
Salt
Freshly ground black pepper

1. Heat the oil in a stockpot deep enough to hold the greens. Add the onions and sauté over medium heat until golden brown, about 8 min-

utes. Add the garlic and cook until fragrant, about 1 minute.

2. Add the damp chard, stir well to coat with the oil, cover, and cook, stirring two or three times, until wilted, about 5 minutes. Season with salt and pepper to taste. If desired, simmer, uncovered, for several minutes to evaporate any excess liquid, or use the liquid to moisten rice, polenta, mashed potatoes, pureed beans, or meat.

VARIATIONS: GARLICKY CHARD, MEXICAN STYLE

In Mexico, this dish is commonly made with quelites, or "lamb's quarters" in English. The earthy flavor of chard is a good substitute for hard-to-find lamb's quarters, as is spinach. As is always the case with chiles, remove the seeds for less heat or leave them if you want this dish to be especially spicy.

Add 1 medium jalapeño chile, stemmed, seeded if desired, and minced, with the garlic. Serve with lime wedges.

GARLICKY CHARD, ASIAN STYLE

Leave these greens a bit soupy and serve them over rice.

Replace the olive oil with an equal amount of roasted peanut oil. Add 1 tablespoon minced fresh gingerroot and 2 medium scallions, sliced thin, with the garlic. Season with pepper as directed but replace the salt with 1 tablespoon soy sauce, or more to taste. Drizzle the greens with a teaspoon or two of toasted sesame oil just before serving.

Chard Stems with Golden Onions and Bread Crumbs

There's no reason to throw out perfectly good chard stems when a recipe calls for just the leaves. The stems can be blanched and then layered into a baking dish with sautéed onions, cream, and bread crumbs. This thrifty dish reveals just how delicious the entire chard plant can be. Chard stems from which the leaves have been removed can be refrigerated in a sealed plastic bag for 1 day, so you can cook the leaves one day and the stems the next.

SERVES 4 AS A SIDE DISH

1 pound chard stems (about 12 large stems), any bruised parts trimmed
Salt
3 tablespoons unsalted butter
2 medium onions, minced
½ cup heavy cream
Freshly ground black pepper
1 cup Fresh Bread Crumbs (page 123)

1. Bring 4 quarts of water to a boil in a large pot. Add the chard stems and salt to taste. Cook until the stems are almost tender, about 8 minutes. Drain and reserve the stems.

2. Preheat the oven to 400 degrees. Use 1 tablespoon of the butter to grease a 13 by 9-inch glass or ceramic baking dish.

3. Melt the remaining 2 tablespoons of butter in a medium skillet. Add the onions and sauté over medium heat until richly colored, about 8 minutes. Add the cream and simmer just until thickened, about 1 minute. Season with salt and pepper to taste.

4. Arrange the chard stems in a single layer in the greased baking dish. Drizzle the onion mixture over the chard. Sprinkle with the bread crumbs. Bake until the crumbs are golden brown and the cream has glazed the chard, 15 to 20 minutes. Serve immediately.

Baked Chard Stems with Butter and Parmesan

This dish is simpler than the last, with the flavors of butter and Parmesan accenting chard stems. Make sure to cook this casserole long enough so that the edges start to brown.

1 pound chard stems (about 12 large stems),
   any bruised parts trimmed
   Salt
3 tablespoons unsalted butter
¾ cup grated Parmesan cheese

1. Preheat the oven to 400 degrees. Bring 4 quarts of water to a boil in a large pot. Lightly grease an 8-inch-square baking dish.

2. Add the chard stems and salt to the boiling water. Cook until the stems are almost tender, about 8 minutes. Drain and reserve the stems.

3. Lay three or four chard stems in the prepared baking dish in a single layer, cutting them as necessary to make them fit. Dot with a little of the butter and sprinkle with some of the cheese. Repeat this process three or four more times, alternating the direction in which you place the stems for each layer, until all the chard, butter, and cheese have been used.

4. Bake until chard is very tender and the top of casserole is lightly browned, about 25 minutes. Serve immediately.

Chayote

This pear-shaped, light green vegetable is grown throughout the tropics, from Brazil to India. It is especially popular in the Caribbean and Mexico. Chayote is a squash that combines the quick-cooking, mild-tasting properties of zucchini with the creamy, dense flesh of winter squash.

The light green chayote that makes its way to American markets is actually underripe fruit. In the Caribbean, the vegetable is often allowed to ripen further on the vine. The skin thickens and becomes yellow. The flesh, however, remains much the same—mildly sweet and vegetal, much like cucumber or zucchini.

The crisp, creamy flesh is often boiled, but I find that it becomes a bit mushy and that boiling washes away the delicate flavor. Better to steam the chayote and then to sauté it with flavorings. Steamed and chilled chayote also makes a refreshing salad.

OTHER COMMON NAMES: Cho-cho, christophene, christophine, chuchu, vegetable pear, and water pear.

AVAILABILITY: Year-round. Many large supermarkets and produce stores stock chayote, as do most Latino grocery stores.

SELECTION: Chayote have a pale green skin that should be unblemished and firm. They come in various sizes, although smaller chayote (a half pound or so) are generally more tender and flavorful.

STORAGE: Chayote will keep in a loosely sealed plastic bag in the refrigerator for a week or so.

BASIC PREPARATION: Use a vegetable peeler to remove the thin but tough green skin. I find it best to then cut the peeled chayote in quarters to expose the large white seed. Once the seed has been pulled out and discarded, the flesh can be sliced or diced as desired.

Some people, myself included, find that a slimy substance just under the skin causes their hands to become numb. (This condition is not dangerous, but it can be annoying.) To prevent this from occurring, you might want to wear gloves when peeling chayote. After dicing or slicing, rinse the chayote until no longer slimy.

BEST COOKING METHODS: Steaming until crisp-tender, then sautéing to flavor and finish cooking. Or steaming until fully cooked for use in salads.

Sautéed Chayote with Onion, Cilantro, and Lime

Creamy, mild-tasting chayote can be steamed and then sautéed with strong flavors to create an interesting side dish.

SERVES 4 AS A SIDE DISH

3 medium chayote (about 1½ pounds), peeled, quartered, pitted, cut into ½-inch cubes, and rinsed
2 tablespoons extra-virgin olive oil
1 medium onion, halved and sliced thin
1 tablespoon minced fresh cilantro leaves
1 tablespoon lime juice
  Salt
  Freshly ground black pepper

1. Place a steamer basket in a wide, deep saucepan. Fill the pan with enough water to reach just below the bottom of the steamer basket. Turn the heat to high and bring the water to a boil. Add the chayote to the basket, cover the pan, and steam until crisp-tender, about 10 minutes. Remove and set aside.
2. Heat the oil in a large skillet. Add the onion and sauté over medium heat until golden, about 5 minutes. Add the chayote and cook, stirring often, until the chayote is tender, about 5 minutes. Add the cilantro, lime juice, and salt and pepper to taste. Serve immediately.

Chayote and Tomato Salad with Lime and Allspice

Steamed chayote wedges can be shocked in ice water and then used to make a composed salad. Allspice and lime is a common combination in the Caribbean and parts of Mexico. The dressing has an exotic, floral flavor that is especially refreshing on a hot day.

SERVES 4 AS A FIRST COURSE OR SIDE DISH

3 medium chayote (about 1½ pounds), peeled, quartered, pitted, cut into long wedges about ½ inch thick, and rinsed
2 medium ripe tomatoes (about 1 pound), cored and sliced crosswise into ½-inch-thick rounds
1 tablespoon lime juice
1 teaspoon ground allspice
  Salt
3 tablespoons extra-virgin olive oil
1 tablespoon minced fresh parsley leaves

1. Place a steamer basket in a wide, deep saucepan. Fill the pan with enough water to reach just below the bottom of the steamer basket. Turn the heat to high and bring the water to a boil. Add the chayote to the basket, cover the pan, and steam until completely tender, about 15 minutes. Remove the chayote from the steamer and place in a bowl of ice water until chilled,

about 2 minutes. Drain and pat dry with paper towels to blot up all the moisture.

2. Arrange the chayote slices in a pinwheel fashion around the perimeter of four salad plates. Place several tomato slices in the center of each plate.

3. Whisk the lime juice, allspice, and salt to taste together in a small bowl. Whisk in the oil until the dressing is smooth. Adjust the seasonings.

4. Drizzle the dressing over the vegetables and sprinkle with the parsley. Serve immediately.

Sautéed Chayote with Fresh Corn, Chile, and Oregano

Chayote and corn are often cooked together in Mexico. A little cream as well as some chiles, garlic, and fresh oregano is enough to create a full-flavored side dish for chicken, fish, or meat.

SERVES 6 AS A SIDE DISH

3 medium chayote (about 1½ pounds), peeled, quartered, pitted, and cut into ½-inch cubes

2 tablespoons unsalted butter

2 medium garlic cloves, minced

1 medium jalapeño chile, stemmed, seeded, and minced

2 medium ears corn, husks and silk removed and discarded; kernels cut away from cobs with a knife (about 1½ cups)

¼ cup heavy cream

2 teaspoons minced fresh oregano leaves

Salt

1. Place a steamer basket in a wide, deep saucepan. Fill the pan with enough water to reach just below the bottom of the steamer basket. Turn the heat to high and bring the water to a boil. Add the chayote to the basket, cover the pan, and steam until crisp-tender, about 10 minutes. Remove and set aside.

2. Melt the butter in a large skillet over medium heat. Add the garlic and chiles and sauté until fragrant, about 1 minute. Add the chayote, corn, and cream. Cover and cook, stirring once or twice, until the vegetables are tender, about 4 minutes. Remove the cover and simmer until most of the liquid in pan evaporates, 1 to 2 minutes. Add the oregano and salt to taste. Serve immediately.

Collard Greens

Collard greens are a Southern staple. Their wide, flat leaves are almost leathery and require more cooking than most other leafy greens. However, traditional recipes that call for simmering collards for 2 hours are not to my taste. I think that prolonged simmering cooks the life out of this mild-tasting green. Twenty minutes will soften collards plenty and still keep their color fairly bright. Best of all, shorter cooking times preserve their unique flavor.

I find that collards have a subtler flavor than most other tough greens, such as kale or turnip greens. They are earthy and almost smoky-tasting, never peppery or hot.

Collards don't cook down as much as other greens. The leaves are tough and don't have tons of moisture to shed. However, the thick stems are inedible, so there is a fair amount of waste up front. Be fairly ruthless about removing the stems. Even the portion that extends up into the leaves can be quite tough and should be discarded if it is thicker than a metal skewer.

OTHER COMMON NAMES: Collards.

AVAILABILITY: Year-round, although fall through spring is the traditional season.

SELECTION: Collard greens should have dark green leaves that show no signs of decay or yellowing. If you have a choice, pick collards with thin stems (there will be less waste).

STORAGE: Collards should be refrigerated in a loosely sealed plastic bag. If they seem very wet when you get them home from the market, blot them dry with paper towels and place them in a dry bag. Collards will stay fresh for a few days at most.

BASIC PREPARATION: Collard stems are quite tough and should be discarded. Even the portion of the stem that runs into the leaf may be quite thick and should be trimmed.

I usually work with collards over a large bowl of water. Working with one stalk at a time, hold the stalk by the end of the stem with the leafy portion pointing down. Use a sharp chef's knife to slice down one side of the stem (the knife is being used like a machete) to strip the leafy green portion away from the tough stem. Repeat the process on the other side of the stem to strip away the remaining leafy portion. When done, discard the bare stems.

The leaves are ready to be washed, chopped, and cooked. Don't bother drying greens like collards that will be cooked in liquid. Simply shake off the excess water over the sink. The remaining moisture becomes part of the cooking liquid.

BEST COOKING METHODS: Boiling (and then braising) or simply braising.

OTHER RECIPES WITH COLLARD GREENS: Any recipe for kale can be adapted to use collards.

Collard Greens, Southern Style

Instead of the traditional slow simmering with smoked pork bones that can take hours, I cook the collards in a modest amount of water until tender and then stir in some sautéed bacon and onion for flavor. The process is simple and retains the full flavor of the greens since there is no excess cooking water to be drained. Serve these soupy greens with corn bread.

SERVES 4 TO 6 AS A SIDE DISH

2½ pounds collard greens, tough stems discarded, washed, shaken to remove excess water, and coarsely chopped
    Salt
4 slices bacon, chopped
1 medium onion, minced
    Freshly ground black pepper
    Red wine vinegar

1. Bring 1 cup of water to a boil in a large casserole or Dutch oven. Add the damp greens and salt to taste. Cover, reduce the heat, and simmer, stirring once or twice, until the greens are very tender, about 15 minutes.

2. While the greens are cooking, fry the bacon in a medium skillet over medium heat until crisp, about 6 minutes. Use a slotted spoon to transfer the bacon to a small plate. Spoon off all but 1 tablespoon of the bacon fat. Add the onion to the pan with the bacon fat and sauté until pieces begin to brown around the edges, about 5 minutes. Remove the pan from the heat.

3. When the greens are tender, add pepper to taste (these greens taste best with a lot of pepper) and simmer, uncovered, until the greens reach the desired consistency, 1 to 2 minutes if you like your greens soupy, 5 minutes if you want them a bit drier. Stir in the reserved bacon and onion. Adjust the seasonings, adding vinegar to sharpen the flavors (use just a teaspoon or so). Serve immediately.

Braised Collards with Tomatoes and Peanuts

Traditional Southern flavors—collard greens, tomatoes, and peanuts—get a new twist here. Use a roasted peanut oil if you really want to highlight the nut flavor in this soupy side dish, which should be served with rice.

SERVES 6 AS A SIDE DISH

2½ pounds collard greens, tough stems discarded, washed, shaken dry to remove excess water, and coarsely chopped
    Salt
2 tablespoons roasted peanut oil or extra-virgin olive oil
1 medium onion, chopped
2 medium garlic cloves, minced
¼ teaspoon cayenne pepper, or to taste
    One 14.5-ounce can diced tomatoes
¼ cup unsalted roasted peanuts, chopped

1. Bring several quarts of water to a boil in a large pot. Add the greens and salt to taste. Cover and cook until the greens are crisp-tender, 5 to 7 minutes. Drain, rinse under cold water, and drain again. Set the greens aside.

2. Heat the oil in a large sauté pan. Add the onion and sauté over medium heat until golden, about 5 minutes. Add the garlic and cayenne and cook until fragrant, about 30 seconds.

3. Add the tomatoes and greens to the pan and stir to combine. Cover and cook, stirring once or twice, until the greens are tender and the flavors have blended, about 10 minutes. Adjust the seasonings. Transfer the greens to a serving bowl, sprinkle with the peanuts, and serve immediately.

Soy-Braised Collards with Five-Spice Powder

Sturdy collards are a good choice for this traditional Asian treatment. More tender greens would turn mush if cooked this way. If you can't find collards, use kale instead. Five-spice powder is a blend of cinnamon, cloves, fennel, star anise, and Szechwan peppercorns. This Chinese seasoning is available in the spice section of many supermarkets. Serve these greens with a pork roast or chops.

SERVES 4 TO 6 AS A SIDE DISH

¼ cup rice wine or sherry
3 tablespoons soy sauce
2 teaspoons sugar
½ teaspoon five-spice powder
2½ pounds collard greens, tough stems discarded, washed, shaken dry to remove excess water, and coarsely chopped
Rice vinegar

1. Bring rice wine, soy sauce, sugar, five-spice powder, and ¼ cup water to a boil in a large casserole or Dutch oven. Add the damp greens. Cover, reduce the heat, and simmer, stirring once or twice, until the greens are very tender, about 15 minutes.

2. Remove the cover and simmer until the greens are no longer soupy, 3 to 4 minutes. Adjust the seasonings, adding rice vinegar to taste. Serve immediately.

Corn

Corn used to be a seasonal crop, available for just a few short months every summer. As a kid, I remember waiting at the farmstand for the farmer to bring in corn from the field. We would rush home and cook it immediately. Why all the fuss?

As soon as corn is picked, the natural sugars begin to convert to starches. In heirloom varieties, the flavor deteriorates within a few hours. Some food snobs insist they can taste the difference between corn picked at 4 P.M. and corn picked at 5 P.M. and then cooked for dinner at 6 P.M. While an hour or two may not have made much difference, a day or two did.

Sugar-enhanced varieties were developed a couple of decades ago. With at least 50 percent more sugar than heirloom varieties, sugar-enhanced varieties taste fine the day after they are picked. In the past decade, a new crop of hybrids, called supersweets, has been developed. With twice as much sugar as the corn of my childhood, it is sweet days after harvesting.

While new varieties may taste sweeter days after picking than heirloom varieties, I'm not sure they taste better. In fact, I find much new corn to be achingly sweet. I taste sugar, but not corn.

So what's the consumer to do? First of all, there is no way to know whether the corn you are buying is an heirloom variety (called normal sweet), sugar-enhanced, or supersweet. I recommend buying corn from a farmstand. They are most likely planting sugar-enhanced corn and it will be delicious as long as you cook it the day you buy it.

AVAILABILITY: Summer through early fall. (You may see supersweet corn at other times of the year, especially the spring. These ears have been grown in Florida or California and trucked to your market. Often, they have been partially husked. Although this corn is sugary sweet, it does not have much corn flavor and I don't buy it.)

SELECTION: You could peel back the husks and silks to examine the kernels, but farmers don't encourage this practice. I find that squeezing the corn with my hand works almost as well. Start at the middle of the ear and work toward the tip. If you pay attention, you can almost feel the kernels through the husks. They should feel plump. Ears with immature kernels at the end are easy to pick out with your hands. These ears also look less full and are thinner than ears with mature kernels right to the tip.

STORAGE: Ideally, corn should be cooked the day it is purchased. Heirloom varieties (which are rarely grown today) must be cooked the day they are picked. New hybrids still taste great a day or two after they are harvested, but letting corn hang out for days in the refrigerator (or supermarket produce aisle) only dulls its flavor. If you must, wrap unhusked ears in a damp cloth and refrigerate them for a day, or two at the most.

BASIC PREPARATION: For all recipes, remove the husks and silks from the corn. (Grilling requires a slightly modified procedure; see page 117.) If you want to remove the kernels from the cob, I find it best to cut the ears in half crosswise with a chef's knife. This way you can stand each piece on its cut end and the corn won't wobble. Slice downward several times to remove all the kernels. (With shorter pieces of corn, the kernels are less likely to fly all over the place—another advantage to cutting the cobs in half before removing the kernels.) Depending on the size of the corn, you will get between ½ cup and ¾ cup of kernels from each ear.

BEST COOKING METHODS: Baking, boiling, braising, grilling, or sautéing.

OTHER RECIPES WITH CORN:
Green Beans and Corn with Tomato-Herb Vinaigrette (page 175)
Zucchini, Corn, and Red Pepper Sauté (page 375)

Boiled Corn

There's not much to this recipe, but it's one of those basic kitchen tasks you will do dozens of times every summer. The key here is to add the corn when the water is at a rolling boil so the cooking time is kept to a minimum. If you have a really large pot (at least 12 quarts), you can double this recipe, but don't try to boil more than eight ears in one pot. Better to cook the corn in batches. Good corn is so sweet and delicious, I find it doesn't even need butter. Pass the butter, as well as the salt and pepper, and let everyone season the corn to his or her own taste.

SERVES 4 AS A SIDE DISH

4 medium ears corn, husks and silks removed
Salt
Freshly ground black pepper
Unsalted butter, if desired

1. Bring 4 quarts of water to a rolling boil in a large pot. (Use more water if cooking more ears of corn.) Add the corn and cook 2 to 4 minutes depending on how tender you like your corn. Use a pair of tongs to lift the corn, one at a time, from the water, letting the excess water drip back into the pot. Transfer the corn to a large platter.
2. Bring the platter to the table and pass the salt and pepper and butter separately.

Grilled Corn with Chili Butter

Grilling is an efficient way to cook corn in the summer, when you are more likely to be outside tending the grill than standing over the stove. The problem is that corn cooked in the husks tends to steam and pick up very little grill flavor. However, husked corn tends to char and burn and the texture can be a bit dry. My friend and colleague Maryellen Driscoll turned me on to this solution: Remove all but the last, thin layer of the husk, which offers protection against burning but permits some browning of the corn kernels. Once the husk blackens, the corn is ready to be husked and silked (be careful, the ears are hot) and served. This recipe can be doubled or even tripled if you like.

The stronger flavor of grilled corn makes it an ideal candidate for more adventurous seasonings, like chili butter. The butter is delicious if you toast and grind your own dried chiles. However, good-quality store-bought chili powder will be fine.

SERVES 4 AS A SIDE DISH

4 medium ears corn
2 tablespoons unsalted butter, softened
½ teaspoon good-quality chili powder
Salt

1. Light a grill fire. Remove all but the innermost layer of the husk from the corn. Twist off the silk at the top of each ear by hand.

2. Place the butter, chili powder, and salt to taste in a small bowl. Use a fork to work the ingredients into a smooth paste.

3. Grill the corn over a medium fire, turning several times, until the husks are charred and beginning to peel away from the ears, about 10 minutes. Remove the corn from the grill.

4. Wearing an oven mitt, peel away and discard the charred husks and silks. Use a butter knife to spread the chili butter lightly over the grilled corn and serve immediately.

VARIATION: GRILLED CORN WITH HERB BUTTER

Good choices are parsley, basil, tarragon, chives, sage, and chervil.

Replace the chili powder with 1½ tablespoons minced fresh herbs.

Grilled Corn, Tomato, and Red Onion Salad

A classic summertime salad, made even better with grilled corn. This juicy salad makes an excellent "relish" to accompany almost any grilled fish. It's also delicious with grilled steaks. Since I really want the charred flavor from the grill, I strip all the husks from the corn before cooking it. The dressing moistens the corn, so there's no worry about the corn becoming dry.

SERVES 4 AS A SIDE DISH

4 medium ears corn, husks and silks removed
2 medium ripe tomatoes, cored and chopped
½ small red onion, minced (about ¼ cup)
2 tablespoons extra-virgin olive oil
1½ teaspoons red wine vinegar
8 large fresh basil leaves, cut into thin strips
  Salt
  Freshly ground black pepper

1. Light a grill fire. Grill the corn over a medium fire, turning several times, until the kernels are tender and lightly charred, about 10 minutes. Remove the corn from the grill. When the corn is cool enough to handle, cut the ears in half with a chef's knife, stand each piece on its cut end, and slice downward several times to remove all the kernels. Place the corn in a large serving bowl; discard the cobs.

2. Add the tomatoes and onion to the bowl with the corn and toss gently. Drizzle the oil and vinegar over the vegetables. Add the basil and salt and pepper to taste. Toss gently and serve. (This salad can be set aside at room temperature for up to 1 hour.)

Sautéed Corn and Sweet Peppers

Fresh corn and bell peppers make an especially attractive and delicious summer side dish. Use two red or one red and one orange bell pepper for the best presentation.

4 medium ears corn

2 tablespoons extra-virgin olive oil

1 medium shallot, minced

2 medium bell peppers, cored, seeded, and chopped fine

1 tablespoon lime juice

1 tablespoon minced fresh cilantro leaves

Salt

Freshly ground black pepper

1. Remove the husks and silks from the corn. Cut the ears in half crosswise with a chef's knife, stand each piece on its cut end, and slice downward several times to remove all the kernels. (Discard the cobs.) You should have about 2½ cups of kernels.

2. Heat the oil in a large skillet. Add the shallot and sauté over medium heat until softened, about 3 minutes. Add the corn and peppers and sauté until crisp-tender, about 6 minutes. Sprinkle with the lime juice and cilantro and season with salt and pepper to taste. Serve hot or at room temperature.

"Creamed" Corn with Onion and Chile

Corn cooked in a thick cream sauce sounds like bad cafeteria food. The sauce usually contains flour so it's extremely thick, and the flavors of the cream and cheese overwhelm the corn. However, creamed corn can be delicious, especially if just a little cream is used to accentuate the flavor of sweet corn. Here, I cook the corn in a little stock and then enrich the liquid with cream to give it some body. The sauce is still thin, perfect for moistening mashed potatoes, chicken, or even grilled flank steak. Mexican flavors are a natural with corn and help keep the dish from tasting too heavy.

SERVES 4 TO 6 AS A SIDE DISH

6 medium ears corn

2 tablespoons unsalted butter

1 medium onion, minced

1 medium jalapeño chile, stemmed, seeded, and minced

¾ cup chicken or vegetable stock

Salt

Freshly ground black pepper

¼ cup heavy cream

1 tablespoon minced fresh cilantro leaves

1. Remove the husks and silks from the corn. Cut the ears in half crosswise with a chef's knife, stand each piece on its cut end, and slice downward several times to remove all the kernels. (Discard the cobs.) You should have about 4 cups of kernels.

2. Melt the butter in a medium skillet. Add the onion and sauté over medium heat until golden, about 6 minutes. Add the chile and cook until softened, about 1 minute. Add the corn, stock, and salt and pepper to taste. Bring to a boil, reduce the heat, cover, and simmer gently, stirring once or twice, until the corn is tender, 6 to 7 minutes.

3. Remove the cover and add the cream to the pan. Simmer until the liquid in the pan thickens, about 1 minute. Add the cilantro and adjust the seasonings. Serve immediately.

Corn and Mushroom Sauté

This dish is heavenly with chanterelles and delicious with most any mushroom, including the lowly button. Serve with grilled meat, especially steaks or burgers.

SERVES 4 TO 6 AS A SIDE DISH

3 medium ears corn
3 tablespoons unsalted butter
2 medium shallots, minced
1 pound fresh mushrooms, sliced thin
   Salt
   Freshly ground black pepper
½ cup chicken or vegetable stock
1 tablespoon minced fresh parsley leaves

1. Remove the husks and silks from the corn. Cut the ears in half crosswise with a chef's knife,

stand each piece on its cut end, and slice downward several times to remove all the kernels. (Discard the cobs.) You should have about 2 cups of kernels.

2. Melt 2 tablespoons of the butter in a large skillet. Add the shallots and sauté over medium heat until softened, about 2 minutes. Add the mushrooms and raise the heat to medium-high. Sauté until golden brown, about 7 minutes. Season with salt and pepper to taste.

3. Add the corn and stock to the skillet. Cook, stirring often, just until the corn is tender and the liquid in the pan has evaporated, about 3 minutes.

4. Remove the pan from the heat. Swirl in the remaining tablespoon of butter and the parsley. Adjust the seasonings and serve immediately.

Fresh Corn Griddle Cakes with Parmesan and Chives

Fresh ears of corn are grated into a chunky puree and then enriched with an egg, some Parmesan, chives, and a little flour. The mixture is like thick pancake batter. The batter is cooked in a skillet with butter to form large, round cakes (they look like pancakes) that are browned and crisp on the exterior and creamy inside. These cakes are delicious with grilled fish or roast chicken. A tomato salad would round out the meal.

SERVES 6 AS A SIDE DISH

4 medium ears corn
1 large egg
¼ cup flour
¼ cup grated Parmesan cheese
1 tablespoon snipped fresh chives
½ teaspoon salt
Freshly ground black pepper
1 tablespoon unsalted butter

1. Remove the husks and silks from the corn. Grate the corn on the large holes of a box grater set over a large bowl until the cobs are clean. (Discard the cobs.) Stir in the egg, flour, cheese, chives, salt, and pepper to taste until the batter is smooth.

2. Melt the butter in a large nonstick skillet. Fill a ¼-cup measure with batter. Use a rubber spatula to scrape the batter into the pan to form a round cake. Repeat using all the batter. (You should get six cakes from the batter.) Cook over medium heat, turning once, until the cakes turn a rich golden brown color on both sides, about 9 minutes. Serve immediately.

Corn-Mango Salsa

This simple salsa can be assembled in 10 minutes and adds a tremendous amount of flavor to grilled fish, chicken, pork, or beef. I especially like this moist, flavorful salsa with a spice-rub pork tenderloin or flank steak. The salsa is so delicious, you will want to eat it like a vegetable side dish. Use this recipe as a starting point for other quick corn salsas. Combine boiled and cooled corn with diced roasted red peppers, extra-virgin olive oil, lemon juice, and parsley. Or, pair corn with black beans, diced tomatoes, chili powder, lime juice, and cilantro.

MAKES 2 GENEROUS CUPS, ENOUGH
FOR AT LEAST 4 SERVINGS

3 medium ears corn
Salt
1 large mango, peeled, pitted, and chopped fine
½ medium jalapeño chile, stemmed, seeded, and minced, or more to taste
2 tablespoons lime juice
1 tablespoon minced fresh cilantro leaves

1. Remove the husks and silks from the corn. Cut the ears in half crosswise with a chef's knife, stand each piece on its cut end, and slice downward several times to remove all the kernels. (Discard the cobs.) You should have about 2 cups of kernels.

2. Bring a quart or two of water to a boil in a medium saucepan. Add the corn and salt to taste and cook until the corn is tender, about 2 minutes. Drain and set the corn aside until cool.

3. Combine the cooled corn with the mango, chile, lime juice, cilantro, and salt to taste. Let stand at room temperature for 10 minutes to allow the flavors to blend. (The salsa can be refrigerated in an airtight container for several days. For the best flavor, bring it to room temperature before using.)

Corn Pudding with Buttered Crumbs

The emphasis is clearly on the corn in this simple recipe, which contains very little "pudding" and lots of corn kernels. You may add a tablespoon or two of minced fresh herbs—chives are particularly good— but there is something to be said for the simplicity of this dish.

SERVES 6 AS A SIDE DISH

2 tablespoons unsalted butter
5 medium ears corn
2 large eggs, lightly beaten
1¼ cups milk
½ teaspoon salt
　 Freshly ground white pepper
1 cup Fresh Bread Crumbs (page 123)

1. Preheat the oven to 325 degrees. Use 1 tablespoon of the butter to grease an 8-inch square baking dish.
2. Remove the husks and silks from the corn. Cut the ears in half crosswise with a chef's knife, stand each piece on its cut end, and slice downward several times to remove all the kernels. (Discard the cobs.) You should have about 3½ cups of kernels.
3. Combine the corn, eggs, milk, and salt and pepper to taste in a medium bowl. Scrape the corn mixture into the buttered dish.
4. Melt the remaining tablespoon of butter in a small saucepan. Place the crumbs in a small bowl.

Drizzle the melted butter over the crumbs and stir until the crumbs are evenly moistened. Sprinkle the buttered bread crumbs over the corn mixture.
5. Bake until the pudding has set in the center and the top has browned lightly, about 1 hour. Serve hot or warm.

FRESH BREAD CRUMBS

Homemade crumbs are far superior to dusty crumbs from a can. They taste like bread and have a coarser and more appealing texture. Use any stale country white bread or baguette without seeds to make the crumbs. Fresh bread has too much moisture to grind properly. To dry out fresh bread, place slices in a 250-degree oven until firm (this will take 10 to 20 minutes, depending on the bread), cool, and the grind.

MAKES ABOUT 2 CUPS

Four ½-inch-thick slices stale country white bread (about 6 ounces), torn into small pieces

Place the pieces of bread in a food processor and process until the crumbs are coarsely ground, about 1 minute. Fresh bread crumbs can be refrigerated in an airtight container for a couple of days.

Corn Chowder with Leeks and Potatoes

Many cooks think good chowder requires a lot of time or effort. However, I find that simpler is better with this recipe that contains just corn, leeks (for added sweetness), potatoes (for thickness), and milk. Simmering the cleaned cobs in the chowder delivers an especially rich corn flavor.

**SERVES 4 AS A LIGHT MAIN COURSE,
6 AS A FIRST COURSE**

5   medium ears corn
2   tablespoons unsalted butter
2   medium leeks, white and light green parts, sliced thin
2   cups milk
¾   pound red potatoes, peeled and cut into ½-inch dice
    Salt
    Freshly ground black pepper
2   tablespoons minced fresh parsley leaves

1. Remove the husks and silks from the corn. Cut the ears in half crosswise with a chef's knife, stand each piece on its cut end, and slice downward several times to remove all the kernels. (Reserve the cobs.) You should have about 3½ cups of kernels.
2. Place the corn cobs and water to cover (about 4 cups) in a large saucepan. Bring to a boil, reduce the heat, partially cover, and simmer gently for 20 minutes. Pick out and discard the corn cobs.

Strain and reserve 3 cups corn broth; discard the remaining broth.
3. Melt the butter in a soup kettle. Add the leeks and sauté over medium heat until softened, about 5 minutes. Add the corn broth, milk, potatoes, and salt and pepper to taste. Bring to a boil, reduce the heat, and simmer gently until the potatoes are almost tender, about 15 minutes. Add the corn kernels and continue to simmer gently until the corn and potatoes are tender, about 10 minutes.
4. Puree 2 cups of the soup in a blender. Return the puree to the soup pot and reheat gently. Stir in the parsley and adjust the seasonings. Serve immediately.

VARIATION: CORN CHOWDER WITH BACON, LEEKS, AND POTATOES

Follow steps 1 and 2. Omit the butter from step 3. Instead, sauté 4 to 6 strips of diced bacon until the fat has rendered, about 3 minutes. Add the leeks and continue to sauté until the bacon is crisp and the leeks have softened, about 5 minutes. Add the corn broth, milk, potatoes, salt, and pepper and proceed as directed.

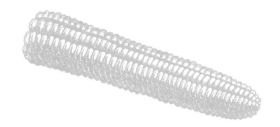

Cucumbers

Cucumbers are the ideal summer vegetable since they are crisp and refreshing and best eaten chilled. The standard supermarket cucumber has a lot of seeds and is waxed. While it is easy to overcome these obstacles (peeling and seeding take just minutes), other varieties may have more appeal.

Long, slender, ridged cucumbers (variously called English, Dutch, or Japanese cucumbers) have few or no seeds and thin skins. Round yellow cucumbers (called lemon cucumbers) are sweet and crunchy. (They get their name from their appearance, not their flavor). If you shop at a farmers' market, you will see a variety of shapes and sizes.

AVAILABILITY: Year-round, although summer is the season for heirloom varieties.

SELECTION: Cucumbers should be very firm and unblemished. Smaller cucumbers tend to have fewer seeds and thus less waste. Cucumbers should feel heavy for the size. If you can buy cucumbers that have not been waxed, do so. They are probably fresher than cucumbers that have been coated with wax to prevent dehydration. Don't worry too much about the wax though; the skin is generally peeled anyway.

STORAGE: Cucumbers can be stored in the vegetable crisper drawer as is. The waxed coating applied by most wholesalers will keep the cucumbers fresh and crisp for at least a week or two. Unwaxed cucumbers are more delicate. Store them in a loosely sealed plastic bag for up to 1 week.

BASIC PREPARATION: Unless the skin is thin and unwaxed (which is unlikely if you shop at a supermarket), always remove the skin with a vegetable peeler. Even if the skin has not been waxed, I often remove it anyway. Peeled cucumbers give marinated salads a better texture.

The seeds are watery and add little to finished dishes. I almost always remove them as well. Cut the peeled cucumber in half lengthwise and then scrape out the seeds with a small spoon. Once the cucumber has been seeded, it can be sliced or diced as desired.

All but one of the recipes that follow call for salting the cucumbers to drive off excess moisture. Cucumbers are almost all water and have a hard time absorbing flavors, especially from a dressing. Salting rids them of some water and gives the cucumbers a pleasingly crunchy texture. Best of all, the cucumbers can soak up some vinaigrette or other dressing, rather than making the dressing watery. I highly recommend that you try this method.

Simply place the sliced cucumbers in a strainer, sprinkle with coarse salt, and then set a zipper-lock plastic bag filled with ice water on top of the cucumbers. The weight of the water helps force liquid out of the cucumbers. I use ice water so the cucumber slices stay cold and refreshing. After about an hour, the cucumber slices will have thrown off several tablespoons of water and are ready to be rinsed, dried, and dressed.

BEST COOKING METHODS: Cucumbers are generally used raw in salads. Their texture is vastly improved by salting and weighting to drive off excess moisture. If you are going to cook cucumbers, sautéing is the best choice. Salting the cucumbers before sautéing delivers the best results.

OTHER RECIPES WITH CUCUMBER:
Tomato and Cucumber Salad with Mint (page 330)

Cucumber Salad with Yogurt and Dill

Thanks to my friend Adam Ried for showing me how to salt and weight cucumbers for the crispest results. To make raita, the Indian cucumber salad often served as a cooling accompaniment to curries, use mint instead of dill.

SERVES 4 TO 6 AS A SIDE DISH

3 medium cucumbers (about 1½ pounds), peeled, halved lengthwise, seeded, and cut on the diagonal ¼ inch thick
1 tablespoon kosher salt
¾ cup plain low-fat yogurt
1 tablespoon extra-virgin olive oil
1 medium garlic clove, minced
1 tablespoon minced fresh dill leaves
Freshly ground black pepper

1. Toss the cucumbers and salt in a large strainer or colander set over a bowl. Fill a gallon-size zipper-lock plastic bag with ice water and set the bag on top of the cucumber slices. Drain for 1 hour.
2. Thoroughly rinse the cucumber slices under cold, running water and pat dry with paper towels. Toss the cucumbers with the yogurt, oil, garlic, dill, and pepper to taste. Serve immediately or refrigerate for up to several hours.

Asian Cucumber Salad with Sesame

This light cucumber salad makes a perfect accompaniment to grilled foods, especially chicken or fish.

SERVES 4 TO 6 AS A SIDE DISH

3 medium cucumbers (about 1½ pounds), peeled, halved lengthwise, seeded, and cut on the diagonal ¼ inch thick
1 tablespoon kosher salt
2 tablespoons rice vinegar
2 tablespoons toasted sesame oil
½ teaspoon sugar
¼ teaspoon hot red pepper flakes
1 tablespoon sesame seeds, toasted in a dry skillet until golden brown

1. Toss the cucumbers and salt in a large strainer or colander set over a bowl. Fill a gallon-size zipper-lock plastic bag with ice water and set the bag on top of the cucumber slices. Drain for 1 hour.
2. Meanwhile, whisk the vinegar, oil, sugar, and pepper flakes together in a small bowl and set the dressing aside, stirring occasionally until the sugar dissolves.
3. Thoroughly rinse the cucumber slices under cold, running water and pat dry with paper towels. Toss the cucumbers with the dressing and toasted sesame seeds. Serve immediately or refrigerate for up to 1 day.

Spicy Cucumber Salad with Peanuts

This traditional Thai salad is served as an accompaniment to meals (it's especially good with chicken and fish) or as a first course. The sugar in the dressing balances the heat of the chile and the sharpness of the raw onion. I find this salad addictive, especially in the hot summer weather. If you can, use a tiny (very hot) red Thai chile. A jalapeño is fine, though.

SERVES 4 TO 6 AS A SIDE DISH OR FIRST COURSE

- 3 medium cucumbers (about 1½ pounds), peeled, halved lengthwise, seeded, and cut on the diagonal ¼ inch thick
- 1 tablespoon kosher salt
- ½ cup rice vinegar
- ½ cup water
- 3 tablespoons sugar
- 1 small fresh chile, stemmed, seeded if desired to reduce the heat, and minced
- 2 tablespoons minced red onion
- 2 tablespoons finely chopped roasted salted peanuts

1. Toss the cucumbers and salt in a large strainer or colander set over a bowl. Fill a gallon-size zipper-lock plastic bag with ice water and set the bag on top of the cucumber slices. Drain for 1 hour.

2. Combine the vinegar, water, and sugar in a small saucepan. Bring the mixture to a boil and cook until the sugar dissolves and the mixture becomes slightly syrupy, and is reduced to about ⅓ cup, about 10 minutes. Cool the mixture to room temperature.

3. Stir the chile, onion, and peanuts into the dressing. Thoroughly rinse the cucumber slices under cold, running water and pat dry with paper towels. Toss the cucumber with the dressing. Serve immediately or refrigerate for up to 1 day.

Sautéed Cucumbers with Shallots and Lemon

Many people gasp at the notion of cooking cucumber. However, crisp slices of seeded and salted cucumber work surprisingly well when sautéed briefly. The secret is to cook the cucumber long enough so that it picks up the flavors of the shallots and lemon but not so long that it becomes mushy. When done properly, sautéed cucumber is crisp-tender. If you can purchase unwaxed cucumbers, leave the peels on for a pretty contrast of colors.

SERVES 4 AS A SIDE DISH

- 3 medium cucumbers (about 1½ pounds), peeled, halved lengthwise, seeded, and cut on the diagonal ¼ inch thick
- 1 tablespoon kosher salt
- 2 tablespoons extra-virgin olive oil
- 3 medium shallots, minced
- 2 tablespoons lemon juice
- 2 tablespoons minced fresh mint leaves
  Ground black pepper

1. Toss the cucumbers and salt in a large strainer or colander set over a bowl. Fill a gallon-size zipper-lock plastic bag with ice water and set the bag on top of the cucumber slices. Drain for 1 hour.

2. Thoroughly rinse the cucumber slices under cold, running water and pat dry with paper towels.

3. Heat the oil in a large skillet. Add the shallots and sauté over medium heat until golden, 2 to 3 minutes. Add the cucumber slices and lemon juice and cook until crisp-tender, 3 to 4 minutes. Stir in the mint and pepper to taste and serve immediately.

Cucumber-Watermelon Salsa

Crunchy cucumbers make an excellent base for salsa, especially if paired with ripe watermelon. I have adapted this recipe from an excellent relish in Salsas, Sambals, Chutneys, and Chowchows *by my friends Chris Schlesinger and John Willoughby. Serve this relish with grilled seafood. It's especially good with shrimp and lobster.*

MAKES ABOUT 4 CUPS, ENOUGH
FOR 6 TO 8 SERVINGS

2 tablespoons rice vinegar
2 teaspoons sugar
1 teaspoon hot red pepper flakes
2 medium cucumbers (about 1 pound), peeled, halved lengthwise, seeded, and diced
2 cups seeded and diced watermelon
¼ cup minced red onion
2 tablespoons minced fresh cilantro or mint leaves
  Salt

1. Combine the vinegar, sugar, and hot red pepper flakes in a small bowl. Let stand, stirring occasionally, until the sugar dissolves, about 10 minutes.

2. Place the cucumbers, watermelon, onion, and cilantro in a large bowl. Drizzle the dressing over the salsa and toss to coat. Add salt to taste. Refrigerate for 1 hour, tossing once or twice, to allow the flavors to develop. (The salsa can be refrigerated in an airtight container for several days.)

Dandelion Greens

Gathering wild dandelion greens is a springtime ritual for many Europeans. It's hard to imagine too many Americans combing roadsides for tender, young greens. In any case, pollution and pesticides make roadside collection of any greens a chancy proposition.

Thankfully, American farmers have taken to cultivating dandelion greens and they have become a popular ingredient in restaurants and supermarkets during the past decade. It's ironic that some people spend hours and countless dollars trying to eradicate the same weed they will happily pay for and enjoy in restaurants and markets.

Dandelion greens are deeply notched (the leaves are said to be saw-toothed) and dark green. A lighter-colored stem rises through the leaf and is generally thin.

Dandelion greens show up in two forms in our markets. Occasionally, you will see young dandelion greens, also called baby dandelions. The leaves are tender enough to eat raw in salads and the stems are extremely thin and tender. The flavor is peppery, but not overly so.

Once the leaves are much longer than 5 inches, they become tough and quite hot. Mature dandelion greens, with leaves that grow to be a foot or so, are best cooked. I usually blanch them to set their color and reduce their sharpness. I then sauté the blanched greens in fat for flavor. You could braise dandelion greens (much as you cook spinach and chard), but the results may be quite spicy.

OTHER COMMON NAMES: Dandelion.

AVAILABILITY: Year-round, although baby or young dandelions are usually found in the spring.

SELECTION: Look for dandelion greens that are dark green and show no signs of yellowing or browning. If you can, buy greens with thinner (and therefore more tender) stems.

STORAGE: Dandelion greens should be refrigerated in a loosely sealed plastic bag. If the greens are damp when you get them home from the market (as is likely if you shop at a supermarket with automatic misters in the produce aisle), pat dry the greens with paper towels and put them into a dry bag. Mature greens may hold up for several days in the refrigerator. Baby greens are more perishable and should be used within a day or two.

BASIC PREPARATION: Use your hands to snap off the tough stems from mature greens. The stems on young or baby greens can be left on. Either way, make sure to wash the greens in a large bowl of cold water. Continue draining the water, adding fresh water, and swishing the greens around until no more grit falls to the bottom of the bowl.

If making salad, dry the greens in a spinner and then with paper towels. If cooking the greens, there's no need to dry them.

BEST COOKING METHODS: Mature greens should be blanched and then sautéed. They can also be braised. Young greens are best eaten raw (or lightly wilted by a warm dressing) in salads.

Dandelion Greens with Bacon and Onion

This recipe demonstrates the flavoring power of bacon. Just two strips flavor a large bunch of dandelion greens. This recipe is designed for mature greens, five inches long or more. Blanch the greens first to tame their pepperiness. The greens are then chopped and cooked with bacon and a little onion. A sprinkling of vinegar balances the other flavors.

SERVES 4 AS A SIDE DISH

1½ pounds mature dandelion greens, washed (tough stems discarded)
1 teaspoon salt
2 strips bacon
1 small onion, minced
2 teaspoons red wine vinegar
   Freshly ground black pepper

1. Bring the water to a boil in a large saucepan. Add the greens and salt to the water. Cook until the greens are tender, about 6 minutes. Drain, cool, and chop coarsely.
2. Cook the bacon in a large skillet over medium heat until crisp, about 5 minutes. Remove the bacon strips from the pan and drain them on paper towels.
3. Add the onion to the bacon fat and sauté until softened, about 4 minutes. Add the greens and cook, tossing well, until heated through and evenly flavored with the bacon fat and onion, 1 to 2 minutes. Add the vinegar and a generous amount of pepper.
4. Remove the pan from the heat. Crumble the bacon over the greens and adjust seasonings. Serve immediately.

Young Dandelion Salad with Warm Shallot Dressing and Croutons

Serve this salad when young dandelion greens are available in the spring. Baby mustard greens (available in the salad section of some supermarkets, usually near the mesclun) are a good year-round substitute. There are a lot of croutons in this salad, but I find that everyone always eats them all.

SERVES 4 AS A FIRST COURSE

10 cups stemmed young or baby dandelion greens, washed and thoroughly dried
3 tablespoons extra-virgin olive oil
2 medium shallots, minced
2 tablespoons red wine or sherry vinegar
   Salt
   Freshly ground black pepper
2½ cups Best Croutons (recipe follows)

1. Place the dandelion greens in a large bowl and set them aside.

2. Heat the oil in a small skillet. Add the shallots and cook over medium heat until lightly browned, about 5 minutes. Remove the skillet from the heat and stir in the vinegar and salt and pepper to taste.

3. Drizzle the warm dressing over the dandelion greens and toss to coat. Add the croutons, toss once or twice, and serve immediately.

BEST CROUTONS

Stale bread can be recycled and turned into the best croutons in the world when cooked with a little olive oil. Many chefs fry the croutons. However, I find that you must use a lot of oil to ensure even coverage. To use less fat, I toss the bread cubes with olive oil on a cookie sheet and then bake the croutons until crisp. Use good olive oil here—it really makes a difference.

MAKES ABOUT 2½ CUPS

Four ½-inch-thick slices stale country
   white bread (about 6 ounces)
2 tablespoons extra-virgin olive oil
Salt

1. Preheat the oven to 400 degrees. Trim and discard the crusts from the bread. Cut the bread into ¾-inch squares. (You should have about 3 cups.) Drizzle the oil over the bread cubes. Toss to coat. Sprinkle with salt to taste.

2. Bake, turning the croutons once, until nicely browned and crisp, about 15 minutes. Drain the croutons on paper towels and use as quickly as possible, certainly within a couple of hours.

VARIATION: GARLIC CROUTONS

Cubes of bread can be tossed with garlic-flavored oil to make delicious croutons. Make sure to strain out the garlic before combining the oil with the bread; if left in, the garlic will burn in the oven. If you like, use 2 tablespoons of commercial garlic oil in place of the olive oil in the recipe for Best Croutons.

Put two peeled garlic cloves through a garlic press. Combine the pressed garlic with 3 tablespoons extra-virgin olive oil and ¼ teaspoon salt in a small bowl. Set the mixture aside for 20 minutes. Pour the oil through a fine-mesh strainer and drizzle directly over the bread cubes on a rimmed cookie sheet. Toss to coat. Proceed as directed.

Eggplant

Creamy eggplant flesh acts like a sponge. It soaks up most any flavor, so it works just as well in a Thai salad with fish sauce and cilantro as it does in a Provençal gratin with onions and tomatoes.

However, care must be exercised when choosing a cooking method for eggplant. It will absorb as much fat as you give it, which means that sautéed or pan-fried eggplant will be heavy and greasy. I avoid this problem by choosing such cooking methods as grilling and broiling, which limit the amount of fat the eggplant can absorb. Yes, you must brush eggplant slices with some oil before grilling or they will stick to the rack and be bland. But with these cooking methods, as well as with stewing and roasting, there is no danger of the eggplant soaking up extra oil as it cooks.

AVAILABILITY: Summer and early fall are the traditional seasons for eggplant, although you can find eggplant in many markets year-round.

SELECTION: Size is the most important issue when shopping for eggplant. I find that large ones are often full of seeds and bitter. When grilling, broiling, or stewing, I always choose small or medium eggplant, weighing eight ounces or less each. Larger ones are fine for roasting whole if making an eggplant puree. Simply remove the seeds from the roasted flesh.

Eggplant should be firm with no soft spots. The different colors may look marvelous at the market, but once cooked the beautiful eggplant with white and mauve streaking looks pretty much the same as a black-skinned eggplant. No matter the color, the skin should be bright, shiny, and taut.

STORAGE: Like tomatoes, I find that eggplant is best stored on the counter. It seems to prefer the warmth of the summer kitchen to the chill of the refrigerator. Fresh eggplant should be fine for a couple of days if kept in a bowl in the kitchen.

BASIC PREPARATION: There's not much preparation here. Trim the green caps from the eggplant and then either slice it lengthwise into long strips or crosswise into rounds. Some sources suggest peeling eggplant. I find this a bother and prefer to keep the skin on. I think the contrast between chewy skin and creamy flesh makes eggplant more interesting to eat. The only time I get rid of the skin is when making an eggplant puree from roasted eggplant.

BEST COOKING METHODS: I prefer to use lower-fat cooking methods with eggplant, such as broiling, grilling, roasting, and stewing. I find that grilling draws off more moisture than broiling and produces a crisper texture. (Broiled eggplant tends to be a bit soft.) Grilling is my first choice for cooking eggplant, but the broiler may be used if necessary.

Grilled Eggplant with Asian Flavors

The eggplant is flavored in a two-step process. The raw eggplant is brushed with a mixture of roasted peanut oil, garlic, and ginger. After grilling, the slices are drizzled with a mixture of hoisin sauce, soy sauce, and scallions. This dish is one of my favorite eggplant preparations. It works especially well with grilled steak.

SERVES 4 AS A SIDE DISH

3 tablespoons roasted peanut oil
2 medium garlic cloves, minced
1 tablespoon minced fresh gingerroot
2 tablespoons hoisin sauce
2 tablespoons soy sauce
2 medium scallions, sliced thin
  Freshly ground black pepper
4 medium eggplant (about 2 pounds total weight)

1. Light the grill. Combine the oil, garlic, and ginger in a small bowl. Set the oil mixture aside until you are ready to grill. Stir the hoisin sauce, soy sauce, and scallions together in another small bowl until smooth. Season with pepper to taste and set aside.
2. Trim the green caps from the eggplant and then slice them lengthwise into ½-inch-thick pieces. Lay the slices on a large baking sheet.
3. When ready to grill, brush the oil mixture over both sides of the eggplant slices. Grill the eggplant over a medium-hot fire, turning once, until marked with dark stripes, 8 to 10 minutes. Transfer the slices to a large platter. Drizzle the hoisin mixture over them. Serve the eggplant hot or at room temperature.

Grilled Eggplant with Italian Flavors

As in the previous recipe, the eggplant is flavored in a two-step process. Before grilling, the raw eggplant slices are brushed with olive oil and garlic. After grilling, the slices are drizzled with a mixture of balsamic vinegar, honey, and thyme.

SERVES 4 AS A SIDE DISH

3 tablespoons extra-virgin olive oil
3 medium garlic cloves, minced
¼ cup balsamic vinegar
1 tablespoon honey
1 teaspoon minced fresh thyme leaves
  Salt
  Freshly ground black pepper
4 medium eggplant (about 2 pounds total weight)

1. Light the grill. Combine the oil and garlic in a small bowl. Set the oil mixture aside until you are ready to grill. Place the vinegar and honey in a small saucepan set over medium heat. Simmer until the vinegar mixture has thickened slightly, about 2 minutes. Stir in

thyme and salt and pepper to taste and set the mixture aside.

2. Trim the green caps from the eggplant and then slice lengthwise into ½-inch-thick pieces. Lay the eggplant on a large baking sheet.

3. When ready to grill, brush the oil mixture over both sides of the eggplant slices. Grill the eggplant over a medium-hot fire, turning once, until marked with dark stripes, 8 to 10 minutes. Transfer the eggplant to a large platter. Drizzle the vinegar mixture over the eggplant slices. Serve hot or at room temperature.

Grilled Eggplant with Garlic, Lemon, and Oregano

For this recipe, thick eggplant rounds are marinated in a heady mixture of minced garlic, lemon juice, olive oil, and minced oregano for an hour. The eggplant is then grilled until crusty and dark. Make sure to cut the slices quite thick so that the inside of each piece of eggplant remains creamy and soft and provides a nice contrast to the grilled exterior.

SERVES 4 AS A SIDE DISH

½ cup lemon juice
¼ cup extra-virgin olive oil
4 medium garlic cloves, minced
1 tablespoon minced fresh oregano leaves
Salt

Freshly ground black pepper
4 medium eggplant (about 2 pounds total weight)

1. Whisk the lemon juice, oil, garlic, oregano, and a generous sprinkling of salt and pepper together in a small bowl.

2. Cut the eggplant into ¾-inch-thick rounds. Place the eggplant in a large zipper-lock bag, add the marinade, and seal the bag. Turn the bag several times to coat the eggplant with the marinade. Set aside, turning the bag occasionally, for 1 hour.

3. Light the grill. Grill the eggplant over a medium-hot fire, turning once, until the eggplant is dark and crusty, about 10 minutes. Transfer the eggplant to a large platter. Serve hot or at room temperature.

Grilled Eggplant Salad with Thai Flavors

This is another one of my favorite eggplant dishes. The smoky flavor of grilled eggplant is the perfect match for aggressive Thai seasonings—in this case, lime juice, fish sauce, chile, scallions, cilantro, and roasted peanut oil. Serve this salad with grilled fish, chicken, or beef. Use a small red Thai chile if you can, but any hot chile is fine. I leave the seeds in for extra heat, but take them out if you like your food mild.

SERVES 4 TO 6 AS A SIDE DISH

2 tablespoons lime juice

1 tablespoon fish sauce

1 small very hot red or green chile, stemmed and minced

1 teaspoon sugar

4 medium eggplant (about 2 pounds total weight)

3 tablespoons roasted peanut oil
  Salt
  Freshly ground black pepper

4 medium scallions, white and light green parts, sliced thin

2 tablespoons minced fresh cilantro leaves

¼ cup roasted unsalted peanuts, chopped

1. Light the grill. Combine the lime juice, fish sauce, chile, and sugar in a small bowl and set aside for the flavors to blend and the sugar to dissolve.

2. Trim the green caps from the eggplant and then slice lengthwise into ½-inch-thick pieces. Lay the eggplant on a large baking sheet. Brush the oil over both sides of the eggplant slices and sprinkle with salt and pepper to taste.

3. Grill the eggplant over a medium-hot fire, turning once, until the surface of the eggplant has become quite dark and crisp, about 10 minutes. Transfer the eggplant to a large cutting board and cool to room temperature. Chop the eggplant into ½-inch squares.

4. Combine the chopped eggplant, scallions, and cilantro in a large serving bowl. Drizzle the dressing over the eggplant mixture and toss to combine. Adjust the seasonings. Sprinkle with the peanuts and serve immediately.

Broiled Eggplant Slices with Parmesan and Oregano Bread Crumbs

This recipe is a good low-fat, no-mess alternative to breaded and fried eggplant slices. Here, eggplant slices are broiled and then topped with a cheesy bread crumb mixture. The slices are put back into the oven and broiled just until the crumb topping is crisp and golden.

SERVES 4 AS A SIDE DISH

4 medium eggplant (about 2 pounds)

5 tablespoons extra-virgin olive oil
  Salt

1½ cups Fresh Bread Crumbs (page 122)

¾ cup grated Parmesan cheese

1 tablespoon minced fresh oregano leaves

1. Preheat the broiler. Trim the green caps from the eggplant and then slice them lengthwise ¾ inch thick. Lay the eggplant on a large baking sheet. Brush lightly on both sides with 3 tablespoons of the oil and season with salt to taste. Make sure that any slices with skin on one side are turned flesh side down on the baking sheet.

2. Combine the bread crumbs, cheese, remaining 2 tablespoons of oil, and oregano in a small bowl. Mix with your fingers until evenly combined and moistened.

3. Broil the eggplant, turning once, until lightly browned, about 10 minutes. Remove the baking

sheet from the oven and spoon the bread crumb mixture evenly over the eggplant. Return the baking sheet to the oven and broil just until the crumbs are lightly browned, no more than a minute or two. (Watch carefully to make sure the crumbs do not burn.) Serve immediately.

Broiled Eggplant Slices with Parsley, Capers, and Garlic

A vinegary green sauce makes a lively seasoning for slices of broiled eggplant. You may grill the eggplant in this recipe if you prefer.

SERVES 4 AS A SIDE DISH

4 medium eggplant (about 2 pounds)
5 tablespoons extra-virgin olive oil
Salt
¼ cup minced fresh parsley leaves
1 tablespoon drained capers, minced
1 medium garlic clove, minced
1 tablespoon red wine vinegar

1. Preheat the broiler. Trim the green caps from the eggplant and then slice them lengthwise ¾ inch thick. Lay the eggplant on a large baking sheet. Brush lightly on both sides with 3 tablespoons of the oil and season with salt to taste.
2. Stir together the parsley, capers, garlic, vinegar, and remaining 2 tablespoons of oil in a small bowl.

3. Broil the eggplant, turning once, until lightly browned, about 10 minutes. Transfer the eggplant to a large platter. Drizzle the green sauce over the eggplant slices. Serve hot or at room temperature.

Middle Eastern Eggplant Puree with Tahini

This is my version of baba ghanoush, the Middle Eastern eggplant dip flavored with tahini, also called sesame paste. You can roast or grill the eggplant for this recipe. Grilling imparts a slightly smoky flavor to the eggplant, but since the skin is discarded once the eggplant has been cooked, the difference is slight. I find it easiest to make this recipe in the food processor, but make sure to pulse the eggplant just a few times. The eggplant should not become a smooth puree. Serve with pita breads or pita chips and/or fresh vegetables (everything from cherry tomatoes to sliced bell peppers and baby carrots). Baba ghanoush is also delicious slathered over slices of grilled or toasted country bread.

MAKES ABOUT 1½ CUPS, ENOUGH FOR 6 TO 8 AS AN HORS D'OEUVRE

2 medium-large eggplant (about 1½ pounds total weight)
3 tablespoons tahini (sesame paste)
2 tablespoons lemon juice
2 medium garlic cloves, chopped

½ teaspoon ground cumin

Salt

1 tablespoon extra-virgin olive oil

1 tablespoon minced fresh parsley leaves

1. Preheat the oven to 450 degrees or light the grill.

2. Use a paring knife to puncture the eggplant in several places to allow the steam to escape. If roasting, place the eggplant on a rimmed baking sheet and roast, turning occasionally, until they have collapsed and the skins have charred in places, about 45 minutes. If grilling, cook the eggplant over a medium-low fire, turning often, until collapsed and charred, about 30 minutes. Either way, set the eggplant aside to cool.

3. When cool enough to handle, remove the ends of the eggplant with a knife and peel away the skin with your fingers. Open the flesh and remove any long strands of seeds. Discard the seeds and any juices.

4. Place the tahini, lemon juice, garlic, cumin, and salt to taste in the work bowl of a food processor and process to combine. Add the eggplant flesh and pulse only until the mixture forms a chunky puree. Scrape the mixture into a bowl and adjust the seasonings. (The puree can be covered and refrigerated for up to 2 days.)

5. When ready to serve, drizzle the oil over the surface of the eggplant puree and sprinkle with the parsley.

Eggplant Puree with Asian Flavors

Roasted or grilled eggplant can be used to make baba ghanoush (see above), but that's just one possible sea-soning route. Soy sauce, rice vinegar, garlic, fresh chile, cilantro, and sesame are equally appealing. Serve this like baba ghanoush, with raw vegetables and crackers or other flat breads.

MAKES ABOUT 1½ CUPS, ENOUGH FOR
6 TO 8 AS AN HORS D'OEUVRE

2 medium-large eggplant (about 1½ pounds total weight)

2 tablespoons rice vinegar

1½ tablespoons soy sauce

2 medium garlic cloves, minced

1 small red or green chile, stemmed, seeded, and minced

2 tablespoons chopped fresh cilantro leaves

Salt

1 teaspoon toasted sesame oil

1 tablespoon sesame seeds, toasted in a dry skillet until golden brown

1. Preheat the oven to 450 degrees or light the grill.

2. Use a paring knife to puncture the eggplant in several places to allow the steam to escape. If roasting, place the eggplant on a rimmed baking sheet and roast, turning occasionally, until the eggplant have collapsed and the skins have charred in places, about 45 minutes. If grilling, cook the eggplant over a medium-low fire, turn-

ing often, until collapsed and charred, about 30 minutes. Either way, set the eggplant aside to cool.

3. When cool enough to handle, remove the ends of the eggplant with a knife and peel away the skin with your fingers. Open the flesh and remove any long strands of seeds. Discard the seeds and any juices.

4. Transfer the eggplant flesh to the work bowl of a food processor. Add the vinegar, soy sauce, garlic, chile, and cilantro and pulse until the mixture forms a chunky puree. Scrape the mixture into a bowl and adjust the seasonings. (The puree can be covered and refrigerated for up to 2 days.)

5. When ready to serve, drizzle the oil over the surface of the eggplant puree and sprinkle with the sesame seeds.

Eggplant and Tomato Gratin with Onion-Herb Jam

This simple yet elegant dish begins with slowly sautéed chopped onions, which are spread in a gratin dish, covered with slices of raw tomato and eggplant, and then baked. The onions become especially sweet, even a bit jam-like, as they soak up the juices from the tomatoes and eggplant in the oven. Serve with beef, chicken, or fish as a summer side dish. Or, serve with grilled bread and a leafy salad as lunch for four.

SERVES 6 AS A SIDE DISH

¼ cup extra-virgin olive oil
3 medium onions, cut into ½-inch dice
2 medium garlic cloves, minced
¼ cup chicken or vegetable stock
1 tablespoon honey
1 tablespoon minced fresh parsley leaves
2 teaspoons chopped fresh thyme leaves
 Salt
 Freshly ground black pepper
2 medium ripe tomatoes (about 1 pound), cored and cut crosswise into ¼-inch-thick slices
3 medium eggplant (about 1½ pounds), cut crosswise into ¼ inch-thick rounds

1. Preheat the oven to 400 degrees.

2. Heat 2 tablespoons of the oil in a large saucepan. Add the onions and sauté over medium-low heat until golden, about 20 minutes. Add the garlic and cook until fragrant, 1 to 2 minutes. Add the stock, honey, parsley, and thyme and raise the heat to medium. Cook just until the onion mixture thickens and becomes jam-like, about 5 minutes. Season with salt and pepper to taste.

3. Spread the onion mixture along the bottom of a shallow (1½-inch-deep) 10-inch round gratin dish. Lay the tomato and eggplant slices over the onion mixture, alternating slices of each and overlapping them quite a lot. Brush the remaining 2 tablespoons oil over the tomatoes and eggplant and season with salt and pepper to taste.

4. Bake until the eggplant and tomatoes soften and brown in spots, about 55 minutes. Let settle for 5 minutes and serve hot, warm, or at room temperature.

Ratatouille

I can't be bothered with cooking each vegetable separately as many classic recipes recommend. I do cook the eggplant first and then add it back at the end so that it doesn't completely fall apart. The perfect addition to any grilled meal, ratatouille is also delicious with eggs, spread on toasted bread as an appetizer, or even used as pasta sauce.

SERVES 6 TO 8 AS A SIDE DISH

¼ cup extra-virgin olive oil
2 medium eggplant (about 1 pound), cut into ½-inch dice
4 medium zucchini (about 1½ pounds), cut into ½-inch dice
2 medium onions, cut into ½-inch dice
2 medium red bell peppers (about ¾ pound), cored, seeded, and cut into ½-inch dice
2 medium garlic cloves, minced
2 small ripe tomatoes (about ¾ pound), cored and cut into small dice
½ cup chicken or vegetable stock
Several sprigs fresh thyme
1 bay leaf
Salt
2 tablespoons minced fresh basil leaves

1. Heat 2 tablespoons of the oil in a large casserole, preferably a nonstick one. Add the eggplant and cook over medium heat, stirring occasionally, until golden brown, about 10 minutes. Transfer the eggplant to a platter and set aside.

2. Heat the remaining 2 tablespoons of oil in the same casserole. Add the zucchini and onions and cook over medium heat, stirring often, until tender and golden, about 10 minutes. Add the peppers and garlic and cook for 2 minutes. Add the tomatoes, stock, thyme, bay leaf, and salt to taste. Simmer, uncovered, until the tomatoes fall apart, about 7 minutes.

3. Return the eggplant to the casserole along with the basil. Simmer, uncovered stirring occasionally, until all the vegetables are soft and the flavors have melded, about 15 minutes. Remove and discard the thyme and bay leaf. Adjust the seasonings. Serve hot, warm, or at room temperature. (Ratatouille can be refrigerated in an airtight container for several days.)

Indian Eggplant and Potato Stew with Chickpeas

This hearty vegetarian main course is subtly spiced. Mustard seeds are frequently used in Indian cooking to provide an earthy, but not spicy flavor to a dish. To release their flavor, the seeds are sautéed in hot oil. Since the seeds pop (it sounds like popcorn as they cook), make sure the cover is in place when the seeds are first cooking in the hot oil. Once the aromatics (in this case, ginger, garlic, and chile) are added to the pan, the popping will stop. Serve this stew with Indian flat breads or warm pitas.

2 tablespoons canola or other tasteless oil

2 teaspoons mustard seeds

2 tablespoons minced fresh gingerroot

4 medium garlic cloves, minced

1 medium jalapeño chile, stemmed, seeded if
  desired to reduce heat, and minced
  One 14.5-ounce can diced tomatoes
  Salt

1 cup water

4 medium eggplant (about 2 pounds total
  weight), cut into ½-inch dice

1 pound red potatoes, cut into ½-inch dice

1 cup drained and rinsed canned chickpeas

2 tablespoons lime juice

2 tablespoons minced fresh mint or cilantro
  leaves

1. Heat the oil in a large casserole or Dutch oven over medium heat. Add the mustard seeds and quickly cover the pot. When the seeds darken in color (after about 30 seconds), remove the cover and add the ginger, garlic, and chile. Sauté until the aromatics are softened, about 2 minutes.

2. Add the tomatoes, salt to taste, and water. Reduce the heat to low and simmer to combine flavors, about 2 minutes. Add the eggplant and potatoes, cover, and simmer gently, stirring occasionally, until the eggplant and potatoes are almost tender, about 25 minutes.

3. Add the chickpeas, as well as more water if the stew looks dry. Continue cooking until the chickpeas are heated through, about 5 minutes. Add the lime juice and mint. Adjust the seasonings and serve immediately.

Endive

Endive is a member of the chicory family and is closely related to radicchio. Endive is grown in the dark and thus lacks color. Like most chicories, it has some bite and can be especially sharp in salads. When cooked, the flavor becomes milder, even a bit sweet, and the texture creamy and satisfying.

There is some confusion regarding the nomenclature used to described endive. Belgian endive (the subject of this chapter) is the leaves grown from a chicory root forced in the dark. It should not be confused with curly endive, a nickname for the dark green, leafy vegetable more commonly called chicory.

Although Belgian endive is often used in salads, it is equally delicious cooked and served as a vegetable side dish.

OTHER COMMON NAMES: Belgian endive, chicory, and witloof.

AVAILABILITY: Year-round, although fall and winter are the traditional season.

SELECTION: Choose endive with crisp, unblemished outer leaves. The leaves should be compact and tightly closed. Look at the stem end. It should be white, with little or no browning. A stem that is brown and soft indicates that the endive is past its prime. The leaves should be as white; some yellow around the edges is fine but avoid endive with green edges. Exposure to light, which is signaled by green leaves, makes endive especially bitter.

STORAGE: Endive will stay fresh in the refrigerator for several days if stored in a loosely sealed plastic bag. If after a few days the outer leaves start to wilt or brown, they can be discarded. The inner leaves will remain crisp for several days more.

BASIC PREPARATION: If cooking the endive as a vegetable (that is, grilling, roasting, or braising), remove any limp outer leaves. Slice the endive in half lengthwise through the core or stem end. Because the leaves are still attached to the core, the endive can be cooked without the individual leaves separating.

For salad, discard any limp outer leaves and then trim a thick slice from the stem end to remove the tough core. Slice the endive in half lengthwise and then crosswise into thin strips.

BEST COOKING METHODS: Braising, grilling, or roasting. Shredded or thinly sliced raw endive also makes an excellent salad ingredient.

OTHER RECIPES WITH ENDIVE:
Arugula, Endive, and Radicchio Salad with Balsamic Vinaigrette (page 203)

Roasted Endive with Gruyère

Endive is roasted in a very hot oven until tender and lightly browned. A light dusting of nutty Gruyère cheese adds richness to this simple dish. Serve with roast chicken.

SERVES 4 TO 6 AS A SIDE DISH

2 tablespoons unsalted butter
4 medium Belgian endive (about
   1¼ pounds)
   Salt
   Freshly ground black pepper
1 cup shredded Gruyère cheese

1. Preheat the oven to 425 degrees. With 1 tablespoon of the butter, grease a baking dish just large enough to hold the endive in a single layer.
2. Remove any limp outer leaves from the endive. Slice the endive in half lengthwise.
3. Place the endive in the prepared dish, cut side down. Cut the remaining 1 tablespoon of butter into small bits and scatter the butter over the endive. Sprinkle with salt and pepper to taste.
4. Bake for 20 minutes. Turn the endive cut side up and sprinkle with the cheese. Bake until the endive is tender and lightly browned, about 15 minutes. Serve immediately.

Cider-Braised Endive

Sweet cider mellows some of the bitter punch of endive. Once the endive is tender, make sure to remove the cover and simmer until the cider has reduced to a thick glaze. The glaze has a complex, rich flavor that complements chicken, duck, or turkey.

SERVES 4 TO 6 AS A SIDE DISH

4 medium Belgian endive (about 1¼ pounds)
2 tablespoons unsalted butter
⅔ cup apple cider
1 teaspoon minced fresh thyme leaves
   Salt
   Freshly ground black pepper

1. Remove any limp outer leaves from the endive. Slice the endive in half lengthwise.
2. Melt the butter in a sauté pan large enough to hold the endive in a single layer. When the butter stops foaming, add the endive, cut side down. Cook, turning once, over medium heat until nicely browned, about 8 minutes.
3. Turn the endive cut side down and add the cider and thyme. Reduce the heat to low, cover, and simmer gently until the endive is tender when skewered with the tip of a paring knife, about 15 minutes. Uncover, raise the heat to high, and cook until the liquid reduces to a thick glaze, 2 to 3 minutes. Season with salt and pepper to taste and serve immediately.

Slow-Cooked Endive with Cream and Parmesan

This unusual cooking method produces endive that is fall-apart tender and rich with the flavors of cream and cheese. It's imperative that the pan have a tight-fitting lid so that the endive will steam in its own juices. Slow-cooked endive is perfect with a roast, especially for a winter meal. Consider cooking the endive in something attractive enough to bring to the table.

SERVES 4 TO 6 AS A SIDE DISH

4 medium Belgian endive (about 1¼ pounds)
2 tablespoons extra-virgin olive oil
  Salt
  Freshly ground black pepper
2 tablespoons heavy cream
½ cup grated Parmesan cheese

1. Remove any limp outer leaves from the endive. Slice the endive in half lengthwise.
2. Heat the oil in an ovenproof sauté pan large enough to hold the endive in a single layer over medium heat. Add the endive, season with salt and pepper to taste, and turn to coat evenly with the oil. Turn the endive cut side down, cover, and reduce the heat to medium-low. Cook, turning once, until the endive is extremely tender and beginning to brown, about 30 minutes.
3. When the endive is almost done, adjust the oven rack to the second-highest position and preheat the broiler.
4. Add the cream to the pan when the endive is done and turn to coat the endive with the cream. Sprinkle the cheese over the endive.
5. Place the pan with the endive under the broiler and broil until the cheese melts and browns, 2 to 3 minutes. Serve immediately.

Grilled Endive

It's imperative to slice the endive lengthwise, through the stem end, so that the piece of the core in each half will hold the leaves together.

SERVES 4 AS A SIDE DISH

4 medium Belgian endive (about 1¼ pounds)
2 tablespoons extra-virgin olive oil
  Salt
  Freshly ground black pepper

1. Light the grill. Remove any limp outer leaves from the endive. Slice the endive in half lengthwise. Brush the endive with the oil. Season with salt and pepper to taste.
2. Grill the endive over a medium fire, turning once, until richly colored and tender at the core, 12 to 15 minutes. Serve hot, warm, or at room temperature.

Grilled Endive with Sweet Balsamic Marinade

A sweet marinade, with balsamic vinegar and honey, balances the tartness of the endive. Brush extra marinade over the endive as they cook.

SERVES 4 AS A SIDE DISH

2 tablespoons balsamic vinegar
1 tablespoon honey
1 medium garlic clove, minced
2 tablespoons extra-virgin olive oil
Salt
Freshly ground black pepper
4 medium Belgian endive (about 1¼ pounds)

1. Light the grill.
2. Whisk the vinegar, honey, and garlic together in a small bowl. Whisk in the oil until the dressing is smooth. Add salt and pepper to taste.
3. Remove any limp outer leaves from the endive. Slice the endive in half lengthwise. Place the endive in a shallow baking dish. Brush the balsamic mixture over the endive and marinate, turning once, for 20 minutes.
4. Grill the endive over a medium fire, turning once and basting with any excess marinade, until richly colored and tender at the core, for 12 to 15 minutes. Serve hot, warm, or at room temperature.

Endive, Watercress, and Pear Salad

This salad is delicious as is but can be modified in several ways. For a stronger nut flavor, replace the olive oil with a mixture of 2 tablespoons walnut oil and 2 tablespoons olive oil. Or, sprinkle ½ cup crumbled goat or mild blue cheese over the salad once it has been plated. With or without cheese, this salad makes a nice first course. With the cheese and fruit, I sometimes like to serve this variation after dinner in place of dessert.

SERVES 4 AS A FIRST COURSE

2 medium Belgian endive (about 10 ounces)
2 cups stemmed watercress
1 large ripe pear
½ cup walnuts, toasted in a dry skillet until fragrant
2 tablespoons lemon juice
Salt
Freshly ground black pepper
¼ cup extra-virgin olive oil

1. Remove any limp outer leaves from the endive. Trim a thick slice from the stem end to remove the core. Slice the endive in half lengthwise and then crosswise into ½-inch-wide strips. Place the endive and watercress in a bowl.
2. Peel, halve, and core the pear. Lay the pear halves cut side down on a board and cut lengthwise into thin strips. Add the pear strips to the

bowl with the endive and watercress. Add the toasted nuts.

3. Whisk the lemon juice and salt and pepper to taste in a small bowl. Whisk in the oil until the dressing is smooth. Drizzle the dressing over the salad and toss. Adjust the seasonings and serve immediately.

Tart Endive and Apple Salad

Shredded endive and apple pieces are tossed with sour cream and a splash of lemon juice to make a tart, refreshing salad. I prefer the bracing flavors in this sophisticated slaw, which is best served as an accompaniment to sandwiches, fish, or chicken. To moderate some of the tartness, use firm, sweet apples instead of the Granny Smiths.

SERVES 6 AS A SIDE DISH

3 medium Belgian endives (about 1 pound)
2 tablespoons lemon juice
2 medium Granny Smith apples, quartered and cored (do not peel)
¼ cup sour cream
Salt and ground black pepper

1. Remove any limp outer leaves the endive. Trim a thick slice from the stem end to remove the core. Using the shredding disk of a food processor, shred the endive. Transfer the endive to a large bowl but do not clean the food processor workbowl. Toss the endive with the lemon juice.

2. Shred the apples in the food processor, cutting the pieces as necessary so they will fit into the feed tube. Add the apples and sour cream to the bowl with the endive. Toss to combine. Add salt and pepper to taste and serve immediately.

Escarole

Escarole is a leafy member of the chicory family. It looks a lot like green-leaf lettuce, although the white stems tend be thicker and crunchier. Escarole is sturdier than most lettuces, which means it can be cooked like spinach or chard in a covered pan until tender. However, escarole is still tender enough to eat raw in salads, especially the pale, inner leaves.

Unlike other chicories (especially endive and radicchio), escarole is not bitter. It has a slight hint of bitterness but is never peppery or sharp. It tastes more like spinach or chard than endive.

AVAILABILITY: Year-round, although traditionally fall through spring.

SELECTION: Escarole should be bright green with crisp outer leaves that show no signs of decay or wilting. For salad, it's best to buy escarole with a significant number of pale inner leaves, which tend to be very tender and mild.

STORAGE: Escarole will keep in the refrigerator in a loosely sealed plastic bag for a day or two. If the escarole looks very damp when you get it home (if you shop at a market that mists vegetables, this is very likely), blot up the excess moisture with paper towels and transfer the escarole to a dry plastic bag.

BASIC PREPARATION: Remove and discard any tough or wilted outer leaves from the head of escarole. Tear the leaves from the head, removing any tough portion of the white stem from each leaf.

Escarole that will be cooked should be washed and shaken dry to remove excess water. (Leave the escarole damp; this liquid will steam the escarole in a covered pot.)

Escarole that will be used in salads should be torn into bite-sized pieces, washed, and spun completely dry.

BEST COOKING METHODS: Braising (wilting in a covered pot when damp) or raw in salads.

OTHER RECIPES WITH ESCAROLE: Damp escarole can be wilted in a covered pan like chard or spinach.

Wilted Escarole with Anchovies and Garlic

A classic Italian preparation that will appeal to cooks and eaters who like big flavors. Serve with grilled fish or perhaps a cheese pizza. Like all greens, escarole really cooks down so make sure to start out with a pot large enough to accommodate the mass of uncooked leaves. If you like heat, add ½ teaspoon hot red pepper flakes just before the escarole goes into the pot.

SERVES 4 AS A SIDE DISH

1 large head escarole (about 1½ pounds)
2 tablespoons extra-virgin olive oil
4 anchovy fillets, minced very fine
2 medium garlic cloves, minced very fine
  Salt
  Freshly ground black pepper

1. Remove and discard any tough outer leaves from the head of escarole. Tear the leaves from the head, removing the tough portion of the white stem from each leaf. Wash the leaves in a bowl of cold water, tearing any large leaves in half. Shake off the excess water but leave the escarole damp. Set it aside in a clean bowl.

2. Heat the oil, anchovies, and garlic in a large casserole or stockpot set over medium-low heat. Cook very slowly, stirring occasionally, until the anchovies begin to dissolve, about 5 minutes. Do not let the garlic brown.

3. Raise the heat to medium and add the damp escarole leaves. Stir to coat the leaves with the flavored oil. Cover the pot and cook, stirring once or twice, until the escarole has wilted, about 5 minutes. Remove the cover and simmer until any liquid in the pan evaporates, about 1 minute. Season with salt (add sparingly) and pepper to taste. Serve immediately.

Escarole and Orange Salad with Sherry Vinaigrette

An especially good (and easy) salad. The slightly bitter flavor of the escarole works well with the oranges. Romaine or Boston lettuce could be used as a substitute, although they are a bit less flavorful.

1 medium head escarole (about 1 pound)
2 medium navel oranges
1 tablespoon sherry vinegar
3 tablespoons extra-virgin olive oil
  Salt
  Freshly ground black pepper

1. Remove and discard any tough or wilted outer leaves from the head of escarole. Tear the leaves from the head, removing any tough portion of the white stem from each leaf. Wash the leaves in a bowl of cold water, tearing the leaves into bite-sized pieces. Spin dry and place in a large bowl. You should have about 8 cups.

2. Using a paring knife, trim thick slices from the ends of the oranges so they can sit flat on a work surface. Slice downward around the oranges to remove the peel and white pith. Slice the peeled fruit crosswise into ¼-inch-thick circles. Place the orange slices in the bowl with the escarole. Pour any juices into a small bowl. (You should have about 2 teaspoons.)

3. Whisk the vinegar into the juices from the oranges. Whisk in the oil until the dressing is smooth. Add salt and pepper to taste.

4. Drizzle the dressing over the salad and toss to coat. Serve immediately.

Fava Beans

This prized bean has its origins in Europe, where it remains a highlight of spring cooking. In Italy, the first beans of the season are shelled and served raw with olive oil and coarse salt as an appetizer. Tender young favas are available only to gardeners in this country. The beans that show up at farmers' markets and some supermarkets are larger and must be cooked before eating.

Fava beans are a member of the pea family. Favas grow in furry pods that are often 5 or 6 inches long. The beans are light green and kidney-shaped.

Fava beans have a pleasantly bitter flavor, with distinct vegetable overtones. If they were not so much work, favas would no doubt be more popular in this country. Given the amount of time needed to shell and skin a pound of favas (and the paltry yield, about 1 cup per pound of beans), I have focused on recipes that deliver true fava flavor with a modest amount of beans.

OTHER COMMON NAMES: Broad beans.

AVAILABILITY: Spring through early fall. Usually best in the spring.

SELECTION: Fava beans often look a little sad in markets. The green pods can be soft and mottled with brown spots. Ideally, the pods will be bright green and unblemished.

A more important sign at the market is plumpness. Gently squeeze the pods to make sure that the beans inside are large and mature. A pod that feels flat will have small beans inside and should be rejected.

STORAGE: Fava beans should be cooked as soon as possible. They can be refrigerated for a day or two in a loosely sealed plastic bag, but the beans will become less sweet and more starchy with each passing day.

BASIC PREPARATION: Favas require a tedious two-step peeling process. First you must separate the beans from the furry pods, much as you shell garden peas or shell beans. Next, the beans must be blanched and peeled by hand to remove a tough, light green sheath that encases each tender, dark green bean.

To accomplish this second peeling step, bring several quarts of water to a boil in a medium saucepan. Add the fava beans and simmer for 2 minutes. Drain and refresh in a bowl of cold water. Drain again and then use your fingers to scrape away part of the outer light green skin on each fava. Squeeze the skin to pop out the dark green bean. The peeled favas may split into two halves, which is fine. They are now ready to be cooked again, briefly, until tender.

BEST COOKING METHODS: Boiling or braising.

Pureed Fava Beans

This recipe showcases fava beans at their purest and their best. If favas weren't so much work, I would make this recipe every week. The skinned beans and some minced shallots are braised in olive oil until tender and then pureed. You could eat the chunky puree by the spoonful (I do), but it's really meant for spreading on crostini (little toasts) or slathering on bruschetta (thick slices of grilled bread).

For crostini, cut a baguette into ½-inch-thick slices and toast the slices on a baking sheet in a 400-degree oven until crisp and lightly browned, about 5 minutes per side.

For bruschetta, brush thick slices of country bread with olive oil and grill until lightly browned, no more than a minute or two per side.

The recipe makes enough spread to cover at least 20 crostini or 6 to 8 bruschetta. I like to serve the crostini as an hors d'oeuvre for a fancier spring meal. Bruschetta spread with fava bean puree makes an excellent lunch with some salad. Plan on two large bruschetta per person.

MAKES 1 GENEROUS CUP

2 pounds fresh fava beans, shelled (about 2 cups)

¼ cup extra-virgin olive oil, plus more as needed

2 medium shallots, minced

Salt

1. Bring several quarts of water to a boil in a medium saucepan. Add the fava beans and simmer for 2 minutes. Drain and refresh in a bowl of cold water. Drain again and then use your fingers to scrape away part of the outer light green skin on each fava. Squeeze the skin to pop out the dark green bean. Set the peeled favas aside.

2. Heat the oil in a medium sauté pan. Add the shallots and sauté over medium heat until golden brown, about 5 minutes. Add the fava beans and salt to taste. Cook, stirring well to coat the favas with the oil. Add ¼ cup water, reduce the heat to medium-low, and cover the pan. Cook, stirring once or twice, until the beans are tender but not mushy, 3 to 6 minutes depending on their age.

3. Place the contents of the pan in a food processor. Pulse, adding more oil as necessary until the favas form a chunky puree. Adjust the seasonings. (The puree can be refrigerated in an airtight container for several days.)

Fava Bean Soup

This light-textured, smooth soup has a rich fava bean flavor. It is ideal as a first course for a spring meal. Although I like the soup as is, you may float some toasted croutons (page 132) in each bowl if you like.

SERVES 4 AS A FIRST COURSE

2 pounds fresh fava beans, shelled (about 2 cups)
2 tablespoons extra-virgin olive oil, plus extra for drizzling
1 medium leek, white and light green parts, sliced thin
3½ cups chicken or vegetable stock
Salt
Freshly ground black pepper
12 large fresh basil leaves, cut into thin strips

1. Bring several quarts of water to a boil in a medium saucepan. Add the fava beans and simmer for 2 minutes. Drain and refresh in a bowl of cold water. Drain again and then use your fingers to scrape away part of the outer light green skin on each fava. Squeeze the skin to pop out the dark green bean. Set the peeled favas aside.

2. Heat the oil in a large saucepan. Add the leek and sauté over medium heat until beginning to brown, about 6 minutes. Add the fava beans, stock, and salt and pepper to taste. Bring to a boil, reduce the heat, cover, and simmer until the favas are quite tender, 5 to 10 minutes depending on the freshness of the beans.

3. Puree the soup in a blender until quite smooth. Return the soup to a clean saucepan and heat through. Adjust the seasonings. Ladle the soup into small bowls. Garnish with some basil and drizzle with a little olive oil. Serve immediately.

Spring Vegetable Ragout with Fava Beans

This dish is a good way to enjoy favas with a minimum of work. The favas are just one component in this dish, but because of the way the vegetables are cooked, each retains its individual flavor and character. In addition to perfectly cooked vegetables, this dish produces plenty of buttery broth. I think it's best to serve this light stew with crusty bread or biscuits as a vegetarian main course.

SERVES 4 AS A MAIN COURSE

1¼ pounds fresh fava beans, shelled (about 1¼ cups)
3 tablespoons unsalted butter
1 medium onion, chopped
2 medium carrots, peeled and sliced on the diagonal ¼ inch thick
¾ pound red potatoes, sliced ¼ inch thick
Salt
Freshly ground black pepper
¾ pound asparagus, tough ends snapped off, then cut on the diagonal into 2-inch pieces
1 cup chicken or vegetable stock
2 tablespoons snipped fresh chives

1. Bring several quarts of water to a boil in a medium saucepan. Add the fava beans and simmer for 2 minutes. Drain and refresh in a bowl of cold water. Drain again and then use your fingers to scrape away part of the outer light green skin on each fava. Squeeze the skin to pop out the dark green bean. Set aside the peeled favas.

2. Heat 2 tablespoons of the butter in a large sauté pan. Add the onion and sauté over medium heat until softened, about 4 minutes. Add the carrots, potatoes, and salt and pepper to taste. Stir to coat the vegetables with the butter. Reduce the heat to medium-low and cover the pan. Cook until the vegetables begin to soften, about 10 minutes.

3. Add the asparagus and stock. Bring to a boil, reduce the heat, cover, and simmer for 3 minutes. Add the favas, cover, and continue simmering until all the vegetables are tender, 2 to 3 minutes. Swirl in the remaining tablespoon of butter and adjust the seasonings. Garnish with the chives and serve immediately.

Fennel

R aw fennel is crisp and crunchy, much like celery. The flavor is quite strong with a clean, not cloying, hint of licorice. Raw fennel is especially refreshing (it tastes best chilled) and works well when cut into strips and served as an appetizer (with a bowl of olives) or used in a salad.

When cooked, the flavor and texture of fennel change completely. Fennel softens slowly but holds its shape. Unlike celery, cooked fennel is not fibrous or stringy. The strong jolt of anise that is the hallmark of raw fennel fades fairly quickly when cooked. What's left is some residual sweetness and a very faint licorice aroma.

OTHER COMMON NAMES: Anise, anise bulb, finocchio, and Florence fennel.

AVAILABILITY: Year-round, although traditionally from fall to spring.

SELECTION: Look for bulbs that are firm and creamy white with little or no discoloration. The stems should be crisp and the feathery fronds bright green. Do not buy bulbs that look dried out.

STORAGE: Fennel will dry out with prolonged storage; in a plastic bag it should stay fresh in the vegetable crisper drawer for several days.

BASIC PREPARATION: The stalks are generally not eaten, although they can be used to lend a mild sweetness to stock. Start by cutting them off at the point where they meet the swollen bulb. Reserve the feathery green fronds and use them, minced, as you would any herb for flavor and garnish.

How you handle the bulb, which is the real focus of the fennel plant, depends on how you are going to cook it. In general, it is necessary to start by removing all tough or blemished outer layers as well as a slice from the root end.

If grilling or braising, the slice from the root end should be quite thin since you want to slice the fennel through the root end into fan-shaped pieces and it is the root end that will keep the slices from falling apart.

If sautéing, stir-frying, or roasting, you can cut a thicker slice from the root end (which can be a little tough) and then slice the bulb in half. At this point, use a small paring knife to cut out the triangular piece of the core that is attached to the bottom of each half. The core rarely softens as quickly as the rest of the bulb, so I prefer to remove it before cooking when possible. The cored fennel halves can now be sliced or diced as desired.

BEST COOKING METHODS: Braising, grilling, roasting, sautéing, and stir-frying. Also good raw in salads.

OTHER RECIPES WITH FENNEL:
Radishes, Fennel, and Olives with Creamy Feta Cheese Spread (page 285)

Fennel and Apple Salad

A sweet, crisp apple, such as a Fuji or Gala, is the best choice for this refreshing salad. For a stronger flavor, use Gorgonzola or another blue cheese instead of goat cheese. This salad is delightful after dinner since it combines fruit, cheese, and nuts.

**SERVES 4 AS A FIRST COURSE
OR AFTER THE MAIN COURSE**

2 medium fennel bulbs (about 2 pounds)
1 large apple
2 tablespoons lemon juice
1 tablespoon extra-virgin olive oil
Salt
Freshly ground black pepper
2 ounces goat cheese
2 tablespoons sliced almonds, toasted in a dry skillet until fragrant

1. Remove and discard the green stems and the fronds from the fennel. Trim any blemished or tough layers from the fennel bulb and remove a thick slice from the base. Cut the fennel bulb in half through the base and use a small, sharp knife to remove the small triangular piece of the core attached to the bottom of each half. With each fennel piece flat side down and your knife parallel to the work surface, slice crosswise to yield several ¼-inch-thick slices. Cut the slices lengthwise to yield long strips about ¼ inch thick. Place the fennel in a medium bowl.
2. Cut the apple into quarters, remove the piece of the core from each piece, and cut it into thin slices. Add the apple slices and lemon juice to the bowl with the fennel and toss. Drizzle with the oil and sprinkle with salt and pepper to taste. Toss and adjust the seasonings.
3. Divide the salad among individual plates. Crumble some of the goat cheese over each portion and sprinkle each plate with some of the toasted almonds. Serve immediately.

Moroccan Fennel and Grapefruit Salad with Olives

Versions of this salad are popular throughout the Mediterranean, wherever fennel grows wild. Use small black olives in brine, such as Niçoise or Gaeta olives. Although I prefer the floral note that mint adds, chopped parsley can be substituted.

SERVES 4 AS A FIRST COURSE

2 large red grapefruits
1 large fennel bulb (about 1¼ pounds)
⅓ cup small black olives
12 large fresh mint leaves, cut into thin strips
Salt
Freshly ground black pepper
Pinch sweet paprika
2 tablespoons extra-virgin olive oil

1. Trim thick slices from the ends of the grapefruits so they can sit flat on a work surface. Slice

downward around the grapefruits to remove the peel and white pith. Slice the peeled fruit crosswise into ½-inch-thick circles, removing any seeds. Place the slices and any juice they have given off in a large bowl.

2. Trim and discard the stems and fronds from the fennel. Trim a thick slice from the base of the bulb and remove any tough or blemished outer layers. Cut the bulb in half through the base and use a small, sharp knife to remove the triangular piece of the core from each half. With each fennel piece flat side down and your knife parallel to the work surface, slice crosswise to yield several ¼-inch-thick slices. Cut the slices lengthwise to yield long strips about ¼ inch thick.

3. Add the fennel, olives, and mint to the bowl with the grapefruits. Season with salt, pepper, and paprika to taste. Drizzle with the oil and toss gently. Serve immediately.

VARIATION: ITALIAN FENNEL AND ORANGE SALAD

In Italy, cooks are more likely to use oranges than grapefruits.

Use 3 navel or blood oranges in place of the grapefruits and omit the paprika.

Fennel Braised in Cider

Fennel cooks slowly in a bit of butter and cider until tender and is then dusted with cheese just before serving. A perfect side dish with pork.

SERVES 4 AS A SIDE DISH

2 large fennel bulbs (about 2½ pounds)
1 tablespoon unsalted butter
  Salt
  Freshly ground black pepper
⅓ cup apple cider
2 tablespoons grated Parmesan cheese

1. Trim and discard the stems and fronds from the fennel. Trim a very thin slice from the base of the bulb and remove any tough or blemished outer layers. Slice the bulb from top to bottom through the base into ¼-inch-thick pieces.

2. Melt the butter in a sauté pan large enough to hold the fennel in a single layer. Add the fennel and sprinkle with salt and pepper to taste. Add the cider and cover the pan. Simmer over medium heat for 15 minutes. Turn the slices and continue to simmer, covered, until the fennel is quite tender and has absorbed most of the liquid in the pan, about 10 minutes.

3. Transfer the fennel, leaving behind any juices in pan, to a platter. Sprinkle the fennel with the cheese and serve immediately.

VARIATION: FENNEL BRAISED IN WHITE WINE

Any flavorful liquid, including stock, wine, or other fruit juices, can be used in place of the cider in this recipe.

Replace the cider with white wine, preferably a Riesling or something fruity and sweet.

Sautéed Fennel with Raisins, Pine Nuts, and Garlic

In this recipe, thinly sliced fennel is sautéed slowly to concentrate its natural sweetness and to allow the fennel to soften nicely without burning the exterior. The garlic and raisins add sweet and savory notes that work well with the lightly caramelized strips of fennel. Serve with fish or pork.

SERVES 4 AS A SIDE DISH

2 medium fennel bulbs (about 2 pounds)

3 tablespoons extra-virgin olive oil

4 medium garlic cloves, minced

2 tablespoons raisins

2 tablespoons pine nuts

Salt

Freshly ground black pepper

1. Trim the stems and fronds from the fennel. Discard the stems; mince enough of the fronds to yield 1 tablespoon. Trim a thick slice from the base of the bulb and remove any tough or blemished outer layers. Cut the bulb in half through the base and use a small, sharp knife to remove the triangular piece of the core from each half. With each fennel piece flat side down and your knife parallel to the work surface, slice crosswise to yield several ½-inch-thick slices. Cut the slices lengthwise to yield long strips about ½ inch thick.

2. Heat the oil in a large skillet. Add the fennel strips and toss to coat them with oil. Cook, stirring often, over medium heat until the fennel has softened considerably but still offers some resistance, about 15 minutes.

3. Add the garlic, raisins, and pine nuts and cook, stirring often, until the garlic is golden, about 1 minute. Season generously with salt and pepper to taste. Stir in the minced fennel fronds and serve immediately.

Stir-Fried Fennel with Orange and Basil

When stir-frying, don't be timid with the heat. You can always turn down the heat or slide the pan off the burner if the smoke and sizzle become too intense. However, a tepid skillet will not sear the fennel and it will steam without browning. For chile heat, add up to 1 teaspoon hot red pepper flakes to the citrus sauce.

2 medium fennel bulbs (about 2 pounds)
1 tablespoon soy sauce
2 teaspoons toasted sesame oil
1 teaspoon grated orange zest
3 tablespoons orange juice
1 tablespoon roasted peanut oil
2 medium garlic cloves, minced
3 medium scallions, sliced thin
10 fresh basil leaves
    Salt
    Freshly ground black pepper

1. Trim and discard the stems and fronds from the fennel. Trim a thick slice from the base of the bulb and remove any tough or blemished outer layers. Cut the bulb in half through the base and use a small, sharp knife to remove the triangular piece of the core from each half. With each fennel piece flat side down and your knife parallel to the work surface, slice crosswise to yield several ½-inch-thick slices. Cut the slices lengthwise to yield long strips about ½ inch thick.

2. Combine the soy sauce, sesame oil, and orange zest and juice in a small bowl and set aside.

3. Set a large nonstick skillet over high heat and heat until a drop of water evaporates on contact with the pan. Add the peanut oil and heat briefly. Add the fennel and stir-fry until crisp-tender, 2 to 3 minutes.

4. Add the garlic and scallions and cook until fra-grant, about 30 seconds. Stir in the reserved orange sauce and basil. Stir to combine and cook just until the sauce coats the fennel, about 15 seconds. Remove the pan from the heat, add salt and pepper to taste, and serve immediately.

VARIATIONS: STIR-FRIED FENNEL WITH LEMON AND GINGER

Lemon and ginger are a good balance for sweet fennel.

Replace the orange zest and juice with an equal amount of lemon zest and 1 tablespoon lemon juice plus 2 tablespoons water. Add 1 tablespoon minced fresh gingerroot with the garlic and scal-lions.

STIR-FRIED SHRIMP AND FENNEL

Serve over steamed rice or Chinese egg noodles. Use the lemon and ginger variation above if you prefer.

SERVES 4 AS A MAIN COURSE

Prepare the recipe as directed through step 2. Heat the skillet and 1 tablespoon of peanut oil as directed in step 3. Add 1 pound shelled medium shrimp and stir-fry until bright pink, 1 to 2 min-utes. Transfer the shrimp to a bowl. Heat another tablespoon of oil in the empty skillet, add the fennel, and proceed as directed, adding the shrimp back to the pan with the sauce and basil in step 4.

Roasted Fennel and Red Onions

Serve this sweet, tender side dish with chicken, pork, veal, or even fish. The last-minute drizzle of balsamic vinegar imparts a caramel flavor to the vegetables.

SERVES 4 AS A SIDE DISH

1 large fennel bulb (about 1¼ pounds)
3 medium red onions, cut into ¾-inch
   wedges
2 tablespoons extra-virgin olive oil
   Salt
1 tablespoon balsamic vinegar

1. Preheat the oven to 425 degrees.

2. Trim and discard the stems and fronds from the fennel. Trim a thin slice from the base of the bulb and remove any tough or blemished outer layers from the bulb. Cut the bulb in half through the base and use a small, sharp knife to remove the triangular piece of the core from each half. With the flat side of the fennel bulb down and your knife parallel to the work surface, slice each fennel half crosswise to yield several ½-inch-thick slices. Cut the slices lengthwise to yield long strips about ½ inch thick.

3. Toss the fennel and onions in a large roasting pan with the oil. Season with salt to taste. Roast for 35 minutes, turning the vegetables once after 25 minutes.

4. Drizzle the vinegar over the vegetables and toss gently. Continue roasting until the vegetables are richly colored and tender, about 5 minutes more. Adjust the seasonings. Serve hot or warm.

Garlic

Garlic is used in all corners of the globe, from China to Mexico to France. In most cuisines, garlic is generally used as a seasoning. It probably appears in 20 percent of the recipes in this book. However, there are a few instances where garlic takes center stage, as the sole or primary vegetable. Recipes for several such dishes follow in this chapter.

AVAILABILITY: Year-round.

SELECTION: There are several varieties of garlic. Some have completely white skins, while others are tinged with purple or even mostly purple. There are flavor differences among these varieties (some are harsher than others), but you rarely have a choice when shopping. In addition, climate and growing conditions affect flavor as much as the variety. The same variety can taste mellow in spring and decidedly hot in summer.

Fresh green garlic, with chive-like stalks still attached, may be available at farmers' markets in the spring. This garlic is very juicy and mild. The white bulb that we generally cook with has been dried. The cloves are more pungent and have a much longer shelf-life. Recipes throughout this chapter and book have been tested with dried bulb garlic.

The most important feature to focus on at the market is firmness. Heads of garlic should be tight and hard. Any softness is a sign that the garlic is past its prime. Since garlic bulbs have been dried by wholesalers to prolong their freshness, the outer skin should be dry and papery. Do not buy garlic with green sprouts emerging from the cloves. (The sprouts are bitter tasting.) If your garlic sprouts at home, cut out the green portion with a paring knife when preparing the garlic.

You may see garlic (called elephant garlic) with especially large cloves. This garlic is generally very mild and I don't particularly like it.

STORAGE: Garlic will last for weeks at room temperature if stored in an open basket that allows for air circulation. Keep heads of garlic dry and do not remove the papery outer skin before you need the cloves.

BASIC PREPARATION: To produce minced garlic (which is how garlic is usually prepared), I start by separating the cloves from the head with my fingers, pulling off and discarding as much papery skin as I can. I then crush each clove with the side of a chef's knife. I hold my hand on the side of the blade and press down on the clove until it flattens. It is now easy to pick off and discard the papery skin and mince the soft flesh. Use a chef's knife to mince garlic, rocking the knife back and forth on a cutting board until the garlic is quite fine.

To help break down the garlic, you can sprinkle it with a little coarse salt as you mince. The coarse crystals keep the garlic pieces from clumping together and will help you achieve a particularly fine mince.

If you are roasting a whole head of garlic, you need to take a different approach. Peel off as much of the papery skin as possible, without causing the cloves to separate. Then, cut a ½-inch-thick slice from the top of each head to expose the cloves. The head of garlic is now ready to roast.

BEST COOKING METHODS: Roasting and sautéing.

OTHER RECIPES WITH GARLIC:
Roasted Kohlrabi with Whole Garlic Cloves (page 191)

Whole Heads of Roast Garlic with Grilled Bread

Roasting turns garlic into a creamy, mild-flavored paste that can be spread on slices of grilled or toasted bread. This is a messy and fun way to begin a meal.

SERVES 4 AS AN APPETIZER

4 whole heads garlic
About ½ cup water or chicken or veg-
    etable stock
3 tablespoons extra-virgin olive oil, plus
    extra for the toasts
    Salt
1 long baguette, cut on the bias into thin
    slices

1. Preheat the oven to 375 degrees.
2. Peel off as much of the papery skin as possible from the garlic without causing the cloves to sep-arate. Cut a ½-inch-thick slice from the top of each head to expose the cloves.
3. Place the garlic heads in a small baking dish. Add enough water or stock to come up ⅛ inch in the dish. Drizzle 2 tablespoons of the oil over the cut garlic and sprinkle with salt to taste. Cover the dish with foil.
4. Bake for 25 minutes. Remove the foil and con-tinue baking until the garlic is quite tender and golden, about 15 minutes. Remove the baking dish from the oven and drizzle the remaining tablespoon of oil over the garlic. Cool the garlic just until it is comfortable to handle it.
5. Meanwhile, lightly brush the bread slices with some oil and grill over a medium fire or toast on a baking sheet in a 400-degree oven until lightly browned on both sides. Serve one roasted garlic head per person along with slices of grilled or toasted bread. Tell everyone to squeeze the garlic cloves directly from the skins onto the bread.

Roasted Garlic and Potato Soup

This rich soup offers a real hit of garlic. Serve it in small portions as a first course or in mugs for lunch with some bread and salad. When making roasted garlic for bread you can roast a couple of extra heads of garlic and then store the extra garlic in an airtight container in the refrigerator for a day or two.

SERVES 6 TO 8 AS A FIRST COURSE

2 heads roasted garlic (page 166), cooled
2 tablespoons extra-virgin olive oil
2 medium onions, chopped fine
2 pounds red potatoes, peeled and diced fine
6 cups chicken or vegetable stock
2 bay leaves
    Salt
    Freshly ground black pepper
2 tablespoons snipped fresh chives

1. Squeeze the garlic cloves from their skins. Discard the skins. You should have about ¾ cup of roasted garlic cloves.

2. Heat the oil in a large soup pot. Add the onions and sauté over medium heat until golden, about 6 minutes. Add the roasted garlic and stir, mashing the cloves with the back of a wooden spoon. Add the potatoes and continue to cook just until coated with the garlic and oil.

3. Add the stock, bay leaves, and salt and pepper to taste to the pot. Bring to a boil, reduce the heat, and simmer until the potatoes are very tender, about 30 minutes.

4. Remove and discard the bay leaves. Puree the soup in batches in a blender until smooth. Stir in chives and adjust the seasonings. Serve immediately.

Spaghetti with Garlic and Oil

This famous Italian pasta sauce, called aglio olio, *is one of the best ways to enjoy garlic. The key is to cook the garlic over moderate heat so that it softens and loses its sharp edge without burning. I use a lot of garlic here, at least seven or eight cloves. Of course, you can use less if you prefer. This basic sauce can be varied almost endlessly; some suggestions follow.*

SERVES 4 AS A MAIN COURSE

⅓ cup extra-virgin olive oil
4 to 8 medium garlic cloves, minced very fine
Salt
1 pound spaghetti or linguine
Freshly ground black pepper

1. Bring 4 quarts of water to a boil in a large pot for cooking the pasta.

2. Place the oil and garlic in a small skillet. Turn the heat to medium-low and cook, stirring occasionally, until the garlic turns golden, about 5 minutes. Lower the heat or remove the skillet from the burner if the garlic starts to burn. Stir in 1 teaspoon salt and set the sauce aside.

3. While preparing the sauce, add 1 tablespoon salt and the pasta to the boiling water. Cook until al dente. Drain, allowing some of the cooking water to cling to the noodles. Return the dripping noodles to the pot and toss with the oil mixture. Season with salt and pepper to taste. Divide among pasta bowls and serve immediately.

VARIATIONS: SPAGHETTI WITH GARLIC AND HOT RED PEPPER

Make this as spicy as you like, or use a small, dried red chile.

Cook ½ teaspoon (or more to taste) hot red pepper flakes with the oil and garlic.

SPAGHETTI WITH GARLIC AND HERBS

If you grow herbs, just walk outside and harvest whatever you like as you wait for the water to boil. Use higher amounts of softer herbs like parsley, basil, mint, chives, and cilantro, and smaller amounts of stronger herbs like oregano, sage, and thyme.

Toss ½ cup minced fresh herbs with the pasta and sauce.

UDON OR SOBA NOODLES WITH GARLIC, GINGER, AND CILANTRO

Use slippery udon noodles (Japanese wheat noodles) or dark soba noodles (Japanese buckwheat noodles).

Cook 1 tablespoon minced fresh gingerroot with the oil and garlic. Toss 2 tablespoons minced fresh cilantro leaves with the pasta and sauce.

Green Beans

As its name suggests, the familiar green bean is related to dried beans (such as cannellini and kidney) and fresh shell beans (such as lima beans). Dried and fresh shell beans are grown for the seeds (what we call the beans) that grow inside pods. The pods are too tough to eat.

Fresh green beans contain seeds but they are immature and sometimes so small they are barely visible. The pod is the thing we enjoy about these beans, which grow either on bushes or vines attached to poles. Green beans once contained an inedible string that ran along the length of the pod, but modern hybrids are stringless.

A number of fresh pole and bush beans are available in supermarkets and farmers' markets. Green beans are the most common (especially during the winter), but during the summer you will see yellow wax beans; purple string beans that actually turn green when cooked; flat, thick Romano beans; and very thin, small haricots verts (also called French green beans).

The recipes in this chapter have been developed for green beans but you can use the other varieties if you make some adjustments. Yellow wax beans and purple string beans can be cooked just like green beans. Romano beans are best braised; the pods are fairly thick and respond best to slow cooking. Delicate haricots verts are best blanched and dressed for salads. Use them in any recipe where green beans are boiled, but reduce the cooking time to just 2 minutes or less.

Green beans respond well to a variety of cooking methods. I strongly suggest that you choose a method based on the age and thickness of the beans. Super-fresh summer green beans are best boiled and then dressed with a vinaigrette. If the beans are thicker or older (as is often the case in the off-season), consider braising or roasting them. These cooking methods might obliterate the delicate sweetness of just-picked beans, but will infuse older beans with flavor.

OTHER COMMON NAMES: Bush beans, pole beans, snap beans, and string beans.

AVAILABILITY: Summer is the height of the season. You will see green beans at other times of the year, but they are generally thick and are best braised or roasted.

SELECTION: Green beans and their relations should be brightly colored and fresh-looking. Snap one in half and taste it. It should really snap (not bend) and the flavor (even when raw) should be sweet. Avoid really thick beans that are swollen with seeds, which will be mealy and bland. Thinner beans are generally sweeter and more tender.

STORAGE: All string beans are highly perishable, losing sweetness within a few days of harvesting. If you must, store fresh beans in a loosely sealed plastic bag in the refrigerator.

BASIC PREPARATION: Old-fashioned green beans had to be "stringed," literally. Modern hybrids need only have their tough ends snapped off by hand (squeeze the thin end of the bean between two fingers) or with a paring knife.

BEST COOKING METHODS: Boiling (and then dressing or sautéing briefly with seasonings), braising, and roasting.

Green Beans with Toasted Walnuts and Tarragon

Green beans are boiled and then tossed with walnut oil, toasted walnuts, and tarragon. The anise notes in the tarragon highlight the sweetness of fresh green beans. Basil or parsley may be used as a substitute.

SERVES 4 AS A SIDE DISH

¼ cup walnuts, toasted in a dry skillet until fragrant, cooled, and chopped
1 tablespoon minced fresh tarragon leaves
1 pound green beans, ends snapped off
Salt
1½ tablespoons walnut oil
Freshly ground black pepper

1. Bring 2½ quarts of water to a boil in a large saucepan.
2. Place the toasted nuts and tarragon in a large serving bowl and set aside.
3. Add the green beans and 1 teaspoon salt to the boiling water. Cook until the beans are tender, about 5 minutes. Drain the beans well and them add to the bowl with the nuts and tarragon.
4. Drizzle the oil over the beans and toss gently to coat them evenly. Sprinkle with salt and pepper to taste and serve immediately.

Greens Beans in Yogurt-Dill Sauce

Beans in a creamy yogurt sauce make a perfect accompaniment to salmon.

SERVES 4 AS A SIDE DISH

1 pound green beans, ends snapped off
Salt
½ cup plain yogurt
1 medium garlic clove, minced
2 teaspoons minced fresh dill leaves
⅛ teaspoon cayenne pepper

1. Bring several quarts of water to a boil in a large saucepan. Add the beans and salt to taste. Cook until crisp-tender, about 5 minutes. Drain, shake dry, and then spread out over a clean towel so they dry quickly. Let the beans cool for several minutes.
2. While the beans are cooling, mix the yogurt, garlic, dill, cayenne, and salt to taste in a small bowl. Place the beans in a large serving bowl. Drizzle the yogurt sauce over the beans, toss, and serve immediately.

Green Beans with Bacon and Onion

This rich dish is a nice addition to a holiday table. If you like, substitute pancetta for the bacon.

SERVES 4 AS A SIDE DISH

- 1 pound green beans, ends snapped off
  Salt
- 4 strips bacon
- 1 medium onion, minced
- 2 tablespoons minced fresh parsley leaves
  Freshly ground black pepper

1. Bring 2½ quarts of water to a boil in a large saucepan. Add the green beans and 1 teaspoon salt. Cook until the beans are tender, about 5 minutes. Drain the beans and set aside for up to several hours.
2. Fry the bacon in a large skillet over medium heat until crisp, about 6 minutes. Remove the bacon from the pan and drain on paper towels. Spoon off all but 1 tablespoon of the fat. Add the onion to the remaining fat in the skillet and sauté until the pieces start to brown around the edges, about 5 minutes.
3. Add the beans and parsley to the pan. Toss to heat through for a minute or two. Crumble the bacon over the pan. Season with salt and pepper to taste and serve immediately.

Braised Green Beans with Soy and Sesame

This recipe is a good use for thicker, older, out-of-season beans. The long cooking time may shock those used to eating crisp (i.e., undercooked) green beans. However, braising makes the beans especially tender and gives them a chance to absorb the flavors from the braising liquid. The result is highly seasoned, very tender (but not mushy) beans. Serve these beans as a side for something plain, such as sautéed chicken breasts, and accompany with plenty of white rice to absorb the potent sauce the braising liquid forms when reduced.

SERVES 4 AS A SIDE DISH

- ⅔ cup chicken or vegetable stock
- 2 tablespoons soy sauce
- 1 tablespoon toasted sesame oil
- 1 tablespoon roasted peanut oil
- 3 medium garlic cloves, minced
- 1 tablespoon minced fresh gingerroot
- 2 medium scallions, sliced thin
- 1 pound green beans, ends snapped off
- 1 tablespoon minced fresh cilantro or basil leaves
  Freshly ground black pepper

1. Combine the stock, soy sauce, and sesame oil in a small bowl and set the mixture aside.
2. Heat the peanut oil in a large sauté pan. Add the garlic, ginger, and scallions and sauté over medium heat until the garlic is golden, about 1

minute. Add the beans and stir to coat them well with the oil and aromatics.

3. Add the stock mixture to the pan and bring the liquid to a boil. Reduce the heat to medium-low, cover the pan, and simmer, stirring two or three times, until the beans are tender but still offer some resistance to the bite, about 20 minutes.

4. Uncover and cook to reduce the remaining liquid to just a tablespoon or two, 2 to 3 minutes. Stir in the cilantro and pepper to taste. Serve immediately.

Braised Green Beans with Tomatoes, Olives, Capers, and Basil

This recipe could be called green beans puttanesca style, since the classic flavors of that popular pasta sauce—tomatoes, olives, capers, and garlic—season a simple braise with green beans. This recipe requires canned tomatoes packed in juice, not puree, since the juice itself serves as the braising medium. Tomatoes packed in juice have a fresher flavor than tomatoes packed in puree, so get into the habit of buying them if you don't already do so. These beans make a great side for grilled steaks, tuna, or swordfish.

SERVES 4 AS A SIDE DISH

1 tablespoon extra-virgin olive oil
3 medium garlic cloves, minced
1 pound green beans, ends snapped off

4 canned tomatoes, chopped, with enough
   packing juice added to equal 1 cup
8 large black olives, such as Kalamatas, pitted and chopped
1 teaspoon drained capers
1 tablespoon minced fresh basil leaves
   Salt
   Freshly ground black pepper

1. Heat the oil in a large sauté pan. Add the garlic and sauté over medium heat until golden, about 1 minute. Add the beans and stir to coat them well with the oil and garlic.

2. Add the tomatoes, olives, and capers to the pan and bring the liquid to a boil. Reduce the heat to medium-low, cover the pan, and simmer, stirring two or three times, until the beans are tender but still offer some resistance to the bite, about 20 minutes.

3. Uncover and cook to evaporate any remaining tomato liquid, 1 to 2 minutes. Stir in the basil and salt and pepper to taste. Serve immediately.

Roasted Green Beans with Garlic and Ginger

High oven heat concentrates the flavor in less-than-prime green beans. They shrivel up slightly and brown just a bit. Even over-the-hill beans end up tasting good. The garlic and ginger do wonders for the beans as does good olive oil. Tender, in-season beans are best blanched, but for thicker beans that don't have much flavor, this is the best technique for bringing them back to life.

2 tablespoons extra-virgin olive oil
2 medium garlic cloves, minced
1 tablespoon minced fresh gingerroot
  Salt
  Freshly ground black pepper
1 pound green beans, ends snapped off

1. Preheat the oven to 450 degrees.
2. Combine the oil, garlic, ginger, and salt and pepper to taste in a small bowl.
3. Place the green beans on a shallow rimmed baking sheet. Drizzle the oil mixture over the beans and toss with your hands to coat them.
4. Place the baking sheet in the oven and roast, turning the beans once, until lightly browned, about 15 minutes. Serve immediately.

Green Beans and Corn with Tomato-Herb Vinaigrette

One of those quintessential summer dishes that requires almost no work, looks great, and tastes even better. Needless to say, only the freshest beans, corn, and tomatoes should be used here. This salad works with most any grilled meats, chicken, or fish.

4 medium ears corn
2 medium ripe tomatoes (about 1 pound), cored and cut into ½-inch cubes
2 tablespoons extra-virgin olive oil
1 tablespoon red wine vinegar
¼ cup minced fresh herbs (especially basil, tarragon, chives, parsley, and cilantro)
  Salt
  Freshly ground black pepper
1 pound green beans, ends snapped off

1. Remove the husks and silks from the corn. Cut the ears in half crosswise with a chef's knife, stand each piece on its cut end, and slice downward several times to remove all the kernels. (Discard the cobs.) You should have about 2½ cups of kernels.
2. Bring several quarts of water to a boil in a large pot. While waiting for the water to come to a boil, combine the tomatoes, oil, vinegar, herbs, and salt and pepper to taste in a large serving bowl. Set aside.
3. Add the beans and salt to taste to the boiling water. Cook for 3 minutes. Add the corn and continue cooking until the vegetables are tender, 2 to 3 minutes longer. Drain, shake dry, and then spread out the vegetables over a clean towel so they dry quickly. Let cool to room temperature.
4. When the beans and corn are just barely warm (this will take about 10 minutes), toss them with the tomato mixture. Adjust the seasonings. Serve at room temperature. (The salad can be covered and set aside for up to 2 hours.)

Green Bean Salad with Tomatoes and Feta Cheese

This lovely dish captures some of the best flavors of summer in one light salad. For the best eye-pleasing results, use a mix of green and yellow wax beans. Serve with plenty of bread to sop up the juices from the salad.

SERVES 4 TO 6 AS A FIRST COURSE

1 pound green beans (preferably a mix of green and yellow beans), ends snapped off
Salt
2 medium ripe tomatoes (about 1 pound), cored and cut into ½-inch cubes
1 small shallot, minced
2 tablespoons extra-virgin olive oil
1 tablespoon lemon juice
2 tablespoons minced fresh parsley leaves
Freshly ground black pepper
2 ounces feta cheese, crumbled (about ½ cup)

1. Bring several quarts of water to a boil in a large saucepan. Add the beans and salt to taste. Cook until crisp-tender, about 5 minutes. Drain, shake dry, and then spread out over a clean towel so they dry quickly. Let the beans cool to room temperature.
2. Combine the tomatoes, shallot, oil, lemon juice, parsley, and pepper to taste in a large serv-ing bowl. Add the beans and adjust the season-ings, using salt sparingly. Sprinkle the feta cheese over the salad and serve immediately.

VARIATION: GREEN BEAN SALAD WITH TOMATOES, GOAT CHEESE, AND WALNUTS

Walnuts add another rich flavor and some crunch to this salad. I find that the walnuts work best with milder goat cheese, or ricotta salata, which is less pungent than feta but has some of that sheepy flavor that goes well with the beans and tomatoes.

Use 1 tablespoon walnut oil and 1 tablespoon extra-virgin olive oil. Sprinkle the salad with ⅓ cup toasted and coarsely chopped walnuts and crumbled goat cheese (instead of the feta) just before serving.

Green Beans and Potatoes with Aioli

Cooking the beans and potatoes in the same pot is a way to save kitchen work. When the potatoes are almost tender, add the beans and cook just until both vegetables are tender. Aioli, pungent garlic mayonnaise, makes an excellent dressing for most any steamed or boiled vegetable. It is especially good with potatoes, which tend to soak up the flavor of the mayonnaise, and beans, which come alive with the strong hit of garlic. Use potatoes the size of golf balls if you can. Serve this with sandwiches (in place of potato salad) or with grilled fish. To make a classic Italian dish, toss the cooked green beans and potatoes with about ½ cup of pesto instead of aioli.

SERVES 4 TO 6 AS A SIDE DISH

1 pound small new potatoes, scrubbed and halved (or quartered if large)
  Salt
1 pound green beans, ends snapped off
½ cup Garlic Mayonnaise (page 8)
2 tablespoons chopped fresh basil leaves

1. Bring several quarts of water to a boil in a large pot. Add the potatoes and a generous amount of salt. Cook until a skewer glides through the potatoes, about 8 minutes. Add the green beans and continue cooking until they are tender, about 5 minutes longer. Drain the potatoes and beans, shaking to remove excess moisture.

2. Transfer the potatoes and beans to a large serving bowl and let cool for several minutes. Stir in the garlic mayonnaise and basil. Adjust the seasonings and serve warm.

Jerusalem Artichokes

This tuber is native to North America but is rarely cooked in this country anymore. Farmers' markets are helping bring some attention to this neglected vegetable which was popular in Colonial times, but even experienced cooks probably pass right by this small, gnarled, light brown tuber, thinking it is gingerroot.

The funny and misleading name does not help. There is some debate about how the name arose. Some sources suggest the name is derived from a corruption of the Italian word for sunflower *(girasole)* coupled with a mild culinary resemblance to artichokes. Other sources suggest otherwise, and the fact that Jerusalem artichokes do not taste like artichokes only confuses the matter.

Jerusalem artichokes are actually the root of a sunflower, hence the alternative name sunchokes, which may in fact be replacing the term Jerusalem artichokes in many parts of the country.

Etymology aside, how do Jerusalem artichokes taste? If you can imagine a gnarled, miniaturized Yukon Gold potato, then you pretty much have the texture and yellowish appearance of the flesh. The flavor is much more complex than a potato, with lots of sugar. Jerusalem artichokes have nutty and vegetal overtones as well.

OTHER COMMON NAMES: Girasole, sunchokes, and sun roots.

AVAILABILITY: Summer through winter.

SELECTION: Look for firm Jerusalem artichokes without blemishes. The smoother they are, the easier they will be to clean. The skin should be tan or light yellow and there should be no signs of sprouting.

STORAGE: They can be refrigerated in a loosely sealed plastic bag for several days.

BASIC PREPARATION: Jerusalem artichokes are tubers and thus can be very dirty. All the little protrusions tend to trap dirt, so I trim any knobs with a paring knife and then scrub the Jerusalem artichokes under cold, running water. It's fine to scrape off some of the skin in the process, but there's no need to peel this tuber.

BEST COOKING METHODS: Roasting or sautéing. Many people have trouble digesting Jerusalem artichokes and they can cause a moderate amount of flatulence. If you have difficulty after eating dried beans, you may want to cook the cubed or sliced Jerusalem artichokes in boiling water until crisp-tender (5 to 15 minutes depending on the size of the pieces). Drain, thoroughly dry, and then proceed with roasting or sautéing. Boiling first before roasting or sautéing won't remove all the flatulence-causing compounds, but some of them will leach into the cooking water.

Roasted Jerusalem Artichokes with Garlic and Mixed Herbs

Roasting makes Jerusalem artichokes especially sweet and crunchy. The garlic and herb mixture is fairly heady so make sure to serve this side dish with a meat, like pork, that matches well with aggressive seasoning.

SERVES 4 AS A SIDE DISH

1¼ pounds Jerusalem artichokes
2 tablespoons sunflower or extra-virgin olive oil
Salt
Freshly ground black pepper
2 medium garlic cloves, minced
1 teaspoon minced fresh rosemary leaves
1 teaspoon minced fresh oregano leaves
1 teaspoon minced fresh thyme leaves

1. Preheat the oven to 425 degrees.
2. Remove the knobby protrusions from the Jerusalem artichokes with a paring knife. Scrub them thoroughly under cold, running water. Cut the Jerusalem artichokes into 1-inch cubes and toss with the oil on a large rimmed baking sheet. Sprinkle with salt and pepper to taste.
3. Roast, stirring two or three times, until the Jerusalem artichokes are golden brown, 30 to 35 minutes. Sprinkle the garlic and herbs over the Jerusalem artichokes. Toss to coat evenly. Continue roasting just until the garlic is golden, about 3 minutes. (Do not let the garlic burn.) Adjust the seasonings and serve immediately.

Sautéed Jerusalem Artichokes with Sunflower Seeds and Lemon Zest

Rounds of Jerusalem artichokes are browned in hot oil until crisp on the exterior and chewy inside. The emphasis here is really on the delicate vegetal flavor of the Jerusalem artichokes. Using sunflower oil helps reinforce the sweet flavor of this unusual tuber.

1 pound Jerusalem artichokes
2 tablespoons sunflower oil or extra-virgin
  olive oil
2 tablespoons roasted salted sunflower seeds
1 tablespoon minced fresh parsley leaves
½ teaspoon grated lemon zest
  Salt
  Freshly ground black pepper

1. Remove the knobby protrusions from the Jerusalem artichokes with a paring knife. Scrub them thoroughly under cold, running water. Cut the cleaned Jerusalem artichokes crosswise into ¼-inch-thick rounds.

2. Heat the oil in a large nonstick skillet. Add the Jerusalem artichokes and sauté over medium-high heat, turning occasionally, until nicely browned and tender but still chewy, about 8 minutes. Stir in the sunflower seeds, parsley, lemon zest, and salt and pepper to taste. Serve immediately.

Jicama

Jicama has become a common item in American markets. The skin on this tropical tuber is thin and tan, while the flesh is crisp, juicy, and white. Crunchy jicama is best used in salads because its porous flesh absorbs flavorful dressings. Although jicama is grown in Asia, in this country we generally think of it in terms of Mexican cooking.

OTHER COMMON NAMES: Sa kot, sha ge, and yam bean.

AVAILABILITY: Throughout the year, especially in stores with a good supply of Latino or Asian vegetables.

SELECTION: Look for jicama that feels heavy for its size and firm. The skin should be smooth and without blemishes.

STORAGE: Jicama can be refrigerated in the vegetable crisper for a week or so.

BASIC PREPARATION: Jicama is covered by a thin, light brown skin that is fairly smooth. The skin could be removed with a vegetable peeler, however, I find that the layer of white flesh right beneath the skin is fibrous and should be removed as well. A paring knife will remove the skin and outer ⅛ inch of white flesh in one motion. Once peeled, the jicama can be sliced or diced as needed. Peeled jicama will eventually discolor, although more slowly than an apple or potato. To keep the color bright white, just toss the jicama with some acid, preferably lime juice.

BEST COOKING METHODS: Jicama is not generally cooked. Its cool crunch is best appreciated in salads and slaws.

Jicama and Carrot Salad with Ginger-Sesame Vinaigrette

This juicy, crunchy slaw is especially good with chicken or fish.

SERVES 4 TO 6 AS A SIDE DISH

2 tablespoons rice vinegar
1 tablespoon soy sauce
2 teaspoons minced fresh gingerroot
1 tablespoon canola or other tasteless oil
2 teaspoons toasted sesame oil
  Freshly ground black pepper
1 large jicama (about 1½ pounds)
1 large carrot, peeled and shredded on the large holes of a box grater
2 medium scallions, sliced thin

1. Whisk the vinegar, soy sauce, and ginger together in a small bowl. Whisk in the oils and add pepper to taste.
2. Using a paring knife, remove the thin brown skin and outer ⅛ inch of flesh from the jicama. Cut the peeled jicama in half through the equator. Lay the halves cut side down and slice into ¼-inch-thick pieces. Slice the jicama as thinly as possible. You want to end up with very thin slivers of jicama that are about 2 inches long.
3. Place the jicama, carrot, and scallions in a large bowl. Drizzle the dressing over the vegetables and toss. Serve immediately or refrigerate up to 4 hours and serve chilled.

Jicama Salad, Mexican Style

Serve this dish as finger food, perhaps as a midday snack. It also makes an excellent hors d'oeuvre. Note that this salad has no fat. You may substitute pink grapefruit rounds or even sliced mango for the orange slices if you like.

SERVES 6 AS AN APPETIZER

1 large jicama (about 1½ pounds)
2 large navel oranges
2 tablespoons lime juice
½ teaspoon chili powder
  Salt
1 tablespoon minced fresh cilantro leaves

1. Using a paring knife, remove the thin brown skin and outer ⅛ inch of flesh from the jicama. Cut the peeled jicama in half through its equator. Lay the halves cut side down and slice into ⅛-inch-thick pieces.
2. Using a paring knife, trim thick slices from the ends of the oranges so they can sit flat on a work surface. Slice downward around the oranges to remove the peel and white pith. Slice the peeled fruit crosswise into ¼-inch-thick circles.

3. Arrange the jicama and orange slices on a large platter. (For an especially attractive presentation, line both sides of the platter with jicama slices and place the orange slices in the center.)

4. Sprinkle the lime juice over the jicama and orange slices. Sprinkle with the chili powder and salt to taste. Sprinkle with the cilantro and serve immediately.

Jicama and Mango Salad with Lime-Cilantro Dressing

This recipe takes its cue from Southeast Asian flavors. The dressing contains fish sauce, sugar, lime juice, and cilantro. For some heat, add hot red pepper flakes if you like. In Thailand or Vietnam, this kind of salad is commonly made with green mangoes or papayas. Sweet ripe mangoes are easier to find and nicely balanced by crunchy jicama. This salad is especially good with grilled fish but works with chicken or pork.

2 tablespoons lime juice

1 tablespoon fish sauce

2 teaspoons sugar

2 tablespoons minced fresh cilantro leaves

1 medium jicama (about 1¼ pounds)

1 large ripe but firm mango (about 1 pound), peeled, peeled, and cut into long, thin strips

1. Combine the lime juice, fish sauce, sugar, and cilantro in a small bowl, stirring occasionally to help dissolve the sugar.

2. Using a paring knife, remove the thin brown skin and outer ⅛ inch of flesh from the jicama. Cut the peeled jicama in half through its equator. Lay the halves cut side down and slice into ¼-inch-thick pieces. Slice the jicama into ¼-inch-thick slivers, each 2 to 3 inches long.

3. Place the jicama and mango in a serving bowl. Drizzle the dressing over the them and toss to coat evenly. Serve immediately.

Kale

K ale has thick, ruffled, dark green leaves. It is a member of the cabbage family. Rather than growing in round heads, kale grows on individual stalks and is sold in bunches. Kale is closely related to collard greens. Although collard greens have flat leaves, the color of the leaves is the same as kale leaves and collard and kale stalks are nearly identical.

Kale has a pleasant cabbagey flavor that is earthy and rich. While it has a little bite, most kale is not bitter or peppery. In fact, when cooked it can even taste a bit sweet.

Unless you grow your own kale and can harvest it very young, most kale has thick, tough leaves that require a lot of cooking to become tender. Make sure to fully cook kale. Undercooked kale is tough and leathery.

AVAILABILITY: Fall and winter are the traditional seasons for kale, although many markets stock kale year-round.

SELECTION: Kale leaves should be dark green and crisp-looking. They should show no signs of wilting, yellowing, or bruising. If you have a choice, choose kale with thinner stalks.

STORAGE: Kale will keep in a loosely sealed plastic bag in the refrigerator for several days. If the kale is very damp when you get it home from the market, blot up the excess moisture with paper towels and place the kale in a dry plastic bag.

BASIC PREPARATION: Kale has an extremely tough stalk and central vein that runs through the middle of the leafy portion. The stalk and thick portion of the central vein must be removed and discarded. I usually start by washing the kale in several changes of cold water and stripping off the leafy green portion from either side of the tough central vein with my hands. Kale is sturdy enough so it won't bruise.

However, if you want more control, hold each stalk upside down (with the leafy portion pointing down) and use a chef's knife to slice the leafy portion off from both sides of the stalk. (Use the knife as if it were a machete.)

Once the tough stalk and vein have been discarded and the leaves washed, they can be chopped or torn by hand as directed in the recipe.

BEST COOKING METHODS: Boiling and then sautéing or braising.

OTHER RECIPES WITH KALE:
Soba Noodles with Spicy Broccoli Rabe (page 53)

Kale may be used in any of the collard recipes.

Kale with Caramelized Onions and Balsamic Vinegar

The assertive flavor of kale is tamed by blanching and then sautéing with sweet caramelized onions and some balsamic vinegar.

SERVES 4 AS A SIDE DISH

1½ pounds kale
    Salt
2 tablespoons extra-virgin olive oil
2 medium onions, halved and sliced thin
½ teaspoon sugar
2 teaspoons balsamic vinegar
    Freshly ground black pepper

1. Bring 4 quarts of water to a boil in a large pot.
2. Wash the kale in several changes of cold water, stripping off the leafy green portion from both sides of the tough central vein. Discard the veins and rip the leafy portions in small pieces. Add the kale and 1 teaspoon salt to the water. Cover and cook, stirring occasionally, until the kale is tender, about 8 minutes. Drain well.
3. Heat the oil in a large skillet set over medium heat. Add the onions and cook, stirring occasionally, until golden brown, 12 to 15 minutes. Sprinkle with the sugar and continue cooking until the onions are a rich brown color, about 10 minutes. Lower the heat if at any time the onions start to burn.
4. Add the kale and cook, tossing well, until heated through and evenly flavored with the onions, 1 to 2 minutes. Add the vinegar and a generous amount of pepper. Adjust the seasonings and serve immediately.

Garlicky Kale with White Beans

A delicious, hearty vegetarian main course. Use this basic recipe to prepare most any beans and greens dish. This dish is a bit brothy, so serve with crusty bread.

SERVES 4 AS A MAIN COURSE

1½ pounds kale
    Salt
2 tablespoons extra-virgin olive oil
4 medium garlic cloves, minced
    Two 15-ounce cans cannellini or other white beans, drained and rinsed
⅔ cup chicken or vegetable stock
    Freshly ground black pepper

1. Bring 4 quarts of water to a boil in a large pot.
2. Wash the kale in several changes of cold water, stripping off the leafy green portion from both sides of the tough central vein. Discard the veins and tear the leafy portions into small pieces. Add the kale and 1 teaspoon salt to the boiling water. Cover and cook, stirring occasionally, until the kale is tender, about 8 minutes. Drain well.

3. Heat the oil and garlic in a large skillet set over medium heat. When the garlic is golden (this will take about 2 minutes), add the kale and cook, tossing well, until heated through and evenly flavored with the garlic, 1 to 2 minutes.

4. Add the beans and stock and simmer just until the beans are heated through, about 5 minutes. Add pepper to taste. Adjust the seasonings and serve immediately.

Kale and Polenta Pie

This unusual side dish is surprisingly easy to make. Kale and instant polenta are cooked together and then poured into a cake pan and baked until firm. The polenta pie is cooled and then cut into wedges. Serve with a roast or turn this dish into a vegetarian entrée for four. Make sure to buy instant or quick-cooking polenta. This Italian product shaves a half hour off the normal cooking time for regular polenta and yields excellent results here.

SERVES 6 TO 8 AS A SIDE DISH

½ pound kale
Salt
1 tablespoon plus 2 teaspoons extra-virgin olive oil
1 cup instant polenta
¼ cup grated Parmesan cheese

1. Preheat the oven to 400 degrees.

2. Bring 3½ cups of water to a boil in a large pot. Wash the kale in several changes of cold water, stripping off the leafy green portion from either side of the tough central vein. Discard the veins and chop the leafy portions finely. Add the kale, ½ teaspoon salt, and 1 tablespoon of the oil to the water. Cover and cook, stirring occasionally, until the kale is tender, about 6 minutes.

3. Reduce the heat to low. Slowly stir in the polenta with a wooden spoon until smooth. (This should take about 1 minute.) Partially cover and cook until the polenta is thick, about 2 minutes.

4. Remove the pot from the heat and stir in the cheese. Taste and adjust the seasonings, adding more salt if necessary. Grease a 9-inch round cake pan with the remaining 2 teaspoons of oil. Scrape the kale-polenta mixture into the cake pan.

5. Bake until the polenta pie is firm and golden brown, about 20 minutes. Let the pie cool until barely warm, at least 30 minutes and up to several hours. (The polenta will firm up as it cools, so don1t rush this process.) Cut into wedges and serve.

Kohlrabi

Kohlrabi is certainly hard to miss when you see it. Round, pale green bulbs give rise to thick stalks and leafy greens. For some reason, it strikes many cooks (me included) as alien-looking. However, kohlrabi has a long tradition around the globe, especially in Central and Eastern Europe.

The bulbs, which are actually a thickened portion of the stalks, are the part of the plant we usually cook. However, if you are lucky enough to find freshly harvested kohlrabi with crisp leaves, the leaves may be cooked separately like chard or spinach.

Kohlrabi is often compared to turnips. The bulbs are about the same size and once peeled the flesh is similar-looking—white, juicy, and crisp. However, unlike turnips, kohlrabi is never hot. It is mildly sweet and has a vegetal flavor that reminds me more of broccoli than anything else.

OTHER COMMON NAMES: Cabbage turnip.

AVAILABILITY: Summer through early fall is the prime season for kohlrabi, although you may see it at other times of the year.

SELECTION: Small kohlrabi is less fibrous and better-tasting than larger bulbs. If possible, select bulbs the size of a peach, or smaller. Kohlrabi the size of grapefruit should be avoided, since it is likely to be woody and/or spongy.

Most kohlrabi bulbs have pale green skin, although a purple-tinged variety will occasionally show up at farmers' markets. Either way, the bulbs should have a bright, even color and be free of blemishes or soft spots. Healthy-looking leaves are the surest sign that the kohlrabi is fresh.

STORAGE: Kohlrabi can be refrigerated in a loosely sealed plastic bag for several days. If the leaves are starting to go, you might want to trim and discard the stems and leaves before refrigerating the bulbs, in order to prevent the spread of rot.

BASIC PREPARATION: Kohlrabi is usually sold with the long stalks and leaves attached. When ready to cook kohlrabi, trim and discard the stalks and leaves. Use a paring knife to remove the green skin and outer ⅛ inch or so of flesh from the bulbs. (The flesh right below the skin is green. This is the flesh you need to remove in order to reveal the white, creamy flesh below.) The peeled bulbs can be sliced, diced, or shredded as desired.

BEST COOKING METHODS: Roasting and sautéing (if shredded).

Shredded Kohlrabi with Butter and Parmesan

A little Parmesan highlights the nutty flavor of kohlrabi without overwhelming this delicate vegetable.

SERVES 4 AS A SIDE DISH

3 medium kohlrabi bulbs (about 1½ pounds without the stalks and leaves)
2 tablespoons unsalted butter
¼ cup grated Parmesan cheese
Salt
Freshly ground black pepper
1 tablespoon minced fresh parsley leaves

1. Peel the kohlrabi with a paring knife, removing the green skin and outer ⅛ inch or so of the flesh. Cut the bulbs so they will fit in the feed tube of a food processor. Shred using the coarse shredding blade.
2. Melt the butter in a large skillet. Add the shredded kohlrabi and cook over medium heat, stirring often, until tender, about 8 minutes. Sprinkle with the cheese and salt and pepper to taste. Toss and cook just until the cheese melts, about 1 minute. Garnish with the parsley and serve immediately.

Roasted Kohlrabi with Whole Garlic Cloves

Roasting cubes of kohlrabi gives them a thick, crusty exterior and tender interior. This recipe really brings out their flavor, which is reminiscent of broccoli stems.

SERVES 4 AS A SIDE DISH

3 medium kohlrabi bulbs (about 1½ pounds without the stalks and leaves)
10 large whole garlic cloves, peeled
2 tablespoons extra-virgin olive oil
Salt

1. Preheat the oven to 450 degrees.
2. Peel the kohlrabi with a paring knife, removing the green skin and outer ⅛ inch or so of the flesh. Cut the bulbs into ¾-inch dice. Toss the kohlrabi, garlic cloves, and oil together on a large rimmed baking sheet.
3. Roast, turning the kohlrabi and garlic two or three times, until well browned, 30 to 35 minutes. Season with salt to taste and serve immediately.

Leeks

eeks look like giant scallions (they are both members of the allium family), but it is probably best to think of them as replacements for onions. They are sweeter and more subtle than onions and lend a delicious flavor to countless dishes.

While minced or sliced leeks are a common seasoning, whole leeks can be cooked and served as a vegetable in their own right. Leeks cooked by dry-heat methods, such as roasting, can be tough. I find they respond best if cooked with some moisture.

Blanching gives leeks a watery texture and washes away much of their flavor. I prefer to steam leeks. They emerge silky smooth from the steamer, with their flavor undiminished.

Once steamed, leeks can be drizzled with vinaigrette or further cooked, usually by sautéing or grilling. Braising leeks in a covered pan with a bit of moisture (the juices from the leeks and some butter is enough liquid) is another good option.

AVAILABILITY: Year-round, although the traditional season is spring through fall.

SELECTION: Leeks should be firm with crisp, dark green leaves. Even though you don't eat the dark green tops, don't buy trimmed leeks. Some markets remove the tops when they wilt and sell just the white portion. Unfortunately, these fully trimmed leeks often have an off flavor. In addition, the roots should still be attached (some markets remove them, but this can cause the bottom of the stalk to soften) and healthy-looking.

If you plan to serve leeks as a side dish or salad, they should be fairly thin—no thicker than an inch. (My preference is to use ¾-inch-thick leeks, what I call "medium leeks.") I generally cut the leeks in half lengthwise for cleaning and then cook the halves in a steamer basket, skillet, or on the grill.

Thicker leeks might seem easier to work with, but they can cook unevenly when prepared by the methods outlined in this chapter. The outside layers become mushy before the inside is tender. If you are chopping leeks for soup or for use as a seasoning, thicker leeks are fine. Note, though, that some very thick leeks may have tough cores, another reason to be wary of jumbo leeks.

Some leeks have a short white area and long green stalks. Others have a longer white portion that shades into light green and eventually into dark green. Since the dark green portion is tough and must be discarded, choose leeks with an elongated white and light green section, at least 6 inches in length and preferably 8 inches.

Markets trim varying amounts of the dark green tops. Because different stores trim leeks differently, they are hard to buy by weight. Six medium leeks can weigh 2 pounds at one store or closer to 3 pounds at another, depending on how they have been trimmed. For this reason, you must shop for leeks by the number and thickness and not weight.

STORAGE: Leeks should be wrapped in plastic and refrigerated in the vegetable crisper. They will stay fresh for several days, if not a week or more. If the leeks are very damp when you get them home, blot up the extra moisture with a paper towel before wrapping them up.

BASIC PREPARATION: Trim and discard the dark green tops and tough outer leaves from the leeks. Remove the roots along with a very thin slice of the nearby white part. (If you are slicing leeks for soup, you can remove a thicker slice. However, if you are cooking halved leeks, don't remove too much from the bottom or the layers will fall apart.)

Halve the leeks lengthwise and wash them under cold, running water. Gently spread apart but do not separate the inner layers to remove all traces of soil. If the leeks are particularly sandy, soak them in several changes of clean water. At this point, the leeks are ready to be cooked or sliced further for use in soups or as a seasoning.

BEST COOKING METHODS: Braising, grilling (with or without first steaming), and steaming (and then either dressing with vinaigrette or sautéing).

OTHER RECIPES WITH LEEKS:
Corn Chowder with Leeks and Potatoes (page 122)
Corn Chowder with Bacon, Leeks, and Potatoes (page 123)

Steamed Leeks with Tarragon-Mustard Vinaigrette

A classic preparation. Steaming retains the most flavor in the leeks and creates a silky, soft (but not mushy) texture. The tarragon is optional but delicious. I like to serve leeks as the first course of a spring meal but they are also delicious with a piece of fish.

SERVES 4 TO 6 AS A FIRST COURSE
OR SIDE DISH

6 medium leeks
1 tablespoon white wine vinegar
1½ teaspoons Dijon mustard
Salt
Freshly ground black pepper
4 tablespoons extra-virgin olive oil
2 teaspoons minced fresh tarragon leaves

1. Trim and discard the dark green tops and tough outer leaves from the leeks. Remove the roots along with a very thin slice of the nearby white part. Halve the leeks lengthwise and wash them under cold, running water. Gently spread apart but do not separate the inner layers to remove all traces of soil. If the leeks are particularly sandy, soak them in several changes of clean water.

2. Bring several inches of water to a boil in a large saucepan. Place the leeks in a single layer in a steamer basket and place the basket in the pan. Cover the pot and steam until the leeks are ten-der, about 15 minutes. Remove the leeks from the steamer basket and transfer to a platter. Pat dry with paper towels. (The leeks may be cooled slightly or covered and refrigerated until well chilled.)

3. While the leeks are steaming, whisk the vinegar, mustard, and salt and pepper to taste together in a small bowl. Whisk in the oil until the dressing is smooth. Whisk in the tarragon and adjust the seasonings.

4. Drizzle the dressing over warm or chilled leeks and serve immediately.

VARIATION: LEEKS WITH TOMATO-OLIVE
VINAIGRETTE

An especially attractive and delicious leek dish. Perfect as part of an Italian or Provençal meal.

Prepare the leeks through step 2. For the dressing, stir together 1 medium tomato, cored, peeled, seeded, and diced very small, 1 tablespoon red wine vinegar, 3 tablespoons extra-virgin olive oil, 8 pitted and chopped Kalamata olives, 1 tablespoon minced fresh parsley leaves, and salt and pepper to taste. Dress as directed in step 4.

Sautéed Leeks

Steaming cooks the leeks and improves their texture by eliminating any stringiness or chewiness. The drained and dried leeks are then sautéed in a little olive oil until golden brown in order to accentuate their sweetness.

6 medium leeks
2 tablespoons extra-virgin olive oil
  Salt
  Freshly ground black pepper

1. Trim and discard the dark green tops and tough outer leaves from the leeks. Remove the roots along with a very thin slice of the nearby white part. Halve the leeks lengthwise and wash them under cold, running water. Gently spread apart but do not separate the inner layers to remove all traces of soil. If the leeks are particularly sandy, soak them in several changes of clean water.

2. Bring several inches of water to a boil in a large saucepan. Place the leeks in a single layer in a steamer basket and place the basket in the pan. Cover the pot and steam until the leeks are tender, about 15 minutes. Remove the leeks from the steamer basket and transfer to a platter lined with several layers of paper towels. Blot the leeks dry. (The leeks may be set aside at room temperature for several hours.)

3. Heat the oil in a skillet large enough to hold the leeks in a single layer. Add the leeks and cook over medium heat, turning once, until golden brown in spots, 8 to 10 minutes. Season the leeks with salt and pepper to taste. Serve immediately.

VARIATION: SAUTÉED LEEKS WITH ORANGE, HONEY, AND SESAME

Serve with roast chicken or fish.

When the leeks are done (after step 3), transfer them to a platter. Add 1 tablespoon sesame seeds to the empty pan and cook, stirring often, until they turn golden brown, about 1 minute. Add ⅓ cup orange juice and 1 tablespoon honey and cook just until the mixture thickens to a glaze, about 2 minutes. Season the glaze with salt and pepper to taste. Pour the glaze over the leeks and serve immediately.

Grilled Leeks, Two Ways

You have two options when grilling leeks. They may be trimmed, brushed with oil, and then grilled as is over a medium-low fire until streaked with grill marks. The texture is crisp and a bit chewy but still pleasant. Personally, I prefer to steam the leeks first and then to grill them briefly over a hotter fire. The leeks are silkier (especially the inner leaves) and the flavor is excellent. The former method works only with small to medium leeks. If working with thick leeks, you must steam them first.

6 medium leeks
2 tablespoons extra-virgin olive oil
  Salt

1. Trim and discard the dark green tops and tough outer leaves from the leeks. Remove the roots along with a very thin slice of the nearby white part. Halve the leeks lengthwise and wash them under cold, running water. Gently spread apart but do not separate the inner layers to remove all traces of soil. If the leeks are particu-

larly sandy, soak them in several changes of clean water.

2. If steaming the leeks, bring several inches of water to a boil in a large saucepan. Place the leeks in a single layer in a steamer basket and place the basket in the pan. Cover the pot and steam the leeks until tender, about 15 minutes. Remove the leeks from the steamer basket and transfer to a platter lined with several layers of paper towels. Blot the leeks dry. (The leeks may be set aside at room temperature for several hours.)

3. Light a grill fire. Brush the leeks with the oil and sprinkle with salt to taste. Steamed leeks may be grilled directly over the hot part of the fire until streaked with grill marks, 3 to 4 minutes per side. If the leeks have not been steamed, place them over a cooler part of the fire and grill, turning once, until crisp and streaked with dark grill marks, about 12 minutes. Serve immediately.

VARIATION: GRILLED LEEKS WITH CITRUS OIL

A flavored oil may be brushed over the leeks to add another element to the dish. This oil is just one example. Consider adding ground spices or minced ginger or herbs instead.

Add the grated zest from one orange or lemon to the oil before brushing it on the leeks.

Pan-Browned Leeks with Butter

The leeks are cooked in a covered pan with a little butter until almost tender, then the lid is removed and the leeks are cooked until lightly browned. Don't try this recipe with leeks thicker than ¾ inch; they won't soften properly. Serve with chicken or fish.

SERVES 4 AS A SIDE DISH

4 medium leeks
2 tablespoons unsalted butter
Salt
Freshly ground black pepper

1. Trim and discard the dark green tops and tough outer leaves from the leeks. Remove the roots along with a very thin slice of the nearby white part. Halve the leeks lengthwise and wash them under cold, running water. Gently spread apart but do not separate the inner layers to remove all traces of soil. If the leeks are particularly sandy, soak them in several changes of clean water.

2. Melt the butter in a large skillet set over medium heat. Place the leeks, cut side down, in the skillet in a single layer. Season with salt to taste. Cover and cook until they are crisp-tender, 8 to 12 minutes depending on the thickness of the leeks.

3. Remove the cover, raise the heat to medium-high, and cook the leeks, turning them once, until lightly browned, 3 to 4 minutes. Season with

pepper to taste. Adjust the seasonings and serve immediately.

VARIATION: CRISPY LEEKS WITH PARMESAN

An excellent accompaniment to egg dishes.

Preheat the broiler. Prepare the leeks as directed, through step 3, cooking them in an ovenproof skillet. Dust the browned leeks with ⅓ cup grated Parmesan cheese and broil until the cheese is golden brown and bubbly, no more than a few minutes. Serve immediately.

Leeks Braised in Red Wine

This richly flavored dish works well with meat or oily fish (like salmon), or as part of a vegetarian meal with eggs. For the best flavor, reduce the sauce until it is quite thick and very potent.

SERVES 6 AS A SIDE DISH

6 medium leeks
2 tablespoons unsalted butter
  Salt
  About 2 cups red wine
1 bay leaf
8 black peppercorns
½ teaspoon dried thyme

1. Trim and discard the dark green tops and tough outer leaves from the leeks. Remove the roots along with a very thin slice of the nearby white part. Halve the leeks lengthwise and wash them under cold, running water. Gently spread apart but do not separate the inner layers to remove all traces of soil. If the leeks are particularly sandy, soak them in several changes of clean water.

2. Melt the butter in a large sauté pan set over medium heat. Add the leeks, piling them up in two layers. Season with salt to taste. Add the 2 cups wine and the bay leaf, peppercorns, and thyme. The wine should just reach the bottom of the top layer of leeks. If not, add more wine.

3. Bring the wine to a boil, reduce the heat, cover, and simmer until the leeks are tender, 10 to 15 minutes, depending on the thickness of the leeks.

4. Use a slotted spoon to transfer the leeks to a serving platter and cover with foil to keep warm. Turn the heat to high and boil the sauce until it becomes syrupy and reduces to about ¼ cup, about 10 minutes. Remove and discard the bay leaf and peppercorns. Add back any accumulated juices on the platter with the leeks and reduce the sauce again if necessary. Adjust the seasonings in the sauce and then drizzle it over the leeks. Serve immediately.

Leek and Potato Soup

A classic soup that relies on just a few ingredients to provide tremendous flavor. Sautéing the leeks brings out the sweetness and contributes mightily to the soup. This soup is hearty enough to serve for dinner with a salad or a vegetable side dish and some bread.

SERVES 4 AS A MAIN COURSE

4 medium leeks
2 tablespoons extra-virgin olive oil
1 pound red potatoes, peeled and cut into
   ½-inch dice
4 cups chicken or vegetable stock
1 bay leaf
   Salt
   Freshly ground black pepper
2 tablespoons minced fresh parsley leaves

1. Trim and discard the dark green tops and tough outer leaves from the leeks. Remove the roots along with a thin slice of the nearby white part. Halve the leeks lengthwise and then cut them crosswise into thin strips. Wash the sliced leeks in a large bowl with several changes of clean water, or until no grit falls to the bottom of the bowl.

2. Heat the oil in a large casserole or Dutch oven. Add the leeks and sauté over medium heat until tender and golden, about 10 minutes. (Do not let the leeks brown.)

3. Add the potatoes, stock, bay leaf, and salt and pepper to taste. Bring to a boil, reduce the heat, and simmer until the potatoes are tender, about 25 minutes.

4. Use the back of a wooden spoon to crush some of the potatoes against the side of the pot to thicken the texture of the soup. Leave some of the potato chunks intact. Remove the bay leaf and stir in the parsley. Adjust the seasonings and serve immediately.

VARIATION: CREAMY LEEK AND POTATO SOUP

Cream makes this soup more refined. Serve in small portions to start a meal.

SERVES 6 TO 8 AS A FIRST COURSE

Prepare the soup through step 3. Remove and discard the bay leaf. Puree the soup in a blender. (Do not puree any longer than necessary or the potatoes will become gluey.) Return the soup to the pot and stir in ½ cup heavy cream and the parsley. Bring almost to a boil, adjust the seasonings, and serve immediately.

Lettuces and Salad Greens

There are dozens of leafy greens in the average American supermarket. The choices include everything from iceberg and Boston lettuce to mizuna and kale. The focus of this chapter is on those lettuces and tender greens we eat in salads. What separates a cooking green from a salad green? It's mostly a question of texture. If the green is at all tough or chewy, we generally cook it. Often, the same green is both a cooking green and a salad green, it is merely a question of size.

Baby mustard greens add a lovely, sharp note to salads, but once the leaves are more than 2 or 3 inches long they become tough and must be cooked. Some salad greens, such as spinach, can be cooked or used in salads.

So how does one make sense of these greens for salad? I divide them into two large categories—lettuces and salad greens—with numerous subdivisions.

Lettuces

There are four main varieties of lettuce.

BUTTERHEAD LETTUCES. These lettuces grow in round heads and have loose outer leaves. The leaves are light or medium green (sometimes streaked with red) and are very mild and tender. Boston and Bibb lettuce are the most common varieties.

LOOSELEAF LETTUCES: The lettuces grow in a loose rosette shape, not a tight head. They have ruffled leaves, that are either green or shade from green at the base to magenta at the top. They have a bit more crunch and flavor than butterhead lettuces, but are still soft and mild. Common varieties include red leaf, green leaf, red oak, and lolla rossa.

ROMAINE LETTUCE: Also called cos lettuce, this lettuce has long leaves that are quite broad at the top. Outer leaves are dark green, while inner leaves are pale. This lettuce is always crisp and has a crunchy texture that stands up well to creamy dressings.

CRISPHEAD LETTUCES: These lettuces grow in round heads and the leaves are tightly packed. Their leaves are crisp.

Salad Greens

Dozens of greens are used in salads. Dandelion, endive, escarole, radicchio, and spinach are also cooked and served as vegetable dishes. Each has its own entry in this book.

In addition, diminutive versions of leafy greens that we usually cook (beet greens, chard, kale, mustard greens, and turnip greens) frequently turn up in salad mixes, especially mesclun. (The term *mesclun* is used to describe any mixture of baby greens, although technically it should include fresh herbs and flowers, as it does in the south of France).

A number of other leafy greens that are generally used in salads, including:

CHICORY: Also known as curly endive, this green looks like a loosehead lettuce. However, the leaves have much more bite than any lettuce and are usually tougher.

FRISÉE: This spiky, miniature chicory has a nutty flavor coupled with a mild bite. The green is small and delicate-looking but fairly crisp and crunchy.

MÂCHE: This tiny chicory has small, dark green leaves and a sweet, nutty flavor. Also called lamb's tongue or lamb's lettuce, this green is most often used in salad mixes.

MIZUNA: A Japanese mustard green with long, dark green leaves that are deeply cut with jagged edges. This green has a strong bite and sturdy texture. If using it in salads, make sure the greens are not too big or tough.

TATSOI: This tiny Asian green is a member of the cabbage family. It has slender white stalks and round dark green leaves. It tastes a bit like bok choy but is usually very tender.

WATERCRESS: This green has long stalks and small, round green leaves. The stalks are usually thick and should be trimmed. The leaves are peppery, somewhat like arugula.

AVAILABILITY: Year-round.

SELECTION: Lettuces and salad greens should be crisp and healthy-looking. Any wilting or browning is a bad sign. These vegetables are extremely perishable and should be purchased in prime condition, especially if you plan to keep them.

STORAGE: Refrigerate lettuces and salad greens in sealed plastic bags until needed. If the greens or lettuces are very damp when you get them home, blot up the excess moisture with paper towels and place them in a dry bag. Tender greens should be used the day they are purchased. Lettuces will keep for several days.

BASIC PREPARATION: Start by separating the leaves from a head of lettuce. Place the lettuce leaves or salad greens in a large bowl of cold water and swish them with your hands. As you wash the greens, remove any thick stems and tear any large leaves into bite-sized pieces. Before dumping out the water, rub your hand along the bottom of the bowl to feel for grit. If you feel any dirt, lift the greens from the water, dump out the water, rinse the bowl, add fresh cold water, and return the greens to the bowl. Repeat until there's no grit in the bowl. The greens must be dried thoroughly. Even lightly damp greens make poor salad. The dressing will roll off the leaves and puddle in the bottom of the bowl.

To dry the greens, lift them from the water and shake dry to remove some liquid. Next, put the greens in a salad spinner and spin until well dried. Finally, turn the greens out on a clean kitchen towel or a double layer of paper towels and gently blot up any remaining moisture. Washed greens can be gently rolled up in dry paper towels and refrigerated in a zipper-lock bag for several hours.

BEST COOKING METHODS: Only the hardiest salad greens (such as dandelion, endive, escarole, radicchio, and spinach) are cooked.

OTHER RECIPES WITH LETTUCES AND SALAD GREENS:
Water Chestnut and Mizuna Salad with Sesame Vinaigrette (page 347)

See also recipes in the arugula, dandelion, endive, escarole, and spinach chapters.

Leafy Salad with Classic Vinaigrette

This is my basic formula for salad. I particularly like sherry vinegar here, but red wine vinegar is delicious as well. This salad is best with a variety of greens that offer a selection of colors and textures. You can vary the salad or dressing in countless ways. Whisk a tea-spoon or two of mustard in with the vinegar and salt and pepper. Change the acid and use citrus juice (lemon is the best choice) or another vinegar. Add a little minced shallot or garlic to the dressing. Add chopped carrots, radishes, or cucumber to the salad. Sprinkle with croutons (page 132).

SERVES 4 TO 6 AS A FIRST COURSE OR
AFTER THE MAIN COURSE

8 cups tender lettuce torn into bite-sized pieces and/or baby greens, washed and thoroughly dried
1 tablespoon red wine or sherry vinegar
Salt
Freshly ground black pepper
¼ cup extra-virgin olive oil

1. Place the greens in a large bowl.
2. Whisk the vinegar and salt and pepper to taste together in a small bowl. Whisk in the oil until the dressing is smooth. Adjust the seasonings.
3. Drizzle the dressing over the salad greens. Toss to coat and serve immediately.

Greek Salad with Feta and Olives

One of my favorite salads, with bright, sharp flavors. The smooth, mild lemon vinaigrette allows the olives, tomato, herbs, and cheese to shine through. If you have some fresh herbs on hand, tear the leaves by hand and add them to the salad. The perfume of a little mint and some oregano is particularly intoxi-cating.

SERVES 4 TO 6 AS A FIRST COURSE

8 cups tender lettuce torn into bite-sized pieces and/or baby greens, washed and thoroughly dried
1 medium tomato, cored and cut into ½-inch wedges
10 large Kalamata olives, pitted and sliced
2 to 3 tablespoons roughly torn fresh herb leaves (parsley, mint, and/or oregano), optional
1½ tablespoons lemon juice
Salt
Freshly ground black pepper
3 tablespoons extra-virgin olive oil
1½ ounces feta cheese, crumbled (about ⅓ cup)

1. Place the greens, tomato, olives, and herbs in a large bowl.
2. Whisk the lemon juice and salt and pepper to taste together in a small bowl. Whisk in the oil until the dressing is smooth. Adjust the seasonings.

3. Drizzle the dressing over the salad greens. Toss to coat. Sprinkle the cheese over the salad and toss lightly. Serve immediately.

Arugula, Endive, and Radicchio Salad with Balsamic Vinaigrette

A classic combination of bitter Italian salad greens. Don't buy cheap balsamic vinegar at the supermarket—it's harsh and tastes like chemicals. Real balsamic vinegar is aged for many years and has a complex flavor with hints of oak, vanilla, and sweetness.

SERVES 4 TO 6 AS A FIRST COURSE OR AFTER THE MAIN COURSE

1 large bunch arugula, leaves stemmed, washed, and thoroughly dried (about 3 cups)

2 medium Belgian endive, leaves separated, washed, thoroughly dried, and sliced crosswise into ½-inch pieces

1 small head radicchio, leaves washed, thoroughly dried, and torn into bite-sized pieces (about 3 cups)

2 teaspoons red wine vinegar

2 teaspoons aged balsamic vinegar

Salt

Freshly ground black pepper

¼ cup extra-virgin olive oil

1. Place the arugula, endive, and radicchio in a large bowl.

2. Whisk the vinegars and salt and pepper to taste together in a small bowl. Whisk in the oil until the dressing is smooth. Adjust the seasonings.

3. Drizzle the dressing over the salad greens. Toss to coat and serve immediately.

Mesclun with Baked Goat Cheese and Herb Vinaigrette

This restaurant classic is remarkably easy to make at home. An excellent way to begin almost any special meal, or fine as a light weekend lunch. Make sure the goat cheese is quite cold before breading it—you want it to be able to stay in the oven long enough to brown the coating but not melt the cheese.

SERVES 4 AS A FIRST COURSE

7 tablespoons extra-virgin olive oil

¾ cup Fresh Bread Crumbs (page 123)

6 ounces chilled goat cheese, cut into 4 rounds

8 cups mesclun or assorted baby greens, washed and thoroughly dried

1 tablespoon red wine or sherry vinegar

Salt

Freshly ground black pepper

2 tablespoons minced fresh parsley, basil, tarragon, thyme, oregano, sage, and/or dill leaves

1. Preheat the oven to 400 degrees. Coat a small baking dish with 1 tablespoon of the oil.

2. Place 2 tablespoons of the oil in a small bowl. Place the bread crumbs in another bowl. Working with one goat cheese round at a time, dip the round into the oil and turn to coat. Lift the round from the oil and gently place it in the bread crumbs. Turn gently to coat. Transfer the goat cheese round to the baking dish. Repeat until all four rounds are in the dish. Sprinkle some of the crumbs over the cheese to cover any bare spots. Bake until the cheese rounds turn golden brown but are still holding their shape, about 8 minutes. (Do not let the goat cheese cook any longer or it will start to melt.)

3. While the goat cheese rounds are baking, place the greens in a large bowl. Whisk the vinegar and salt and pepper to taste together in a small bowl. Whisk in the remaining 4 tablespoons of oil until the dressing is smooth. Whisk in the herbs and adjust the seasonings.

4. Drizzle the dressing over the salad greens. Toss to coat. Divide the greens among four salad plates. Place one warm goat cheese round on each plate and serve immediately.

Caesar Salad

The dressing should be made with a coddled (or lightly boiled) egg. Coddling causes the egg to thicken slightly and gives the dressing its characteristic creaminess. If you don't eat eggs that have not been fully cooked, see the tofu variation (page 205). Make sure to mince the garlic very fine or, better yet, put it through a garlic press.

SERVES 4 AS A FIRST COURSE

CAESAR DRESSING

3 tablespoons lemon juice
1 teaspoon Worcestershire sauce
¼ teaspoon salt
8 grindings fresh black pepper
1 small garlic clove, pressed or minced fine
4 anchovy fillets, minced fine
1 large egg
⅓ cup extra-virgin olive oil

2 medium heads romaine lettuce or 2 large romaine hearts
⅓ cup grated Parmesan cheese
2½ cups Garlic Croutons (page 132)

1. Whisk the lemon juice, Worcestershire sauce, salt, pepper, garlic, and anchovies together in a medium bowl. Bring several cups of water to a boil in a small saucepan. Carefully slide the egg into the boiling water and cook for 45 seconds. Remove the egg with a slotted spoon and cool very briefly. Crack the egg into the bowl with

the other ingredients and whisk until smooth. Add the oil in a slow, steady stream, whisking constantly until smooth. Adjust the seasonings. (The dressing may be refrigerated in an airtight container for 1 day; shake before using.)

2. Discard the bruised outer leaves from the romaine heads, if using. Tear the large, crisp inner leaves crosswise into four pieces; tear smaller leaves into three pieces. Wash the lettuce in a bowl of cold water until free of grit. Spin dry. There should be about 10 cups. (The lettuce may be refrigerated in a zipper-lock plastic bag for up to 4 hours.)

3. When ready to serve, place the lettuce in a large bowl. Drizzle half the dressing over the lettuce and toss to coat lightly. Sprinkle with the cheese and drizzle with the remaining dressing. Toss until the leaves are well coated with the dressing and cheese. Add the croutons, toss several times, and divide the salad among four individual plates. Serve immediately.

VARIATIONS: GRILLED CHICKEN CAESAR SALAD

This dish makes an excellent lunch entree or summer dinner. The recipe can easily be doubled.

SERVES 3 AS A MAIN COURSE

Remove excess fat from two boneless, skinless chicken breast pieces (about ¾ pound). Brush the chicken with 1 tablespoon olive oil and sprinkle with salt and pepper to taste. Grill or broil, turning once, until cooked through, about 10 minutes. Cool the chicken to room temperature and slice crosswise into ½-inch strips. Add the chicken to the salad along with the cheese.

EGGLESS CAESAR DRESSING

Use this recipe in place of Caesar Dressing (page 204). Since it is made without eggs, the dressing will keep for a week in the refrigerator.

MAKES GENEROUS ½ CUP

2 ounces drained soft tofu, crumbled (about ⅓ cup)
3 tablespoons lemon juice
1 teaspoon Worcestershire sauce
¼ teaspoon salt
8 grindings fresh black pepper
1 small garlic clove, pressed or minced very fine
4 anchovy fillets, minced fine
⅓ cup extra-virgin olive oil

1. Place the tofu, lemon juice, Worcestershire sauce, salt, pepper, garlic, and anchovies in the work bowl of a food processor. Process, scraping down the sides as needed, until the mixture is smooth and the tofu is fully incorporated into the other ingredients, about 1 minute.

2. With the motor running, add the oil in a slow, steady stream and process until smooth. Adjust the seasonings. (The dressing may be refrigerated in an airtight container for 1 week; stir before using.)

Malanga

Malanga is a popular tuber in the Caribbean, especially in Cuba, Puerto Rico, and the Dominican Republic. It is shaped somewhat like a potato but is covered with patchy, hairy brown skin. The flesh is most often white, but there is a yellow variety that appears regularly in American markets. I have seen malanga with rose-tinted flesh in the Caribbean, but only rarely in American markets.

Personally, I prefer the white variety. It is quite similar to a potato, with crisp white flesh that can be boiled and mashed, sliced and fried for chips, or grated and made into fritters. White malanga has a mild flavor and is a bit starchier than a russet potato. Yellow malanga has a stronger, earthier flavor.

OTHER COMMON NAMES: Malanga amarilla (yellow malanga), malanga blanca (white malanga), and yautia.

AVAILABILITY: Year-round, mostly in markets catering to Latino shoppers.

SELECTION: Malanga should be very hard with no signs of mold, even on the ends. Malanga generally weigh about a pound or so, sometimes a bit less. Size is not really an issue when shopping, although shape is. Tubers that are fairly smooth and evenly shaped will be easier to peel with less waste.

STORAGE: Malanga can be kept in a cool, well-ventilated spot for several days. Do not refrigerate.

BASIC PREPARATION: Start by rinsing the malanga to remove any loose dirt and hairy fibers. Working with one malanga at a time, use a paring knife to remove the shaggy brown skin and outer ⅛-inch layer of flesh; remove any blemishes. It helps to rinse the malanga as you work to flush out any bits of the skin. Cut the malanga as desired and drop the chunks into a bowl of cold water to prevent browning.

BEST COOKING METHODS: Boiling or frying.

OTHER RECIPES WITH MALANGA: Malanga can be sliced thin and fried to make chips like taro (page 320). Malanga also works well cut into chunks and used in soups and stews as a thickener. Malanga is closely related to taro. The two can be used interchangeably.

Mashed Malanga

Like all tubers, malanga can be peeled, cut into chunks, boiled until soft, and then mashed with milk and butter. Although malanga flesh is usually bright white, the color muddies a bit when the vegetable is prepared this way. I add a little ground allspice (which is a traditional Caribbean seasoning) and serve this dish with a juicy stew. (Grated nutmeg could be used if you prefer.) While my palate prefers mashed potatoes in most instances (the texture of mashed potatoes is silkier and less starchy), I do like malanga with Caribbean dishes.

SERVES 4 AS A SIDE DISH

2 pounds malanga
Salt
2 tablespoons unsalted butter, softened
½ cup milk, warmed
Pinch ground allspice

1. Working with one malanga at a time, use a paring knife to remove the hairy brown skin and outer ⅛-inch layer of flesh. Cut the malanga into 1-inch cubes and drop them into a bowl of cold water.

2. Drain the malanga and place it in a large saucepan. Add enough water to cover by about 2 inches. Add a generous amount of salt and bring the water to a boil. Cook until the malanga is tender, about 20 minutes. Drain the malanga.

3. Return the malanga to the empty saucepan set over low heat. Add the butter and use a potato masher to turn the malanga into fine bits. Stir in the milk and the allspice with a wooden spoon until smooth. Adjust the seasonings. Serve immediately.

Malanga Fritters with Chiles and Garlic

This is one of my favorite recipes in this book, if only because the results are so unexpected and the effort is so minimal. Many Americans find malanga too starchy, especially when mashed. However, all that starch is put to good use in this recipe. Peeled malanga is shredded in a food processor and then combined with a little flour, a lot of garlic, and some fresh chile to make a simple fritter batter. Unlike potato fritters (which require eggs to hold them together), malanga is so starchy that eggs are unnecessary. The result is a crisp, wispy fritter with a clean flavor. Because there are no eggs, these fritters are especially light. I find these fritters thoroughly addictive. If you use a habanero chile (which would be very authentic), these fritters will be quite hot. A jalapeño or serrano chile delivers plenty of chile flavor but less heat.

SERVES 6 TO 8 AS AN APPETIZER

1½ pounds malanga
4 medium garlic cloves, minced
1 small fresh chile, stemmed, seeded, and minced
¼ cup flour
Salt

About 1 cup vegetable or peanut oil for frying

Lime wedges

1. Working with one malanga at a time, use a paring knife to remove the hairy brown skin and outer ⅛-inch layer of flesh. Cut the malanga into 1-inch cubes and drop them into a bowl of cold water.

2. Drain the malanga. Using the coarse shredding disk on a food processor, shred the peeled malanga. Transfer the malanga to a large bowl. Toss with the garlic, chile, flour, and salt to taste.

3. Heat about ¼ inch of oil in a large skillet until shimmering. Take a rounded tablespoon of the malanga mixture and carefully drop into it the hot oil, forming the mixture into a round disk as you work. Repeat until the pan is filled with fritters. Fry, turning once, until golden brown, about 5 minutes. Drain the fritters on paper towels. Repeat with the remaining batter, adding more oil as needed. You should be able to make about 24 small fritters. Serve immediately with the lime wedges and ice-cold beers.

Mushrooms

A decade ago, most supermarkets stocked just one kind of mushroom—the familiar white button. Now, most supermarkets offer at least three or four kinds of fresh mushrooms. Here are the varieties you are most likely to see.

BUTTON: This white mushroom is fairly bland and soft, which means that it must be cooked with flavorful ingredients in order to taste like much. High-heat cooking methods, such as roasting and sautéing, help this watery mushroom shed liquid and improve its texture.

CREMINI: This mushroom looks like a light brown button mushroom. However, it is far more flavorful and has a firmer texture than a button mushroom. Given that cremini cost just a little more than button mushrooms, they are my all-purpose mushroom.

PORTOBELLO: This giant mushroom is actually an oversized cremini. It has a meaty texture and strong, earthy flavor. While smaller buttons and cremini are usually sliced for cooking, portobellos are often cooked whole, either on the grill or under the broiler.

SHIITAKE: These Asian mushrooms have umbrella-shaped, dark brown caps. The caps are chewy and delicious when cooked; however, the stems are tough and should be removed before cooking.

DRIED: Many markets sell small packets of dried mushrooms. Dried porcini (an Italian mushroom rarely sold fresh in this country) have an intoxicating aroma and flavor when reconstituted. Dried shiitakes are also quite good, as are mixed dried mushrooms.

In addition to these varieties, there are dozens of other fresh mushrooms that appear at farmers' markets and gourmet shops. Some cost as much as $20 a pound. For the most part, you can prepare any of the "fancy" mushrooms like regular button or cremini mushrooms.

Since chanterelles, hen of the woods, and other specialty mushrooms can be so expensive, I like to cook them as simply as possible, usually just sautéing them in butter (see the recipe on page 212). Although we call these mushrooms "wild," many are raised in darkened cellars and caves and are not picked in forests.

AVAILABILITY: Year-round, although the spring and fall are the traditional seasons for wild mushrooms.

SELECTION: Mushrooms should be firm and dry, never soft or spongy. If shopping for white button mushrooms, examine the underside of the cap. If the mushroom is fresh, the cap will still be attached to the stem and the gills won't be visible. Gills will be visible on other mushrooms, so this tip applies only to button mushrooms. When shopping for expensive mushrooms, give them a whiff. They should smell like the woods, not moldy or sharp.

Dried mushrooms are sold in small plastic packages. Look for packages with large mushroom pieces and a minimum of dust or crumbled pieces.

STORAGE: Dampness will make mushrooms go soft and slimy. When you get home from the market, blot up any excess moisture on paper towels. Refrigerate mushrooms in a paper bag. (Plastic bags trap moisture and should not be used.) Mushrooms can be held for several days.

BASIC PREPARATION: Mushrooms are best wiped clean with a damp paper towel. You can rinse them briefly under cold water if they are very dirty, but make sure to dry them well since damp mushrooms will become soft and spongy very quickly.

Once the mushrooms are clean, I check the ends of the stems. If they look dried out, I remove a thin slice with a paring knife. If the mushrooms are very fresh, this step is not necessary. When preparing shiitakes and portobellos, I remove the entire stem, which is tough and chewy on the shiitakes, and woody on the portobellos.

Rehydrating dried mushrooms takes about 15 minutes. Place the dried mushrooms in a small bowl and cover with hot tap water. (Don't use boiling water; I find it can turn the mushrooms limp.) Set aside to soak until the mushrooms have softened but are still firm and chewy, about 15 minutes. Transfer the mushrooms from the soaking liquid to a cutting board with a fork. (If the mushrooms look or feel gritty, they can be rinsed briefly.)

Don't throw out the flavorful soaking liquid. Strain it through a sieve lined with a coffee filter or a single paper towel and set it aside for use in soups, stews, and rice dishes.

BEST COOKING METHODS: Broiling, grilling, roasting, and sautéing.

OTHER RECIPES WITH MUSHROOMS:
Browned Baby Artichokes and Mushrooms with Garlic (page 5)
Stir-Fried Broccoli and Mushrooms with Oyster Sauce (page 47)
Braised Burdock with Dried Shiitake Mushrooms (page 60)
Corn and Mushroom Sauté (page 120)
Peas with Onion and Mushrooms (page 247)
Spinach Salad with Mushrooms, Croutons, and Warm Lemon Dressing (page 312)

Oven-Roasted Mushrooms

Roasting evaporates the water in mushrooms and concentrates their woodsy flavor. The resulting dish might be called "essence of mushrooms," albeit with a crisp, chewy exterior. This method works well with all kinds of mushrooms, but is especially appropriate for relatively bland button mushrooms. This recipe doubles easily, making it the preferred way to cook mushrooms for a crowd.

SERVES 4 AS A SIDE DISH

1¼ pounds white button or cremini mushrooms, wiped clean and halved (or quartered if large)

2 tablespoons extra-virgin olive oil

Salt

Freshly ground black pepper

1. Preheat the oven to 400 degrees.
2. Spread the mushrooms out over a large, rimmed baking sheet. Drizzle the oil over the mushrooms and toss with your hands to coat evenly. Sprinkle with salt and pepper to taste.
3. Roast, turning once, until the mushrooms are golden brown, for about 20 to 25 minutes. Serve immediately.

VARIATIONS: OVEN-ROASTED MUSHROOMS WITH GARLIC, THYME, AND BALSAMIC VINEGAR

The vinegar gives the mushrooms a dark sheen and the garlic and thyme really boost their flavor.

Roast the mushrooms as directed. When the mushrooms are golden brown, sprinkle with 3 minced garlic cloves, 1 teaspoon chopped fresh thyme leaves, and 1 tablespoon balsamic vinegar and mix well. Continue roasting for 2 minutes to allow the mushrooms to absorb the seasonings. Serve immediately.

OVEN-ROASTED MUSHROOMS WITH FIVE-SPICE POWDER AND SOY SAUCE

These Asian-flavored mushrooms are perfect with roast chicken and rice.

Roast the mushrooms as directed, seasoning them sparingly with salt before cooking. When the mushrooms are golden brown, sprinkle with 1 tablespoon soy sauce, ½ teaspoon five-spice powder, and 2 medium scallions, sliced thin, and mix well. Continue roasting for 2 minutes to allow the mushrooms to absorb the seasonings. Serve immediately.

Sautéed Mushrooms with Butter and Onion

Although not as crisp and chewy as roasted mushrooms, sautéed mushrooms are softer and juicier. This is the best way to cook "expensive" mushrooms, such as chanterelles. This method works well with regular button or cremini mushrooms, too. This dish is an ideal accompaniment to vegetarian meals, chicken, or roasts. Make sure that the mushrooms become nicely browned in spots. The caramelized bits of onion, butter, and mushroom juices that thicken and stick to the pan (and the mushrooms) make this dish a special treat. (So does the butter; the flavor isn't the same with oil.) My favorite herb here is thyme but almost anything will work. Adjust the amount depending on the intensity of the herb, using small amounts of thyme, oregano, and marjoram but larger amounts of parsley or chives.

SERVES 4 AS A SIDE DISH

2 tablespoons unsalted butter
1 medium onion, chopped fine
1 pound mushrooms, wiped clean and halved
   (or quartered if large)
   Salt
   Freshly ground black pepper
1 teaspoon to 1 tablespoon minced fresh
   thyme, oregano, marjoram, parsley, or
   chives

1. Heat the butter in a large skillet. When the butter has melted, add the onion and cook over medium heat until softened, about 3 minutes.

2. Add the mushrooms and salt and pepper to taste. Raise the heat to medium-high and sauté until the juices that the mushrooms give off have evaporated and the mushrooms are nicely browned in spots, about 8 minutes. Stir in the herb and adjust the seasonings. Serve immediately.

Mexican Mushroom Soup with Chiles, Tomatoes, and Cilantro

This soup is heady with the flavors of two kinds of chiles. Anaheim chiles are long and light green in color. Their flavor is fruity with only a modest amount of heat. The jalapeño or serrano provides a stronger burst of chile heat. The broth is light and spicy, while the mushrooms provide some heft and chewy textures. Make sure to prepare this soup in a wide casserole so the mushrooms will brown quickly.

SERVES 4 AS A LIGHT MAIN COURSE
OR 6 AS A FIRST COURSE

2 tablespoons extra-virgin olive oil
1 medium onion, chopped
1 medium Anaheim chile, stemmed, seeded, and minced
1 medium jalapeño or serrano chile, stemmed, seeded, and minced
1½ pounds assorted mushrooms, such as shiitakes, cremini, chanterelles, and oysters, wiped clean and sliced thin (if using shiitakes, discard their stems)

Salt

Freshly ground black pepper

3 cups chicken or vegetable stock

One 14.5-ounce can diced tomatoes

2 tablespoons minced fresh cilantro leaves

1. Heat the oil in a large, wide casserole or Dutch oven. Add the onion and chiles and sauté over medium heat until softened, about 4 minutes. Raise the heat to medium-high, add the mushrooms, and sauté until golden brown, about 8 minutes. Season the mushrooms with salt and pepper to taste.

2. Add the stock and tomatoes and bring to a boil. Reduce the heat and simmer until the flavors have blended, about 10 minutes. Stir in the cilantro and adjust the seasonings. Serve immediately.

Brothy Udon Noodles with Mushrooms

Wheaty, slippery udon noodles match up well with the intense flavor and chewy texture of dried and fresh mushrooms. Although this dish is fairly brothy, it is not a soup. You can still eat these noodles with a fork, but serve them in a wide, shallow soup bowl to hold the brothy "sauce" in place.

SERVES 4 AS A MAIN COURSE

1 ounce dried shiitake mushrooms

12 ounces udon noodles

2 tablespoons roasted peanut oil

1 medium onion, minced

¾ pound assorted fresh mushrooms, such as shiitakes, cremini, portobellos, and buttons, wiped clean and sliced thin (if using shiitakes, discard their stems)

2 tablespoons sake or sherry

2 tablespoons soy sauce

3 medium scallions, sliced thin

2 tablespoons minced fresh cilantro leaves

1. Place the dried mushrooms in a small bowl and cover with 2 cups of hot tap water. Set aside for 15 minutes to soak. Transfer the mushrooms to a cutting board with a fork and chop. Strain the liquid through a sieve lined with a coffee filter or paper towel and set aside separately.

2. Meanwhile, bring 4 quarts of water to a boil in a large pot. Add the noodles and cook until al dente, about 6 minutes. Drain and rinse under warm, running water to remove the excess starch. Set the noodles aside.

3. Heat the oil in a large wok or nonstick skillet. When the oil is quite hot, add the onion and stir-fry until lightly browned, about 1 minute. Add the fresh mushrooms and stir-fry until golden brown, about 4 minutes. Add the rehydrated shiitake mushrooms and stir-fry for 30 seconds to bring out their flavor.

4. Add the shiitake soaking liquid, sake, soy sauce, and scallions and bring the liquid to a boil. Add the noodles and toss in the broth to reheat, about 1 minute. Stir in the cilantro and serve immediately, transferring the noodles and broth to wide, shallow soup bowls.

Hearty Mushroom Stew

This dish again demonstrates the power of a small handful of dried mushrooms. They transform relatively plain vegetables into a richly flavored stew. Porcini are my first choice but any dried mushrooms (shiitakes, chanterelles) would work. Mixed dried mushrooms (as sold in many markets) are another good choice. Butter stirred into the stew just before serving gives the sauce some body but can be omitted. If you like, stir in ¼ cup cream in place of the butter for an even richer stew. Serve over noodles, polenta, or with plenty of good bread.

SERVES 4 AS A MAIN COURSE

1 ounce dried porcini mushrooms

2 tablespoons extra-virgin olive oil

1 medium onion, diced

2 teaspoons minced fresh rosemary leaves

1 pound assorted fresh mushrooms, wiped clean and sliced thick

Salt

Freshly ground black pepper

3 cups chicken or vegetable stock

10 ounces peeled baby carrots

½ pound turnips, peeled and cut into ½-inch dice

2 tablespoons minced fresh parsley leaves

1 tablespoon unsalted butter (optional)

1. Place the dried mushrooms in a small bowl and cover with 2 cups of hot tap water. Set aside for 15 minutes to soak. Transfer the mushrooms to a cutting board with a fork and chop. Strain the liquid through a sieve lined with a coffee filter or paper towel and set aside separately.

2. Heat the oil in a large casserole or Dutch oven. Add the onion and rosemary and sauté over medium heat until softened, about 3 minutes. Add the fresh mushrooms and sauté until golden brown, about 8 minutes. Add the softened dried mushrooms and salt and pepper to taste and stir-cook for 1 minute.

3. Add the reserved mushroom liquid along with the stock, carrots, and turnips. Bring to a boil, reduce the heat, and simmer until the carrots and turnips are tender but not mushy, about 30 minutes. Stir in the parsley and butter and adjust the seasonings. Serve immediately.

Broiled or Grilled Portobello Mushrooms with Asian Flavors

Broiled portobello mushroom caps make a meaty, juicy side dish for most any meal. They also can be used as a sandwich filling or as a light vegetarian entree when served with rice and a vegetable side dish, such as steamed broccoli.

SERVES 4 AS A SIDE DISH OR SANDWICH FILLING OR 2 AS A MAIN COURSE

3 tablespoons rice vinegar

2 tablespoons soy sauce

1 tablespoon toasted sesame oil

4 medium portobello mushrooms (about 1 pound), stems discarded and caps wiped clean

1 tablespoon sesame seeds, toasted in a dry skillet until golden brown

1. Preheat the broiler (the rack should be about 6 inches from the broiler) or light the grill.
2. Combine the vinegar, soy sauce, and sesame oil in a shallow baking dish just large enough to hold the mushrooms in a single layer. Add the mushrooms and marinate, turning occasionally, for 10 minutes.
3. Broil the mushrooms in the baking dish or take them out of the marinade and grill over a medium-hot fire. Cook, turning once, until lightly browned, 8 to 10 minutes. Sprinkle with the sesame seeds and serve immediately.

VARIATION: BROILED OR GRILLED PORTO-
BELLOS AND BABY SPINACH SALAD

I like this dish so much I often divide the greens and mushrooms between two large plates and make this dish dinner for two.

SERVES 4 AS FIRST COURSE
OR LIGHT LUNCH

While the mushrooms are cooking, toss 8 cups stemmed, washed, and dried baby spinach or other tender greens with 2 tablespoons toasted sesame oil and salt and pepper to taste in a large bowl. Divide the greens among four plates. Cut each cooked mushroom in half and then into ½-inch slices. Arrange a portion of the mushrooms over each salad and serve immediately.

Portobello Mushrooms with Red Wine and Oregano

Serve juicy portobello mushrooms as an accompaniment to meat that requires some sort of sauce. For instance, these mushrooms are ideal with pork or veal roast. They also work well with sliced steak or beef tenderloin.

SERVES 6 AS A SIDE DISH

2 tablespoons extra-virgin olive oil
1 medium onion, chopped
1 tablespoon minced fresh oregano leaves
6 medium portobello mushrooms (about 1½ pounds), stems discarded; caps wiped clean and sliced thin
½ cup red wine
½ cup chicken or vegetable stock
Salt
Freshly ground black pepper

1. Heat the oil in large sauté pan. Add the onion and oregano and sauté over medium heat until softened, about 3 minutes. Add the mushrooms and raise heat to medium-high. Cook, stirring often, until the mushrooms soften and are lightly browned, about 8 minutes.
2. Add the wine, then the stock and salt and pepper to taste. Simmer until the liquid thickens but the mushrooms are still juicy, about 3 minutes. Adjust the seasonings and serve immediately.

When ladled over polenta, sautéed portobello mush-rooms become a hearty vegetarian main course. Reg-ular polenta takes over half an hour to cook. In contrast, instant polenta, which has been precooked and dried, cooks in just 3 minutes. The secrets to lump-free polenta are to whisk constantly as you add the polenta to the simmering water and to add the polenta in a slow, steady stream.

SERVES 4 AS A MAIN COURSE

Prepare the mushrooms as directed. At the same time, bring 6 cups of water to a boil in a large saucepan. Add 1 teaspoon salt. Reduce the heat to low and slowly whisk in 1½ cups instant polenta until smooth. (This should take about 1 minute.) Partially cover and cook until the polenta is thick, about 3 minutes. Divide the polenta among four individual bowls and spoon some mushrooms over each portion. Serve with grated Parmesan cheese if desired.

Duxelles

The classic French treatment takes plain button mush-rooms, minces them extremely fine, and then cooks them until all the juices have been driven off. A pound of mushrooms cooks down to just 1½ cups. What's left is concentrated mushroom essence. Stir a spoonful or two into a pot of soup or some stew. Combine duxelles with stale bread and herbs to make a poultry stuffing or stir them into some mashed potatoes or rice. Use dux-elles as the base for a soufflé or an omelet filling. To save a lot of time and energy, use the pulse button on the food processor to mince the mushrooms.

MAKES ABOUT 1½ CUPS

2 tablespoons extra-virgin olive oil
¼ cup minced onion or shallots
1 teaspoon minced fresh rosemary leaves
1 pound white button mushrooms, wiped
  clean and minced very fine
  Salt
  Freshly ground black pepper

1. Heat the oil in a large skillet. Add the onion and rosemary and sauté over medium heat until softened, about 3 minutes.

2. Add the mushrooms and cook, stirring occa-sionally, until they shed their liquid and brown, about 15 minutes. Season with salt and pepper to taste. Use immediately or refrigerate in an air-tight container for several days.

Scrambled Eggs with Duxelles

Eggs are often used as a medium to showcase truffles. They work equally well with duxelles, revealing their full flavor.

SERVES 2 FOR BREAKFAST OR BRUNCH

4 large eggs
¼ cup Duxelles (see above)
2 tablespoons milk
Salt
Freshly ground black pepper
1 tablespoon unsalted butter

1. Lightly beat the eggs, duxelles, milk, and salt and pepper to taste together in a medium bowl.
2. Place a medium nonstick skillet over medium heat for 2 minutes. Add the butter and swirl in the pan until it melts.
3. Add the egg mixture and cook, folding the eggs over frequently with a plastic spatula, until the eggs are set, about 2 minutes if you like loose scrambled eggs and about 3 minutes if you like them drier and fully cooked. Serve immediately.

Roasted Chicken Breasts with Duxelles

Duxelles can be stuffed under the skin of split chicken breasts. As the chicken cooks, the mushrooms keep the delicate white meat moist and give it a terrific flavor.

SERVES 6 AS A MAIN COURSE

1 cup Duxelles (page 218)
3 tablespoons unsalted butter, softened
6 split skin-on, bone-in chicken breasts
Salt
Freshly ground black pepper

1. Preheat the oven to 400 degrees.
2. Use a fork to mash the duxelles and the butter together in a medium bowl.
3. With your fingers, gently lift up the skin on one chicken breast, making sure not to detach the skin. The idea is to loosen the membrane that attaches the skin to the meat so that you create enough space for the duxelles. With your fingers, smear several tablespoons of the duxelles under the skin and directly over the meat. Place the stuffed chicken breast, skin side up, in a roasting pan. Repeat the process with the remaining breasts and duxelles. Season the chicken breasts with salt and pepper to taste.
4. Roast until the juices run clear when the chicken is pierced with a knife, about 40 to 45 minutes. (If using an instant-read thermometer, the temperature should register 165 to 170 degrees.) Serve immediately.

Mustard Greens

There are dozens of greens that can be called mustard greens. Some varieties are bright green, others are tinged with red or purple. Some have flat leaves, others have scalloped or frilly leaves.

The most common variety available in American supermarkets has bright green leaves and curly edges. This mustard green is medium-hot. It looks a lot like kale, but the leaves are lighter in color and not quite as leathery.

Mustard greens have long been popular in the South. They also are widely used in Asia. (To find some of the more exotic-looking mustards with green and chartreuse leaves, go to Chinatown.)

All mature mustard greens have a fairly strong bite. In fact, while they are bitter like other tougher greens (turnips, kale, collard, etc.), I find that they are also hot and really do taste like prepared mustard.

The recipes that follow are designed to accommodate the sharp flavor of this delicious green. I find that mustard greens taste best when paired with equally potent seasonings.

While the focus of the chapter is on bunches of mature mustard greens, baby mustard greens do regularly appear in mesclun salad mixes. Baby red mustard is also sold separately in many markets, as is mizuna, an Asian mustard green variety (see page 200). Use this spicy green in salads, much as you would use arugula.

OTHER COMMON NAMES: Chinese mustard greens, curly mustard, mustard cabbage, and mustard spinach.

AVAILABILITY: Fall through spring.

SELECTION: Look for mustard greens with a brilliant color and crisp leaves. There should be no signs of yellowing or rot. Try to pick greens with fairly thin stems. Very young or baby mustard greens can be used in salads. Mizuna is a type of young mustard green.

STORAGE: Mustard greens can be refrigerated in a loosely sealed plastic bag for several days. If the greens are very damp when you get them home from the market, blot dry with paper towels and place in a dry bag.

BASIC PREPARATION: As always with leafy greens, wash mustard greens in a bowl of cold water, changing the water as necessary until no grit falls to the bottom of the bowl. As you wash the greens, strip off the leafy green portion from either side of the tough central stalk with your hands or a knife. Discard the stalks and tear the leafy portions in small pieces.

Shake the greens to remove the excess water but do not bother to dry them with a towel. This moisture will help cook the greens in a covered pan.

BEST COOKING METHODS: In the recipes that follow, I have assumed you are buying fairly mature, tough mustard greens. In that case, braising is the best cooking method. You could also blanch tougher mustard greens and then sauté them with seasonings (see recipes for turnip greens). If you happen to find very tender mustard greens, you can skip the blanching step and just sauté them in oil like spinach or chard.

OTHER RECIPES WITH MUSTARD GREENS:

Young Dandelion Salad with Warm Shallot Dressing and Croutons (page 131)—use only baby mustard greens

Mustard greens can be used in any recipe that calls for turnip greens.

Curried Mustard Greens with Tomatoes

The rich flavors in this dish complement the strong bite of mustard greens. This dish is a bit soupy. Serve with rice, steamed couscous, or Indian flat breads.

SERVES 4 TO 6 AS A SIDE DISH OR 2 TO 3 AS A MAIN COURSE

2 pounds mustard greens
2 tablespoons canola oil
1 medium onion, halved and sliced thin
1 tablespoon minced fresh gingerroot
1 teaspoon curry powder
   One 14.5-ounce can diced tomatoes
   Salt
   Freshly ground black pepper
   Lime wedges

1. Wash the mustard greens in several changes of cold water, stripping off the leafy green portion from either side of the tough central stalk. Discard the stalks and rip the leafy portions into small pieces. Shake to remove the excess water.

2. Heat the oil in a large casserole or Dutch oven. Add the onion and sauté over medium heat until golden, about 6 minutes. Add the ginger and curry powder and cook, stirring often, until fragrant, about 1 minute.

3. Add the damp greens to the pan and stir to coat with the aromatics. Add the tomatoes and salt and pepper to taste. Reduce the heat, cover, and simmer, stirring occasionally, until the greens are wilted and tender, about 10 minutes.

4. Remove the cover and simmer briskly until the excess liquid has evaporated, 1 to 2 minutes. Adjust the seasonings and serve immediately with the lime wedges.

Soy-Braised Mustard Greens

The strong flavor of soy and the sweetness of mirin are the perfect foil for the heat of the mustard greens. Mirin is sweetened Japanese rice wine packaged in small bottles and available in most supermarkets. (Look for it near the soy sauce.) Serve these moist greens with rice.

SERVES 4 AS A SIDE DISH

2 tablespoons soy sauce
2 tablespoons mirin (Japanese sweet rice wine)
1½ pounds mustard greens
2 tablespoons roasted peanut oil
2 medium garlic cloves, minced
1 tablespoon minced fresh gingerroot

1. Combine the soy sauce and mirin in a small bowl and set the mixture aside.

2. Wash the mustard greens in several changes of cold water, stripping off the leafy green portion from either side of the tough central stalk. Discard the stalks and rip the leafy portions into small pieces. Shake to remove the excess water.

3. Heat the oil in a large, deep sauté pan. Add the garlic and ginger and sauté over medium-high just until fragrant, about 30 seconds. Add the damp greens and stir to coat with the oil and the aromatics, about 30 seconds.

4. Add the soy mixture, cover, reduce the heat, and cook, stirring once, until the greens are tender, 5 to 7 minutes. Remove the cover and simmer briskly until the excess liquid has evaporated, 1 to 2 minutes. Adjust the seasonings and serve immediately.

Black-Eyed Peas and Mustard Greens

Black-eyed peas and greens are a classic Southern combination. Typically, the peas and greens are cooked with ham or bacon. I have used bacon because most cooks are likely to have a few stray slices on hand. However, if you have some good-quality ham in the refrigerator, sauté the onion and celery in two tablespoons of oil and then stir in ¼ to ½ cup chopped ham with the greens. Mustard greens work well in this dish, as would collard greens, kale, turnip greens, or even dandelion. You may need to adjust the wilting time in step 3 depending on the green used. Cornbread is the natural accompaniment to this slightly soupy dish.

SERVES 4 AS A MAIN COURSE

1½ pounds mustard greens
4 strips bacon, chopped
1 tablespoon canola oil
1 medium onion, chopped fine
1 medium celery stalk, chopped fine
1½ cups chicken or vegetable stock
2 15-ounce cans black-eyed peas, drained and rinsed
1 to 2 tablespoons cider or red wine vinegar
Salt
Freshly ground black pepper

1. Wash the mustard greens in several changes of cold water, stripping off the leafy green portions from either side of the tough central stalk. Discard the stalks and rip the leafy portions into small pieces. Shake to remove the excess water.

2. Cook the bacon and oil in a medium casserole or Dutch oven over medium heat until the bacon is crisp, about 6 minutes. Add the onion and celery and cook until softened, about 6 minutes.

3. Add 1 cup stock and the mustard greens, stir well, and cover the pan. Cook, stirring once or twice, until the greens have wilted, about 4 minutes.

4. Stir in the black-eyed peas and remaining ½ cup stock and cover the pan again. Cook, stirring two or three times, until the peas are heated through and the greens are tender, about 5 minutes. Stir in the vinegar and salt and pepper to taste. Serve immediately.

Okra

Okra has a long history in the South but until recently most of the country rarely saw fresh okra, at least in supermarkets. In the past decade, farmers' markets have taken up the cause and okra is reliably available during the summer.

Okra's most famous use is in gumbo. There, its slippery (some say slimy) texture is put to good use as a thickener. Although some experts say that okra is always slippery, I disagree. While "tricks" such as soaking okra in a water and vinegar solution do nothing to reduce okra's gelatinous properties, choosing a dry-heat cooking method does. If okra is sliced and braised or stewed, it will be thick and slippery. However, if the whole pods are grilled or quickly sautéed, they remain crisp and the interior is only a tad slippery.

Although I like slow-cooked okra, I prefer it crisp-cooked on the grill or in a hot skillet so I can appreciate its sweet vegetal flavor and delicate crunch, which reminds me of green beans.

OTHER COMMON NAMES: Lady's fingers (a Southern term that refers to the long, slender shape of okra).

AVAILABILITY: Summer, into the fall in some locations.

SELECTION: Size is probably the most important consideration when shopping for okra. Really long okra are often tough and very gelatinous. Ideally, choose okra that are 3 inches long or less. A 4-inch-long okra will probably be fine, but I don't bother with 6-inch okra. Okra should be firm and dry, with no brown spots or blemishes visible. Most okra will be green, although there is a magenta-colored variety available at some farmers' markets.

STORAGE: Okra should be cooked as soon as possible. It can be refrigerated in a paper bag for a day or two if necessary but it does not hold well.

BASIC PREPARATION: Okra has a thin stem at one end that must be trimmed. Be careful to leave the cap just below the stem in place, especially if cooking the okra whole. When the pod is not opened during preparation, okra cooks up crisp and not gelatinous, especially if the cooking time is kept to a minimum. If you like that slippery texture, slice the okra before cooking or cook until it is very soft and start to falling apart.

BEST COOKING METHODS: Braising, grilling, pan-frying, and sautéing.

Grilled Okra

Simple yet delicious, with a minimum of the sticky texture that some people (mostly Northerners) object to. Make sure to trim the thin stem but leave the cap intact to prevent the seeds and juicy inner flesh from escaping.

SERVES 4 TO 6 AS A SIDE DISH

1 pound small okra (preferably less than 3 inches long), stems removed
2 tablespoons extra-virgin olive oil
 Salt
 Freshly ground black pepper
 Lemon wedges

1. Light the grill.
2. Toss the okra and oil in a medium bowl. Sprinkle with salt and pepper to taste. Thread the okra crosswise onto two skewers at the same time so that okra will be easy to turn on doubled skewers. You should be able to fit six or seven okra per set of skewers.
3. Grill over a medium-hot fire, turning once, until the exterior blackens and blisters in spots, about 8 minutes. Serve hot or warm with lemon wedges.

Sautéed Okra with Garlic and Hot Red Pepper Flakes

Like grilling, sautéing whole okra quickly over a high heat prevents the formation of the gelatinous texture inside the okra. The strong flavor of okra is a natural with garlic and hot red pepper flakes.

SERVES 4 TO 6 AS A SIDE DISH

2 tablespoons extra-virgin olive oil
1 pound small okra (preferably 3 inches long or less), stems removed
2 medium garlic cloves, minced
½ teaspoon hot red pepper flakes
 Salt

1. Heat the oil in a large skillet. When the oil is quite hot, add the okra and sauté over medium-high heat until almost crisp-tender, 3 to 4 minutes.
2. Stir in the garlic, hot red pepper flakes, and salt to taste. Continue cooking until the okra is crisp-tender and the garlic is golden, about 1 minute. Do not let the garlic burn. Adjust the seasonings and serve immediately.

Cornmeal-Crusted Okra

Anyone who thinks they don't like okra will be won over by this classic Southern dish. Sliced okra is dusted with cornmeal then pan-fried in hot oil until golden brown and crisp. The fried okra slices are chewy and crunchy—almost like good french fries. The cornmeal coating—the okra is not dipped first in the eggs, so the cornmeal merely dusts the okra—is light and delicious. I love to serve okra as a snack with cold beers when everyone is gathered in the kitchen waiting for dinner.

SERVES 4 TO 6 AS A SNACK

1 cup cornmeal
  Coarse salt
  Freshly ground black pepper
1 pound small okra (preferably 3 inches long or less), stems removed
  About 1 cup peanut oil for frying
  Lemon wedges

1. Place the cornmeal and salt and pepper to taste in a small brown paper or plastic bag. Cut the okra crosswise into ½-inch pieces. Drop the okra into the bag with the cornmeal and shake to coat. Dump the okra into a large strainer and shake gently over the sink or a bowl to remove the excess cornmeal.

2. Heat ¼ inch of oil in an 11- or 12-inch skillet over high heat. When the oil is shimmering, add half the okra and fry, turning occasionally, until golden brown and crisp, about 4 minutes. Use a slotted spoon to transfer the okra to a platter lined with paper towels. Repeat the process with the remaining okra. Sprinkle the fried okra with salt to taste and serve immediately with the lemon wedges.

Stewed Okra and Tomatoes

This juicy Southern dish is perfect over rice. In the summer, I can eat this for dinner (this recipe will serve two to three as a main course). It's more traditional to use the okra and rice as accompaniments to chicken or fish.

SERVES 4 TO 6 AS SIDE DISH

2 tablespoons extra-virgin olive oil
1 medium onion, chopped
1 medium jalapeño chile, stemmed, seeded, and minced
1 pound small okra (preferably 3 inches long or less), stems removed
3 medium ripe tomatoes (about 1½ pounds), cored, peeled, seeded, and chopped
½ cup water
  Salt
  Freshly ground black pepper
2 tablespoons minced fresh basil or parsley leaves

1. Heat the oil in a large sauté pan. Add the onion and chile and sauté over medium heat until the onion is golden, about 5 minutes.

2. Add the okra and sauté just until it begins to soften, about 3 minutes. Add the tomatoes, water, and salt and pepper to taste. Bring to a boil, reduce the heat, cover, and simmer until the okra is tender, about 15 minutes.

3. Remove the cover, raise the heat, and boil briskly until the liquid in the pan thickens, about 5 minutes. (Remember, you want this dish to be juicy, so simmer just until the liquid in the pan is no longer watery.) Stir in the basil, adjust the seasonings, and serve immediately.

Traditional recipes call for bacon fat, not olive oil. Here's how to make this Southern classic.

Fry six slices of bacon in a sauté pan until crisp. Remove the bacon with a slotted spoon, drain, crumble, and reserve. Omit the olive oil and follow the above recipe, cooking the onion and chile in the bacon fat. Stir in the crumbled bacon along with the basil.

Onions

Onions are used as an aromatic seasoning in most every cuisine around the globe. When sautéed (often with garlic, carrots, and/or celery), they form the basis for soups, sauces, stews, and countless meat, poultry, and fish preparations. This chapter focuses on dishes where the onion is the star, not just part of the supporting cast.

Most onions in our markets have been dried, or cured. These are the most important varieties:

YELLOW ONIONS: This is the standard onion for most American cooks. It is sweet when cooked but never cloying. I think yellow onions have the richest flavor.

RED ONIONS: Red onions are a bit milder than yellow onions and sweeter. If you are going to use a little minced raw onion in a salsa or salad, this is the one.

WHITE ONIONS: Hotter than yellow or red onions, these onions don't have much sweetness.

PEARL OR BOILING ONIONS: Small versions of yellow, red, and white cooking onions are called pearl or boiling onions. (Boiling onions are usually white and slightly larger, but this is not a hard-and-fast rule.) These onions are hard to peel (they must be blanched first) but are sweet and delicious when braised or roasted whole. Also, look for cipolline (they have flattened ends and resemble flying saucers); these Italian onions are especially delicious and can be used in any recipe calling for boiling or pearl onions.

SPANISH: This oversized yellow onion is very mild. One onion yields two or even three cups when chopped—more than is required in most recipes. Spanish onions do make great onion rings.

VIDALIA: This Georgia sweet onion gets a lot of press, but others are just as delicious—Mauis, Walla Wallas, and Texas Sweets. Sweet onions are best saved for dishes where onions are the main attraction.

AVAILABILITY: Year-round.

SELECTION: Choose onions with dry, papery skins. Onions should be rock-hard, with no soft spots or powdery mold on the skin. Avoid onions with green sprouts.

STORAGE: Onions should be stored in a cool, well ventilated spot. In the summer when bugs can be a problem, I store onions in a loosely sealed plastic bag in the crisper drawer. They lose a bit of their flavor when kept this way and will go soft more quickly; however, this method is fine if you plan to use the onions within a week or so.

BASIC PREPARATION: With the exception of tiny boiling or pearl onions (which must be blanched first, see page 232), I start by making a slit from one pole to the other (the poles are the flatter or tapered ends of the onion), peeling off the papery skin.

At this point, the onions can be cut into wedges, rounds, halved and then sliced thin, or chopped. To chop an onion, first cut it in half through the poles. Lay one half cut side down on the board and make one or two cuts parallel to the cutting board. Next, slice the onion from end to end into strips. Then turn your knife 90 degrees and make closely spaced cuts. To mince the onion, keep the cuts very closely spaced.

BEST COOKING METHODS: Braising, frying, grilling, roasting, or sautéing.

OTHER RECIPES WITH ONIONS:
Eggplant and Tomato Gratin with Onion-Herb Jam (page 140)
Ratatouille (page 141)
Roasted Fennel and Red Onions (page 163)
Stewed Peppers with Tomato and Onion *(Peperonata)* (page 251)

Grilled Onions

Almost any onion can be grilled. The key is to hold the slices together with toothpicks. Also, make sure to almost burn the edges of the onion slices. This ensures that the center is really cooked through and tender. Oversized Spanish or sweet onions are the easiest varieties to work with in this recipe.

SERVES 6 TO 8 AS A SIDE DISH

4 large onions (about 3½ pounds), cut cross-wise into ¾-inch rounds
2 tablespoons extra-virgin olive oil
Salt
Freshly ground black pepper

1. Light a grill fire. Stick toothpicks through the sides of the onion slices to hold the rings in place. Brush the onions with the oil and sprinkle with salt and pepper to taste.
2. Grill the onions over a medium-hot fire, turning once, until lightly charred on the exterior, about 15 minutes. Serve immediately, warning everyone at the table to remove the toothpicks first.

VARIATION: GRILLED ONIONS WITH CHILI BUTTER

Grilled onions are delicious straight from the grill. A light brush with a flavored butter makes them divine.

While the onions are grilling, melt 2 tablespoons butter in a small saucepan. Add 1 teaspoon chili powder and salt to taste and cook over low heat for 30 seconds. Remove the pan from the heat. When the onions are done, transfer them to a serving platter and brush with the butter on both sides. Serve immediately.

Roasted Onions with Balsamic Vinegar and Rosemary

If possible, use a mixture of red and yellow onions. They have different flavors (the red onions are sweeter when roasted) and the contrasting colors makes an attractive presentation. No matter the choice of onions, make sure to cut the onions through the poles (their somewhat flattened ends) so that the wedges will stay together as much as possible. These onions make an especially good side with a pork roast or chops.

SERVES 4 AS A SIDE DISH

1½ pounds onions, preferably a mix of yellow and red
2 tablespoons extra-virgin olive oil
2 tablespoons balsamic vinegar
1½ teaspoons minced fresh rosemary leaves
½ teaspoon salt

1. Preheat the oven to 425 degrees.
2. Peel the onions and cut them through the poles (the ends) into wedges. Cut small-to-medium onions into quarters; larger onions should be cut into six or eight wedges. Place the

onions in a large baking dish and drizzle the oil over them. Gently toss the onions and oil with your hands to coat them evenly.

3. Place the baking dish in the oven. Bake, stirring the onions once, for 40 minutes.

4. Combine the vinegar, rosemary, and salt in a small bowl. Drizzle the vinegar mixture over the onions, stir gently, and return the dish to the oven. Bake until nicely browned, about 10 minutes. Adjust the seasonings, adding more salt or vinegar if desired. Serve hot or warm.

Browned Boiling or Pearl Onions

Small boiling or pearl onions are cooked by a three-step process that requires a fair amount of work, but the results are worth the effort. First, the onions are blanched to help loosen their papery skins. The peeled onions are then browned for flavor and color. Finally, liquid is added to the pan and the onions are braised until tender. A little maple syrup creates a thick sauce for the onions that can also be used to flavor meat. These sweet, tender onions are ideal with roast pork or chicken.

SERVES 4 AS A SIDE DISH

1 pound small boiling or pearl onions
2 tablespoons extra-virgin olive oil
½ cup chicken or vegetable stock
2 tablespoons maple syrup
1 bay leaf

Several sprigs fresh thyme
1 tablespoon minced fresh parsley leaves
Salt
Freshly ground black pepper

1. Bring several quarts of water to a boil in large saucepan. Add the onions and cook for 2 minutes. Drain the onions and place them in a bowl of ice water. When cool, drain the onions and slip off their peels with your fingers.

2. Heat the oil in a large skillet. Add the onions and cook over medium heat, stirring occasionally, until lightly browned, 5 to 7 minutes.

3. Add the stock, syrup, bay leaf, and thyme. Bring to a boil, reduce the heat, cover, and simmer until the onions are tender and the liquid has reduced to a thick glaze, about 15 minutes. (If the onions are tender but the liquid has not reduced sufficiently, raise the heat and simmer, uncovered, for a minute or two.) Remove and discard the bay leaf and thyme sprigs. Stir in the parsley and season with salt and pepper to taste. Serve immediately.

VARIATIONS: CREAMED ONIONS

A holiday classic that is sweet and rich. Consider adding a squirt of lemon juice to balance the sweetness; this step is not traditional but recommended.

Prepare the onions as directed. When glazed in step 3, add ¼ cup heavy cream to the pan and simmer just until the sauce thickens, about 2 minutes. Remove and discard the bay leaf and thyme sprigs, stir in the parsley, and season with salt and pepper to taste.

This southern Italian dish works well with pork, chicken, and white-fleshed fish.

Prepare the onions as directed, making the following changes. Replace the maple syrup with 2 tablespoons red wine vinegar. Omit the bay leaf and thyme and add ¼ cup raisins in their place.

Onion Rings

I don't like onion rings coated with a heavy batter. A quick dip in milk to moisten the onions, then a roll in some flour and cornmeal, and the rings are ready to be fried. They emerge from the hot oil crisp and crunchy, and taste like onions, not coating. For the best results, coat the onions just before putting them into the oil and fry in small batches. This means the cook will need to tend the stove, while everyone else enjoys the hot onion rings.

SERVES 4 TO 6 AS A SIDE DISH

2 large Spanish onions (about 2 pounds)
About 6 cups peanut or vegetable oil for frying
1 cup milk
1 cup flour
1 cup cornmeal
Salt
Freshly ground black pepper

1. Peel and slice the onions crosswise about ¼ inch (or slightly wider) thick. Separate the onions into rings and place them in a large bowl.

2. Heat 2 inches of oil in a deep 6-quart pot set over medium-high heat.

3. While the oil is heating, pour the milk into a bowl. Combine the flour, cornmeal, and salt and pepper to taste in another bowl.

4. When the oil almost reaches a temperature of 365 degrees, drop a large handful of the onions into the milk. Swish the onions to make sure they are evenly moistened. Lift the onions from the milk and drop them into the bowl with flour mixture. Toss lightly with your hands to coat. Lift up the onions and gently shake off any excess coating. (The coating process should take less than 30 seconds.)

5. Carefully add the onion rings to the 365-degree oil, making sure not to crowd the onions. Fry, stirring occasionally, until golden brown and crisp, 3 to 4 minutes. Use a slotted spoon to transfer the onions rings to a platter lined with paper towels. Repeat the process with the remaining onions. (You will need to cook the onions in five or six batches.) Sprinkle the onion rings with salt and pepper to taste and serve immediately.

Caramelized Onions

Slowly browned, sweet onions have dozens of uses in my kitchen. I spread them on slices of grilled bread to make bruschetta, use them as a pizza topping, or enrich them with a little heavy cream and fresh herbs to make a rich sauce for fresh fettuccine. Caramelized onions are also a wonderful addition to eggs, rice, beans, or soups. Many cooks burn onions when trying to caramelize them. The onions must be cooked slowly so that they soften, then brown. Crunchy, burnt onions are a disaster. My trick is to cook the onions with a bit of white wine in a covered pot until they are soft. This way they can't burn. I then remove the cover, cook off the wine, and sauté the onions until richly browned.

MAKES ABOUT 2 CUPS

2 tablespoons unsalted butter or extra-virgin olive oil

3 pounds yellow onions, halved and sliced thin

1 teaspoon salt

½ cup white wine

Freshly ground black pepper

1. Heat the butter in a large, heavy casserole or Dutch oven. Add the onions and cook over medium heat until they just begin to soften, about 8 minutes. Add 1 teaspoon salt and the wine. Reduce the heat to medium-low, cover, and cook, stirring occasionally, until the onions are quite soft, about 30 minutes.

2. Remove the cover, raise the heat to medium, and cook, stirring more often, until well browned, 25 to 30 minutes. As the onions cook, scrape the bottom of the pot with a wooden spoon to loosen the brown bits and incorporate them back into the onions. Add pepper to taste and adjust the seasonings. Serve immediately or refrigerate in an airtight container for several days. If using the onions as a topping or condiment, gently reheat them in a small saucepan until warm. For other uses, cold onions can be stirred directly into soups or sauces.

French Onion Soup

This is my streamlined version of the classic soup. I don't like too much gooey cheese on top of onion soup. Others (including my wife) disagree and would sprinkle twice as much cheese over each bowl. Homemade beef stock is the traditional (and delicious) choice here. If using canned broth, stick with chicken or vegetable stock. Canned beef broth is far too salty and lacks flavor. It's fine if the caramelized juices from the onions scorch a bit in the pot. The brandy will loosen them and they will become incorporated into the soup.

SERVES 6 AS A FIRST COURSE
OR FOR LUNCH

2 tablespoons unsalted butter

1 tablespoon extra-virgin olive oil

3 pounds yellow or red onions, halved and sliced thin

1 teaspoon salt

½ cup cognac

5 cups chicken, beef, or vegetable stock

2 sprigs fresh thyme

2 bay leaves

4 sprigs fresh parsley

Freshly ground black pepper

6 thick slices French bread, toasted

8 ounces Gruyère cheese, shredded (about 2 cups)

1. Heat the butter and oil in a large, heavy casserole or Dutch oven. Add the onions and cook, stirring often, over medium heat until they wilt and start to brown, about 10 minutes. Sprinkle with 1 teaspoon salt and raise the heat to medium-high. Continue to cook, stirring more often, until the onions are very soft and nicely browned, about 15 minutes. As the onions cook, make sure to scrape the browned bits from the bottom of the pot back into the onions.

2. Add the cognac and simmer until the liquid evaporates, about 2 minutes. Add the stock, thyme, bay leaves, parsley, and pepper to taste. Bring to a boil, reduce the heat, and simmer until the flavors have blended, about 10 minutes. Adjust the seasonings.

3. While the soup is simmering, adjust the oven rack to the second-highest position and preheat the broiler. Set six deep ovenproof bowls or crocks into a rimmed baking sheet. Ladle the hot soup into the bowls. Float a piece of toasted bread in each bowl. Sprinkle ⅓ cup cheese over each bowl and place the baking sheet in the oven. Broil until the cheese begins to brown, no more than a few minutes. (Watch carefully to prevent burning.) Serve immediately.

Parsnips

P arsnips look like ivory-colored carrots. In fact, they are related to carrots and are quite sweet like their orange cousins. While we eat carrots raw, parsnips have a tougher texture right out of the ground and are always cooked. When roasted, steamed, or braised, parsnips become smooth and creamy, like a potato but not as starchy.

Parsnips are sweet, but they also have buttery and nutty notes. Add some to a tray of roasted vegetables or use them in soups or stews.

AVAILABILITY: Year-round, although the best season is fall through winter.

SELECTION: Shop for parsnips much the way you choose carrots. They should be rock-hard without any mold or soft spots. (Parsnips that bend are way past their prime.) Smaller parsnips are better than larger ones for several reasons. First of all, they are sweeter and have a creamier texture when cooked. Second, thicker parsnips have a tough central core that will need to be trimmed before cooking.

If you have a choice, select parsnips that weigh 4 ounces each, rather than those that weigh 8 ounces or more. (Some parsnips can weigh a pound each.) If you must select larger parsnips, be prepared to cut out the cores as directed below.

At farmers' markets, you may see parsnips with their greens attached. If the greens look healthy, you can be assured that the parsnips were recently dug. Trim the greens at home.

STORAGE: Parsnips can be refrigerated in a loosely sealed plastic bag for a week, if not longer.

BASIC PREPARATION: Parsnips are prepared and cooked much like carrots. If they are quite small, you can simply remove the peel with a vegetable peeler and then cut them as desired.

While the light-colored core in every carrot softens nicely when cooked, the core in many thicker parsnips can be tough and woody. I find it best to remove the core from parsnips that are more than 1½ inches across at the broad end. If you have any doubts, open up the parsnip. If the core is thick and easily visible, poke it with a paring knife. If it seems tough or woody, remove it.

To remove the core, quarter the parsnips lengthwise and then use a paring knife to shave off the portion of the core that is attached to each quarter. (There's no core attached to the bottom of each quarter; so shave off the core near the broad end only.) Cut the cored parsnips into chunks as needed.

BEST COOKING METHODS: Boiling (for soups and stews), braising, roasting, and steaming (for purees).

Pureed Parsnips with Butter and Nutmeg

Steamed parsnips can be whipped into a thick, white puree that resembles mashed potatoes but with a sweeter, richer flavor. This puree is especially good with roast pork. Don't boil parsnips for this dish; they become too watery and mushy.

SERVES 4 AS A SIDE DISH

1½ pounds parsnips
2 tablespoons unsalted butter, softened
¼ cup milk, warmed
Salt
Pinch grated nutmeg

1. Peel the parsnips. If they are quite small, you can simply cut them into 2-inch chunks. Larger parsnips will probably have a tough woody core that needs to be removed. (You can see the core when you cut open the parsnips.) To remove the core, quarter the parsnips lengthwise and then use a paring knife to shave off the portion of the core that is attached to each quarter. Cut the cored parsnips into 2-inch chunks.
2. Place a steamer basket inside a wide, deep saucepan. Fill the pan with enough water to reach just below the bottom of the steamer basket. Turn the heat to high and bring the water to a boil. Add the parsnips to the basket, cover the pan, and steam until tender, about 15 minutes. Transfer the parsnips to the work bowl of a food processor.

3. Add the butter, milk, salt to taste, and nutmeg to the food processor. Process, scraping down the sides of the bowl as necessary, until smooth. Scrape the puree into a bowl. Adjust the seasonings and serve immediately.

Roasted Parsnips with Balsamic Vinegar and Rosemary

Parsnips become chewy and a bit crunchy when roasted, almost like oven fries. The balsamic vinegar glazes the roasted parsnips and keeps them from tasting overly sweet. Roasted parsnips are especially good with meat or poultry.

SERVES 4 TO 6 AS A SIDE DISH

2 pounds parsnips
2 tablespoons extra-virgin olive oil
Salt
Freshly ground black pepper
2 tablespoons balsamic vinegar
2 teaspoons minced fresh rosemary leaves

1. Preheat the oven to 425 degrees.
2. Peel the parsnips. If they are quite small, you can simply cut them into 1½-inch chunks. Larger parsnips will probably have a tough woody core that needs to be removed. (You can see the core when you cut open the parsnips.) To remove the core, quarter the parsnips lengthwise and then

use a paring knife to shave off the portion of the core that is attached to each quarter. Cut the cored parsnips into 1½-inch chunks.

3. Toss the parsnips and oil on a large rimmed baking sheet. Sprinkle with salt and pepper to taste. Roast, turning once, until golden brown, about 40 minutes.

4. Combine the vinegar and rosemary in a small bowl. Drizzle the mixture over the roasted parsnips on the baking sheet and toss to coat. Continue to roast just until the parsnips are glazed, about 3 minutes. Adjust the seasonings and serve immediately.

Honey-Glazed Parsnips with Ginger

Like carrots, parsnips can be glazed in a covered pan. A little ground ginger keeps honey-glazed parsnips from tasting like candy. Serve with roasted chicken or turkey, or with any pork dish.

SERVES 4 TO 6 AS A SIDE DISH

2 pounds parsnips
1 tablespoon unsalted butter
1 cup chicken or vegetable stock
2 tablespoons honey or maple syrup
½ teaspoon ground ginger
  Salt
  Freshly ground black pepper

1. Peel the parsnips. If they are quite small, you can simply cut them into 1-inch chunks. Larger parsnips will probably have a tough woody core that needs to be removed. (You can see the core when you cut open the parsnips.) To remove the core, quarter the parsnips lengthwise and then use a paring knife to shave off the portion of the core that is attached to each quarter. Cut the cored parsnips into 1-inch chunks.

2. Melt the butter in a large sauté pan over medium heat. Add the parsnips and cook just until coated with butter, about 1 minute. Add the stock, honey, ginger, and salt and pepper to taste. Bring the liquid to a boil. Reduce the heat, cover the pan, and simmer, stirring once, until the parsnips are tender, 10 to 12 minutes.

3. Remove the cover, raise the heat, and boil briskly until the liquid in the pan reduces to a thick glaze, about 2 minutes. Adjust the seasonings and serve immediately.

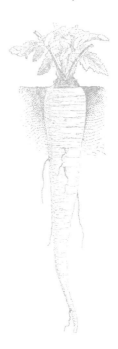

Curried Parsnip Soup

This suave, silky soup makes an excellent lunch or first course during the drab days of winter. Since the parsnips are simmered until extremely tender, there's no need to remove the core unless it is excessively tough. The curry powder in this recipe is subtle. It disguises the poor color of parsnip soup and helps tame the sweetness of this vegetable.

SERVES 8 AS A FIRST COURSE

2 tablespoons extra-virgin olive oil
1 medium onion, diced
1 tablespoon minced fresh gingerroot
2 medium garlic cloves, minced
1½ teaspoons curry powder
2 pounds parsnips, peeled and cut into 1-inch chunks
6½ cups chicken or vegetable stock
   Salt
2 tablespoons minced fresh cilantro leaves
1 cup plain yogurt

1. Heat the oil in a soup pot. Add the onion and sauté over medium heat until golden, about 6 minutes. Add the ginger, garlic, and curry powder and cook until fragrant, about 1 minute.

2. Add the parsnips, stock, and salt to taste. Bring to a boil, reduce the heat, and simmer until the parsnips are very tender, about 35 minutes.

3. Puree the soup, in batches, in a blender. Stir in the cilantro and adjust the seasonings. Ladle the soup into individual bowls. Float a dollop of yogurt in each bowl and serve immediately.

Peas

Sweet green peas come in three distinct forms in our markets. Traditional shelling peas (also called garden peas or English peas) have become something of a rarity. This is the pea we see in the frozen food aisle. Over with the fresh vegetables, they make a brief appearance in late spring and early summer.

Part of the problem is labor. It takes a long time to shell peas and most people would rather not bother. The other problem is flavor. Shelling peas start to lose their sweet flavor as soon as they are harvested. Peas picked last week will be starchy and mealy. If you want to buy shelling peas, buy from a source that picks them locally and frequently. For these reasons, many cooks stick with frozen peas, knowing they will never be great but that they won't be horrible either. Peas freeze better than most vegetables and are a decent option.

Thankfully, there are other fresh peas. Two kinds of edible-pod peas are available in many areas throughout the year. Snow peas are pale green and fairly flat. Inside the pods (which are the main attraction with snow peas) are tiny, immature peas, really nothing more than tiny seeds or bumps. We generally stir-fry snow peas, which may explain why some stores label them Chinese peas.

The other option is the sugar snap pea, which is a cross between the shelling pea and the snow pea. Like snow peas, sugar snap peas are completely edible, pod and all. However, inside the bright green pods are round, little peas that are especially sweet and tender when properly cooked.

Flat snow peas are best stir-fried without precooking. However, sugar snap peas taste better when blanched first and then stir-fried or sautéed. Blanching sets the bright green pod color and helps cook the tiny peas inside the pods, which otherwise can be tough if these peas are stir-fried or sautéed without precooking.

AVAILABILITY: Snow peas and sugar snap peas are available year-round, although summer is the best season for them. Shelling peas are usually available only in the late spring and early summer.

SELECTION: All peas should be brightly colored and crisp. Snow peas will be flexible, while sugar snap and shelling peas should be firm. It's a good idea to taste one or two peas before buying. Peas should be crisp and sweet. If buying shelling peas, open the pod and taste a few. They should be sweet, not starchy or mealy. The peas should fill out the pods, but you don't want swollen peas either; they tend to be starchy.

STORAGE: All three kinds of peas can be refrigerated in a loosely sealed plastic bag. Shelling peas start losing flavor as soon as they are picked and are best used immediately. Snow and sugar snap peas will keep for a few days in the refrigerator.

BASIC PREPARATION: Snow peas are quick to prepare—simply pull the strings off the ends like a zipper. The same thing holds true for sugar snap peas; sometimes they also have a piece of the stem attached, which needs to be removed.

As their name suggests, shelling peas must be removed from their pods, a tedious step that yields a very small amount of peas for quite a bit of effort. Grasp hold of the bit of the stem at the end of the pod and pull to open the pods like a zipper. You may need to force the pods open with your fingers by applying pressure on the seam where the string was.

BEST COOKING METHODS: Snow peas are best stir-fried. Sugar snap peas should be blanched and then sautéed or stir-fried. Shelling peas are best boiled and buttered, braised, or used in soups and stews.

OTHER RECIPES WITH PEAS:
Indian Spiced Potatoes and Peas (page 275)
Stir-Fried Water Chestnuts and Snow Peas (page 347)

Sesame Stir-Fried Snow Peas

A Chinese restaurant classic that is delicious when made at home with good ingredients.

SERVES 4 TO 6 AS A SIDE DISH

¼ cup chicken or vegetable stock
1 tablespoon soy sauce
2 teaspoons toasted sesame oil
1 tablespoon roasted peanut oil
1 pound snow peas, strings pulled off
3 medium garlic cloves, minced
1 tablespoon minced fresh gingerroot
2 tablespoons sesame seeds, toasted in a dry skillet until golden brown

1. Combine the stock, soy sauce, and sesame oil in a small bowl and set the mixture aside.
2. Heat the peanut oil in a large nonstick skillet over medium-high heat until shimmering but not smoking. Add the peas and stir-fry for 30 seconds to coat them with the oil. Add the garlic and ginger and stir-fry until fragrant, about 20 seconds.
3. Add the stock mixture, quickly cover the pan, reduce the heat to medium, and cook until the peas are tender, about 2 minutes. Cook, uncovered, to reduce the sauce to just a tablespoon or two, 1 to 2 minutes. Sprinkle with the sesame seeds, toss, and adjust the seasonings. Serve immediately.

Spicy Stir-Fried Snow Peas with Cashews

Use unsalted cashews if you have a choice. Peanuts may be substituted for the cashews.

SERVES 4 TO 6 AS A SIDE DISH

¼ cup chicken or vegetable stock
1 tablespoon soy sauce
1 tablespoon chile paste
½ teaspoon sugar
1 tablespoon roasted peanut oil
1 pound snow peas, strings pulled off
¼ cup cashews
3 medium garlic cloves, minced
1 tablespoon minced fresh gingerroot
2 medium scallions, sliced thin
1 tablespoon rice vinegar

1. Combine the stock, soy sauce, chile paste, and sugar in a small bowl and set the mixture aside.
2. Heat the oil in a large nonstick skillet over medium-high heat until shimmering but not smoking. Add the peas and cashews and stir-fry for 30 seconds to coat them with oil. Add the garlic, ginger, and scallions and stir-fry until fragrant, about 20 seconds.
3. Add the stock mixture, quickly cover the pan, reduce the heat to medium, and cook until the peas are tender, about 2 minutes. Stir in the rice vinegar. Cook, uncovered, to reduce the sauce to just a tablespoon or two, 1 to 2 minutes. Adjust the seasonings and serve immediately.

Sugar Snap Peas with Walnuts and Basil

I find that blanching sugar snap peas before sautéing them guarantees that the peas are cooked through and tender. Shocking the blanched peas prevents them from overcooking and ensures that their exterior remains bright green and does not pucker or shrivel.

SERVES 4 AS A SIDE DISH

1 pound sugar snap peas, stems and strings removed
Salt
2 tablespoons unsalted butter
2 tablespoon finely chopped walnuts
2 tablespoons finely shredded fresh basil leaves
Freshly ground black pepper

1. Bring the water to a boil in a large saucepan. Meanwhile, prepare a bowl of ice water. Add the peas and salt to taste to the boiling water and cook until crisp-tender, about 1½ minutes. Drain and plunge the peas into the bowl of ice water. When cool, drain the peas and set aside.
2. Melt the butter in a large skillet. Add the walnuts and cook over medium heat until fragrant, about 2 minutes. Stir in the peas and cook until heated through, about 2 minutes. Stir in the basil and season with salt and pepper to taste. Serve immediately.

Sugar Snap Peas with Pancetta and Onion

Peas have a real affinity for bacon and onions. I like the meatier flavor of pancetta (unsmoked Italian bacon), but you can use American bacon with good results.

SERVES 4 AS A SIDE DISH

1 pound sugar snap peas, stems and strings removed
Salt
2 tablespoons extra-virgin olive oil
2 ounces thin-sliced pancetta, minced
1 medium onion, minced
1 tablespoon minced fresh parsley leaves
Freshly ground black pepper

1. Bring 2 quarts water to a boil in a large saucepan. Meanwhile, prepare a bowl of ice water. Add the peas and salt to taste to the boiling water and cook until crisp-tender, about 1½ minutes. Drain and plunge the peas into the bowl of ice water. When cool, drain the peas and set aside.
2. Heat the oil, pancetta, and onion in a large skillet. Sauté until the pancetta is crisp and the onion is golden, about 6 minutes. Stir in the peas and cook until heated through, about 2 minutes. Stir in the parsley and season with salt and pepper to taste. Serve immediately.

Pureed Pea Soup

Fresh shelling peas are a lot of work for a side dish. I much prefer to use sugar snap or snow peas. However, for this luxurious soup, only the best, farm-fresh summer garden peas will do. Many pea soup recipes are weighed down with cream and other extraneous ingredients that mask the delicate flavor of the peas. If you are going to bother shelling peas, I think the soup better taste like peas. My trick is simple. Simmer the empty pods with the stock to make an especially rich-tasting base. The other trick here is to use only a small amount of aromatic vegetables (onion, carrot, and celery) so that the focus stays on the peas. This thick soup is quite rich, so serve it in small bowls as a first course. The crouton garnish is worth the extra 5 minutes of work.

SERVES 6 AS A FIRST COURSE

2 pounds fresh shelling peas in pods, shelled
    (about 2¼ cups), with pods reserved
4½ cups water
    Several sprigs fresh thyme
2 bay leaves
2 tablespoons extra-virgin olive oil
1 small onion, minced
1 small carrot, minced
½ medium celery stalk, minced
1 tablespoon chopped fresh parsley leaves
    Salt
2½ cups Best Croutons (page 132)
1 tablespoon snipped fresh chives

1. Place the empty pea pods, water, thyme, and bay leaves in a large saucepan. Bring to a boil, reduce the heat, cover, and simmer for 15 minutes. Strain through a colander to remove the solids. Reserve the stock and discard the solids. You should have about 3 cups of stock.

2. Heat the oil, onion, carrot, celery, and parsley in a large saucepan. Sauté over medium heat until the vegetables have softened, about 6 minutes. Add the stock and simmer for 5 minutes to blend the flavors. Add the peas and cook just until they are tender, 3 to 4 minutes.

3. Puree the soup in batches in a blender until perfectly smooth. Season with salt to taste. (Reheat briefly if the soup has cooled too much.) Ladle the soup into small bowls. Float several croutons in each bowl and garnish with chives. Serve immediately.

Stewed Peas with Garlic and Pancetta

This recipe breaks most of the usual rules about cooking peas. Slow-braising infuses the peas with the flavors of garlic and pancetta and gives them a lovely soft texture. Thawed frozen peas may be used in this recipe, but you will need to reduce the braising time to just 10 minutes.

SERVES 4 AS A SIDE DISH

2 tablespoons extra-virgin olive oil
2 medium garlic cloves, minced

1½ ounces pancetta or bacon, diced
2 pounds fresh shelling peas in pods, shelled (about 2¼ cups)
½ cup chicken or vegetable stock
2 tablespoons minced fresh parsley leaves
Salt
Freshly ground black pepper

1. Heat the oil in a medium sauté pan. Add the garlic and pancetta and cook over medium heat until the garlic is lightly colored and the pancetta has rendered some of its fat, about 2 minutes.

2. Add the peas and stock to the pan. Bring the liquid to a simmer, reduce the heat to medium-low, and cover. Cook, stirring occasionally, until the peas are extremely tender, 20 to 30 minutes.

3. Uncover the pan and stir in the parsley and salt and pepper to taste. Raise the heat to high and cook briskly for a minute or two to evaporate some of the liquid. Adjust the seasonings and serve immediately.

Italian Rice and Pea Soup (*Risi e Bisi*)

This simple Venetian soup is quite thick—somewhere between risotto and a regular soup. You can omit the prosciutto, but it melts into the base and gives the soup a lovely flavor. If you like, substitute a 10-ounce package of frozen peas that have been thawed for the shelling peas. Add them when the rice is just a minute or two shy of being completely cooked.

SERVES 4 AS A MAIN COURSE OR 6 TO 8 AS A SUBSTANTIAL FIRST COURSE

2 tablespoons unsalted butter
1 tablespoon extra-virgin olive oil
1 medium onion, minced
2 ounces thin-sliced prosciutto, diced
1½ cups arborio rice
6 cups chicken or vegetable stock
2 pounds fresh shelling peas, shelled (about 2¼ cups)
2 tablespoons minced fresh parsley leaves
Salt
Freshly ground black pepper
Grated Parmesan cheese

1. Heat the butter and oil in a soup pot or kettle. Add the onion and prosciutto and sauté over medium heat until the onion has softened, about 5 minutes. Add the rice and stir-cook for 2 minutes.

2. Add the stock and bring the liquid to a boil. Reduce the heat, cover, and simmer, stirring once or twice, until the rice is almost tender, about 15 minutes.

3. Add the peas and cook, uncovered, until the rice and peas are tender, about 7 minutes. Stir in the parsley and salt and pepper to taste. Ladle the soup into bowls and serve immediately with the grated cheese passed separately at the table.

Buttered Peas with Fresh Herbs

Peas plain and simple. The best way to treat frozen peas and marvelous with fresh peas.

SERVES 4 AS A SIDE DISH

One 10-ounce package frozen peas or 2 pounds fresh shelling peas, shelled (about 2¼ cups)
Salt
1 tablespoon unsalted butter
2 tablespoons minced fresh parsley, basil, tarragon, chives, and/or mint
Freshly ground black pepper

1. Bring several quarts of water to a boil in a large saucepan. Add the peas and salt to taste and cook until tender, about 2 minutes for frozen peas, a couple minutes more for fresh. Drain the peas.
2. Melt the butter in a large skillet. Add the peas and cook, shaking to coat them with butter, until hot, about 1 minute. Add the herb and salt and pepper to taste. Serve immediately.

Peas with Onion and Mushrooms

Onion and mushrooms elevate peas to a classic.

SERVES 4 TO 6 AS A SIDE DISH

One 10-ounce package frozen peas or 2 pounds fresh shelling peas, shelled (about 2¼ cups)
Salt
2 tablespoons extra-virgin olive oil
1 medium onion, minced
6 ounces mushrooms, wiped clean and sliced thin
Freshly ground black pepper
1 tablespoon unsalted butter
2 tablespoons minced fresh parsley, basil, tarragon, chives, and/or mint

1. Bring several quarts of water to a boil in a large saucepan. Add the peas and salt to taste and cook until tender, about 2 minutes for frozen peas, a couple minutes more for fresh. Drain the peas.
2. While preparing the peas, heat the oil in a large skillet. Add the onion and cook over medium heat until softened, about 3 minutes. Add the mushrooms and raise the heat to medium-high. Sauté until the mushrooms are golden brown, about 6 minutes. Season with salt and pepper to taste.
3. Add the peas and butter to the skillet. Cook, shaking the pan occasionally to coat the peas with butter, until hot, about 1 minute. Add the herb and adjust the seasonings. Serve immediately.

Peppers

Bell peppers are the most important sweet pepper in our markets and the ones we cook and serve as a vegetable dish. (Spicy chile peppers are generally used as a seasoning.) Bell peppers come in five colors—green, red, yellow, orange, and purple. Green bell peppers are actually red, yellow, or orange peppers that have been picked before they had a chance to ripen. They are bitter and have a strong vegetal flavor. Red, orange, and yellow peppers are sweeter and much more flavorful than green peppers. They cost more but are worth every penny. Don't spend the extra money on purple peppers. They lose their pretty color when cooked and turn green.

Smaller chile peppers are used as a seasoning in countless dishes. The bright green jalapeño is hot but not overly so and widely available. Smaller, bright green serranos are similar in flavor to jalapeños. Bite for bite, serranos are hotter.

Tiny red, orange, or yellow Thai chiles are quite spicy and delicious, with a fruity flavor. Orange, red, yellow, and green Scotch bonnets look like miniature bell peppers, but they are exceedingly hot. Habaneros look like Scotch bonnets but have a floral flavor to accompany all that heat. Long, dark green poblanos are mild and have a pepper flavor.

Fresh chiles can be dried. As with fresh chiles, there are countless dried chiles available. Most have a leathery or brittle texture and reddish-brown color. Anchos (dried poblanos) have an earthy, sweet flavor and are perhaps the most widely available dried chile. All dried chiles must be toasted in a hot skillet, soaked in liquid (water or stock), and then stemmed and seeded before being used in a dish.

The one exception is chipotle chiles (dried, smoked jalapeños) packed in adobo sauce (a vinegary tomato sauce) and sold in cans. These smoky chiles can simply be minced and added to dishes like fresh chiles. Use some of the flavorful packing medium as well.

AVAILABILITY: Year-round, although peppers are best in the summer and early fall.

SELECTION: Peppers should be firm, with no soft spots.

STORAGE: Peppers should be refrigerated in a loosely sealed plastic bag. They will keep for several days, if not a week.

BASIC PREPARATION: The stem and seeds must be removed from a bell pepper before cooking. Use a paring knife to cut around the stem and then grasp hold of the green stem and pull out the core (with many seeds attached). Cut the pepper in half through the core end and scrape out any remaining seeds. Use a paring knife to remove any pithy white membranes on the inside of the pepper and then slice or chop as directed.

See page 252 for details on roasting peppers.

Because of their size, chile peppers are handled a bit differently. Start by cutting off a thin slice from the stem end. Next, halve the pepper through the stem end. If you like heat, don't bother scraping out the seeds, which contain much of the chile's spicy flavor. The chile can now be minced or sliced as needed.

Chile oil will easily transfer to your hands, and eventually your eyes or face if you don't wash your hands immediately after preparing a chile. It may be a good idea to wear rubber gloves when handling chiles. In any case, don't rub your eyes or nose, or touch your lips.

BEST COOKING METHODS: Baking (when stuffed), braising, broiling or grilling (to roast), sautéing, and stir-frying.

OTHER RECIPES WITH PEPPERS:
Sautéed Corn and Sweet Peppers (page 118)
Ratatouille (page 141)
Zucchini, Corn, and Red Pepper Sauté (page 375)

Sautéed Bell Peppers

A mixture of yellow, orange, and red peppers delivers the sweetest and best results. You can use a green pepper or two, but personally I don't like their bitter, vegetal flavor all that much. Balsamic vinegar highlights the sweetness of the peppers, while sharper sherry vinegar tames some of the sweetness.

SERVES 4 AS A SIDE DISH

2 tablespoons extra-virgin olive oil
4 medium bell peppers (about 1½ pounds), cored, seeded, and cut into ½-inch-wide strips
2 medium garlic cloves, minced
2 tablespoons balsamic or sherry vinegar
Salt
Freshly ground black pepper
8 large fresh basil leaves, cut into thin strips

1. Heat the oil in a large skillet. Add the peppers and sauté over medium-high heat until the peppers begin to brown in spots, about 4 minutes. Add the garlic, reduce the heat to low, and cover the pan. Cook, stirring once, until the peppers are tender but not mushy, about 10 minutes.
2. Uncover the pan, raise the heat to high, and add the vinegar. Cook just until the vinegar evaporates, about 1 minute. Season with salt and pepper to taste. Serve hot or at room temperature, garnishing with the basil just before serving.

Sautéed Bell Peppers with Greek Flavors

As with the previous dish, I prefer a mix of red, orange, and yellow peppers. Here, the strong flavors of garlic, lemon, black olives, and oregano contrast with the sweetness of the peppers.

SERVES 4 AS A SIDE DISH

2 tablespoons extra-virgin olive oil
4 medium bell peppers (about 1½ pounds), cored, seeded, and cut into ½-inch-wide strips
2 medium garlic cloves, minced
2 tablespoons lemon juice
8 large black olives, such as Kalamatas, pitted and chopped
1 teaspoon minced fresh oregano leaves
Freshly ground black pepper
2 ounces feta cheese, crumbled (about ½ cup)

1. Heat the oil in a large skillet. Add the peppers and sauté over medium-high heat until the peppers begin to brown in spots, about 4 minutes. Add the garlic, reduce the heat to low, and cover the pan. Cook, stirring once, until the peppers are tender but not mushy, about 10 minutes.
2. Uncover the pan and add the lemon juice, olives, and oregano. Cook just until the lemon juice evaporates, about 1 minute. Season with pepper to taste. Turn the peppers into a serving bowl. Serve hot or at room temperature, sprinkling with the cheese just before serving.

Stewed Peppers with Tomato and Onion (*Peperonata*)

Peppers cooked slowly with tomatoes and onions become tender and yielding, almost like roasted peppers but with far less work. These peppers are particularly good with scrambled eggs as well as with simply cooked chicken, fish, or pork that needs some moistening and added flavor. In fact, you can use peperonata as a combination vegetable side dish and sauce. If possible, use a mix of red, yellow, and orange peppers.

SERVES 4 TO 6 AS A SIDE DISH

- 3 tablespoons extra-virgin olive oil
- 2 medium onions, halved and sliced thin
- 4 medium bell peppers (about 1½ pounds), cored, seeded, and cut into 1-inch-wide strips
- 3 medium ripe tomatoes (about 1½ pounds), cored, peeled, seeded, and diced
- 1 teaspoon chopped fresh thyme leaves
  Salt
  Freshly ground black pepper

1. Heat the oil in a large sauté pan. Add the onions and peppers and sauté over medium heat until softened, about 6 minutes. Add the tomatoes, thyme, and salt and pepper to taste. Reduce the heat to medium-low, cover, and cook, stirring once or twice, until the peppers are tender, 15 to 20 minutes.

2. Uncover and simmer just until the juices from the tomatoes thicken a bit, about 5 minutes. (*Peperonata* should be saucy, so don't try to simmer off all the tomato juice.) Adjust the seasonings and serve hot or at room temperature.

Stuffed Peppers with Bulgur, Walnuts, and Lemon

Many stuffed pepper recipes are labor-intensive (my favorite recipe requires that you first make saffron risotto) or made heavy by cheese and bread crumb fillings. No-cook bulgur (soaking this cracked wheat in hot water softens the grains) makes a quick and light filling for peppers. Serve each pepper as a main course with a salad. Make sure to buy fine-grain bulgur, the same kind you would use to make tabbouleh.

SERVES 4 AS LIGHT MAIN COURSE

- 1¼ cups fine bulgur
- 4 tablespoons extra-virgin olive oil
- 2 tablespoons lemon juice
- ½ cup chicken or vegetable stock
- ½ cup walnuts, toasted in a dry skillet until fragrant, cooled, and chopped
- 3 tablespoons minced fresh parsley leaves
- 1 teaspoon ground cumin
  Salt
  Freshly ground black pepper
- 4 large red bell peppers (about 2 pounds)

1. Place the bulgur in a large bowl. Cover with hot water and soak until softened, about 20 minutes. Drain the bulgur. Combine the bulgur with 3 tablespoons of the oil as well as the lemon juice, stock, walnuts, parsley, cumin, and salt and pepper to taste.

2. Preheat the oven to 400 degrees.

3. Cut off and discard a ½-inch-thick slice from the top of each pepper, which should include the stem and most of the seeds. Scrape out any remaining seeds and white pith from the inside of each pepper.

4. With the remaining tablespoon of oil, grease a baking dish just large enough to hold the peppers. Divide the stuffing among the peppers. Place them, stuffed side up, in the dish. Cover the baking dish with foil.

5. Bake until the peppers are tender, about 40 minutes. Remove the dish from the oven, remove the foil, and let the filling settle for 5 minutes. Serve the peppers hot, warm, or at room temperature.

SIMPLE USES FOR ROASTED PEPPERS

Sliced or chopped roasted peppers can be added to salads, salsas, egg dishes, pasta sauces, or sandwiches. Pureed roasted peppers make an excellent spread or dip. If pureed with more liquid (such as oil, vinegar, cream, or stock), roasted peppers can be turned into a sauce or dressing.

Here are some specific recipes using roasted peppers, all of which are open to improvisation.

Roasted Peppers

This recipe (actually a technique) is best with red, yellow, and orange peppers. Don't roast green peppers (they are much too bitter for this purpose) or purple peppers (which turn green when cooked). If you have the grill lit for another reason, consider roasting the peppers outside as directed in the recipe that follows. Don't try roasting more than six peppers at once in the broiler. Most broilers are hottest in the center and peppers left at the edges of large baking sheets won't really cook properly. Better to roast a mess of peppers in batches, or turn to the grill, which can accommodate as many as twelve peppers at once.

1 to 6 red, yellow, or orange bell peppers

1. Adjust the oven rack to the top position and heat the broiler. Place the peppers on a rimmed, foil-lined baking sheet so that the peppers are an inch or two from the heating element. Broil, turning carefully several times with tongs and taking care not to puncture the peppers, until the skins are lightly charred but not ashen on all sides, about 15 minutes.

2. Place the charred peppers in a large bowl, cover the bowl with plastic wrap, and set the peppers aside to steam for about 10 minutes or until the skins pucker.

3. When cool enough to handle, peel the peppers with your fingers (although rinsing makes this job easier, it also washes away some flavor and should be avoided), then core and seed them, working over a large bowl to catch their juices.

Place the peppers in the bowl with the juices. Use immediately or cover the peppers with a film of extra-virgin olive oil and refrigerate in an air-tight container for up to 3 days.

Roasted Red Pepper Spread with Goat Cheese and Herbs

Excellent spread on pieces of bread or used as a dip for raw vegetables. This recipe can be doubled or even tripled for large parties.

MAKES ABOUT 1 CUP

2 medium red bell peppers (about ¾ pound), roasted, steamed, peeled, cored, and seeded (juices reserved)
3 ounces goat cheese
1 small garlic clove, peeled
6 large fresh basil leaves
   Salt
   Freshly ground black pepper

Puree the peppers and their juices along with the cheese, garlic, and basil in a food processor until smooth. Add salt and pepper to taste. (This spread can be refrigerated in an airtight container for several days.)

Roasted Red Pepper Spread with Near Eastern Flavors

This addictive spread is inspired by a recipe in Paula Wolfert's The Cooking of the Eastern Mediterranean, *the best cookbook on the cuisine of this region. The pomegranate molasses, which is available in Middle Eastern grocery shops and some gourmet stores, is essential here. Its sweet, sour, and musky flavor has no substitutes. This spread is ideal with toasted pita breads or pita chips. The recipe can be doubled or tripled.*

MAKES ABOUT 1¼ CUPS

2 medium red bell peppers (about ¾ pound), roasted, steamed, peeled, cored, and seeded (juices reserved)
½ cup walnuts, toasted in a dry skillet until fragrant
1 tablespoon pomegranate molasses
1 tablespoon extra-virgin olive oil
1 teaspoon lemon juice
¼ teaspoon ground cumin
   Salt

Puree the peppers and their juices along with the walnuts, pomegranate molasses, oil, lemon juice, and cumin in a food processor until smooth. Add salt to taste. (This spread can be refrigerated in an airtight container for several days.)

Peppers Roasted on the Grill

There is one potential pitfall when roasting peppers on the grill. If you turn them with a fork it's easy to puncture the peppers and cause them to loose precious juices. Roll the peppers around the grill with a spatula or turn them with tongs. Grilling is the best method for roasting a lot of peppers at once.

1 to 12 red, yellow, or orange bell peppers

1. Light a grill fire.
2. Place the peppers on the preheated grill and roast over a medium fire. Grill, turning carefully several times with tongs and taking care not to puncture the peppers, until the skins are lightly charred but not ashen on all sides, about 15 minutes.
3. Place the charred peppers in a large bowl, cover the bowl with plastic wrap, and set the peppers aside to steam for about 10 minutes or until the skins pucker.
4. When cool enough to handle, peel the peppers with your fingers (although rinsing makes this job easier, it also washes away some flavor and should be avoided), then core and seed them, working over a large bowl to catch their juices. Place the peppers in the bowl with the juices. Use immediately or cover the peppers with a film of extra-virgin olive oil and refrigerate in airtight container for up to 3 days.

Mozzarella and Roasted Pepper Sandwiches with Basil

Because they are so moist and juicy, roasted peppers are an excellent addition to sandwiches. They can take the place of a sandwich spread since they will moisten the bread. This is just one possible sandwich; roasted red peppers can be added to most any sandwich for flavor and moisture. Place roasted peppers on top of grilled bread to make bruschetta or use roasted peppers as a pizza topping. Use red, orange, and/or yellow peppers here.

SERVES 4 FOR LUNCH

1 pound fresh mozzarella cheese packed in water
4 crusty sandwich rolls or pieces of focaccia, split
2 medium bell peppers (about I pound), roasted, steamed, peeled, cored, seeded, and cut into thin strips (juices reserved)
8 large fresh basil leaves
Salt
Freshly ground black pepper

1. Remove the mozzarella from the water and pat it dry with paper towels. Cut the cheese into thin slices.
2. Cover the bottom piece of each roll with some roasted peppers and their juices. Layer the cheese and whole basil over the peppers. Sprinkle the

filling with salt and pepper to taste. Set the top of each roll in place, cut rolls in half, and serve immediately.

Roasted Peppers with Sherry Vinegar, Green Olives, and Capers

The sharp Spanish flavors in this dish work especially well with sweet roasted peppers. Arrange the peppers on a platter or just serve them in a tangle as part of an antipasto. The peppers are delicious served over slices of grilled, oiled bread.

SERVES 6 AS AN APPETIZER

2 medium red bell peppers (about ¾ pound), roasted, steamed, peeled, cored, seeded, and cut into 1-inch wide strips (juices reserved)

2 medium yellow bell peppers (about ¾ pound), roasted, steamed, peeled, cored, seeded, and cut into 1-inch wide strips (juices reserved)

1 tablespoon sherry vinegar

2 tablespoons extra-virgin olive oil

6 large green olives, pitted and chopped

1 tablespoon drained capers

1 tablespoon minced fresh parsley leaves

Salt

Freshly ground black pepper

Place the peppers and their juices in a large bowl. Add the vinegar, oil, olives, capers, parsley, and salt and pepper to taste. Serve immediately or cover and set aside at room temperature for several hours to allow the flavors to develop. The peppers may be refrigerated for several days. Bring to room temperature before serving.

Roasted Pepper Sauce for Pasta

Use a mix of red, yellow, and orange peppers here. Change the herb as you like.

ENOUGH FOR 1 POUND OF PASTA
(PREFERABLY FETTUCCINE)

6 medium bell peppers (about 2¼ pounds), roasted, steamed, peeled, cored, seeded, and cut into thin strips (juices reserved)

¼ cup extra-virgin olive oil

12 large fresh basil leaves, cut into thin strips

Salt

Freshly ground black pepper

Combine the roasted peppers and their juices in a large bowl with the oil, basil, and salt and pepper to taste. (The sauce can be covered and set aside for several hours before tossing with cooked and drained pasta.)

Roasted Peppers with Onion

This Mexican dish is called rajas, which translates as "strips." The tangle of roasted bell and poblano peppers (the two kinds of peppers should be roasted together; follow the directions on page 252) can be used in fajitas, with sliced flank steak and tortillas, served with eggs, or enjoyed on its own as a side dish with meat, chicken, or fish. Some versions are made with just dark green poblanos. I find that a couple of sweet red bell peppers contrast with the mildly spicy, vegetal flavor of the poblanos. The combination of red and green peppers also has visual appeal.

SERVES 4 TO 6 AS A SIDE DISH

2 tablespoons canola or other tasteless oil
1 medium onion, halved and sliced thin
2 medium garlic cloves, minced
5 medium poblano chiles (about 1 pound), roasted, steamed, peeled, cored, seeded, and cut into thin strips (juices reserved)
2 medium red bell peppers (about ¾ pound), roasted, steamed, peeled, cored, seeded, and cut into thin strips (juices reserved)
½ teaspoon dried oregano
   Salt
1 tablespoon lime juice

1. Heat the oil in a large skillet. Add the onion and sauté over medium-high heat until lightly browned, about 8 minutes. Add the garlic and cook until golden, about 1 minute.

2. Add the peppers and their juices along with the oregano and salt to taste. Stir-cook just until the peppers are heated through and evenly seasoned, about 1 minute. Add the lime juice and adjust the seasonings. Serve hot, warm, or at room temperature.

Roasted Red Pepper Soup with Basil Cream

This chilled, pureed soup captures the full flavor of roasted red peppers with a minimum of distractions. Some shallots are added for sweetness, a little paprika for color and additional pepper flavor, and mild potatoes for texture. However, each spoonful tastes squarely of roasted peppers. The basil cream (just pureed sour cream or yogurt and basil) adds a tangy contrast to the soup.

SERVES 6 AS A FIRST COURSE

2 tablespoons extra-virgin olive oil
4 medium shallots, minced
6 medium red bell peppers (about 2¼ pounds), roasted, steamed, peeled, cored, seeded, and cut into ½-inch-wide strips (juices reserved)
1 teaspoon sweet paprika
2 medium russet potatoes (about 1 pound), peeled and diced
4 cups chicken or vegetable stock

Salt

½ cup sour cream or plain yogurt

15 large fresh basil leaves

1 tablespoon milk, as needed

1. Heat the oil in a large saucepan. Add the shallots and sauté over medium heat until golden, about 4 minutes. Add the peppers and their juices and the paprika and sauté for 1 minute. Add the potatoes, stock, and salt to taste. Bring to a boil, cover, reduce the heat, and simmer until the potatoes fall apart, about 20 minutes.

2. Puree the soup in batches in a blender until smooth. Transfer the soup to a container and cool to room temperature. Adjust the seasonings. Cover the container and refrigerate the soup until well chilled, at least 4 hours or overnight.

3. When ready to serve, puree the sour cream and basil in a blender until smooth, scraping down the sides as necessary. If the basil refuses to liquefy, add the milk and continue to whip the sour cream and basil into a smooth, light green sauce. Ladle the chilled soup into individual bowls and swirl some of the basil cream into each bowl. Serve immediately.

Plantains

Plantains are increasingly available in supermarkets, even those with few Latino shoppers. There is a good reason for this trend. Plantains are delicious and remarkably easy to prepare. Although technically a fruit, we treat plantains as a vegetable.

At first glance plantains look like standard sweet bananas, but they are a bit larger and have more pronounced ridges. Unlike sweet bananas, plantains are sold individually, not in bunches.

Like sweet bananas, plantains pass through several stages of ripeness. Green plantains are very firm and starchy, almost like a root vegetable or potato. They are best fried or stewed in plenty of liquid. They have a pleasantly starchy flavor but are not at all sweet.

As the plantain ripens, the skin becomes yellow, then brown, then black. At each stage, the flesh becomes sweeter and more banana-like, but unlike a sweet banana the flesh remains firm. Even the blackest plantain will be firm and a bit starchy. Plantains, no matter how ripe, are always cooked.

Once peeled, the flesh will be cream-colored and look a lot like a sweet banana. Occasionally, I see plantains with a pale-orange flesh but you cannot pick out this variety by looking at the skin and it tastes the same as the cream-colored flesh.

OTHER COMMON NAMES: Plátanos.

AVAILABILITY: Year-round.

SELECTION: Plantains come in various shades of green, yellow, brown, and black. All are the same plant, just in different stages of ripeness. Like bananas, plantains are picked green and will slowly ripen over the course of several weeks. You can catch plantains at various stages in their ripening process. Buy green plantains and cook them that day or wait until they are ripe. Black plantains should be cooked within a day or two of their purchase, so plan accordingly. Plantains are remarkably sturdy. Unless they look damaged or cracked, they are fine. Remember, the blackest plantains offer some of the best eating.

STORAGE: Plantains should be stored at room temperature in order to allow ripening to proceed. Green plantains will eventually blacken and ripen on the counter, although this process may take a week or more. Once plantains have reached the desired stage of ripeness, they can be held in the refrigerator for several days. Cold temperatures will prevent further ripening.

BASIC PREPARATION: Although a plantain looks like a banana, it is a bit trickier to skin. On green plantains, the peel is firmly attached to the flesh. Even on ripe plantains, the skin often won't peel away from end to end like a banana.

Start by trimming the pointed ends from the plantain. (I often cut the plantains into manageable chunks at this point, but this step is not mandatory.) Next, slit the skin from one cut end to the other cut end with a paring knife. You want to cut through the skin but not into the flesh. Make one slit on each side of the plantain. Starting at one end, lift up a piece of the peel and carefully strip it from the flesh. Repeat the process, stripping the skin away from the flesh in long pieces. Once peeled, the chunks can be sliced as directed.

BEST COOKING METHODS: Green plantains are best fried or cut into chunks and cooked in stews or soups. Ripe plantains can be baked, grilled, or sautéed.

Sautéed Plantains

Chunks of ripe plantains are sautéed until dark brown and then seasoned with a little minced cilantro, a sprinkle of salt, and a squirt of lime juice—unbelievably simple and delicious. Use only the ripest, black or mostly black plantains for this recipe. Serve sweet sautéed plantains with pork or chicken, or with rice and beans for a typical Caribbean meal.

SERVES 4 AS A SIDE DISH

2 large ripe plantains (yellowish black or black)
3 tablespoons canola or other tasteless oil
1 tablespoon minced fresh cilantro leaves
  Salt
  Lime wedges

1. Trim the pointed ends from the plantains. Cut the plantains into 2-inch chunks. Use a paring knife to slit the skin lengthwise in several places on each piece. Carefully remove the skin with your fingers and discard it. Cut each 2-inch chunk in half lengthwise.
2. Heat the oil in a large nonstick skillet. Add the plantains and cook, turning once, over medium heat until quite browned but not burned, about 8 minutes. Transfer the plantains to a platter, sprinkle with the cilantro and salt to taste, and serve immediately with the lime wedges.

Baked Plantains

Most Caribbean cooks fry or sauté plantains. However, ripe plantains can be baked right in their skins. Baked plantains seasoned with butter, hot sauce, lime juice, and salt and are the perfect accompaniment to roast pork, grilled fish, or chicken. Plantains are quite rich and I find that half a large plantain is enough for one serving. However, hearty eaters may want a whole plantain. Adjust this recipe, baking as many plantains as you like. Don't try this recipe with underripe green plantains. The flesh will be dry and unpleasantly starchy.

SERVES 2 TO 4 AS A SIDE DISH

2 large ripe plantains (yellowish black or black)
  Butter
  Salt
  Tabasco or other hot sauce, optional
  Lime wedges

1. Preheat the oven to 425 degrees.
2. Prick the plantains in several places with a fork. Place the plantains on a foil-lined baking sheet and bake until tender when skewered with the tip of a paring knife, about 20 minutes.
3. To serve, split each plantain in half crosswise to yield four pieces total. Slit open each piece as if opening a baked potato. Use a fork to lightly mash the tender flesh. Season with a pat of butter, a generous sprinkle of salt, and a drop or two of hot sauce if desired. Serve immediately with the lime wedges.

Grilled Plantains with Citrus Glaze

Ripe plantains take extremely well to the grill. You could serve them as is (seasoned with just salt), but I like to brush a not-too-sweet citrus glaze over the pieces when they are almost done. (Don't brush on the glaze earlier, or it will burn.) Grilled plantains are great with grilled pork, beef, or chicken.

SERVES 4 AS A SIDE DISH

½ cup orange juice
2 tablespoons lime juice
1 tablespoon brown sugar
2 large ripe plantains (yellowish black or black)
1 tablespoon canola or other tasteless oil
Salt

1. Light a grill fire.
2. Combine the orange juice, lime juice, and brown sugar in a small saucepan. Bring to a boil, stirring to dissolve the sugar. Simmer until the mixture thickens to the consistency of a thin syrup, about 3 minutes. Remove from the heat and set aside.
3. Trim the pointed ends from the plantains. Cut the plantains into 3-inch chunks. Use a paring knife to slit the skin lengthwise in several places on each piece. Carefully remove the skin with your fingers and discard it. Cut each 3-inch chunk in half lengthwise. Toss the plantains, oil, and salt to taste in a large bowl.

4. Grill the plantains over a medium-hot fire, turning once, until browned, about 7 minutes. Brush the glaze over the plantains and continue to grill, turning once, until richly colored, about 2 minutes. (It's fine if the plantains blacken in spots.) Serve immediately.

Fried Green Plantains

This dish, called tostones, *is served in Puerto Rico, Cuba, the Dominican Republic, and elsewhere in the Caribbean. Thick green plantain rounds are fried, flattened, and fried again. (The same technique is used with potatoes—frying at a lower temperature to cook through, then frying at a higher temperature to brown.) These smashed rounds can be served with pork roast, chicken, or stews. In hip Latino restaurants,* tostones *are dolloped with crème fraîche and caviar. The combination of crisp exterior and tender flesh (think steak fries, only better) is addictive.*

SERVES 4 AS A SIDE DISH

2 large green plantains
About 4 cups peanut or vegetable oil for frying
Coarse salt

1. Slice off the narrow tip from each end of the plantains. Slit the skin lengthwise in several places. Carefully remove the skin with your fingers and discard it. Slice the flesh on the bias into ½-inch-thick rounds.

2. Heat 1½ inches of oil in a deep, 4-quart saucepan to 325 degrees. Add the plantain rounds and fry until golden, about 4 minutes. Use a slotted spoon to transfer the plantain rounds to a platter lined with paper towels. Turn off the heat but do not discard the oil.

3. When the plantains are cool enough to handle, crush each round with the flat end of a rolling pin or the bottom of skillet until it is about ¼ inch thick.

4. Heat the oil to 375 degrees. Add about half the smashed plantain rounds, making sure not to crowd the pan, and fry until deep golden brown and crisp, about 4 minutes. Use a slotted spoon to transfer the plantain rounds to a platter lined with clean paper towels. Repeat the process with the remaining rounds. Sprinkle with salt and serve hot.

Plantain Chips

Throughout Latin America, green plantains are sliced very thin and fried to make potato-like chips. Make sure to use firm plantains, to slice them thin (the food processor is best for this), and then to fry them in small batches. Add the sliced plantain pieces to the hot oil one at a time so they don't stick together.

2 large green plantains
About 4 cups peanut or vegetable oil for frying
Coarse salt

1. Slice off the narrow tip from each end of the plantains. Slit the skin lengthwise in several places. Carefully remove the skin with your fingers and discard it. Using the slicing disk on a food processor, cut the peeled plantains into very thin rounds between $1/16$ and $1/8$ inch thick.

2. Heat 1½ inches of oil in a deep, 4-quart saucepan to 375 degrees. Add the plantain slices one at time so they don't stick together, and fry, stirring once in a while to make sure the chips don't stick together, until golden brown and crisp, 2 to 3 minutes. Don't crowd the pan; fry only as many slices as fit comfortably in the pan. Use a slotted spoon to transfer the chips to a brown paper bag or a platter lined with paper towels. Repeat the process with the remaining chips. While still hot, sprinkle the fried chips with salt to taste. Serve warm or at room temperature.

Potatoes

The potato is America's most popular vegetable and with good reason. There's hardly a way you can't cook potatoes and they almost always taste great. When shopping for potatoes keep in mind that different potatoes have different uses. Basically potatoes are divided into three groups based on their starch content.

BAKING POTATOES: These potatoes have the most starch and cook up dry and fluffy. They are ideal for baking or mashing but tend to fall apart when used in salads or when stewed. Russet potatoes (also called Idahos) are the most commonly sold.

BOILING POTATOES: These least starchy potatoes have a waxy, firm texture when cooked, ideal for salads or roasting. All red-skinned potatoes are boiling potatoes.

ALL-PURPOSE POTATOES: These potatoes have less starch than baking potatoes but more starch than boiling potatoes. When cooked, they share some of the traits of both types of potatoes, only to lesser degrees. All-purpose potatoes can be baked, but the texture won't be quite dry and fluffy. They can be roasted as well but they will look a bit ragged, although not as much as russet potatoes.

Yukon Golds are the most famous all-purpose potato. With their buttery flavor and golden appearance, they are good for baking or mashing, although the texture of russet potatoes is better in these dishes. Yukon Golds work very well in potato pancakes or gratins. You can use them in place of red potatoes when roasting, but I would not use Yukon Golds in salads or other recipes where firm texture is a consideration.

Despite what some markets say, red and new potatoes are not the same thing. Occasionally potatoes are harvested before they have developed their full complement of starch. These new potatoes can come from any of the three categories mentioned above. However, these potatoes are always waxy, even if they are a high-starch variety.

Although all new potatoes are small, not all small potatoes are new. If the skin feels thin and you can rub it off with your fingers, you are holding a new potato. New potatoes have a lot of moisture and their flesh is almost juicy when cut.

AVAILABILITY: Year-round.

SELECTION: Choose firm potatoes with no signs of sprouting. Potatoes with a greenish tinge beneath the skin have had too much exposure to light and should be avoided.

STORAGE: Keep potatoes in a cool, well-ventilated spot out of the sun. New potatoes should be used within a week, while other varieties should hold for weeks. Refrigeration speeds up the softening and sprouting process. Potatoes will be fine for a week or so in the refrigerator, but they won't keep as long as potatoes stored in a cool pantry.

BASIC PREPARATION: If you plan on cooking potatoes with their skins on, scrub them under cold, running water to remove any dirt. If you are removing the skin, do so with a vegetable peeler and then rinse the peeled potato.

BEST COOKING METHODS: Baking, boiling, braising, frying, and roasting.

OTHER RECIPES WITH POTATOES:
Roasted Artichokes and New Potatoes (page 4)
Crisp Beet and Potato Cake (page 31)
Mashed Celery Root and Potatoes (page 99)
Corn Chowder with Leeks and Potatoes (page 122)
Corn Chowder with Bacon, Leeks, and Potatoes (page 123)
Indian Eggplant and Potato Stew with Chickpeas (page 141)
Spring Vegetable Ragout with Fava Beans (page 156)
Roasted Garlic and Potato Soup (page 167)
Green Beans and Potatoes with Aioli (page 176)
Leek and Potato Soup (page 197)
Creamy Leek and Potato Soup (page 198)
Sorrel and Potato Soup (page 301)
Pureed Turnips (page 344)

Classic Mashed Potatoes

Simple and delicious. Make sure to warm the milk (a microwave is perfect for this job) and to mash the potatoes back in the empty saucepan set over low heat so they dry out a bit.

SERVES 4 AS A SIDE DISH

2 pounds russet potatoes, peeled and cut into 1-inch chunks
Salt
3 tablespoons unsalted butter, softened and cut into several pieces
⅓ cup milk, warmed

1. Place the potatoes in a large saucepan and add enough water to cover by about 2 inches. Add a generous amount of salt and bring the water to a boil. Reduce the heat slightly and cook until the potatoes are tender, about 15 minutes. Drain the potatoes.
2. Return the potatoes to the empty saucepan set over the warm burner. Add the butter and use a potato masher to turn the potatoes into fine bits. Beat in the milk and salt to taste with a wooden spoon. Serve immediately.

VARIATIONS: BUTTERMILK MASHED POTATOES

Nonfat buttermilk gives mashed potatoes the mouth feel of buttery mashed potatoes. It also gives the potatoes a pleasant tang. This recipe contains only a mod-est amount of fat, so you can make mashed potatoes as often as you want without guilt.

Reduce the amount of butter to 1 tablespoon and replace the milk with ½ cup warmed buttermilk.

GARLIC AND ROSEMARY MASHED POTATOES

The garlic flavor is fairly mild since the cloves are cooked along with the potatoes.

Cook four peeled garlic cloves with the potatoes. Drain the potatoes and garlic and return them to the saucepan. Mash with 4 tablespoons olive oil and 1 teaspoon minced fresh rosemary. (Omit the butter and milk.) Season with salt and serve.

PARMESAN MASHED POTATOES

Buttery, nutty-tasting Parmesan blends easily into mashed potatoes and gives them a great flavor. For the best results, use only the finest Parmigiano-Reggiano.

Replace the butter with ½ cup grated Parmesan cheese and increase the amount of milk to ½ cup.

Mashed Potato Croquettes

With two children in my house, I'm always making mashed potatoes. Occasionally, I have leftovers.

When that happens, this is what my wife and I have for lunch the next day. Mashed potatoes can be refrigerated for up to 2 days in an airtight container. The mashed potatoes must be cold to form proper croquettes.

SERVES 2 FOR LUNCH

½ cup Fresh Bread Crumbs (page 109)
2 tablespoons minced fresh parsley leaves
Salt
Freshly ground black pepper
1 large egg
1⅓ cups cold mashed potatoes
2 tablespoons extra-virgin olive oil

1. Combine the bread crumbs, parsley, and salt and pepper to taste in a shallow bowl. Beat the egg with a fork in another shallow bowl.
2. Take ⅓ cup of the mashed potatoes and shape it into a 3-inch cake. Dip the potato cake in the beaten egg, letting the excess egg drip back into the bowl. Dredge the potato cake in the seasoned bread crumbs, patting the crumbs into the potatoes as necessary. Repeat with the remaining potatoes to form a total of four cakes.
3. Heat 1 tablespoon of the oil in a medium nonstick skillet over medium heat. When the oil is hot, add the potato croquettes. Cook until golden brown on the bottom, about 4 minutes. Carefully flip the croquettes and then drizzle the remaining 1 tablespoon oil down the sides of the pan. Cook until the cakes are golden brown on the second side, about 4 minutes. Serve immediately.

Baked Potatoes

As simple as you can get, but still delicious. Don't ever wrap potatoes in foil as they bake. They steam and the skin becomes mushy and inedible. I usually season baked potatoes with salt and butter, but you can top them with sour cream, plain yogurt, grated cheese, crumbled bacon, minced chives, or most anything that appeals to you.

SERVES 4 AS A SIDE DISH

4 medium russet potatoes (about 2 pounds), scrubbed
Salt
Unsalted butter

1. Preheat the oven to 400 degrees.
2. Use a fork to prick each potato in several places so that steam can escape in the oven. (I have had an unpricked potato "explode" in the oven, so don't skip this step.) Bake until the potatoes are tender when pierced a skewer, about 1 hour.
3. Slit open the potatoes lengthwise and push on the sides to loosen the flesh. Sprinkle with salt to taste and add a pat of butter to each potato. Serve immediately.

Creamy Twice-Baked Potatoes

This simplified version of an American classic relies on yogurt for creaminess rather than the traditional sour cream and butter. The result is a dish that is low in fat but high in flavor. Thanks to my colleagues at Cook's Illustrated, Adam Ried and Anne Yamanaka, for tips about how to handle the potatoes in this dish. A note about the serving yield. In my family, my wife and I each eat two potato shells and my daughters split the other potato. If you are serving a lot of food, you can get away with one potato shell per person—the filling is creamy and rich-tasting, after all. Of course, two shells (or one potato) per adult is not unreasonable either.

SERVES 3 TO 6 AS A SIDE DISH

3 russet potatoes (about 8 ounces each), scrubbed
  Canola oil for coating the potatoes
⅔ cup plain yogurt
½ cup shredded Cheddar cheese
2 medium scallions, sliced thin
  Salt
  Freshly ground black pepper

1. Preheat the oven to 400 degrees.
2. Lightly rub the potatoes with the oil and place them on a small baking sheet. Use a fork to prick each potato in several places so that steam can escape in the oven. Bake the potatoes until the skin is crisp and the potatoes feel cooked through when lightly squeezed, about 1 hour. (Do not test the potatoes with a skewer; you don't want to pierce the skin again.) Remove the potatoes from the oven and heat the broiler.
3. Wearing oven mitts to protect your hands, cut the potatoes in half lengthwise. Scoop out the flesh with a spoon, making sure not to pierce the skin. (It's wise to leave a little of the flesh attached to the skin to prevent this.) Place the flesh in a large bowl and return the empty potato shells, interior facing up, to the baking sheet.
4. Mash the potato flesh with a potato masher or a large fork. Stir in the yogurt, cheese, and scallions. Add salt and pepper to taste. Spoon the potato mixture back into the potato shells, mounding it slightly above each potato shell.
5. Place the baking sheet with the filled potato shells on the top oven rack, 2 to 3 inches below the broiler. Broil until the potato filling begins to brown, 5 to 7 minutes. Serve immediately.

Oven Fries

Thick potato wedges will become crisp if oiled lightly and cooked in a hot oven. There are two "tricks" to this recipe. First, preheat a large baking sheet in the oven as it comes up to temperature so that the potatoes sizzle when they are placed in the pan. Second, don't turn the potatoes too much. You want them to stay in place long enough to really brown. This means one turn, preferably with a pair of tongs rather than a fork. These "fries" are surprisingly crisp and are a great accompaniment for burgers.

SERVES 4 AS A SIDE DISH

4 medium russet potatoes (about 2 pounds), scrubbed
3 tablespoons extra-virgin olive oil
Salt

1. Place a large rimmed baking sheet in the oven. Preheat the oven to 425 degrees.

2. Meanwhile, cut the potatoes in quarters lengthwise and then cut the quarters lengthwise into ½-inch-thick wedges. Toss the potato wedges with 2 tablespoons of the oil and salt to taste in a large bowl.

3. When the oven has come up to temperature, carefully brush the remaining tablespoon of oil evenly over the baking sheet. Dump the potatoes onto the oiled sheet and spread them apart so that each potato wedge is in direct contact with the baking sheet.

4. Bake for 25 minutes. Using a pair of tongs, turn each potato wedge. Continue baking until quite brown and crisp, about 25 minutes longer. Season with more salt if desired and serve immediately.

VARIATION: SPICY OVEN FRIES

Toss the potato wedges with the oil and salt to taste as directed, adding ½ teaspoon cayenne pepper and 1 teaspoon sweet paprika along with the salt. Make sure to mix well to distribute the spices evenly among the potato wedges.

French Fries

Nothing is better or more satisfying than good french fries. Despite what you might think, the best fries are made at home. In restaurants, fries often sit around and become soggy. At home, you can eat fries as soon as they come out of the oil. Don't skip the soaking and drying steps—the potatoes will spit hot fat if you do—and try to use kosher or another coarse salt here. Also, don't try frying the potatoes just once. Double-frying ensures that the fries are cooked through, crisp, and not greasy. I find that peanut oil works best for deep-frying and tastes delicious; however, corn oil is a close second. Make sure to fry in batches—the oil will stay safely in the pot when small batches of potatoes are added and the potatoes cook up crisper and are less greasy.

SERVES 4 AS A SIDE DISH

4 medium russet potatoes (about 2 pounds), scrubbed or peeled
About 6 cups peanut oil for frying
Salt, preferably kosher or other coarse salt

1. Cut the potatoes from end to end into ovals between ¼ and ⅛ inch thick. Slice the ovals

lengthwise to yield long, slender strips between ¼ and ⅛ inch thick. Place the potatoes in a large bowl of ice water and soak for 30 minutes. Drain and pat dry to remove every drop of moisture.

2. Pour about 2 inches of oil in a deep 4½- to 5-quart saucepan. Turn the heat to medium-high and heat the oil to 325 degrees.

3. Add about one quarter of the potatoes to the hot oil, making sure not to crowd the pan, and cook until they begin to color, about 3 minutes. (Adjust the heat as necessary as the potatoes cook; the temperature should not rise above 325 degrees, nor should it drop below 290 degrees.) Use a skimmer or slotted spoon to transfer the fries to a platter lined with paper towels or a brown paper bag. Repeat the process with the remaining fries. Let the fries cool completely, at least 15 minutes and for up to 1 hour. (Turn off the heat but keep the oil in the pot.)

4. Reheat the oil to 365 degrees. Add about one quarter of the fries, making sure not to crowd the pan, and cook until golden brown, about 2 minutes. Use a skimmer or slotted spoon to transfer the fries to a platter lined with clean paper towels or a second brown paper bag. Sprinkle with salt and serve immediately. Repeat with the remaining fries.

Purest Potato Pancake

I love small potato pancakes made from a batter enriched with eggs, matzo meal, and other seasonings (see below). However, for pure potato flavor, I often cook shredded potatoes into a single, thin, crisp, over-sized pancake. The only seasonings are salt and some butter in the pan. This pancake should be cut into wedges and served alongside slices of meat or with roast chicken or fish.

SERVES 4 TO 6 AS A SIDE DISH

  2 pounds russet potatoes
1½ teaspoons salt
  2 tablespoons unsalted butter

1. Peel the potatoes. Using the shredding disk on the food processor or the large holes on a box grater, cut the potatoes into thin shreds. Toss the potatoes with the salt in a medium bowl.

2. Heat 1 tablespoon butter in a 10-inch non-stick skillet. When the foam subsides, distribute the potatoes evenly in the pan. Use a spatula to press down on the potatoes to form a compact circle. Cook over medium heat, occasionally pressing down on the potatoes with a spatula, until the underside is crisp and nicely browned, 10 to 12 minutes.

3. Slide the pancake onto a large plate. Invert the pancake onto a second large plate. Add the remaining tablespoon of butter to the pan and heat briefly. Slide the pancake, browned side up, back into the pan. Cook until the second side is nicely browned, about 10 minutes. Slide the pancake on a large plate, cut it into wedges, and serve immediately.

Latkes

Everyone I know has a favorite latkes recipe. This creamy potato pancake is popular among descendants of Eastern European Jews in this country. In many families, it is a must at Hanukkah. I find that many latkes are soggy and leaden. I prefer something a bit more crisp, especially around the edges. Squeezing the shredded potatoes to remove excess moisture is the trick. The potatoes and minced onion are enriched with eggs and then bound with some matzo meal. Of course, the oil must be hot. It should really shimmer before you add any of the batter. If you like, test the oil by adding a cube of bread; it should sizzle immediately and brown in less than a minute. This recipe makes sixteen medium-sized latkes, enough for four to six people in my house, served with either applesauce or sour cream. If you own a small food processor, you may need to grate the potatoes in batches. An 11-cup model can accommodate 2 pounds of potatoes.

SERVES 4 TO 6 AS AN APPETIZER OR SIDE DISH

2 pounds russet potatoes, peeled

1 medium onion, peeled and quartered

2 large eggs, lightly beaten

¼ cup matzo meal

1½ teaspoons salt

Freshly ground black pepper

About 1 cup vegetable or peanut oil for frying

1. Slice the potatoes lengthwise into chunks small enough to fit through the feed tube in a food processor. Grate the potatoes with the shredding blade attachment of a food processor. Transfer the grated potatoes to a mesh strainer set over a large bowl. Squeeze the potatoes with your hands to extract as much liquid as possible. (You should be able to squeeze out at least ½ cup of liquid.) Discard the liquid and then place the drained potatoes in the bowl. (There's no need to wash the bowl.)

2. Fit the food processor with the metal blade and mince the onion. Add the onion to the bowl with the potatoes. Stir in the eggs, matzo meal, and the salt and pepper to taste.

3. Heat ¼ inch of oil in a large skillet until quite hot. When the oil is shimmering, generously fill a metal ¼ cup measure with the potato mixture. Carefully drop the potato mixture into the oil, pressing down lightly with the back of the metal measuring cup to shape the mixture into a 3-inch pancake. Repeat until the pan is filled with four or five latkes. Fry, turning once, until deep golden brown and crisp, 5 to 6 minutes. (Don't pull the latkes from the pan too early; you want them as crisp as possible without burning.)

4. Transfer the latkes to a platter lined with paper towels. Serve hot. Repeat the process with the remaining batter, leaving behind any liquid that leaches out of potatoes in the bowl and adding more oil to the skillet as needed.

Simplest Potato Gratin

This French recipe highlights the creaminess and starchiness of potatoes. Thinly sliced potatoes are bound together with cheese and cream to form a rich "cake" that is the perfect accompaniment to a special roast. The recipe depends on thinly sliced potatoes. Use a mandoline or a sharp chef's knife to ensure that the potatoes are cut properly. This dish is rich, so a little goes a long way.

SERVES 6 TO 8 AS A SIDE DISH

1 large garlic clove, crushed and peeled
1 tablespoon unsalted butter
2 pounds russet potatoes, scrubbed and cut crosswise into ⅛-inch-thick rounds
Salt
Freshly ground black pepper
6 ounces Gruyère cheese, shredded (about 1½ cups)
1 cup heavy cream, warmed

1. Preheat the oven to 375 degrees.
2. Rub the garlic clove around the inside of 9-inch cake pan or gratin dish. Smear the butter around the bottom and sides of the dish. Layer one quarter of the potato slices into the dish so that the slices overlap slightly. Sprinkle with salt and pepper to taste and ¼ cup of the cheese. Drizzle ¼ cup of the cream over the potatoes, making sure to coat each potato slice. Repeat two more times. For the fourth and final layer, arrange the remaining potatoes, sprinkle with salt and pepper to taste as well as the remaining ¾ cup cheese. Drizzle the remaining ¼ cup cream over the top.
3. Bake, uncovered, until the top layer of potatoes is crisp and nicely browned, about 50 minutes. Let settle for several minutes, then cut into small wedges and serve immediately.

Roasted Potatoes with Rosemary and Garlic

There are three keys to making good roast potatoes. First, use creamy red potatoes, which will hold their shape during the long cooking time. Second, leave the potatoes alone as they roast, turning them just once, so that the exterior of each potato cube can develop a thick brown crust. Lastly, add the seasonings, especially garlic, when the potatoes are almost done to prevent them from burning and tasting bitter.

SERVES 4 AS A SIDE DISH

1½ pounds red potatoes, scrubbed and cut into 1-inch chunks
3 tablespoons extra-virgin olive oil
4 medium garlic cloves, minced
1 tablespoon minced fresh rosemary leaves
1 teaspoon salt

1. Preheat the oven to 425 degrees.
2. Place the potatoes on a large rimmed baking sheet. Drizzle 1½ tablespoons of oil over the potatoes and toss with your hands to coat them evenly.

3. Place the baking sheet in the oven. Roast the potatoes, turning once, until golden brown, about 45 minutes.

4. Meanwhile, combine the remaining 1½ tablespoons of oil in a small bowl with the garlic, rosemary, and salt. Remove the potatoes from the oven. Drizzle this mixture over the potatoes, turn the potatoes to coat them with the seasoned oil, and return the baking sheet to the oven. Bake until the potatoes are have absorbed the seasoned oil and become crisp, about 5 minutes longer.

5. Transfer the potatoes to a serving bowl and serve immediately.

Roasted Potato Salad with Mustard-Balsamic Vinaigrette

This potato salad works better with grilled summer foods than the standard recipe with mayonnaise. The dressing, which contains olive oil, balsamic and red wine vinegars, and mustard, is far lighter than mayonnaise. Make sure to use both kinds of vinegar here. The balsamic adds some sweetness, while the red wine vinegar gives the salad a sharp, acidic flavor.

SERVES 6 AS A SIDE DISH

2 pounds red potatoes, scrubbed and cut into 1-inch chunks

6 tablespoons extra-virgin olive oil

1 tablespoon balsamic vinegar

2 teaspoons red wine vinegar

2 teaspoons Dijon mustard
 Salt

¼ cup snipped fresh chives

1. Preheat the oven to 425 degrees.

2. Place the potatoes on a large rimmed baking sheet. Drizzle 1½ tablespoons of the oil over the potatoes and toss with your hands to coat them evenly.

3. Place the baking sheet in the oven. Roast the potatoes, turning once, until golden brown, about 45 minutes.

4. Meanwhile, whisk the vinegars, mustard, and salt to taste in a small bowl. Whisk in the remaining 4½ tablespoons oil until smooth. Adjust the seasonings.

5. Transfer the roasted potatoes to a large bowl. Rewhisk the dressing and drizzle it over the potatoes. Sprinkle with the chives and mix well. Adjust the seasonings and serve warm or at room temperature.

Creamy Potato Salad with Southwestern Flavors

There are times when you want a creamy potato salad. However, to keep all that mayonnaise from dominating the dish, I like to add sparkle with some chipotle chiles, lime juice, and cilantro. I have borrowed the idea of sprinkling the warm potatoes with something acidic and salt and pepper from my friend Pam Anderson. The potatoes pick up these flavors best when still warm.

SERVES 6 AS A SIDE DISH

2 pounds red potatoes, scrubbed
¼ cup lime juice
   Salt
   Freshly ground black pepper
½ cup mayonnaise
1 chipotle chile in adobo sauce, minced with
   1 teaspoon sauce
4 medium scallions, sliced thin
2 tablespoons minced fresh cilantro leaves

1. Place the potatoes in a large saucepan. Cover with cold water and bring to a boil. Reduce the heat and simmer until a skewer glides easily through the potatoes, 15 to 20 minutes depending on the size of the potatoes. Drain and cool slightly. Slip off the skins with your fingers and discard. Cut the potatoes into ¼-inch-thick rounds. As you work, place the sliced, peeled potatoes in a large bowl and sprinkle with a little lime juice (using a total of 2 tablespoons for all the potatoes) and salt and pepper to taste. Cool to room temperature.

2. Add the mayonnaise, the remaining 2 tablespoons lime juice, the chipotle chile, scallions, and cilantro. Toss gently to coat the potatoes with the dressing. Serve immediately. (The salad is best served right away but can be refrigerated for several hours. Bring to room temperature before serving.)

Boiled New Potatoes with Butter and Chives

Freshly dug new potatoes have so much flavor they can be boiled in their skins and then just tossed with butter and chives. Don't peel the potatoes or they will become soggy.

SERVES 4 TO 6 AS A SIDE DISH

2 pounds small new potatoes, scrubbed
1½ tablespoons unsalted butter
2 tablespoons snipped fresh chives
   Salt

1. Place the potatoes in a large saucepan and add enough water to cover them by several inches. Bring the water to a boil over high heat. When the water starts to bubble, lower the heat to medium to keep the water at a moderate boil. Cook until a skewer slides easily through the largest potato, 15 to 20 minutes, depending on the size of the potatoes.

2. Drain the potatoes well and return them to the empty saucepan. Cook over medium heat to drive off some excess water, about 30 seconds. Add the butter and chives. Cook, stirring to coat the potatoes well, until the butter has melted. Add salt to taste and serve immediately.

Stewed Summer Potatoes with Tomato

In August, farmers where I live on Long Island begin to pull "new" potatoes from the ground. These small round nuggets meld well with the other flavors of the season. In this dish, these small potatoes have been braised with tomatoes, onion, and herbs. The resulting dish is perfect for those cool nights at the end of the summer. I especially like these juicy potatoes with scrambled eggs or a frittata for a light supper.

SERVES 6 AS A SIDE DISH

3 tablespoons extra-virgin olive oil
1 medium onion, halved and sliced thin
1 pound ripe tomatoes, cored, peeled, seeded, and chopped
1 teaspoon minced fresh rosemary leaves
1 teaspoon minced fresh oregano leaves
1 teaspoon minced fresh thyme leaves
   Salt
   Freshly ground black pepper
2 pounds small new potatoes (no larger than a golf ball), halved
½ cup water

1. Heat the oil in a large sauté pan. Add the onion and cook over medium heat until golden, about 6 minutes. Add the tomatoes, herbs, and salt and pepper to taste. Cook just until the tomatoes soften, about 3 minutes.

2. Add the potatoes and water. Cover the pan and cook over medium heat, stirring once or twice, until the potatoes are tender, about 20 minutes. Adjust the seasonings and serve hot or warm.

Pan-Cooked New Potatoes with Garlic and Rosemary

Small new potatoes, or fingerlings that have been cut into 1-inch cubes, are best in this recipe. You want a firm, waxy potato that will hold its shape during the two-step cooking process. The potatoes are stewed with a little water in a covered pan just until soft. The cover is removed, the liquid is allowed to evaporate, and the potatoes will crisp up and brown. The best "home fries" imaginable.

SERVES 4 AS A SIDE DISH

2 tablespoons extra-virgin olive oil
4 medium garlic cloves, sliced thin
1 teaspoon minced fresh rosemary leaves
1½ pounds small new potatoes (about the size of a golf ball), halved
¼ cup water
   Salt

1. Heat the oil in a large sauté pan. Add the garlic, rosemary, and potatoes and stir to combine the ingredients. Sprinkle generously with salt and add the water. Reduce the heat to medium-low, cover, and cook, stirring once, until the potatoes are tender, 20 to 25 minutes. (If the pan dries

out before the potatoes are done, add several tablespoons of water.)

2. Uncover the pan and raise the heat to medium-high. Cook, stirring occasionally, until potatoes and garlic have browned a bit, about 5 minutes. Adjust the seasonings and serve immediately.

Indian Spiced Potatoes and Peas

For this dish, cooked potatoes and peas are sautéed with spices while being mashed with a wooden spoon. Garam masala is an Indian spice mixture sold in many supermarkets and natural food stores. It usually contains black pepper, cinnamon, cardamom, cumin, coriander, and cloves and lends an earthy, almost sweet flavor to the potato filling. Curry powder or another spice mixture may be substituted.

SERVES 4 TO 6 AS A SIDE DISH

1½ pounds red potatoes, scrubbed and cut into ½-inch dice
    Salt
1¼ cups frozen peas (do not thaw)
 2 tablespoons canola or other tasteless oil
 1 tablespoon cumin seeds
 2 teaspoons garam masala or other spice powder
 2 tablespoons minced fresh cilantro leaves

1. Bring several quarts of water to a boil in medium saucepan. Add the potatoes and salt to taste and cook until tender but not mushy, about 10 minutes. Stir in the peas and cook until tender, about 1 minute. Drain the vegetables and set aside.

2. Heat the oil in a large skillet. Add the cumin seeds and cook until they are a rich brown color, 1 to 2 minutes. Stir in the garam masala and cook until fragrant, about 30 seconds.

3. Add the potatoes and peas to the pan and cook, stirring with a wooden spoon and mashing slightly, until well seasoned with the spices and warm, about 2 minutes. Stir in the cilantro and adjust the seasonings. Serve immediately.

Smoky Potato and Zucchini Stew

This stew gets its unusual flavor from chipotle chiles in adobo sauce, a condiment made in Mexico and sold in cans in U.S. markets, especially those that cater to Latino shoppers. Chipotles are smoked, dried jalapeños. Adobo sauce is a vinegary tomato sauce. The combination is unbeatable. This thick stew should be served in bowls and accompanied with warm flour tortillas, which can be used to scoop up the stew if you like.

SERVES 4 AS A MAIN COURSE

 2 tablespoons extra-virgin olive oil
 1 medium onion, chopped
 4 medium zucchini (about 1½ pounds), cut into ¾-inch dice

1 chipotle chile in adobo sauce, minced with
2 teaspoons sauce
2 medium garlic cloves, minced
2 teaspoons minced fresh oregano leaves
2½ cups chicken or vegetable stock
1 pound red potatoes, scrubbed and cut into
½-inch dice
2 tablespoons minced fresh cilantro leaves
Salt
8 large flour tortillas (at least 8 inches in
diameter)

1. Preheat the oven to 375 degrees.

2. Meanwhile, heat the oil in a large sauté pan. Add the onion and zucchini and sauté over medium-high heat until lightly browned, about 7 minutes. Add the chile and adobo sauce, garlic, and oregano and sauté until fragrant, about 1 minute.

3. Add the stock and bring to a boil. Add the potatoes, cover, and simmer briskly over medium heat for 10 minutes. Uncover and continue to simmer until the stew thickens and the potatoes are tender, about 5 minutes. Stir in the cilantro and salt to taste. (The stew can be covered and set aside for several hours. Reheat before serving.)

4. While the stew is cooking, wrap the tortillas in aluminum foil and place them in the oven. Warm for 15 minutes. Remove the packet from the oven and set aside until ready to eat.

5. Ladle the stew into bowls. Unwrap the tortillas and place in a cloth-lined basket. Serve immediately.

Radicchio

Radicchio has become widely available in American supermarkets in the past decade. While many cooks use this bitter member of the chicory family in salads, it's also delicious cooked.

There are actually several varieties of this crisp chicory with ivory and magenta or crimson leaves. We generally see a round variety (it looks like a miniature cabbage) called *rossa di Verona*. If you shop at gourmet stores or farmers' markets, you may see an elongated variety (it looks like purple endive) called *rossa di Treviso*.

Both varieties are pleasantly bitter although when cooked this bitterness fades a bit (as does the bright color). I think cooked radicchio has a slight sweet flavor as well as some smoky notes, especially if the leaves are caramelized a bit. Cooked radicchio still tastes bitter, but the flavor is much more complex.

OTHER COMMON NAMES: Red chicory.

AVAILABILITY: Year-round.

SELECTION: Look for tightly closed heads of radicchio with crisp outer leaves. Avoid heads that shows any signs of decay or browning on the outer leaves.

STORAGE: Radicchio can be refrigerated in a loosely sealed plastic bag for several days, if not a week. Just make sure that the radicchio is dry when you put it into the refrigerator. Any moisture will cause the leaves to soften and rot prematurely, so do not wash radicchio until you are ready to use it.

BASIC PREPARATION: Start by pulling off and discarding any limp or brown outer leaves. For salad, keep pulling off the leaves, tearing them in bite-sized pieces, and then washing them. To cook radicchio, you need to prepare it differently.

One option is to cut the radicchio into wedges. Halve the radicchio lengthwise through the core and then continue to cut the halves lengthwise to yield wedges of the desired size. By making all the cuts through the core or stem end, you ensure that the layers of leaves will stay together when grilled or sautéed.

The other option when cooking radicchio is to shred it, like cabbage. Start by halving the radicchio through the core. Next, cut out and discard the portion of the hard core attached to each half. The halves can be turned over onto their flat sides and then sliced crosswise into thin strips.

BEST COOKING METHODS: Braising, grilling, roasting, and sautéing.

OTHER RECIPES WITH RADICCHIO:
Arugula, Endive, and Radicchio Salad with Balsamic Vinaigrette (page 203)

Grilled Radicchio

An unexpected but delightful way to prepare this vegetable. Make sure to cut the heads through the stem end so that they do not fall apart over the hot coals. The exterior of the radicchio will char a bit, but this adds flavor and ensures that the center is cooked through. Serve as is or drizzle with a little high-quality balsamic vinegar when done.

SERVES 4 TO 6 AS A SIDE DISH

3 medium heads radicchio (about 1¼ pounds)
⅓ cup extra-virgin olive oil
Salt
Freshly ground black pepper

1. Light a grill fire.
2. Discard any limp outer leaves from the radicchio. Cut the radicchio in half through the stem end. Cut the radicchio in half again through the stem end. Place the radicchio quarters in a large baking dish and brush them with the oil. Sprinkle with salt and pepper to taste.
3. Use tongs to transfer the radicchio pieces to the grill. Grill the radicchio wedges over a medium fire, turning them twice so that each side spends some time directly facing the fire, until they are lightly charred on all sides, about 8 minutes. Transfer the radicchio to a platter and serve immediately.

Pan-Seared Radicchio with Balsamic Vinegar

The only tricky part of this recipe is cutting the radicchio properly. You want to slice the radicchio into wedges that are thin enough to cook through, but large enough—and with a piece of the core—to hold together in the pan. Start by cutting each head of radicchio in half through the core end. Lay the halves cut side down and cut into three or four wedges.

SERVES 4 AS A SIDE DISH

2 medium heads radicchio (about ¾ pound)
3 tablespoons extra-virgin olive oil
2 tablespoons balsamic vinegar
Salt
Freshly ground black pepper

1. Discard any limp outer leaves from the radicchio. Cut the radicchio in half through the stem end. Cut each half lengthwise (through the stem end) to make several 1½-inch-thick wedges.
2. Heat the oil in a skillet large enough to accommodate all the radicchio in a single layer. When the oil is hot, add the radicchio. Sauté over medium-high heat, turning several times with tongs, until lightly browned on all sides, 3 to 4 minutes.
3. Drizzle the vinegar over the radicchio and continue cooking just until it has evaporated, about 30 seconds. Season the radicchio with salt and pepper to taste and serve immediately.

Radicchio with Pancetta and Onion

Radicchio makes an especially rich and flavorful side dish when it is sweated in a covered pan with onion, oil, and pancetta. Because there's no liquid in the pan, the radicchio will start to brown and stick to the bottom. Don't worry; the browned bits are extremely flavorful.

SERVES 4 TO 6 AS A SIDE DISH

3 medium heads radicchio (about 1¼ pounds)
2 tablespoons extra-virgin olive oil
2 ounces thin-sliced pancetta, chopped fine
1 medium onion, chopped fine
2 tablespoons minced fresh parsley leaves
Salt
Freshly ground black pepper

1. Discard any limp outer leaves from the radicchio. Halve the radicchio lengthwise through core. Cut out and discard the portion of the hard white core attached to each half. Lay the halves cut side down on a cutting board and slice crosswise into ¼-inch-wide strips.

2. Place the oil, pancetta, and onion in a large casserole or Dutch oven. Turn the heat to medium and sauté until the pancetta is crisp and the onion is golden, about 7 minutes.

3. Stir in the radicchio, making sure to coat the leaves evenly with the oil, pancetta, and onion. Cover and cook, stirring occasionally, until the radicchio has wilted and browned, about 5 minutes. Stir in the parsley and season with salt and pepper to taste.

Risotto with Radicchio, Pancetta, and Onion

A traditional dish where radicchio actually tastes sweet and a bit smoky. Keep the stock warm in a saucepan over low heat as you make the risotto.

**SERVES 4 AS A MAIN COURSE OR
6 TO 8 AS A FIRST COURSE**

1 recipe Radicchio with Pancetta and Onion (see above)
1½ cups arborio rice
½ cup dry white wine
6 cups chicken or vegetable stock, warmed
2 tablespoons unsalted butter
½ cup grated Parmesan cheese, plus more for the table, optional

1. Prepare the radicchio as directed but reserve the parsley. When the radicchio has browned, stir in the rice with a wooden spoon and cook for 1 minute. Add the wine and simmer just until the alcohol burns off, 1 to 2 minutes.

2. Ladle ½ cup of the warm stock into the pot with the rice. Cook, stirring frequently, until the rice absorbs the liquid. Continue adding stock in ½-cup increments, stirring often, until the rice is

creamy and soft but still a bit al dente, 20 to 25 minutes. (Add hot water if you run out of stock.)

3. Remove the pot from the heat and vigorously beat in the butter and cheese with a wooden spoon. Stir in the reserved 2 tablespoons minced fresh parsley and adjust the seasonings. Serve immediately, passing more cheese at the table if you like.

Shredded Radicchio with Caramelized Onion Dressing

A hot dressing gently wilts thinly sliced radicchio and gives it a pleasing texture. This wintery dish makes an excellent accompaniment to roast chicken, pork, or beef. It could also be served as a first course salad, but you would want to dress up each plate with some tender greens, such as baby spinach or leaf lettuce.

SERVES 6 AS A SIDE DISH

3 large heads radicchio (about 1½ pounds)
⅓ cup extra-virgin olive oil
1 medium onion, minced
1 teaspoon sugar
2 tablespoons red wine vinegar
 Salt
 Freshly ground black pepper

1. Discard any limp outer leaves from the radicchio. Cut the radicchio in half through the stem end. Cut the radicchio in half again through the stem end. Cut out and discard the portion of the hard white core attached to each piece. Lay the radicchio cut side down on a cutting board and slice crosswise into ¼-inch-wide strips. Place the shredded radicchio in a medium bowl.

2. Place the oil and onion in a medium skillet. Turn the heat to medium and cook, stirring occasionally, until the onion pieces are beginning to brown around the edges, about 8 minutes. Stir in the sugar and continue cooking until the onion pieces are nicely browned, about 5 minutes. Add the vinegar and salt and pepper to taste.

3. Pour the warm onion dressing over the radicchio and toss to coat. Serve immediately.

Radishes

There are at least a dozen major varieties of radishes grown around the world. If you shop at a supermarket, you are likely to see familiar round red radishes as well as the elongated, white daikon, which can grow to be a foot long and weigh 2 pounds or more.

Stop at a farmers' market and you will see tiny French breakfast radishes, which are easily recognized because their elongated shape shades from bright red at the stem end to white at the root. Icicle radishes are white like a daikon but much smaller, about the size of your thumb. Easter egg radishes are round and come in various shades of red, pink, white, and purple. All of the small red, pink, white, and purple varieties can be used like the common red radish. They can be sliced thin and added raw to salads, pickled, or cooked.

Crisp, hot radishes are fine raw, but you can only eat so much. When cooked, however, radishes can be consumed (and enjoyed) in much greater amounts. Braising and roasting are the best choices, with both methods yielding creamy-textured radishes that are sweet, not peppery.

The huge daikon is commonly used in Asian cooking and should be treated slightly differently because of its size, firmer texture, and spicier flavor. In some respects, daikon is handled more like a turnip than a tiny red radish.

AVAILABILITY: Year-round, although best in the spring and fall.

SELECTION: The easiest way to buy radishes is to look at their greens. If the greens are healthy and crisp, the radishes have been freshly dug. Unfortunately, radishes are often sold without their greens. If this is the case, make sure they are firm (not spongy) and that the skin is smooth, not cracked or dry. Trimmed radishes sold in plastic bags are not necessarily bad, but they lose some flavor as they sit in the produce aisle. Avoid really large radishes, which can be woody. Anything bigger than a walnut is suspect.

STORAGE: Radishes can be refrigerated in a loosely sealed plastic bag for several days, if not a week. If the greens are attached, you may want to remove them when you get home. The greens can collect moisture and may hasten softening of the bulbs.

BASIC PREPARATION: Start by trimming and discarding the stems and leaves. Next, wash the radishes well and use a paring knife to cut off any tiny white rootlets. Basic red radishes do not need to be peeled.

Long daikon radish is handled a bit differently. I find the ivory peel to be thicker and not very flavorful. Just run a vegetable peeler over this radish to remove it. Peeled daikon can be sliced or shredded as desired.

BEST COOKING METHODS: Braising or roasting. Raw radishes are also used in salads and hors d'oeuvres.

OTHER RECIPES WITH RADISHES:
Avocado, Orange, and Radish Salad with Lime-Chile Dressing (page 24)

Braised Red Radishes

The flavor of cooked radishes is delicious. When braised, the white flesh turns light pink and the sharpness fades. What's left is pure radish flavor. This recipe is unexpectedly good.

SERVES 4 AS A SIDE DISH

20 medium radishes, leaves, stems, and rootlets removed (about 1 pound when trimmed)
 1 tablespoon unsalted butter
 1 medium shallot, minced
 ½ cup chicken or vegetable stock
 1 tablespoon honey
   Salt
 1 tablespoon minced fresh parsley leaves

1. Unless very small, halve the radishes lengthwise from stem to root end.

2. Melt the butter in a large sauté pan. Add the shallot and sauté over medium heat until softened, about 2 minutes. Add the radishes and stir-cook until well coated with butter, about 1 minute.

3. Add the stock and honey, cover, and cook until the radishes are tender but not soft, about 10 minutes. Remove the cover, season with salt to taste, and simmer to allow any juices in the pan to reduce to a glaze, about 1 minute. Garnish with the parsley and serve immediately.

Roasted Radishes with Soy and Sesame Seeds

Like other root vegetables, radishes take well to roasting. Even the hottest radishes will emerge mild and creamy from the oven. Tossing the radishes with a little soy sauce as they finish cooking creates a syrupy glaze and seasons them perfectly. Serve these radishes with fish, chicken, or even steak.

SERVES 4 AS A SIDE DISH

20 medium radishes, leaves, stems, and rootlets trimmed (about 1 pound when trimmed)
1½ tablespoons roasted peanut oil
 2 tablespoons soy sauce
 2 medium scallions, sliced thin
 1 tablespoon sesame seeds, toasted in a dry skillet until golden brown

1. Preheat the oven to 425 degrees.

2. Unless very small, halve the radishes lengthwise from stem to root end. Toss them with the oil on a large rimmed baking sheet. Roast, turning once or twice, until the radishes are tender and beginning to brown, about 25 minutes. Remove the radishes from the oven (but do not turn it off).

3. Drizzle the soy sauce over the radishes and sprinkle with the scallions. Toss well and continue roasting for 5 minutes longer. Turn the radishes and any juices on the baking sheet into a serving bowl. Sprinkle with the sesame seeds and serve immediately.

Radishes, Fennel, and Olives with Creamy Feta Cheese Spread

Spicy radishes, sweet fennel, salty olives, and sharp feta cheese tempered with some plain yogurt make an appealing hors d'oeuvre, especially if accompanied by pita breads. Soaking the radishes in ice water makes them especially crunchy and helps tame some of their spiciness.

SERVES 6 TO 8 AS AN APPETIZER

15 medium radishes, leaves, stems, and rootlets trimmed (about ¾ pound or so when trimmed)
 4 ounces feta cheese, crumbled (about 1 cup)
¼ cup plain yogurt
 1 small garlic clove, minced
    Freshly ground black pepper
 1 small fennel bulb (about ¾ pound)
18 large Kalamata olives
 4 large pita breads, cut into wedges

1. Halve the radishes lengthwise from stem to root end. Place them in a large bowl of ice water for 30 minutes.

2. While the radishes are soaking, use a fork to mash the cheese, yogurt, and garlic together in a small bowl. When the mixture comes together, add pepper to taste. Place the cheese mixture in a small ramekin or dish. Put the dish in the center of a large serving platter.

3. Remove and discard the green stems and the fronds from the fennel. Remove any blemished or tough layers from the fennel bulb and remove a thick slice from the base. Cut the fennel bulb in half through the base and use a small, sharp knife to remove the small triangular piece of the core attached to the bottom of each half. With each fennel piece flat side down and your knife parallel to the work surface, slice crosswise to yield several ½-inch-thick slices. Cut the slices lengthwise to yield long strips about ½ inch thick.

4. Arrange the fennel and olives around the cheese spread. Drain and pat dry the radishes with paper towels. Arrange them on the platter with the fennel and olives. Serve with the pita breads in a basket.

Sweet-and-Sour Radishes

These crisp radish "pickles" are perfect with cocktails. Salting the radishes tames some of their heat and allows them to absorb the flavors of the sugar, vinegar, and sesame oil marinade.

SERVES 6 TO 8 AS PART
OF AN HORS D'OEUVRE SPREAD

20 medium radishes, leaves, stems, and rootlets trimmed (about 1 pound when trimmed)
1 teaspoon kosher salt
½ cup rice vinegar
3 tablespoons sugar
2 teaspoons toasted sesame oil

1. Cut the trimmed radishes into ¼-inch-thick circles. Toss the radishes and salt in a medium bowl and set aside, stirring occasionally, for 45 minutes. Drain off the liquid; there should be about ¼ cup of salty juices.
2. Meanwhile, bring the vinegar and sugar to a boil in a small saucepan, stirring just until the sugar dissolves. Remove the pan from the heat and cool the mixture to room temperature. Whisk in the oil.
3. Pour the vinegar mixture over the drained radishes. Marinate, stirring occasionally, for 30 minutes. Drain the radishes if desired (the pickles are less messy to eat this way) and serve immediately.

Radish and Orange Salad with Paprika

Moroccan flavors turn radishes into a lovely condiment-style salad, perfect with grilled fish or chicken, or with sandwiches at lunchtime.

SERVES 4 TO 6 AS A SIDE DISH

2 medium oranges
1 teaspoon honey
8 radishes, leaves, stems, and rootlets removed (about 6 ounces when trimmed)
1 tablespoon extra-virgin olive oil
½ teaspoon sweet paprika
Salt

1. Trim thick slices from the ends of the oranges so they will sit flat on a cutting board. With a paring knife, slice downward around the oranges to remove the peel and white pith. Chop the peeled oranges and transfer them to a bowl with their juices. Drizzle the honey over the oranges and toss gently.
2. Cut the trimmed radishes into very thin circles. Add the radishes to the bowl with the oranges and toss again. Drizzle with the oil and sprinkle with the paprika and salt to taste. Toss and serve immediately.

Braised Daikon with Ginger and Soy

This is perhaps the most "Western" way to prepare daikon and perhaps the most appealing for Americans. The daikon retains some of its peppery bite but the flavors are softened by the soy and sugar.

SERVES 4 TO 6 AS A SIDE DISH

- 1 tablespoon roasted peanut oil
- 2 medium garlic cloves, minced
- 1 tablespoon minced fresh gingerroot
- 2 medium scallions, sliced thin
- 1 pound daikon radishes, peeled and cut into ½-inch cubes
- ¼ cup chicken or vegetable stock
- 1 tablespoon soy sauce
- ½ teaspoon sugar
  Salt
  Freshly ground black pepper

1. Heat the oil in a large sauté pan. Add the garlic, ginger, and scallions and sauté over medium heat until fragrant, about 1 minute. Add the radishes and sauté until the radishes are coated with the oil and aromatics, about 1 minute.

2. Add the stock, soy sauce, and sugar to the pan. Cover, reduce the heat, and simmer until the radishes are crisp-tender, about 5 minutes. Remove the cover and simmer until the liquid in the pan evaporates, about 2 minutes. Add salt (sparingly) and pepper to taste. Serve immediately.

Shredded Daikon Salad with Sesame Seeds

This Japanese salad is commonly served with sushi. I like this slaw just as well with a piece of grilled or sautéed fish. Make sure to drain the shredded daikon well, or the salad will be watery. If you like, shred a carrot along with the radishes for some color.

SERVES 6 AS A SIDE DISH

- 1½ pounds daikon radishes
- 2 tablespoons soy sauce
- 1 tablespoon rice vinegar
- 2 teaspoons mirin (Japanese sweet rice wine)
- 1 teaspoon toasted sesame oil
  Freshly ground white pepper
- 1 tablespoon sesame seeds, toasted in a dry skillet until golden brown

1. Peel and cut the radishes into chunks that will fit in the feed tube of a food processor. Shred the radishes using the shredding disk. Turn the shredded daikon into a colander and let drain for at least 5 minutes, squeezing out any excess moisture with your hands. Turn the daikon into a medium bowl.

2. Whisk the soy sauce, vinegar, mirin, oil, and pepper to taste together in a small bowl. Pour the dressing over the daikon and toss. Sprinkle with the toasted sesame seeds and serve immediately.

Rutabagas

Although rutabagas are cooked like turnips and often labeled "yellow turnips" in markets, they are not turnips. They are related, but rutabagas have a gentle sweetness and are rarely peppery, as are turnips. The cooking methods for turnips and rutabagas are pretty much the same. Rutabaga flesh is creamy and starchy and takes well to mashing as well as braising and roasting.

OTHER COMMON NAMES: Swedes or yellow turnips.

AVAILABILITY: Fall through spring.

SELECTION: They are almost always huge (a pound or more) and covered with wax to prevent the loss of moisture. If you can buy small, unwaxed rutabagas do so. You peel off the wax with the tough skin and even mammoth rutabagas usually taste fine. Do avoid any rutabagas with cracks or specimens that look old and shriveled.

STORAGE: Rutabagas can be refrigerated for at least a week in the vegetable drawer. Because they are generally coated with wax, they may stay fresh for a couple of weeks.

BASIC PREPARATION: Use a paring knife to remove the wax, skin, and a thin layer of flesh. You want to remove the greenish-white flesh right under the skin and expose the yellowish-orange flesh. Once peeled, the rutabaga can be sliced as desired.

BEST COOKING METHODS: Boiling, braising, or roasting.

OTHER RECIPES WITH RUTABAGAS: Use in any recipe for turnips.

Mashed Rutabaga with Orange and Ginger

Rutabaga makes a brilliant-looking puree, especially if that puree is enriched with orange juice. The orange juice and ground ginger bring out the mildly sweet flavor of the rutabaga. This recipe is an excellent addition to a holiday meal that features turkey or goose.

SERVES 4 TO 6 AS A SIDE DISH

- 1 large rutabaga (about 2 pounds), peeled and cut into 1-inch chunks
  Salt
- 2 tablespoons unsalted butter, softened and cut into several pieces
- 1 teaspoon grated orange zest
- ¼ cup orange juice
- ½ teaspoon ground ginger

1. Place the rutabaga chunks in a large saucepan and add enough water to cover by 2 inches. Add a generous amount of salt and bring the water to a boil. Reduce the heat a bit and cook until the rutabaga is very tender, 25 to 30 minutes. Drain.
2. Return the rutabaga to the empty saucepan set over low heat. Add the butter and orange zest and use a potato masher to turn the rutabaga into fine bits. Stir in the orange juice and ginger with a wooden spoon and add salt to taste. Serve immediately.

Mashed Rutabaga and Apples with Sautéed Onions

This Central European dish is appealing and satisfying. Use a sweet apple, such as Golden Delicious, to bring out the sweetness of the rutabaga. Serve with a pork or veal roast.

SERVES 4 TO 6 AS A SIDE DISH

- 1 large rutabaga (about 2 pounds), peeled and cut into 1-inch chunks
  Salt
- 1 medium sweet apple, peeled, quartered, and cored
- 3 tablespoons unsalted butter
- 1 tablespoon canola or other tasteless oil
- 2 medium onions, halved and sliced thin
- ¼ cup milk or half-and-half, warmed

1. Place the rutabaga chunks in a large saucepan and add water to cover by 2 inches. Add a generous amount of salt and bring the water to a boil. Reduce the heat a bit and cook for 15 minutes. Add the apple and continue cooking until the rutabaga and apple are very tender, 10 to 15 minutes.
2. While the rutabaga is cooking, heat 1 tablespoon butter and the oil in a large skillet. Add the onions and cook over medium heat until golden brown, about 10 minutes. Season with salt to taste. Cover and keep warm.

3. When the rutabaga and apple are tender, drain them well. Return them to the empty saucepan set over low heat. Add the remaining 2 table-spoons of butter and use a potato masher to turn the rutabaga into fine bits. Stir in the milk with a wooden spoon and add salt to taste.

4. Transfer the mashed rutabaga and apple to a serving bowl. Top with the onions and serve immediately.

Rutabaga "Fries" with Warm Spices

Thick slabs of rutabaga make excellent oven fries. The mildly sweet flavor of the rutabaga fries works especially well with earthy spices such as cinnamon, paprika, and cumin. Serve with pork, chicken, or beef.

SERVES 4 AS A SIDE DISH

1 large rutabaga (about 2 pounds)
3 tablespoons extra-virgin olive oil
½ teaspoon ground cinnamon
½ teaspoon sweet paprika
¼ teaspoon ground cumin
Salt

1. Place a large rimmed baking sheet in the oven. Preheat the oven to 425 degrees.

2. Peel the rutabaga and then cut it in half through the flat ends. Lay each half cut side down on a cutting board. Slice crosswise to yield ½-inch-thick half circles. Cut the half circles in half lengthwise to yield long pieces that are about 1 inch across and ½ inch thick. (They will look like steak fries.) Toss the rutabaga wedges with 2 tablespoons of the oil, the spices, and salt to taste in a large bowl.

3. When the oven has come up to temperature, carefully brush the remaining 1 tablespoon of oil evenly over the baking sheet. Dump the rutabaga onto the oiled sheet and spread the pieces apart so that each one is in direct contact with the bak-ing sheet.

4. Bake for 25 minutes. Using a pair of tongs, turn each rutabaga wedge. Continue baking until the rutabaga wedges are quite brown and crisp, about 20 minutes longer. Season with more salt if desired and serve immediately.

Stewed Rutabaga with Chard and Garlic

This dish looks as good as it tastes. Bright yellow cubes of stewed rutabaga are cooked with Swiss chard to create a hearty side dish of contrasting colors, tex-tures, and flavor. In fact this dish—which is savory not sweet, like many dishes made with rutabagas—is so substantial, it could be turned into a vegetarian main course for three or four. If you like, use turnips and spinach in place of the rutabaga and chard for a similar effect.

SERVES 6 AS A SIDE DISH

2 tablespoons extra-virgin olive oil
1 medium rutabaga (about 1½ pounds), peeled and cut into 1-inch cubes
3 medium garlic cloves, minced
1 cup chicken or vegetable stock
  Salt
  Freshly ground black pepper
1 pound chard (preferably with red stalks), stems and thick ribs discarded; leaves washed, shaken to remove excess water, and chopped roughly (about 6 cups)

1. Heat the oil in a large, deep sauté pan. Add the rutabaga and cook, stirring occasionally, over medium heat until lightly browned, about 8 minutes. Add the garlic and cook until fragrant, about 1 minute.

2. Add the stock and salt and pepper to taste. Cover the pan, reduce the heat, and simmer gently until almost all the liquid has evaporated and the rutabaga is almost tender, about 35 minutes.

3. Add the chard, cover, and continue cooking, stirring once, until the chard has wilted, about 6 minutes. Uncover, raise the heat, and cook briskly until the excess liquid in the pot evaporates, 1 to 2 minutes. Adjust the seasonings. Serve immediately.

Salsify and Scorzonera

S alsify and scorzonera are two root vegetables that resemble each other, and to some extent parsnips. Salsify has buff-colored skin and creamy white flesh. Scorzonera (sometimes called black salsify, although this plant is not a type of salsify) has dark brown, almost black skin and tan flesh.

Both salsify and scorzonera are tapered like parsnips, and salsify has basically the same coloring as parsnips. However, these unusual root vegetables taste nothing like parsnips. While parsnips are sweet, salsify and scorzonera (which taste and cook pretty much the same) are much more savory, even meaty. Some old cookbooks call these vegetables white and black "oyster plant" because of their flavor. Frankly, these roots taste nothing like oysters, but they are unusual tasting, more like an artichoke heart in texture and flavor than anything else.

Salsify and scorzonera are used in many European countries, especially France and Belgium. Where I live in New York, salsify is more popular, so that's the name I have attached to the recipes in this chapter. However, you may use scorzonera with no modifications or adjustments.

OTHER COMMON NAMES: Salsify is sometimes called white salsify (although this is redundant since all real salsify has white flesh), oyster plant, or vegetable oyster. Scorzonera is sometimes called black salsify or black oyster plant.

AVAILABILITY: Fall through early spring, mostly at farmers' markets and gourmet produce shops.

SELECTION: Salsify and scorzonera should be firm, not flabby, and without any bruises or soft spots. Extremely narrow roots will have little usable flesh once peeled. However, very thick roots can be tough and fibrous. I've had the best success with roots that measure between 1 and 1½ inches across at the very top when the greens are trimmed. Buy roots roughly the size of medium carrots and you will be fine.

Some salsify and scorzonera can be highly gnarled or even forked. These roots are very difficult to peel and the amount of waste is tremendous. For the best results, buy roots that taper fairly evenly, with a minimum of bumps and no branches or forks.

STORAGE: If the salsify was purchased with the grass-like greens still attached, remove and discard them when you get home. Scorzonera is usually sold without the greens attached, but remove them if the farmer has left them on. Refrigerate the roots in a loosely sealed plastic bag for several days, perhaps up to a week if they have been freshly dug.

BASIC PREPARATION: Salsify and scorzonera are usually quite muddy and covered with tiny white rootlets. Although the skin is thin and edible, it's so difficult to remove all the dirt from tiny crevices in the skin and trim all those rootlets that you must peel both roots.

Both salsify and scorzonera will discolor almost immediately when cut. (In this way, they are exactly like artichokes.) The cream-colored flesh will turn rust brown in minutes. To prevent most of the discoloration, drop each peeled root into a bowl of cold water with some lemon juice added.

BEST COOKING METHODS: Boiling (and then sautéing) or braising.

Sautéed Salsify with Butter and Herbs

In this recipe, salsify is peeled, boiled whole in water (spiked with lemon juice to prevent discoloration), drained, cut into 2-inch pieces, and sautéed until lightly browned. The gentle flavor of butter and fresh herbs ensures that the focus stays on the salsify. Instead of thyme, try a little tarragon or chervil, or replace the thyme and parsley with some snipped chives. The weight here is for the roots only and does not include any green tops.

SERVES 4 AS A SIDE DISH

½ lemon
1¼ pounds salsify (about 10 roots)
1½ tablespoons unsalted butter
1 tablespoon minced fresh parsley leaves
1 teaspoon minced fresh thyme leaves
Salt
Freshly ground black pepper

1. Squeeze the lemon half into a large pot filled with a couple of quarts of water. Drop the lemon half into the pot. Working with one root at a time, remove the green top if present. Use a vegetable peeler to remove the buff-colored skin and tiny white rootlets. (Don't be too ruthless; a few rust-colored blemishes are fine.) If the root tapers down to almost nothing, trim and discard the last inch or two of the root. Drop the root into the pot of acidulated water. Repeat until all the salsify are in the water.

2. Turn the heat to high and bring the water to a boil. Reduce the heat a bit and cook until the salsify are tender but still holding their shape, 10 to 15 minutes depending on the freshness and thickness of the roots. Drain and set aside. When cooled slightly, blot the roots dry on paper towels and then slice them on the bias into 2-inch lengths. Any thick chunks from the wide end of the root should be halved lengthwise.

3. Melt the butter in a large skillet set over medium heat. As soon as the butter foams, add the salsify and cook, stirring occasionally, until golden brown in spots, about 5 minutes. Sprinkle with the herbs and salt and pepper to taste. Serve immediately.

Glazed Salsify
with Cream

This dish is simple to prepare because the salsify is cooked once, not twice as in the previous recipe. However, it can be a bit tricky because salsify absorbs liquid differently based on its freshness and thickness. The idea here is for the salsify chunks to braise in the stock and cream until tender. By the time they are tender, almost all of the liquid should have either been absorbed by the salsify or evaporated. If the salsify is not tender but all the liquid has cooked off (which can happen if you are cooking older or thicker roots), just add a few tablespoons more stock or water and continue cooking with the cover on. On the other hand, if the salsify is very fresh and/or tender, it may cook more quickly and absorb less liquid. If this happens, remove the cover once the salsify is tender and cook off the extra liquid. The weight here is for the roots only and does not include any green tops.

SERVES 4 AS A SIDE DISH

½ lemon
1¼ pounds salsify (about 10 roots)
1 tablespoon unsalted butter
2 medium shallots, minced
½ cup chicken or vegetable stock
2 tablespoons heavy cream
⅛ teaspoon grated nutmeg
Salt
1 tablespoon minced fresh parsley leaves

1. Squeeze the lemon half into a bowl of cold water. Drop the lemon half into the bowl of water. Working with one root at a time, remove the green top if present. Use a vegetable peeler to remove the buff-colored skin and tiny white rootlets. (Don't be too ruthless; a few rust-colored blemishes are fine.) If the root tapers down to almost nothing, trim and discard the last inch or two of the root. Cut the salsify into 1-inch chunks and immediately drop the pieces into the bowl of acidulated water. Repeat until all the salsify is in the bowl.

2. Melt the butter in a large sauté pan. Add the shallots and sauté over medium heat until softened, about 3 minutes. Drain the salsify (it should not be dripping wet, but there's no need to dry it) and add it to the pan. Cook, stirring often, to coat the salsify with the butter and shallots, about 1 minute.

3. Add the stock, cream, nutmeg, and salt to taste to the pan. Bring the liquid to a boil. Reduce the heat, cover the pan, and simmer gently, stirring once or twice, until the salsify is tender, 10 to 15 minutes depending on the freshness and thickness of the salsify.

4. Remove the cover and boil briskly until any liquid in the pan has evaporated and the salsify pieces are becoming lightly glazed, no more than a couple of minutes. Stir in the parsley and adjust the seasonings. Serve immediately.

Shallots

Shallots are sweeter and more flavorful than onions, to which they are closely related. Shallots look like small, tear-shaped bulbs and are covered with copper-colored, papery skin.

I use minced shallots as a seasoning in many dishes. When sautéed in butter or oil, shallots become especially sweet. They can be used in almost any dish that calls for minced onion. If you don't have shallots on hand, you can substitute minced onion, preferably red onion.

A little minced shallot can also be stirred into a vinaigrette or sprinkled over a salad. While onions are too hot to use this way, shallots are mellow enough to use raw, especially if you keep the amount quite small.

Although shallots are almost always used as a seasoning, they can stand on their own as a vegetable side dish when braised or roasted. They are sweet and delicious and have a lovely creamy texture when cooked whole. Given their price, shallots can be a luxury when prepared this way, but one worth trying since the results are so good.

AVAILABILITY: Year-round.

SELECTION: Look for shallots with dry papery skins. Shallots should be firm and shiny-looking. Shallots with green sprouts rising from the tips are old and should be avoided.

STORAGE: Keep shallots with the onions in a cool spot in the kitchen with good ventilation. They should stay firm and fresh for at least a week or two.

BASIC PREPARATION: To peel a shallot, trim off the tip and any roots at the base with a paring knife. Make a shallow incision down the length of shallot (from the tip to the root end) and then peel away the papery skin with your fingertips. Most shallots actually contain two bulbs. If this is case, separate the shallot into two pieces by pulling apart the bulbs.

BEST COOKING METHODS: Braising and roasting.

OTHER RECIPES WITH SHALLOTS: Shallots can be used in place of pearl onions in most any recipe. Shallots are larger than pearl onions so you will need fewer of them (by number, not weight). In addition, there's no need to blanch shallots to loosen their papery skins—a tedious but necessary step when preparing pearl onions.

Glazed Shallots with Port

A good addition to the holiday table, especially if turkey, duck, or goose is being served. The port reduces to a thick, rich syrup that complements the shallots perfectly. If the shallots can be separated into two pieces after peeling, do so.

SERVES 4 AS A SIDE DISH

2 tablespoons extra-virgin olive oil
1 pound small shallots, peeled
⅓ cup port
⅓ cup water
1 teaspoon chopped fresh thyme leaves
Salt
Freshly ground black pepper

1. Heat the oil in a large skillet. Add the shallots and cook over medium heat, stirring occasionally, until lightly browned, about 7 minutes.
2. Add the port, water, and thyme to the pan. Bring to a boil, reduce the heat, cover, and simmer, stirring once or twice, until the shallots are tender and the liquid has reduced to a thick glaze, about 20 minutes. (If the shallots are tender but the liquid has not reduced sufficiently, raise the heat and cook, uncovered, for a minute or two.) Season with salt and plenty of pepper to taste. Serve immediately.

Roasted Shallots with Vinegar

The vinegar in this recipe balances the intense sweetness of roasted shallots. If the shallots can be separated into two pieces after peeling, do so. Serve with roast pork or chicken. I prefer the oaky, nuanced flavor of sherry vinegar here, but good aged red wine vinegar is delicious, too.

SERVES 4 AS A SIDE DISH

1½ pounds shallots, peeled
1 tablespoon extra-virgin olive oil
Salt
1 to 2 teaspoons sherry vinegar or red wine vinegar, or to taste

1. Preheat the oven to 400 degrees.
2. Toss the shallots and oil in a baking dish just large enough to hold the shallots in a single layer.
3. Roast the shallots in the preheated oven, turning once or twice, until richly browned, about 50 minutes. Season with salt and vinegar to taste. Serve immediately.

Sorrel

Sorrel looks a bit like other tender, leafy greens (especially spinach or arugula), but it behaves quite differently in the kitchen. Because elongated, dark green sorrel leaves have a large amount of oxalic acid (the same substance is found in rhubarb), they are quite sour, hence its nickname, sour grass. In addition to being sour, sorrel has a strong lemon flavor.

Perhaps the most unusual thing about sorrel is what happens when it is cooked. (Sorrel is so strong-tasting that it is rarely added raw to salads.) When the sorrel is heated, it immediately loses its bright green color and dissolves. A pile of bright green sorrel will reduce to a small army-green puree in a matter of minutes.

Because of the way sorrel acts when cooked, it is best used in soups and sauces, rather than on its own as a vegetable side dish. Sorrel's strong lemon flavor also benefits from being tamed with other ingredients, especially potatoes, cream, and butter.

Sorrel is popular in France and other parts of Europe but unknown in many parts of this country. Farmers' markets and gourmet supermarkets are your best bet for finding this tasty leafy green.

OTHER COMMON NAMES: Sour grass.

AVAILABILITY: Spring through fall, although you are most likely to see this green during the spring and summer at a farmers' market. Hothouse sorrel may pop up at other times of the year, but you cannot count on finding sorrel even when it is in season.

SELECTION: Buy sorrel that has crisp, brightly colored leaves. Bunches with wilted or bruised leaves should be avoided.

STORAGE: Sorrel is highly perishable. It can be refrigerated in a loosely sealed plastic bag for a day or two, but not much longer.

BASIC PREPARATION: Handle sorrel as you would any tender leafy green. Pinch off the tough stems then wash, dry, and chop the leaves as directed.

BEST COOKING METHODS: Braising (until it collapses into a coarse puree) or boiling (for soup).

OTHER RECIPES WITH SORREL: If you like, cook a handful or two of sorrel with spinach. The sorrel will dissolve but its lemony flavor lingers. Try adding a little sorrel to Wilted Spinach with Yellow Raisins and Pine Nuts (page 309) or Spinach with Brown Butter and Walnuts (page 310).

Sorrel and Potato Soup

Sorrel has a strong lemony flavor that works especially well with mild potatoes. Arugula may be substituted for the sorrel, along with a tablespoon or two of lemon juice just before serving, but the effect is not the same. Serve this chunky soup hot, or puree it and serve a smooth, silky soup chilled on a hot summer's night.

SERVES 4 TO 6 AS A FIRST COURSE

- 2 tablespoons extra-virgin olive oil
- 2 medium leeks, white and light green parts, halved and sliced crosswise into thin strips
- 1 pound russet potatoes, peeled and cut into ½-inch cubes
- 4 cups chicken or vegetable stock
  Salt
  Freshly ground black pepper
- 4 cups stemmed sorrel leaves, washed and chopped

1. Heat the oil in a large saucepan. Add the leeks and sauté over medium heat until completely softened, about 8 minutes.

2. Add the potatoes, stock, and salt and pepper to taste and bring to a boil. Reduce the heat, partially cover, and simmer until the potatoes are extremely tender, about 30 minutes.

3. Stir in the sorrel and continue cooking until the sorrel has wilted, 2 to 3 minutes. Adjust the seasonings. Serve hot or cool slightly, puree in a blender, chill, and then serve ice cold.

Sorrel Sauce

This thick lemony sauce works well with fish (especially cod or other firm, white-flesh fish), with sautéed chicken cutlets, or with eggs.

MAKES ABOUT ¼ CUP

- 2 tablespoons unsalted butter
- 1 medium shallot, minced
- ½ pound sorrel, washed, spun dry, stemmed, and chopped (about 5 cups)
- 2 tablespoons heavy cream
  Salt
  Freshly ground black pepper

1. Place the butter and shallot in a medium sauté pan over medium heat. Cook just until the butter melts and the shallot softens, about 3 minutes. Add the sorrel, cover, and cook, stirring once or twice, until completely wilted, about 4 minutes.

2. Remove the cover, stir in the cream, and continue cooking, stirring occasionally, until the sorrel loses its shape and forms a coarse puree, 1 to 2 minutes. Season with salt and pepper to taste. Use immediately.

Frittata with Sorrel

This recipe is a bit of a culinary hybrid. A sorrel omelet is a traditional French dish. If you like, you can make individual two- or three-egg omelets, seasoning the beaten eggs with a little sorrel sauce. Frankly, I was never very good at making omelets. I much prefer the no-fuss Italian egg dish called a frittata. No folding or complicated turning and no need to make individual portions. Six eggs are cooked at once and then the round frittata is sliced into wedges. The sorrel sauce gives this frittata a creamy texture and pleasant lemony flavor.

SERVES 3 TO 4 AS A LIGHT MAIN COURSE

6 large eggs
½ cup Sorrel Sauce (page 300)
  Salt
  Freshly ground black pepper
1 tablespoon unsalted butter

1. Beat together the eggs, sorrel sauce, and salt and pepper to taste in a medium bowl just until combined.

2. Adjust the oven rack to the top position and preheat the broiler.

3. Melt the butter in a 10-inch nonstick skillet with an ovenproof handle. Swirl the butter to coat the bottom of the pan evenly. Add the egg mixture. Cook over medium-low heat, occasionally sliding a spatula around the edges of the pan to loosen the frittata as it sets. Continue cooking until the frittata is set, except for the top, about 8 minutes.

4. Place the pan directly under the broiler and cook just until the top is golden brown and set, 1 to 2 minutes. Do not let the frittata burn. Slide the frittata onto a large platter. Cut it into wedges and serve. (The frittata may be cooled to room temperature and then cut and served.)

Soybeans

Soybeans are one of the world's most important food crops. There are literally dozens of varieties, which are used for dozens of purposes—everything from feeding animals to making cooking oil and tofu.

If you shop at natural food stores, you may have seen dried black soybeans. These tiny, round beans take a long time to soften and don't have much flavor. I much prefer black beans.

However, fresh green soybeans, which are popular in Japan and are increasingly available in this country, are a treat. Like lima beans or fava beans, fresh green soybeans are a shell bean. They have a rich, earthy, sweet flavor and creamy yet slightly crunchy texture. Anyone who has tried steamed fresh green soybeans in a Japanese restaurant (they are usually called edamame) knows what I mean when I say that fresh soybeans are definitely worth seeking out.

Fresh soybeans show up in two forms in American markets. You may occasionally run across the freshly picked beans, which look a bit like furry garden peas. You are more likely to see the whole pods frozen at Asian markets or natural food stores. These "fresh" soybeans have been blanched in their pods and then frozen. They have much more flavor than beans that are shelled and then frozen, which I don't recommend buying.

I always have a pound of frozen soybeans in the freezer. Edamame is a standard snack food at my home—as addictive as popcorn but more delicious and far healthier. Best of all, even my four-year-old loves this snack. There's something so inviting about shelling cooked soybeans to reveal those sweet beans.

OTHER COMMON NAMES: Edamame and sweet beans.

AVAILABILITY: Frozen soybeans are sold in many natural food stores and Asian markets and are available year-round. Chinatown is your best bet for fresh soybeans, although they occasionally show up in well-stocked natural food stores and farmers' market, especially in the summer and early fall.

SELECTION: If buying frozen soybeans, inspect the package for signs of freezer burn. The pods should be smooth and bright green. If buying fresh soybeans, try to select pods that are uniformly green. The beans inside pods with yellow or brown spots still taste fine but the pods don't look very attractive when steamed. Avoid fresh soybeans that are soft or cracked. Gently squeeze the pod to make sure you can feel two or three firm beans.

STORAGE: Frozen beans will keep for several months in the freezer. Fresh beans can be refrigerated in a loosely sealed plastic bag for several days. Make sure there's no moisture in the bag and don't wash fresh soybeans until you are ready to use them.

BASIC PREPARATION: Frozen soybeans can be taken straight from the freezer and added to a steamer basket. Fresh soybeans should be washed in successive bowls of cold water until the water is no longer dirty. Pick through fresh soybeans to remove any foreign matter (stems, etc.) and any cracked or open pods.

Frozen pods can be thawed slightly and shelled. Fresh pods can be shelled right away, but the pods are easier to open after steaming so I usually cook them first. Either way, open the pods as you open garden peas. Each pod will contain two or three small beans, each slightly larger than a garden pea.

BEST COOKING METHODS: Braising if shelled, or steaming if still in the pods.

Fresh Soybeans, Japanese Style

Edamame is a favorite snack or appetizer in Japanese restaurants. A mound of steamed fresh soybeans in their pods and ice cold beers are the perfect way to wind down at home. There's something therapeutic about opening the pods one by one (either with your hands or better still your teeth) and pulling out the beans. Edamame are usually pretty salty. The crystals of coarse salt cling to the pods. As you pop the pods into your mouth to scrape out the beans, you will get a good hit of salt. I have chosen a middle road here, but you should adjust the amount of salt as desired. Frozen soybeans are uniformly green and a bit easier to prepare. Fresh soybean pods are often mottled with yellow and brown spots but the beans are richer-tasting, with hints of grain and even oatmeal.

SERVES 4 TO 6 AS A SNACK OR APPETIZER

1 pound fresh or frozen soybeans in their
   pods
½ teaspoon kosher or coarse sea salt

1. If using fresh soybeans, wash them well in successive bowls of cold water until the water is clean. Pick out and discard any foreign material, stems, or broken pods.

2. Fit a wide saucepan with a steamer basket and add enough water so that it comes to within ½ inch of the basket. Cover the pan and bring the water to a boil. Place the soybeans (there's no need to defrost beans that have been frozen) in the basket, cover, and steam until the soybeans inside the pods are tender (test as you go along), 4 to 5 minutes for frozen beans and 9 or 10 minutes for fresh.

3. Drain any water in the steamer basket and transfer the beans to a bowl. Toss with the salt and mix gently. Serve immediately.

Soybeans and Spinach with Onion and Sesame Oil

Pale green soybeans and dark green spinach make an attractive and delicious pairing. I usually buy frozen soybeans in the pod and then shell them for this dish. If you prefer you can steam fresh soybeans (see above), cool them, and then shell them. Serve this soupy dish with plenty of rice. I especially like this side dish with seafood.

1 pound frozen soybeans in their pods
1 tablespoon canola or other tasteless oil
1 medium onion, minced
1 pound spinach, preferably flat-leaf, stems removed unless they are very thin, washed, and shaken dry to remove excess water (about 6 cups, tightly packed)
1 tablespoon soy sauce
1 teaspoon toasted sesame oil

1. Place the frozen soybean pods in a bowl of cool water and set aside until they have thawed enough to open easily with your hands, about 10 minutes. Use your fingers to open the pods and remove the beans. You should have about 1½ cups of shelled soybeans. Discard the pods.

2. Heat the canola oil in a large, deep sauté pan. Add the onion and sauté over medium heat until golden, about 5 minutes. Add the spinach and stir just until it starts to wilt, about 1 minute.

3. Add the soybeans, cover, and cook until the spinach is tender and the soybeans are heated through, 3 to 4 minutes. Remove the cover and cook to evaporate some of the liquid in the pan, about 2 minutes. Add the soy sauce.

4. Transfer the soybeans and spinach to a serving bowl. Drizzle the sesame oil over the mixture and serve immediately.

Spinach

Spinach is the most commonly available leafy green, used in salads, side dishes, pasta and rice dishes, and much more. The recent history of spinach is a good example of the improved quality and selection typical of produce in this country.

Not long ago, curly leaves packed in cellophane bags were the only option in most markets. But now flat-leaf spinach sold in bundles is just as common and many stores stock bins of baby spinach. Each kind of spinach has a different texture and therefore different uses.

Curly-leaf spinach packed in cellophane bags has chewy, ruffled leaves and thick, fibrous stems. It is too tough and dry to use raw in salads. Curly spinach must be cooked, and since its flavor is usually nondescript I try to reserve it for dishes, such as fresh spinach pasta or gnocchi, where the flavor of the spinach is not paramount.

Flat-leaf spinach has a sweeter, more earthy flavor. The spade-shaped leaves are tender and the stems are thin and often edible, especially if the spinach is going to be cooked. Flat-leaf spinach is moist enough (almost like lettuce) to use raw in salads.

Baby spinach—a miniature flat-leaf variety sold in many supermarkets in bulk, often near the mesclun—has very tender leaves that are suited to use in salads. Baby spinach has little or no stems and is usually fairly clean (a quick rinse is sufficient in most cases), so the preparation takes less time than either of the large-leaf varieties.

AVAILABILITY: Year-round, although traditionally during temperate fall and spring weather.

SELECTION: Spinach should be a deep green color (never yellow) with smooth (never slimy) leaves and crisp stems. It should smell fresh and earthy, not musty or sour.

STORAGE: Spinach is highly perishable and should be used as quickly as possible. Curly varieties in a cellophane bag will last the longest, especially if the bag is not opened. Flat-leaf and baby spinach should be stored in a dry, open plastic bag. Moisture will hasten its decline, so if the bag is full of water when you get home from the market, blot the spinach dry and place it in a new bag.

BASIC PREPARATION: Grit is the main issue when preparing spinach. Wash spinach thoroughly or risk a ruined recipe. Washing leaves in successive bowls of cold water until no sand can be felt on the bottom of the bowl is required. Spinach destined for the salad bowl should be spun and then towel dried. If cooking spinach in water, there is no need to dry it. Wilted or braised spinach should be shaken dry to remove excess water but can still be damp.

Depending on the age and variety, the stems should be removed during the washing process. The stems on all baby spinach and some flat-leaf spinach are quite thin and tender and taste fine, even in salads. Thicker, more fibrous stems on bagged spinach should be pinched off by hand while washing the spinach. If you want to remove the straight stems from flat-leaf spinach, use a knife to chop off most of the stems and then pinch off any remaining bits by hand.

While thin stems may be left on mature spinach that will be cooked, all stems should, no matter how tiny, should be removed from mature spinach destined for the salad bowl.

BEST COOKING METHODS: Boiling, braising, and stir-frying. Also used raw in salads.

OTHER RECIPES WITH SPINACH:
Stir-Fried Cauliflower and Spinach with Red Curry Sauce (page 91)
Broiled or Grilled Portobellos and Baby Spinach Salad (page 217)
Soybeans and Spinach with Onion and Sesame Oil (page 305)

Spinach can also be used in place of chard leaves in any recipe.

Wilted Spinach with Garlic and Chiles

Spinach can be cooked in the water that clings to the leaves after they are washed. Since this process occurs in a covered pan, the technique is braising, although most cooks use the term wilting. Remember that spinach will shrink down to a fraction of its original volume, so don't be alarmed by the amount of uncooked leaves and do use a large, deep pot.

SERVES 4 AS A SIDE DISH

2 tablespoons extra-virgin olive oil

3 medium garlic cloves, minced

½ teaspoon hot red pepper flakes or 1 small dried red chile, minced

2½ pounds spinach, preferably flat-leaf, stems removed, washed, and shaken dry to remove any excess water (about 15 cups, tightly packed)

Salt

1. Heat the oil in a deep stockpot. Add the garlic and hot red pepper flakes and sauté over medium heat until the garlic is golden, about 1 minute. Add the spinach leaves and stir to coat evenly with the oil. Sprinkle with salt to taste.
2. Cover and cook, stirring occasionally, until the spinach is partially wilted, about 5 minutes. Remove the cover and cook for another minute or two or until any liquid in the pot has evaporated. Adjust the seasonings and serve immediately.

NOTE ABOUT BAGGED SPINACH

If you insist on using bagged spinach, you will need less since there is so little waste (i.e., no stems) with this product. One 10-ounce bag of spinach yields the same amount of usable spinach leaves as a 1¼-pound bunch of flat-leaf spinach. Adjust the recipes in this chapter accordingly if using stemmed spinach leaves sold in bags.

VARIATIONS: WILTED SPINACH WITH YELLOW RAISINS AND PINE NUTS

This is a typical Italian preparation.

Omit the hot red pepper flakes. Add 2 tablespoons yellow raisins and 2 tablespoons pine nuts when removing the cover in step 2.

WILTED SPINACH WITH GARLIC, GINGER, AND SOY

Cook a minced chile with the garlic and ginger if you like.

2 tablespoons roasted peanut oil

3 medium garlic cloves, minced

1 tablespoon minced fresh gingerroot

2½ pounds spinach, preferably flat-leaf, stems removed unless they are very thin, washed, and shaken dry to remove any excess water (about 15 cups, tightly packed)

1 tablespoon soy sauce

1. Heat the oil in a deep stockpot. Add the garlic and ginger and sauté over medium heat until the garlic is golden, about 1 minute. Add the spinach leaves and stir to coat evenly with the oil.

2. Cover and cook, stirring occasionally, until the spinach is partially wilted, about 5 minutes. Remove the cover, stir in the soy sauce, and cook for another minute or two or until any liquid in the pot has evaporated. Adjust the seasonings, adding more soy sauce if necessary, and serve immediately.

WILTED SPINACH WITH PASTA

Wilted spinach is an excellent sauce for pasta. Use linguine or spaghetti if making the Italian spinach recipes with chiles or raisins. The variation with soy sauce works well with slippery udon noodles.

SERVES 4 AS A MAIN COURSE

Prepare one of the previous spinach recipes, increasing the amount of oil to ¼ cup and reducing the amount of spinach to 1½ pounds. While preparing the spinach, bring 4 quarts of water to a boil in large pot. Add 1 pound pasta and salt to taste and cook until al dente. Reserve ½ cup cooking water and drain the pasta. Toss the pasta with the cooked spinach, adding as much of the reserved cooking water as necessary to moisten the pasta.

Spinach with Brown Butter and Walnuts

Instead of braising spinach in its own liquid, it is also possible to boil it in abundant water, drain it when tender, and then briefly reheat the shrunken mass in fat. In this case, butter infuses the cooked spinach with flavor rather quickly. Heating the butter until the solids become golden brown gives it an intense dairy flavor and aroma.

SERVES 4 AS A SIDE DISH

2½ pounds spinach, preferably flat-leaf, stems removed unless they are very thin, and washed (about 15 cups, tightly packed)
     Salt
3 tablespoons chopped walnuts
2 tablespoons unsalted butter

1. Bring 4 quarts of water to a boil in a large saucepan. Add the damp spinach and 2 teaspoons salt. Cook, stirring to submerge all the leaves, until tender, about 2 minutes. Drain and set the spinach aside. (The spinach can be set aside at room temperature for up to 2 hours.)

2. Place the walnuts in a medium skillet set over medium heat. Toast, shaking the pan occasionally to turn the nuts, until fragrant, about 5 minutes. Transfer the nuts to a plate.

3. Reduce the heat to medium-low and add the butter to the empty pan. Cook, swirling the pan occasionally, until the butter turns golden brown, about 4 minutes. Stir in the toasted walnuts and

spinach. Use two forks to pull apart the spinach leaves and coat them evenly with the butter. Cook until the spinach is heated through, about 2 minutes. Add salt to taste and serve immediately.

Sesame Spinach

This dish is very simply seasoned and delicious.

SERVES 4 AS A SIDE DISH

2½ pounds spinach, preferably flat-leaf, stems removed unless they are very thin, and washed (about 15 cups, tightly packed)
     Salt
  2 tablespoons sesame seeds
  2 tablespoons toasted sesame oil

1. Bring 4 quarts of water to a boil in a large saucepan. Add the damp spinach and 2 teaspoons salt. Cook, stirring to submerge all the leaves, until tender, about 2 minutes. Drain and set the spinach aside. (The spinach can be set aside at room temperature for up to 2 hours.)
2. Place the sesame seeds in a medium skillet set over medium heat. Toast, shaking the pan occasionally to turn the seeds, until lightly browned, about 3 minutes.
3. Add the oil to the pan and heat briefly. Stir in the spinach. Use two forks to pull apart the spinach leaves and coat them evenly with the oil and sesame seeds. Cook until the spinach is heated through, about 2 minutes. Add salt to taste and serve immediately.

Stir-Fried Spinach with Caramelized Shallots and Scallions

When stir-frying spinach, leave enough moisture on the greens so they don't dry out in the hot pan. Also, add the spinach in batches to prevent cooling the pan.

SERVES 4 AS A SIDE DISH

 ¼ cup chicken or vegetable stock
  2 tablespoons soy sauce
  1 tablespoon dry sherry or sake
2½ tablespoons roasted peanut oil
2½ pounds spinach, preferably flat-leaf, stems removed unless they are very thin, washed, and shaken dry to remove excess water (about 15 cups, tightly packed)
  4 medium shallots, peeled and sliced thin
  2 medium scallions, white and light green parts, sliced thin

1. Combine the stock, soy sauce, and sherry in a small bowl and set it aside.
2. Heat ½ tablespoon of the oil in a wok or large nonstick skillet set over high heat. Add one quarter of the spinach and cook, turning the leaves with tongs, just until wilted, about 1 minute. Transfer the cooked spinach to a colander set over a large bowl and repeat the process, adding more oil as needed, until all of the spinach has been cooked and transferred to the colander.

3. Heat the remaining ½ tablespoon of oil in the empty pan. Add the shallots and stir-fry until golden brown, 2 to 3 minutes. Add the scallions and cook just until tender, about 30 seconds. Add the cooked spinach and reserved sauce to the pan. Stir-fry until heated through, about 1 minute. Serve immediately.

VARIATION: STIR-FRIED SPINACH WITH SCALLOPS OR TOFU

Serve with rice or noodles.

SERVES 4 AS A MAIN COURSE

Before cooking the spinach, stir-fry 1 pound scallops or firm tofu, drained well and cut into ½-inch cubes, in 1 tablespoon peanut oil. The scallops should be cooked until opaque, about 1 minute; the tofu until golden brown, about 5 minutes. When cooked, transfer the scallops or tofu to a bowl. Proceed with the recipe (using the same pan). Add back the scallops or tofu with the cooked spinach and sauce to heat through.

Spinach Salad with Mushrooms, Croutons, and Warm Lemon Dressing

Woodsy cremini mushrooms are a first choice here, but blander white button mushrooms will be fine since the dressing is so flavorful. Whole baby spinach leaves may be used if desired.

SERVES 4 AS A FIRST COURSE

1½ pounds flat-leaf spinach, stemmed, washed, dried, and torn into large pieces (about 9 cups, tightly packed)
½ pound cremini or white button mushrooms, wiped clean and sliced thin
¼ cup extra-virgin olive oil
2 medium garlic cloves, minced
2 tablespoons lemon juice
　Salt
　Freshly ground black pepper
2½ cups Best Croutons (page 132)

1. Place the spinach and mushrooms in a large bowl and set the bowl aside.
2. Heat the oil and garlic in a small skillet over medium-low heat until the garlic is golden, about 4 minutes. Remove the pan from the heat and whisk in the lemon juice and salt and pepper to taste.
3. Pour the warm dressing over the salad and toss gently. Add the croutons and toss again. Serve immediately.

Spinach Salad with Shrimp, Mango, and Red Onion

This Asian-style dish calls for cooked and peeled shrimp. If you decide to do this yourself, buy slightly more than 1 pound of shrimp with the shells on.

SERVES 4 AS A MAIN COURSE

1½ pounds flat-leaf spinach, stemmed, washed, dried, and torn into large pieces (about 9 cups, tightly packed)

1 pound cooked peeled medium shrimp

1 large ripe mango, peeled, pitted, and cut into thin strips

½ small red onion, sliced thin

2 tablespoons rice vinegar

1 teaspoon grated orange zest

2 tablespoons orange juice

1 tablespoon minced fresh gingerroot
Salt and ground black pepper

¼ cup canola or other tasteless oil

1 tablespoon toasted sesame oil

1. Place the spinach, shrimp, and mango in a large bowl and set the bowl aside.

2. Place the onion slices and 1 tablespoon vinegar in a small bowl. Soak the onion until pink, about 5 minutes. Drain and set the onion aside.

3. Whisk the remaining tablespoon of vinegar, orange zest and juice, ginger, and salt and pepper to taste together in a small bowl. Whisk in the oils until the dressing is smooth. Adjust the seasonings.

4. Add the quick-pickled onion slices to the salad. Pour the dressing over the salad and toss gently. Serve immediately.

Sweet Potatoes

Sweet potatoes are not related to potatoes. In fact, these tubers are a member of the morning glory family. In addition, sweet potatoes are *not* yams. Yams are a tropical tuber with thick, bark-like and starchy flesh.

There are several kinds of sweet potatoes. An orange-fleshed variety is the most common in our markets, but sweet potatoes can have yellow or even white flesh. In general, the darker the color of the flesh, the moister and sweeter it will be.

OTHER COMMON NAMES: Yams (although this name is incorrect; see page 359).

AVAILABILITY: Year-round, although most reliably from fall through spring.

SELECTION: Choose firm sweet potatoes with skins that are taut, not wrinkled.

STORAGE: Sweet potatoes must be stored in a cool, dark, well-ventilated spot. They should keep for a week or so. Don't put sweet potatoes in the refrigerator. They soften and become moldy remarkably fast.

BASIC PREPARATION: Sweet potatoes require a minimum of preparation. If you are cooking the sweet potatoes with their skins on, scrub them well under cold, running water. If you want to remove the skin, just run a vegetable peeler over the sweet potatoes.

BEST COOKING METHODS: Baking, boiling (for purees), braising, frying, grilling (after boiling), and roasting.

Baked Sweet Potatoes

This is simple and delicious. Add a green vegetable or salad and you have an excellent lunch or a light dinner.

SERVES 4 AS A SIDE DISH

4 medium sweet potatoes (about 3 pounds), scrubbed
Salt
Unsalted butter

1. Preheat the oven to 425 degrees.
2. Line a rimmed baking sheet with foil. Place the sweet potatoes on the baking sheet. Bake until the sweet potatoes are tender when pierced with a skewer, about 1¼ hours.
3. Slit open the potatoes lengthwise and push on the sides to loosen the flesh. Sprinkle with salt to taste and add a pat of butter. Serve immediately.

VARIATIONS: BAKED SWEET POTATOES WITH GINGER BUTTER

This is unusual and delicious. Try other ground spices, such as nutmeg, allspice, cinnamon, or cardamom with sweet potatoes, adjusting the amount of spice as desired.

While the sweet potatoes are baking, mash 3 tablespoons softened butter, salt to taste, and ¾ teaspoon ground ginger together in a small bowl. Slit the baked sweet potatoes as directed and top with a dollop of the flavored butter. Serve immediately.

BAKED SWEET POTATOES WITH CHIPOTLE BUTTER

Spicy but not overpowering.

While the sweet potatoes are baking, mash 3 tablespoons softened butter, salt to taste, 1 minced chipotle chile in adobo sauce, and 1 teaspoon of the adobo sauce together in a small bowl. Slit the baked sweet potatoes as directed and top with a dollop of the flavored butter. Serve immediately.

BAKED SWEET POTATOES WITH LIME-CILANTRO BUTTER

Sweet potatoes and tropical flavors are a good match.

While the sweet potatoes are baking, mash 3 tablespoons softened butter, salt to taste, ½ teaspoon grated lime zest, 2 teaspoons lime juice, and 1 tablespoon minced fresh cilantro leaves together in a small bowl. Slit the baked sweet potatoes as directed and top with a dollop of the flavored butter. Serve immediately.

Sweet Potato Puree with Ginger and Chiles

Sweet potatoes can be boiled and mashed into a creamy puree just like regular potatoes. Their sweet flavor is a good foil for such strong flavors as ginger and chiles, which might overwhelm russet potatoes. I like the butter in this recipe (you could use peanut oil if you like) but find that the milk commonly used to smooth out mashed potatoes is a bit odd here. I prefer to reserve some of the sweet potato cooking water for this purpose. Pureed sweet potatoes are especially good with pork but also work nicely with most chicken dishes.

SERVES 4 AS A SIDE DISH

2 pounds sweet potatoes, peeled and cut into 1-inch cubes
    Salt
2 tablespoons unsalted butter
1 tablespoon minced fresh gingerroot
1 small jalapeño or other fresh chile, stemmed, seeded, and minced
1 tablespoon minced fresh cilantro leaves

1. Place the sweet potatoes in a large saucepan and add enough water to cover by about 2 inches. Add a generous amount of salt and bring the water to a boil. Reduce the heat slightly and cook until the sweet potatoes are tender, about 15 minutes.

2. Meanwhile, heat the butter in a large skillet until foamy. Add the ginger and chile and sauté over medium heat until fragrant, about 1 minute. Remove the pan from the heat.

3. Drain the sweet potatoes, reserving ½ cup of the cooking liquid. Place the sweet potatoes in a large bowl and use a potato masher to turn the sweet potatoes into fine bits. Add ¼ cup of the cooking liquid and continue mashing until the sweet potatoes form a fairly smooth puree. Add the remaining cooking liquid as needed to work the sweet potatoes into a smooth puree.

4. Set the skillet back over medium-high heat. When the ginger and chile start to sizzle, add the sweet potato puree and cook, stirring constantly, just until the ginger, chiles, and butter have been evenly incorporated into the sweet potatoes, about 1 minute. Stir in the cilantro and salt to taste and serve immediately.

Sweet Potato Puree with Orange and Brown Sugar

I prefer this traditional American puree just barely sweet. Increase the brown sugar to 2 or 3 tablespoons for a puree that is truly sweet.

SERVES 4 AS A SIDE DISH

2 pounds sweet potatoes, peeled and cut into 1-inch cubes
    Salt
1 tablespoon unsalted butter, softened

1 teaspoon grated orange zest
¼ cup orange juice
1 tablespoon brown sugar

1. Place the sweet potatoes in a large saucepan and add enough water to cover by about 2 inches. Add a generous amount of salt and bring the water to a boil. Reduce the heat slightly and cook until the sweet potatoes are tender, about 15 minutes. Drain thoroughly.

2. Return the sweet potatoes to the empty saucepan set over the warm burner. Add the butter and orange zest and use a potato masher to turn the sweet potatoes into fine bits. Add the orange juice and brown sugar and continue mashing until the sweet potatoes form a fairly smooth puree. Adjust the seasonings and serve immediately.

Sweet Potato Fries

I like these fries just as much as regular french fries. They are delicious seasoned with just salt but the sweet, caramelized flavors also work well with spices. Sweet potatoes don't need to be twice-cooked like regular potatoes. Cut them thin and fry them until very brown (the sugars make them look more cooked than they really are) and they will be cooked through.

SERVES 4 AS A SIDE DISH

1½ pounds sweet potatoes, scrubbed
     About 6 cups peanut oil for frying
     Salt, preferably kosher or other coarse salt

1. Cut the sweet potatoes from end to end into ovals about ¼ inch thick. Slice the ovals lengthwise to yield long, slender strips about ¼ inch thick.

2. Heat about 2 inches of oil in a deep 6-quart pot to 365 degrees.

3. Add about one quarter of the sweet potatoes to the hot oil, making sure the pan is not crowded, and cook until they are well browned, about 4 minutes. (Adjust the heat as necessary as the sweet potatoes cook—the temperature should not rise above 365 degrees, nor should it drop below 340 degrees.) Use a skimmer or slotted spoon to transfer the fries to a platter lined with paper towels. Sprinkle with salt to taste and serve immediately. Repeat with the remaining sweet potatoes.

VARIATION: SPICY FRIES

Add more cayenne for really spicy fries.

Mix 2 teaspoons chili powder, 2 teaspoons sweet paprika, cayenne pepper to taste (at least ¼ teaspoon), and salt to taste in a small bowl. As the fries come out of the oil, sprinkle them with some of this mixture and toss to coat evenly. Serve immediately.

Roasted Sweet Potato "Fries"

Thick wedges of sweet potatoes will caramelize and become crisp if oiled lightly and cooked in a hot oven. There are two "tricks" to this recipe. First, preheat a large baking sheet in the oven as it comes up to temperature so that the potatoes sizzle when they are added to the pan. Second, don't turn the potatoes too much. You want them to stay in place long enough to brown nicely. These "fries" are a great accompaniment to chicken, pork, or burgers.

SERVES 4 AS A SIDE DISH

3 medium sweet potatoes (about 2 pounds)
3 tablespoons extra-virgin olive oil
  Salt

1. Place a large rimmed baking sheet in the oven. Preheat the oven to 425 degrees.
2. Meanwhile, cut the potatoes in quarters lengthwise and then cut the quarters lengthwise into ½-inch-thick wedges. Toss the sweet potato wedges with 2 tablespoons of the oil and salt to taste in a large bowl.
3. When the oven has come up to temperature, carefully brush the remaining 1 tablespoon of oil evenly over the baking sheet. Dump the sweet potatoes onto the oiled sheet and spread them apart so that each sweet potato wedge is in direct contact with the baking sheet.
4. Bake for 25 minutes. Using a pair of tongs, turn each sweet potato wedge. Continue baking

until the sweet potato wedges are quite brown and crisp, about 20 minutes. Season with more salt if desired and serve immediately.

Sweet Potato Casserole with Maple and Ginger

This is a sweet but not cloying version of this perennial holiday favorite.

SERVES 6 TO 8 AS A SIDE DISH

3 pounds sweet potatoes, scrubbed
3 tablespoons unsalted butter, plus extra for greasing the baking dish
1 tablespoon minced fresh gingerroot
⅓ cup maple syrup
⅓ cup water
  Salt
  Freshly ground black pepper

1. Place the sweet potatoes in a large pot and cover with several inches of water. Bring to a boil, reduce the heat, and simmer until a skewer slides through the sweet potatoes with just a little resistance, about 15 minutes. Drain and cool.

2. While cooking the potatoes, melt the butter in a small saucepan. Add the ginger and sauté over medium heat until fragrant, about 1 minute. Stir in the maple syrup and water. Remove the pan from the heat. Season with salt and pepper to taste.

3. Preheat the oven to 375 degrees. Butter a 13 by 9-inch baking dish.

4. When cool, peel and cut the sweet potatoes in half lengthwise. Cut the sweet potato halves crosswise into 1-inch chunks. Place the sweet potatoes in the baking dish. Pour the maple mixture over the potatoes. Cover the dish with aluminum foil and bake, stirring once, for 45 minutes. Remove the foil, stir the sweet potatoes, and continue to bake until the sweet potatoes are completely tender and the glaze has thickened, about 15 minutes. Serve immediately.

Taro

Taro and malanga are closely related and are often confused by food writers and shopkeepers. The two are often mislabeled in stores, which can be frustrating to the novice cook. Thankfully, taro and malanga can be used interchangeably. However, it is helpful to be able to distinguish the two.

Both taro and malanga are covered with hairy, brown skin. Taro is barrel-shaped, while malanga often has rounded ends like a potato. Malanga flesh is most frequently white but can be yellow or even pink. Taro has ivory-colored flesh, which is often speckled with tiny brown dots.

I find that taro tastes a lot like a potato and it can be cooked pretty much the same way as a potato, often with better results. Taro makes an especially suave, silky soup; unlike potatoes, taro doesn't become gummy when pureed. Taro makes the crispest, lightest chips imaginable and produces wispy, lacy fritters.

Of all the tropical root vegetables now available in this country, taro probably has the widest appeal because of its light (not-too-starchy) texture and mild flavor.

OTHER COMMON NAMES: Dasheen, eddo, malanga isleña, and woo tau.

AVAILABILITY: Year-round, mostly in markets that cater to Latino or Asian shoppers.

SELECTION: Look for firm taro that are at least as large as a russet potato, if not larger. Small taro, the size of a new potato and often sold as eddo, are very difficult to peel. By the time you remove all the skin and blemishes, there's nothing left to cook. Small taro should be avoided.

STORAGE: Taro can be kept in a cool, well-ventilated spot for several days. Do not refrigerate.

BASIC PREPARATION: Start by rinsing the taro under cool, running water to remove any loose dirt. Working with one taro at a time, use a paring knife to remove the brown skin and outer ⅛-inch layer of flesh. You want to remove any blemishes. It helps to rinse the taro as you work to flush out any bits of the skin. Cut the peeled taro as desired and drop the chunks into a bowl of cold water to prevent browning.

BEST COOKING METHODS: Boiling, frying, or steaming and then sautéing.

OTHER RECIPES WITH TARO: Taro can be used in any of the malanga recipes. Like malanga, it turns gray when boiled and mashed.

Taro Soup

The texture of this soup is silky and suave. Taro becomes grayish when cooked so I've added carrots here to give the soup a light orange color. The sweetness of the carrots (and leeks) also works well with the tropical flavors of chile, coconut milk, and cilantro. Serve this rich soup in small portions. Use light or regular coconut milk as desired.

SERVES 6 TO 8 AS A FIRST COURSE

1 pound large taro
2 tablespoons extra-virgin olive oil
2 medium leeks, white and light green parts, sliced thin
2 medium carrots, peeled and chopped
2 medium garlic cloves, minced
1 medium jalapeño or other fresh chile, stemmed, seeded, and minced
1 tablespoon minced fresh gingerroot
4 cups chicken or vegetable stock
Salt
Freshly ground black pepper
½ cup coconut milk
2 tablespoons minced fresh cilantro leaves

1. Working with one taro at a time, use a paring knife to remove the skin and outer ⅛-inch layer of flesh. Cut the taro into 1-inch chunks and drop them into a bowl of cold water.

2. Heat the oil in a large stockpot. Add the leeks and carrots and sauté over medium heat until softened, about 10 minutes. Add the garlic, chile, and ginger and sauté until fragrant, about 1 minute.

3. Drain the taro and add it to the pot along with the stock and salt and pepper to taste. Bring to a boil, reduce the heat, cover, and simmer until the taro is very tender, about 30 minutes.

4. Puree the soup, in batches if necessary, in a blender until smooth. Return the soup to the pot and stir in the coconut milk. Adjust the seasonings. (The soup can be cooled and refrigerated for 1 day or frozen for several weeks.) Reheat. Ladle the soup into bowls as soon as the soup is hot. Garnish the bowls with the cilantro and serve immediately.

Sautéed Taro with Garlic, Chiles, and Sour Orange Sauce

This is my version of a Caribbean dish that starts with steamed taro chunks that are then sautéed and cooked with garlic, lots of fresh chile, and sour orange juice. A combination of sweet orange juice and lime juice approximates the flavor of the Caribbean fruit typically used here. The habanero is the authentic choice but is too hot for most American palates. The jalapeño delivers a similar result but with far less heat. Taro chunks must be cooked before sautéing, but they fall apart and become mushy if boiled. Steaming works beautifully. Serve with a Caribbean pork roast, with chicken, or even with fish.

1 pound large taro
2 tablespoons extra-virgin olive oil
3 medium garlic cloves, minced
1 habanero or jalapeño chile, stemmed,
    seeded, and minced
⅓ cup orange juice
2 tablespoons lime juice
  Salt

1. Working with one taro at a time, use a paring knife to remove the skin and outer ⅛-inch layer of flesh. Cut the taro into 1-inch chunks and drop them into a bowl of cold water.

2. Bring an inch or so of water to a boil in a wide saucepan. Drain the taro and place it in a steamer basket. Lower the basket into the pan, cover the pan, and steam until the taro is just tender, about 10 minutes. Remove the taro from the steamer and set it aside. Blot the taro dry on paper towels.

3. Heat the oil in a large skillet. Add the taro and cook over medium heat, turning the pieces two or three times, until lightly browned, about 8 minutes. Stir in the garlic and chile and cook until fragrant, about 20 seconds. Add the juices and cook until they reduce to a glaze, 1 to 2 minutes. Add salt to taste and serve immediately.

Taro Chips

These are crisper and lighter than potato chips. Make sure to buy regularly shaped taro without too many knobs or protrusions. Log-shaped taro, about 2 inches thick, are ideal here. You can cut the taro with a mandoline, but a heavy-duty vegetable peeler will also work.

SERVES 4 TO 6 AS A SNACK

1 pound large taro
  About 4 cups peanut oil for frying
  Salt

1. Working with one taro at a time, use a paring knife to remove the skin and outer ⅛-inch layer of flesh. Cut a thick slice off one end of the taro to make a flat surface. Working against this cut surface, use a mandoline or strong vegetable peeler to slice the taro into thin chips. (If using a vegetable peeler, make sure to press fairly hard so that the slices are not too thin and are complete circles.)

2. Heat 1½ inches of oil in a deep, 4-quart pot to a temperature of 375 degrees. Add a handful of taro slices and stir with a mesh skimmer to separate them. (Add as much taro as will fit in a single layer across the surface of the oil.) Fry, turning occasionally, until the chips are golden brown, 1 to 2 minutes.

3. Use a skimmer or slotted spoon to transfer the chips to a platter lined with paper towels. Sprinkle generously with salt and gently roll the chips around on the paper towels to soak up the excess oil. Transfer the chips to a serving bowl. Repeat the process with the remaining taro. (You will be making at least eight batches here.) Serve the chips within an hour or two for maximum crispness.

Tomatillos

Tomatillos look like small green tomatoes but they are not. Like tomatoes, tomatillos are technically a fruit, not a vegetable. However, they are sharp-tasting (there's not even a trace of sweetness in a tomatillo) and we use them like a vegetable in savory dishes.

The tomatillo is green and round, between the size of a golf ball and a plum. Its most distinctive feature is the papery yellow husk that covers each tomatillo.

Tomatillos have a bright, lemon flavor and thick, pulpy texture when pureed, either before or after cooking. They make an excellent salsa and salad dressing and can be used in soups or stews.

OTHER COMMON NAMES: Tomato verde. (Tomatillos are not simply green tomatoes as this name suggests but a different species in the same family.)

AVAILABILITY: Year-round.

SELECTION: Choose tomatillos that are still in their husks. Tomatillos that are mature at harvest time will fill out their husks and should be selected. The fruit should feel firm when squeezed. I find that smaller tomatillos, about the size of a golf ball, are marginally more flavorful than larger specimens. Occasionally, you might see a tomatillo blushed with purple. This variety is popular in Mexico but rarely reaches U.S. markets. They taste the same as all-green tomatillos.

STORAGE: Unhusked tomatillos will keep in the refrigerator for at least a week.

BASIC PREPARATION: Remove the papery husk that covers each tomatillo and rinse the sticky substance that covers the fruit, especially near the stem end.

BEST COOKING METHODS: Boiling, broiling, or roasting. Raw tomatillos can be pureed for salad dressing.

OTHER RECIPES WITH TOMATILLOS: Chilled Avocado-Tomatillo Soup (page 25)

Roasted Tomatillo Salsa with Ancho Chiles

It's hard to believe that there are just four ingredients, plus salt, in this rich, flavor-packed, nonfat salsa. Roasting the tomatillos and toasting the chile and garlic really adds depth here. Serve this thick, chunky salsa with a basket of chips, drizzle some over cheese quesadillas or grilled fish, or stir some into scrambled eggs. Any dried chile will work here, but I prefer an ancho or New Mexico chile.

MAKES ABOUT 1½ CUPS

1 medium dried chile, about 3 inches long
2 medium garlic cloves, unpeeled
1 pound tomatillos, husked and rinsed
1 tablespoon minced fresh cilantro leaves
Salt

1. Place a medium nonstick skillet over medium heat. Add the chile to the hot skillet and toast, turning once, until fragrant, about 2 minutes. Transfer the chile to a bowl and cover with hot tap water. Soak for 30 minutes.
2. Add the garlic cloves to the hot skillet and toast, turning occasionally, until the skins blacken, about 5 minutes. Remove the garlic from the pan and set aside to cool.
3. Preheat the broiler. Place the tomatillos on a rimmed baking sheet and broil, turning occasionally, until the skins blacken in spots, about 8 minutes. Set the tomatillos aside to cool.

4. When the chile has softened, drain and place it on a cutting board. Remove the stem, halve lengthwise, and discard the seeds. Place the chile in a food processor. Peel the garlic and place it in the food processor along with half the tomatillos. Puree until smooth. Add the remaining tomatillos and pulse once or twice to form a chunky salsa. Scrape the salsa into a bowl and stir in the cilantro and salt to taste. Serve immediately or cover and refrigerate for up to 2 days. Bring to room temperature before serving.

Tomatillo Dressing

This thick and smooth dressing can be used with salad greens, shrimp salad, or chicken salad. Pour some into an avocado half instead of a traditional vinaigrette. This dressing is sharp-tasting but not acidic.

MAKES ABOUT 1 CUP

⅓ pound tomatillos (about 4 medium), husked, rinsed, and quartered
1 tablespoon lime juice
¼ cup extra-virgin olive oil
Salt
Freshly ground black pepper

Place the tomatillos, lime juice, and oil in a food processor or blender and puree until smooth. Add salt and pepper to taste. Use the dressing immediately or refrigerate it in a covered container for several days. Shake well before using.

Tomatoes

Fresh tomatoes are a summer fruit that we treat as a vegetable. If you want to cook with tomatoes at other times of the year, use canned. I know this sounds simple, but someone must be buying all those rock-hard, mealy, flavorless tomatoes that fill supermarkets, even in the dead of winter.

Scientists and plant breeders have tried everything (including inserting DNA from other organisms into tomatoes to keep them from softening after they ripen) but nothing has worked. If you want a good tomato, buy a tomato that has been grown locally.

There are numerous heirloom tomatoes, with all kinds of colors and patterns at farmers' markets. For the most part, all of these tomatoes can be used like the basic round, red tomato. Some may be sweeter or more acidic than others, but the differences are fairly slight. One notable exception is the tiny cherry tomato. Because of their size, cherry tomatoes are the one tomato that I cook whole in a hot skillet with a little oil and seasonings.

If you garden, you may find yourself with a surfeit of green tomatoes at the end of the year. As long as green tomatoes are not rock-hard, they can be coated, Southern style, with cornmeal and pan-fried. They can also be used to make interesting (and tart) chutneys.

Although all the recipes in this chapter call for fresh tomatoes, I use canned tomatoes as a seasoning or cooking medium throughout this book. Until fairly recently, I relied on canned whole tomatoes in juice. I drained the tomatoes, chopped them, and then added them to dishes, often with some of the packing liquid, which is tomato juice. (I find that canned tomatoes in juice have a fresher flavor than canned tomatoes in puree.)

Although I still like canned whole tomatoes in juice, I have found an equally good product that saves much bother and mess. Muir Glen Diced Tomatoes are nothing more than diced tomatoes packed in tomato juice and flavored with a bit of salt.

AVAILABILITY: Summer through early fall.

SELECTION: Never buy tomatoes at a supermarket. This may sound drastic, but this advice will serve you well in 99 out of 100 supermarkets in this country.

If you care about tomatoes, you want to buy tomatoes that are locally grown. That means waiting until it is tomato season in your area and then buying at a farm stand or a produce market that buys directly from local growers. Almost no supermarkets do this. Even though I live in an agricultural region that produces stunning summer tomatoes, my local super-market (which otherwise has a superb produce section) sells rock-hard tomatoes that have been trucked hundreds if not thousands of miles in August. Go figure.

Tomatoes should be richly colored and their skins should be smooth. When shopping, give the tomatoes a sniff; they should smell sweet and delicious. Gently squeeze the tomatoes; they should not feel mushy or rock-hard. Ideally, they will give slightly to gentle pressure.

STORAGE: Tomatoes should never be refrigerated. Cold temperatures make them mushy and ruin their flavor. Keep tomatoes in a basket on the counter. If they are not fully ripe, they will continue to ripen and soften over the course of several days or even a week. Fully ripe tomatoes should be used sooner, within a few days, or you risk having them become soft.

BASIC PREPARATION: There are several ways to prepare a round tomato. Most recipes start by removing the core. Use a paring knife to cut around the stem end and sim-ply pull out the brown spot on the top of the tomato and the piece of core that is attached. At this point, the tomato can be: cut into wedges, by slicing down through the hole left by the core; chopped or diced—handle a tomato the same way you would an onion, by cutting it in half, laying each half flat side down on a cutting board, making one or two slices par-allel to the board, and then turning the knife and slicing down through the tomato slices and then across the slices to turn out cubes; or cut into round slices, by slicing the tomato crosswise through (not across) the imaginary equator of the tomato.

All of these methods assume you are using all parts of the tomato. However, in some cases, you will want to remove the peels and/or seeds.

To remove just the seeds, cut the cored tomato in half through the equator and then pull out the seeds and surrounding gelatinous material with your fingers.

To remove the skins and seeds, you have two options. The classic technique is to drop the whole tomatoes in a pot of simmering water for about 20 seconds to loosen the skins. Turn the tomatoes at least once while they are in the water to ensure that that all parts of the tomato have come into direct contact with the water. The tomatoes are retrieved with a slotted spoon, cooled slightly, and then cored as usual. With the skin exposed at the top of the tomato (where the core piece was removed), you can scrape away the skin with your fingers. The tomato is then halved through the equator and the seeds removed.

Unless the tomatoes are really ripe and soft, I don't bother with the blanching step. My Oxo Good Grips vegetable peeler is quite sharp and will remove skin from any tomato that is at all firm. Remove the core with a paring knife. Starting at the top of the tomato where the skin has been cut, gently but firmly glide the vegetable peeler down the side of the tomato to remove a wide swath of skin. Repeat the process, always starting at the top of the tomato where the flesh has been exposed. If you feel that your vegetable peeler is not sharp enough or that the tomato is too soft, you can always bring a quart of water to a boil and blanch the tomatoes.

Cherry tomatoes are usually sold with their green stems attached. Remove the stems, wash the tomatoes, and then use them whole (for sautéing) or slice in half for salads.

BEST COOKING METHODS: Baking, broiling, grilling, roasting, and sautéing. Raw tomatoes are used in salads.

OTHER RECIPES WITH TOMATOES:
Simplest Arugula and Tomato Salad (page 11)
Fusilli with Arugula and Tomato Sauce (page 13)
Shrimp and Avocado Salad with Grapefruit Dressing (page 25)
Chayote and Tomato Salad with Lime and Allspice (page 109)
Grilled Corn, Tomato, and Red Onion Salad (page 118)
Eggplant and Tomato Gratin with Onion-Herb Jam (page 140)
Ratatouille (page 141)
Green Beans and Corn with Tomato-Herb Vinaigrette (page 175)
Green Bean Salad with Tomatoes and Feta Cheese (page 176)
Green Bean Salad with Tomatoes, Goat Cheese, and Walnuts (page 176)
Greek Salad with Feta and Olives (page 202)
Stewed Okra and Tomatoes (page 227)
Stewed Peppers with Tomato and Onion (*Peperonata*) (page 251)
Stewed Summer Potatoes with Tomato (page 274)
Zucchini and Tomato Gratin with Pesto (page 373)

Tomato and Cucumber Salad with Mint

Tomato and cucumbers are a natural summer pairing. I like the extra crispness of salted cucumbers. Without the cucumber seeds and juices, the dressing tastes more clearly of tomatoes, which to my mind is preferable. See page 125 for more information on salting cucumbers. Serve this salad with almost anything from the grill.

SERVES 4 TO 6 AS A SIDE DISH

2 medium cucumbers (about 1 pound), peeled, halved lengthwise, seeded, and cut on the diagonal ¼ inch thick

2 teaspoons kosher salt, plus more to taste

4 small ripe tomatoes (about 1 pound), cored and cut into ¾-inch-thick wedges

½ small red onion, diced (about ¼ cup)

8 large fresh mint leaves, cut into thin strips

2 tablespoons extra-virgin olive oil

1 tablespoon lemon juice

Freshly ground black pepper

1. Toss the cucumbers and 2 teaspoons salt in a large strainer or colander set over a bowl. Fill a gallon-size zipper-lock plastic bag with ice water and set the bag on top of the cucumber slices. Drain for 1 hour.

2. Thoroughly rinse the cucumber slices under cold, running water and pat dry.

3. Place the tomatoes in a large bowl and sprinkle lightly with salt to taste. Add the cucumbers, onion, and mint and toss gently. Drizzle the oil and lemon juice over the salad and toss gently. Season with pepper to taste and serve immediately.

Sliced Tomato Salad with Parmesan and Basil

A favorite summer salad in my house that relies on top-notch ingredients—ripe tomatoes, fragrant basil, extra-virgin olive oil, and Parmigiano-Reggiano. (The tomatoes have enough acidity that the salad needs no vinegar.) I like this salad so much I often serve it for lunch with some grilled bread. It is also wonderful as a first course to a summer supper, followed by most anything—grilled fish, chicken, steak. As a side dish, I prefer this tomato, cheese, and basil salad to the version made with mozzarella, since the emphasis here is on the tomatoes with the cheese as an seasoning.

SERVES 4 AS A FIRST COURSE OR SIDE DISH

4 medium ripe tomatoes (about 2 pounds), cored and cut crosswise into ½-inch-thick slices

8 large fresh basil leaves, cut into thin strips
Salt
Freshly ground black pepper

1 small hunk Parmesan cheese

2 tablespoons extra-virgin olive oil

1. Arrange the tomato slices on a large serving platter. Scatter the basil over the tomatoes and sprinkle with salt and pepper to taste.

2. Using a vegetable peeler, remove thin shavings of cheese from the hunk of Parmesan. Shower several dozen cheese curls directly over the tomatoes. (You will use about an ounce of cheese.) Drizzle with the oil and serve immediately.

Sautéed Cherry Tomatoes with Garlic and Basil

The technique could not be simpler—just warm whole cherry tomatoes in a hot skillet. This recipe relies on the simplest flavorings—garlic and basil. The dish is especially good as part of an Italian meal.

SERVES 4 AS A SIDE DISH

1 tablespoon extra-virgin olive oil
1 pint cherry tomatoes, stems removed
3 medium garlic cloves, minced
8 large fresh basil leaves, cut crosswise into thin strips
Salt
Freshly ground black pepper

1. Heat the oil in a large skillet over medium-high heat. When the oil is hot, add the tomatoes and cook, stirring often, just until the tomatoes are almost heated through and the skins are beginning to brown in spots, about 2 minutes.

2. Add the garlic and continue to cook for another 30 seconds, taking care not to let the garlic burn. Add the basil and salt and pepper to taste. Serve immediately.

Sautéed Cherry Tomatoes with Onion, Olives, and Feta Cheese

Greek flavors are used to create a rich, satisfying tomato side dish that works especially well with lamb. Because feta cheese is generally so salty, this recipe does not call for any added salt.

SERVES 4 AS A SIDE DISH

2 tablespoons extra-virgin olive oil
1 medium onion, minced
1 pint cherry tomatoes, stems removed
12 large Kalamata olives, pitted and chopped
1 tablespoon minced fresh parsley leaves
Freshly ground black pepper
2 ounces feta cheese, crumbled (about ½ cup)

1. Heat the oil in a large skillet. Add the onion and sauté over medium heat until golden, about 5 minutes.

2. Raise the heat to medium-high and add the tomatoes. Cook just until the tomatoes are

heated through and the skins are beginning to brown in spots, about 2 minutes. Add the olives, parsley, and pepper to taste.

3. Transfer the tomato mixture to a wide, shallow serving bowl. Sprinkle the cheese over the tomatoes and serve immediately.

Simplest Broiled Tomatoes with Parmesan

Too many broiled tomato recipes go wrong because the tomatoes are placed too close to the heating element. The result is a charred top crust and a lukewarm interior. Moving the oven rack 6 inches from the broiling element gives the tomatoes a chance to heat through completely and to soften a bit by the time the top becomes golden brown and crisp. Depending on what else is being served, a halved tomato will yield two modest portions or one large portion.

SERVES 4 TO 8 AS A SIDE DISH

4 medium ripe tomatoes (about 2 pounds), cored and halved crosswise through the equator
1 cup grated Parmesan cheese
½ teaspoon salt
Freshly ground black pepper

1. Adjust the oven rack so that it is about 6 inches from the broiling element. Preheat the broiler. Place the tomatoes on a lightly oiled rimmed baking sheet and set aside briefly.

2. Combine the cheese and salt and pepper to taste in a small bowl. Sprinkle the cheese mixture over the tops of the tomatoes.

3. Broil the tomatoes, watching them carefully to make sure they are not burning, just until the tomatoes soften a bit and the tops become nicely browned, 5 to 6 minutes. Serve hot or warm.

Broiled Tomatoes with Blue Cheese and Parsley

The contrast between soft, juicy tomato and pungent blue cheese is delicious. I prefer a creamier blue cheese, such as a young Gorgonzola or Saga blue here, but you can use a crumbly, more potent blue cheese if you prefer. Serve with lamb chops or steak.

SERVES 4 TO 8 AS A SIDE DISH

4 medium ripe tomatoes (about 2 pounds), cored and halved crosswise through the equator
4 ounces blue cheese, crumbled (about 1 cup)
1 tablespoon minced fresh parsley leaves
Freshly ground black pepper

1. Adjust the oven rack so that it is about 6 inches from the broiling element. Preheat the broiler. Place the tomatoes on a lightly oiled rimmed baking sheet and set aside briefly.

2. Use a fork to mash together the cheese, parsley, and pepper to taste in a small bowl. Pat the cheese mixture over the tops of the tomatoes.

3. Broil the tomatoes, watching them carefully to make sure they are not burning, just until the tomatoes soften a bit and the tops become nicely browned, 5 to 6 minutes. Serve hot or warm.

Baked Tomatoes with Herbed Bread Crumb Stuffing

This old-fashioned recipe tastes thoroughly modern when fresh bread crumbs and fresh herbs are used in place of the standard dried bread crumbs and herbs. I like the combination of parsley, basil, and oregano, but use whatever you have on hand, including thyme, tarragon, marjoram, dill, or sage. As with broiled tomatoes, a single tomato will yield two modest portions or one large portion.

SERVES 4 TO 8 AS A SIDE DISH

4 medium ripe tomatoes (about 2 pounds), cored and halved crosswise through the equator
1 cup Fresh Bread Crumbs (page 109)
¼ cup grated Parmesan cheese
2 tablespoons minced fresh parsley leaves
2 tablespoons minced fresh basil leaves
1 tablespoon minced fresh oregano leaves
1 large garlic clove, minced

Salt
Freshly ground black pepper
2 tablespoons extra-virgin olive oil, plus extra for greasing the baking dish

1. Preheat the oven to 425 degrees.

2. Use your fingers to pull the seeds and surrounding liquid material out of the tomatoes halves. Set the seeded tomatoes aside.

3. Combine the bread crumbs, cheese, herbs, garlic, and salt and pepper to taste in a small bowl. Drizzle the oil over the mixture and combine with your fingers just until the bread crumb mixture is moistened.

4. Carefully spoon the mixture into the seeded tomatoes, patting the stuffing over the tops. Place the tomatoes, cut side up, in a lightly greased baking dish.

5. Bake just until the tomatoes are heated through and the stuffing is crisp and golden brown, about 20 minutes. Let the tomatoes settle for 10 minutes. Serve warm.

Fresh Tomato Soup for Summer

In this recipe, the flavor of fresh tomatoes is distilled into a creamy pureed soup with minimal distractions. Onion, carrot, and celery provide some backbone, along with fresh thyme or oregano, but there's no cream here to interfere with the tomato flavor. Although you may serve this soup hot, I think it's best well chilled with a couple of croutons floated in each bowl. If you must have some dairy, float a dollop of sour cream or crème fraîche in each bowl.

SERVES 4 TO 6 AS A FIRST COURSE

2 tablespoons extra-virgin olive oil
1 small onion, minced
1 small carrot, peeled and minced
1 small celery stalk, minced
1 teaspoon minced fresh thyme or oregano
3 pounds ripe tomatoes, cored, peeled, seeded, and chopped (about 4 cups pulp)
  Salt
  Freshly ground black pepper
2 cups chicken or vegetable stock
2½ cups Best Croutons (page 132)
  Shredded fresh basil leaves

1. Heat the oil in a large saucepan. Add the onion, carrot, and celery and sauté over medium heat until softened, about 5 minutes. Add the thyme and tomatoes and cook until the tomatoes lose their shape, about 10 minutes. Season with salt and pepper to taste.

2. Add the stock and simmer until the flavors have blended, about 5 minutes. Puree the soup in a blender until quite smooth. Adjust the seasonings. Serve immediately, garnishing the bowls with croutons and basil. Better yet, refrigerate the soup until well chilled (at least 4 hours and up to 2 days) and add the croutons and basil just before serving.

Fresh Tomato Salsa with Chipotle Chile

My favorite all-purpose tomato salsa, perfect with tortilla chips, grilled fish, or steak. I like the smoky flavor of the chipotle chile, but you can substitute a minced fresh jalapeño if you prefer. The amount of chipotle chile called for in this recipe makes a spicy but not incendiary salsa. Adjust the amount as desired.

MAKES ABOUT 3 CUPS

1½ pounds ripe tomatoes, cored and diced very small
1 chipotle chile in adobo sauce, minced with 1 teaspoon sauce, or to taste
1 small red onion, minced
¼ cup minced fresh cilantro leaves
3 tablespoons lime juice
  Salt

Combine all the ingredients, including salt to taste, in a medium bowl. Serve immediately. (The salsa can be covered and set aside at room temperature for several hours or refrigerated for a day or two. Bring to room temperature before serving.)

Fresh Tomato Sauce

The key to great tomato sauce is to keep the cooking time to a minimum and thus retain the flavor of fresh tomatoes. This chunky sauce works best with short, tubular or curly pasta shapes such as penne, ziti, or fusilli. For a smooth-textured sauce (that will work better with spaghetti or linguine), puree the sauce in a blender or food processor.

If you have a lot of tomatoes on hand, you may double this recipe, using a large (12-inch) sauté pan. Freeze any extra sauce in small airtight containers and defrost in the refrigerator as nezeded. Reheat the sauce gently. It's best to add the basil just before using the sauce, so omit this ingredient from sauce destined for the freezer.

ENOUGH FOR 1 POUND OF PASTA

2 tablespoons extra-virgin olive oil
2 medium garlic cloves, minced very fine
2 pounds ripe tomatoes, cored, peeled,
   seeded, and cut into ½-inch dice
2 tablespoons chopped fresh basil leaves
   Salt

1. Heat the oil and garlic in a medium sauté pan over medium heat until fragrant but not brown, about 2 minutes.

2. Stir in the tomatoes and cook briskly until any liquid thrown off by the tomatoes has evaporated and the tomato pieces have lost their shape and formed a chunky sauce, about 10 minutes. (If desired, puree the sauce in a blender or food processor.) Stir in the basil and salt to taste. Toss with drained pasta.

VARIATIONS: SPICY FRESH TOMATO SAUCE

Cook ¾ teaspoon hot red pepper flakes (or more or less to taste) with the oil and garlic.

FRESH TOMATO SAUCE WITH ANCHOVIES, OLIVES, AND CAPERS

Cook 3 minced anchovy fillets with the oil and garlic. Add 8 large black olives (such as Kalamatas), pitted and chopped, and 1 tablespoon drained capers along with the basil. Add salt sparingly.

FRESH TOMATO SAUCE WITH BACON AND ONION

Use pancetta (unsmoked Italian bacon) or regular bacon, as you like. If using American bacon (which is fattier than pancetta), reduce the oil in step 1 to just 1 tablespoon.

Replace the garlic with 1 medium onion, minced. Cook the onion and 4 ounces chopped pancetta or bacon in the oil until the onion pieces begin to brown around the edges and the pancetta or bacon has rendered all its fat, about 8 minutes. Add the tomatoes and proceed with the recipe, replacing the basil with an equal amount of parsley. Add salt sparingly.

FRESH TOMATO SAUCE WITH CREAM

Butter and cream give this sauce a totally different character. The emphasis here is as much on the dairy as on the tomatoes. This sauce is especially good with fresh fettuccine or cheese ravioli. It is also delicious on dried pasta.

Replace the olive oil with an equal amount of butter and substitute 1 medium onion, minced, for the garlic. Sauté the onion in the butter until golden, about 5 minutes. Add the tomatoes and proceed with the recipe. When the tomatoes have formed a chunky sauce, add ½ cup heavy cream and simmer just until the sauce thickens, 2 to 3 minutes. Finish the sauce with the basil and salt as directed.

Slow-Roasted Tomato Sauce

I consider this the best tomato sauce in my repertoire. Yes, it takes 3 hours to make, but the actual hands-on work is about 10 minutes. Slow-roasting sliced, salted tomatoes drives off excess moisture and concentrates the flavor of the tomatoes without actually changing their flavor the way that high-heating roasting does. The tomatoes are then put through a food mill to remove the seeds and skins and enriched with a little fresh basil and olive oil. Since the oil is not cooked, use the finest extra-virgin oil in your pantry. This sauce is good with all kinds of pasta, but I especially like it with egg fettuccine.

MAKES ABOUT 2 CUPS, ENOUGH FOR 1 POUND OF PASTA

5 large ripe tomatoes (about 3¼ pounds), cored and cut crosswise into ½-inch-thick slices

1 teaspoon kosher salt

Freshly ground black pepper

2 tablespoons extra-virgin olive oil

1 tablespoon chopped fresh basil leaves

1. Preheat the oven to 250 degrees. Line two large rimmed baking sheets with parchment paper.

2. Spread the tomatoes out over the baking sheets in a single layer. Sprinkle with the salt and pepper to taste. Roast, turning the baking sheets occasionally and switching their position in the oven once, until the tomatoes are extremely condensed and shriveled, about 3 hours.

3. Carefully transfer the roasted tomatoes to a food mill fitted with the medium blade, set over a large bowl. Puree the tomatoes to a smooth, thick sauce; discard the seeds and skins left in the food mill. Stir in the oil and basil. The sauce is best used the day it is made but can be refrigerated in an airtight container for several days or frozen for several months.

Spiced Tomato Chutney

This recipe is an extraordinarily delicious way to use up extra tomatoes. Chopped, peeled tomatoes are simmered for several hours with vinegar, brown sugar, and spices. The result is a thick, jam-like chutney that can be served with grilled fish (it's especially good with salmon), steak, or chicken. Leave all the whole spices, except the cinnamon stick, right in the chutney. After two and a half to 3 hours of simmering, the peppercorns, cloves, and coriander seeds will have become soft and their flavor is delicious. I like this recipe so much I buy extra tomatoes just to use them up in this long-lasting chutney.

MAKES ABOUT 2¾ CUPS

3 pounds ripe tomatoes, cored, peeled, and chopped
1½ cups cider vinegar
1½ cups packed light brown sugar
½ cup raisins
1 cinnamon stick, about 4 inches long
1 tablespoon black peppercorns
1 teaspoon whole cloves
1 teaspoon coriander seeds
1 teaspoon hot red pepper flakes, or more to taste
1 tablespoon minced fresh gingerroot

1. Place all the ingredients in a large, heavy-bottomed saucepan. Bring to a boil, reduce the heat to low, and cook at a gentle simmer, stirring occasionally, until the mixture thickens to a jam-like consistency, 2½ to 3 hours.
2. Transfer the mixture to an airtight container, cool, and refrigerate for up to 2 weeks.

Fried Green Tomatoes

This version is lighter than the traditional Southern dish cooked in bacon fat. I think that olive oil pro-duces a crisper crust and the flavor works better with modern cooking. I like fried tomatoes as a side dish with almost any summer meal but their tart flavor is especially good with fish. The cornmeal coating makes the exterior crunchy and light. The interior is soft and full of tomato flavor.

SERVES 4 AS A SIDE DISH

1 pound green tomatoes
½ cup cornmeal
1 tablespoon minced fresh oregano or thyme leaves
Salt
Freshly ground black pepper
1 large egg
1 tablespoon water
⅓ cup extra-virgin olive oil

1. Remove a ¼-inch slice from the stem end of each tomato. Cut the tomatoes crosswise into ½-inch-thick slices. Lay the tomatoes out on a couple of layers of paper towels.
2. Combine the cornmeal, herb, and salt and pepper to taste in a shallow, wide bowl. Beat the egg and water in another shallow, wide bowl.
3. Heat the oil in a large, nonstick skillet over medium-high heat. Dip the tomato slices in the egg and then dredge the slices in the cornmeal mixture, making sure that both sides are well coated. Place the slices in the hot oil. Cook over medium-high heat, turning once, until golden brown and crisp on both sides, about 5 minutes. Serve immediately.

Turnip Greens

Although turnip greens have a long history in the rural South, they do not enjoy the same popularity or wide availability as most other greens. They are quite leathery and tough, especially in the winter months when they make their way to most supermarkets. Perhaps more important (at least in terms of their poor reputation), they are quite strong-tasting.

However, for those cooks who like bitter flavors (myself included), turnip greens are a favorite, especially during the winter months when good vegetables can be scarce. Although I occasionally find tender greens in the spring, which can be wilted in hot oil like spinach or chard, most turnip greens are too tough for this treatment. I almost always cook turnip greens in salted boiling water, drain them well, and then sauté or braise them with seasonings.

Boiling the greens makes them tender, although they will never be silky like spinach or chard. Expect these greens to have some chew. Boiling also washes away some of the bitterness, which can be overpowering in tougher greens.

Older cookbooks suggest stewing turnip greens with bacon or another pork product for an hour or more in a covered pot. I find this method is overkill, at least to my palate. I like my greens to have some texture and color. Like collards, turnip greens must be cooked thoroughly but not to death. If you want to flavor turnip greens with bacon, follow the collard green recipe on page 113, adding more water as needed to cook the turnip greens until tender.

OTHER COMMON NAMES: Turnip tops.

AVAILABILITY: Late fall through winter.

SELECTION: Look for turnip greens with relatively thin stems and bright green leaves. Pass by any bunches with yellow or limp leaves. Turnip greens should look fresh and crisp.

Most turnip greens sold in bunches at markets are a special variety grown specifically for the greens. You may occasionally see turnips sold with their tops still attached at farmer's markets. When you get the turnips and their greens home, slice off the greens and use them quickly, within a day or two. (The turnips can be held for several days.) You are unlikely to get more than a few ounces of greens from a bunch of turnips. I usually add these turnip greens (which tend to be more delicate than bunched turnip greens) to another greens recipe.

STORAGE: Turnip greens can be refrigerated in a loosely sealed plastic for a day or two. If the greens are very moist when you get them home, blot up the excess water with a paper towels and place the greens in a dry plastic bag.

BASIC PREPARATION: Like all greens, turnip greens are sandy. Wash the greens in a large bowl of cold water, changing the water several times or until no grit falls to the bottom of the bowl. As you wash the greens, strip off the leafy green portion from either side of the tough central stalk. Discard the stalks and rip the leafy portions into small pieces.

BEST COOKING METHOD: Boiling (in order to make them tender and mellow some of their punch) and then sautéing or braising with seasonings. Very young, tender greens can be wilted in hot oil like spinach or chard.

OTHER RECIPES WITH TURNIP GREENS: Turnip greens can be used in any of the recipes calling for mature mustard greens.

Turnip Greens with Toasted Walnuts

Rich, slightly bitter walnuts bring out the strong, earthy flavor of the greens. If you want to soften the bite of turnip greens, see the following recipe.

SERVES 4 AS A SIDE DISH

1½ pounds turnip greens
 Salt
½ cup walnuts
2 tablespoons extra-virgin olive oil
 Freshly ground black pepper

1. Bring 4 quarts of water to a boil in a large pot.
2. Wash the greens in several changes of cold water, stripping off the leafy green portion from either side of the tough central stalk. Discard the stalks and rip the leafy portions into small pieces. Add the greens and 1 teaspoon salt to the boiling water. Cook until the turnip greens are tender, about 8 minutes. Drain well.
3. Place the walnuts in a large skillet set over medium heat. Toast, shaking the pan occasionally to turn the nuts, until fragrant, about 4 minutes. Transfer the nuts to a small plate. Cool and chop.
4. Heat the oil in the empty skillet. Add the turnip greens and cook, turning often, over medium heat until coated with the oil and no longer damp, about 2 minutes. Season with salt and pepper to taste. Stir in the toasted walnuts and serve immediately.

Turnip Greens with Creamy Mustard Sauce

The cream and mustard soften the bite of the greens and create a delicious sauce that can be served with pork, veal, or a strong-tasting fish such as cod.

SERVES 4 AS A SIDE DISH

1½ pounds turnip greens
 Salt
2 tablespoons unsalted butter
1 medium onion, minced
 Freshly ground black pepper
¼ cup heavy cream
1 tablespoon Dijon mustard

1. Bring 4 quarts of water to a boil in a large pot.
2. Wash the greens in several changes of cold water, stripping off the leafy green portion from either side of the tough central stalk. Discard the stalks and rip the leafy portions into small pieces. Add the greens and 1 teaspoon salt to the boiling water. Cook until the turnip greens are tender, about 8 minutes. Drain well.
3. Melt the butter in a large skillet. Add the onion and cook over medium heat until golden, about 5 minutes. Add the greens and toss to coat with the butter and onion. Season with salt and pepper to taste.
4. Whisk the cream and mustard together in a small bowl. Add this mixture to the skillet and cook just until the greens absorb some of the sauce, 3 to 4 minutes. Adjust the seasonings and serve immediately.

Turnips

Turnips are widely available, easy to prepare (just peel and dice), and their flavor is delicious. Depending on their size and variety, turnips can taste mild and sweet or slightly peppery, but never hot.

When cooked, turnips have a dense, creamy flesh like potatoes, but without all that starch. They make an especially light, smooth puree. Turnips do an excellent job of absorbing flavors (which is why braising is such a good way to cook them), but still hold on to their character and flavor, even when seasoned aggressively.

AVAILABILITY: Year-round, although spring and fall are the best times for turnips.

SELECTION: Choose turnips with smooth, unblemished skins. If the greens are still attached, they should look fresh and crisp. If the greens have been trimmed, check the scar on the top of the turnips. It should look fresh, not dark brown or soft.

Small turnips (less than 2 inches in diameter) are generally less tough than larger specimens, which can be quite woody. Try to buy small turnips if you are braising, which will turn out creamier than really big turnips. Roasting and boiling are more forgiving of imperfections in large turnips.

STORAGE: Turnips can be refrigerated in a loosely sealed plastic bag for at least a week, if not longer.

BASIC PREPARATION: If turnips are sold with the tops, cut off the stems and leafy greens, saving the greens to cook later. Most turnips have fairly thin skin, which can be removed with a peeler. (If you have purchased really young, small turnips, you can leave the skin on.) If you prefer, use a paring knife to cut away the skin. Larger turnips may have some fibrous material right under the skin, which should be trimmed away. This is easier to do with a knife.

BEST COOKING METHODS: Boiling, braising, and roasting.

OTHER RECIPES WITH TURNIPS:
Roasted Carrots and Turnips (page 83)
Hearty Mushroom Stew (page 216)

Turnips can be used in rutabaga recipes, especially Stewed Rutabaga with Chard and Garlic (page 291). Turnips can be roasted like other root vegetables. I like to roast them in combination with something sweet, like carrots, but they can be roasted alone. Refer to the parsnips recipe on page 238.

Maple-Braised Turnips and Carrots

In this recipe, the liquid is a mixture of stock and maple syrup, which reduces to a thick glaze coating the turnips and carrots. This recipe makes an excellent side dish for roast pork.

SERVES 4 TO 6 AS A SIDE DISH

1 tablespoon unsalted butter
1 pound turnips (preferably small turnips), peeled and cut into ¾-inch cubes
3 medium carrots (about ½ pound), peeled, cut crosswise into 1-inch lengths, thick pieces halved lengthwise
⅔ cup chicken or vegetable stock
2 tablespoons maple syrup
Salt
Freshly ground black pepper

1. Melt the butter in a large sauté pan. Add the turnips and cook, turning occasionally, over medium heat until lightly browned, about 8 minutes.

2. Add the carrots, stock, maple syrup, and salt and pepper to taste. Cover the pan, reduce the heat, and simmer until the turnips and carrots are tender, 15 to 20 minutes.

3. Remove the cover, raise the heat to high, and cook until the liquid in the pan reduces to a thick glaze, about 2 minutes. Adjust the seasonings and serve immediately.

Braised Turnips with Mustard-Cream Sauce

The mustard and cream reduce to a thick glaze on the turnips in this French recipe. The mustard accentuates the peppery flavor of the turnips. Serve with beef or veal.

SERVES 4 TO 6 AS A SIDE DISH

1 tablespoon unsalted butter
1½ pounds turnips (preferably small turnips), peeled and cut into ¾-inch cubes
⅔ cup chicken or vegetable stock
2 tablespoons heavy cream
1 tablespoon Dijon mustard
2 tablespoons minced fresh chives
Salt
Freshly ground black pepper

1. Melt the butter in a large sauté pan. Add the turnips and cook, turning occasionally, over medium heat until lightly browned, about 8 minutes.

2. Add the stock and cream. Cover the pan, reduce the heat, and simmer until the turnips are tender, 15 to 20 minutes.

3. Remove the cover, raise the heat to high, and cook until the liquid in the pan reduces to a glaze, about 2 minutes. Stir in the mustard and chives and season with salt and pepper to taste. Serve immediately.

Braised Turnips with Tomatoes and Cumin

Turnips soak up North African flavors in this dish. Pair this saucy dish with couscous and roasted or grilled chicken for a complete meal.

SERVES 4 TO 6 AS A SIDE DISH

2 tablespoons extra-virgin olive oil
1 medium onion, minced
1½ pounds turnips (preferably small turnips), peeled and cut into ¾-inch cubes
½ teaspoon ground cumin
One 14.5-ounce can diced tomatoes
Salt
Freshly ground black pepper
2 tablespoons minced fresh cilantro or pars-ley leaves

1. Heat the oil in a large sauté pan. Add the onion and cook over medium heat until softened, about 3 minutes. Add the turnips and cook, turning occasionally, over medium heat until lightly browned, about 8 minutes.
2. Add the cumin and cook, stirring to coat the turnips with the cumin, for about 1 minute. Add the tomatoes and salt and pepper to taste. Cover the pan, reduce the heat, and simmer, stirring occasionally, until the turnips are tender, 15 to 20 minutes.
3. Remove the cover, raise the heat to high, and cook until the liquid in the pan reduces to a thick sauce, 2 to 3 minutes. Stir in the cilantro and adjust the seasonings. Serve immediately.

Pureed Turnips

Pureed turnips are a revelation to anyone who has never had this dish. Turnips yield a puree that is bright white and silky smooth. The consistency is far lighter than mashed potatoes and the puree tastes as if it is loaded with butter and cream, but it's not. The single potato is added because turnips pureed by themselves are a bit too thin. Unlike mashed potatoes, pureed turnips will not turn to glue as they cool. In fact, you can prepared pureed turnips an hour or two in advance and then reheat the puree in a microwave. For this reason (and many others), pureed turnips are a better choice than potatoes for holiday meals.

SERVES 4 AS A SIDE DISH

1½ pounds turnips, peeled and cut into 1-inch chunks
1 medium russet potato (about 8 ounces), peeled and cut into 1-inch chunks
Salt
2 tablespoons unsalted butter, softened
Grated nutmeg, optional

1. Place the turnips and potato in a large saucepan and add enough water to cover by 2 inches. Add a generous amount of salt and bring the water to a boil. Reduce the heat a bit and cook until the turnips and potatoes are tender, about 15 minutes. Drain thoroughly.
2. Place the turnips and potatoes in the work bowl of a food processor. Add the butter and process until smooth. Scrape the puree into a bowl and adjust the seasonings, adding a pinch of nutmeg if desired. Serve immediately.

Water Chestnuts

Fresh water chestnuts have all the crunch of the commonly served canned variety but are also full of flavor. They are increasingly available at Chinese and Asian markets. Although water chestnuts might look like regular chestnuts, they are not nuts but rather corms, or small bulbs. In fact, upon closer inspection, fresh water chestnuts look a bit like mahogany-colored tulip bulbs.

Peeled water chestnuts can be used raw in salads, where their crunchy texture (akin to jicama or a firm apple, but creamier) and unusual flavor (surprisingly sweet and earthy tasting) can really shine. Peeled water chestnuts can also be stir-fried. They remain crunchy and sweet but also absorb other flavors from the sauce.

OTHER COMMON NAMES: Ma tai.

AVAILABILITY: Sporadically sold throughout the year in Asian markets.

SELECTION: Choose water chestnuts that are firm, not at all soft or shriveled. The skins should be smooth although the skins at the tufted top may be a bit loose and papery.

STORAGE: Water chestnuts will keep in a paper bag in the refrigerator for at least a week if not longer. Don't let them become soft though.

BASIC PREPARATION: Although water chestnuts are quite hard and may look difficult to peel, they are not. Start by washing them in a bowl of cold water to remove any caked-on mud. (Water chestnuts are grown in flooded fields and can be quite dirty.) Next, use a paring knife to trim away the brown skin and any discoloration from the water chestnuts. I find it helpful to work under cool, running water, which washes away bits of skin as you work. Once you have removed all brown or yellow material (the flesh should be ivory-colored), slice the water chestnut as directed.

Like an apple, cut water chestnuts will eventually brown when exposed to air. I put them in a bowl of cold water, which also keeps them crunchy and juicy. If you are going to use the water chestnuts immediately (within 20 minutes or so), you can skip this step. Sliced water chestnuts can be refrigerated in a bowl of cold water overnight.

BEST COOKING METHODS: Stir-frying or raw in salads.

Water Chestnut and Mizuna Salad with Sesame Vinaigrette

A revelation to anyone who has never had fresh water chestnuts. Sweet, crunchy water chestnuts work especially well with the slightly bitter flavor of mizuna. However, tatsoi and baby spinach are excellent as well. This salad makes a light, refreshing first course before an Asian meal.

SERVES 6 AS A FIRST COURSE

- 1 pound fresh water chestnuts
- 2 tablespoons rice vinegar
- 2 teaspoons very finely minced fresh ginger-root
- 1 teaspoon soy sauce
  Freshly ground black pepper
- 3 tablespoons canola or other tasteless oil
- 1 tablespoon toasted sesame oil
- 8 cups mizuna, tatsoi, or baby spinach, washed and thoroughly dried

1. Wash the water chestnuts to remove as much caked-on mud as you can. Working under cool, running water, use a paring knife to remove the brown skin from the water chestnuts. Lay the water chestnuts on a flat side and slice crosswise into very thin ovals. Place the slices in a bowl of cold water to prevent discoloration.

2. Whisk the vinegar, ginger, soy sauce, and pepper to taste together in a small bowl. Whisk in the oils until the dressing is smooth. Adjust the seasonings.

3. Place the mizuna in a large bowl. Drain the water chestnuts and blot dry with paper towels. Add to the bowl with the mizuna. Drizzle the dressing over the salad and toss to coat. Serve immediately.

Stir-Fried Water Chestnuts and Snow Peas

Szechwan peppercorns have a lovely floral flavor that works especially well with water chestnuts. Toast the peppercorns in a dry skillet over medium heat until fragrant (about 2 minutes), cool, then grind in a coffee grinder or spice mill. Szechwan peppercorns are one of the spices in five-spice powder, a preground spice blend sold in many supermarkets. You can use ¼ teaspoon of five-spice powder in place of the Szechwan peppercorns, but the effect is not the same. Check out an Asian market for Szechwan peppercorns.

SERVES 4 AS A SIDE DISH

1 pound fresh water chestnuts
3 tablespoons chicken or vegetable stock
1 tablespoon soy sauce
1 teaspoon Szechwan peppercorns, toasted and ground
2 teaspoons sugar
1 tablespoon roasted peanut oil
½ pound snow peas, strings pulled off
3 medium garlic cloves, minced
1 tablespoon minced fresh gingerroot
2 medium scallions, sliced thin

1. Wash the water chestnuts to remove as much caked-on mud as you can. Working under cool, running water, use a paring knife to remove the brown skin from the water chestnuts. Cut the water chestnuts into ¼-inch rounds and place them in a bowl of cold water to prevent discoloration.
2. Combine the stock, soy sauce, Szechwan peppercorns, and sugar in a small bowl and set the mixture aside. Drain the water chestnuts.
3. Heat the oil in a large nonstick skillet until shimmering but not smoking. Add the peas and stir-fry for 30 seconds to coat them with the oil. Add the water chestnuts and continue stir-frying for 30 seconds. Add the garlic, ginger, and scallions and stir-fry until fragrant, about 20 seconds.
4. Add the stock mixture, quickly cover the pan, reduce the heat to medium, and cook until the peas are tender, about 2 minutes. Cook, uncovered, to reduce the sauce to just a tablespoon or two, 1 to 2 minutes. Adjust the seasonings. Serve immediately.

Stir-Fried Water Chestnuts, Shrimp, and Cashews in Spicy Orange Sauce

Crisp slices of water chestnuts take center stage in a stir-fry of contrasting textures and flavors. This dish requires a fair amount of preparation but it makes a delicious dinner. Serve with rice.

SERVES 4 AS A MAIN COURSE

1 pound fresh water chestnuts
½ teaspoon grated orange zest
¼ cup orange juice
1 tablespoon soy sauce
2 teaspoons toasted sesame oil
2 teaspoons sugar
2 tablespoons roasted peanut oil
1 pound medium shrimp, peeled
½ cup roasted cashews
3 medium garlic cloves, minced
1 tablespoon minced fresh gingerroot
2 medium scallions, sliced thin
1 medium jalapeño chile, stemmed, seeded, and minced

1. Wash the water chestnuts to remove as much caked-on mud as you can. Working under cool, running water, use a paring knife to remove the brown skin from the water chestnuts. Cut the water chestnuts into ¼-inch rounds and place

the rounds in a bowl of cold water to prevent discoloration.

2. Combine the orange zest and juice, soy sauce, sesame oil, and sugar in a small bowl and set the mixture aside. Drain the water chestnuts.

3. Heat 1 tablespoon of the oil in a large nonstick skillet until shimmering but not smoking. Add the shrimp and stir-fry until bright pink, about 2 minutes. Use a slotted spoon to transfer the shrimp to a bowl. Add the cashews to the empty skillet and stir-fry in the remaining oil in the pan until lightly browned, about 30 seconds. Transfer the nuts to the bowl with the shrimp.

4. Heat the remaining tablespoon of peanut oil in the empty skillet. Add the water chestnuts and stir-fry until they begin to brown, about 1 minute. Add the garlic, ginger, scallions, and chile and stir-fry until fragrant, about 20 seconds.

5. Return the shrimp and cashews to the pan. Add the orange sauce and stir-fry until everything is heated through and nicely glazed, about 1 minute. Adjust the seasonings and serve immediately.

Winter Squash
and Pumpkin

The term winter squash includes any squash with a thick, tough skin that allows the squash to be kept for several months, traditionally from harvesttime in the fall through the winter. Winter squash are related to zucchini and summer squash, although the latter lack the protective skin and their flesh is more watery. Pumpkins are simply round winter squash with orange skin and flesh.

Most winter squash have dense yellow or orange flesh. Some varieties are sweeter than others, but I think texture is the most important consideration. Some squash, such as butternut, cook up creamy and smooth. Others, especially pumpkins and often acorn squash, can be stringy, fibrous, and/or watery when cooked.

There are dozens of squash varieties grown across the country. The following are the most common.

ACORN: Acorn squash are usually pretty small (1 to 2 pounds) and easily recognized because of their dark green color (sometimes covered with orange patches) and deep ridges. The flesh is yellowish-orange and sweet, but not overly so, and often a bit coarse or watery.

BUTTERCUP: This squash is dark green and round. The flesh is orange and very sweet, similar to a butternut. Most buttercups weigh about 3 pounds, but there is a tremendous range. Kabocha squash are similar.

BUTTERNUT: This is my favorite squash. The light tan skin can be peeled, so you can use chunks of butternut squash in soups, casseroles, and braises—dishes where the peel must come off before cooking. The bright orange flesh is dense and creamy (never stringy) and sweet. Butternut squash range in size from less than 2 pounds to 5 pounds. The smaller squash are easier to cut. Unlike other squash, butternuts are available most of the year.

DELICATA: This elongated squash has yellow or cream-colored skin streaked with green dark strips. It is small, usually weighing less than a pound. The flesh is yellow and has a fine, creamy texture. Sweet dumpling squash is similar.

HUBBARD: The skin has an unusual bluish-gray or gray color but the flesh is smooth, sweet, and orange. Traditional varieties weigh at least 10 pounds, although a new hybrid comes in at 3 or 4 pounds. The thick, bumpy skin makes Hubbard squash a challenge to prepare, but the results are worth the effort.

PUMPKINS: Any ridged, round winter squash with orange skin and orange flesh can be called a pumpkin, a name that covers at least two dozen varieties. Mini pumpkins, also called Jack-Be-Littles, are the easiest to prepare and offer the best flavor and texture of any pumpkins (see page 357 for details). Larger pumpkins are difficult to work with and are usually stringy and bland.

SPAGHETTI: With their smooth yellow skin, spaghetti squash are easy to spot. They look like overgrown footballs. When cooked, the pale gold flesh turns into long, stringy fibers that resemble pasta. Spaghetti squash cannot be substituted for any other squash. See page 356 for details on preparing this unusual vegetable.

AVAILABILITY: Fall through early spring.

SELECTION: Choose squash that are hard; any soft spots are a sign that the squash have been mishandled. Squash should feel heavy for their size, an indication that the flesh is moist and dense.

STORAGE: Winter squash can be stored in a cool, well-ventilated spot in the kitchen for several weeks.

BASIC PREPARATION: In most recipes, remove the stringy fibers and seeds in the center of all winter squash before cooking. The easiest way to do this is to cut the squash in half. Use a really heavy chef's knife or a cleaver and expect to exert some pressure to accomplish this task. Cut long squash like butternut in half lengthwise, from narrow end to narrow end. Cut round squash like acorn in half crosswise, through the equator. Once the squash has been opened, use a large spoon to scrape out and discard the strings and seeds.

There are instances when you will want to peel squash before cooking. Ridged squash like acorn are too hard to peel before cooking—the task is impossible with a peeler and the waste is tremendous if you use a knife. Better to cook these squash with the skin on, then scoop out the flesh once it has cooked.

Smooth-skinned squash, such as butternuts, can be peeled with a vegetable peeler or paring knife. The thin tan skin comes off in one stroke, although you may want to go back over the same area two or three times to remove the whitish-green flesh underneath the skin. Once you reveal the bright orange, the squash is ready to be chopped and cooked.

BEST COOKING METHODS: Boiling (for soup), braising, and roasting,

OTHER RECIPES WITH WINTER SQUASH: Butternut or delicata squash can be used in any of the calabaza recipes.

Oven-Roasted Butternut Squash with Maple Glaze

I like to cook butternut squash cut side down to promote caramelization. Once the squash is cooked through, I flip it cut side up, brush it with a little seasoned melted butter and maple syrup, and let it bake just until the glaze sets. Even the most finicky child will eat this vegetable. It tastes like a less sweet version of candied sweet potatoes—minus the marshmallows and all that work. This squash is especially good with pork and turkey. Use two small acorn squash in place of the butternut if you like. See the following recipe (below) for instructions on handling acorn squash.

SERVES 4 AS A SIDE DISH

Nonstick cooking spray
1 medium butternut squash (about 2 pounds), halved lengthwise, strings and seeds scooped out with a spoon and discarded
1 tablespoon unsalted butter
2 tablespoons maple syrup
Salt
Freshly ground black pepper

1. Preheat the oven to 400 degrees. Lightly coat a baking sheet with cooking spray.
2. Place the squash halves, cut side down, on the baking sheet. Bake until a skewer glides easily through the squash, 45 to 55 minutes.
3. Meanwhile, melt the butter in a small skillet. Add the maple syrup and salt and pepper to taste and turn off the heat.
4. When the squash is cooked through, remove it from the oven (don't turn the oven off). Carefully turn the halves cut side up and brush the maple syrup mixture over the orange flesh. Return the squash to the oven and bake until the glaze has set, about 5 minutes.
5. Cut each squash half into two pieces and serve immediately.

Oven-Roasted Acorn Squash with Cumin

The earthy flavor of cumin tempers some of the sweetness of the squash and gives it a mildly exotic flavor. Acorn squash halves make excellent individual portions, provided that you can find small squash that weigh about 1 pound each. If only large squash (each weighing about 2 pounds) are available, buy just one squash and then cut it in half and seed as directed. When the squash is tender (it might need an extra 10 minutes or so), cut each half into two pieces, brush with the cumin butter, and serve. If desired, use one 2-pound butternut squash here.

Nonstick cooking spray
2 small acorn squash (about 2 pounds total), halved crosswise, strings and seeds scooped out with a spoon and discarded
2 tablespoons unsalted butter
1 teaspoon ground cumin
Salt
Freshly ground black pepper

1. Preheat the oven to 400 degrees. Lightly coat a baking sheet with cooking spray.
2. Place the squash halves, cut side down, on the baking sheet. Bake until a skewer glides easily through the squash, about 45 minutes.
3. Meanwhile, melt the butter in a small skillet. Add the cumin and cook for 30 seconds. Turn off the heat and add salt and pepper to taste.
4. When the squash are cooked through, carefully turn the halves cut side up and brush the cumin butter over the yellow flesh. Serve immediately.

Pureed Squash

This recipe is an excellent way to handle difficult-to-peel acorn squash or even pumpkin because there's no need to the peel the squash before cooking and because the food processor eliminates small strings and fibers. The puree is silky smooth and rich, perfect with a holiday turkey, chicken, pork, or duck. Squash with very creamy, dense flesh, such as a butternut, could be mashed with a potato masher. However, even but-ternut squash makes a creamier puree in the food processor.

Nonstick cooking spray
3 pounds squash or pumpkin, halved, strings and seeds scooped out with a spoon and discarded
2 tablespoons unsalted butter, cut into bits
2 tablespoons milk
Salt
Freshly ground black pepper

1. Preheat the oven to 400 degrees. Lightly coat a baking sheet with cooking spray.
2. Place the squash halves, cut side down, on the baking sheet. Bake until a skewer glides very eas-ily through the squash, 50 to 60 minutes. (Bet-ter to overcook than undercook the squash; it needs to be very soft in order to puree properly.)
3. As soon as the squash is cooked through, use a spoon to scoop out the hot flesh and place it in a food processor. Discard the skin. Add the but-ter and milk to the processor and puree until per-fectly smooth, about 30 seconds. Add salt and pepper to taste and serve immediately. (The squash puree can be scraped into a serving bowl, covered with plastic wrap, set aside up to 1 hour, and then reheated briefly in a microwave.)

VARIATIONS: SQUASH PUREE WITH PARMESAN AND THYME

The cheese and herb really tone down the sweetness of the squash. Use fresh sage or rosemary in place of the thyme if desired.

Replace the butter with ½ cup grated Parmesan cheese and 2 teaspoons chopped fresh thyme leaves. Add the milk and salt and pepper as directed.

SQUASH PUREE WITH ORANGE AND ALLSPICE

The orange zest and juice highlight the sweetness of the squash, while allspice adds a savory note.

Add the butter as directed. Replace the milk with 2 tablespoons orange juice, ½ teaspoon grated orange zest, and ¼ teaspoon ground allspice. Add the salt and pepper as directed.

SQUASH PUREE WITH CHIPOTLE CHILE AND LIME

A chipotle chile gives the puree a great smoky flavor and some heat.

Replace the butter with 1 minced chipotle chile in adobo sauce. Replace the milk with 2 tablespoons lime juice. Add the salt and pepper as directed.

Roasted Squash Pieces with Fresh Herbs

This method, one of my favorite ways to cook squash, works well with butternut squash because relative to other squash it is easy to peel. You could also use delicata squash, or any other variety with smooth skin. Serve with meat or chicken, or with eggs as part of a vegetarian dinner.

SERVES 4 AS A SIDE DISH

1 medium butternut squash (about 2 pounds)
2 tablespoons extra-virgin olive oil
Salt
Freshly ground black pepper
2 teaspoons minced fresh rosemary or sage leaves

1. Preheat the oven to 400 degrees.
2. Halve the squash lengthwise. Use a spoon to scoop out and discard the strings and seeds. Cut the squash into pieces about the size of your hand. Remove the skin and a layer or two of flesh (you want to remove any whitish or green flesh right beneath the skin) with a vegetable peeler or paring knife. Cut the peeled squash into 1-inch cubes.
3. Place the squash on a rimmed baking sheet lined with foil. Drizzle the oil over the squash and sprinkle with salt and pepper to taste. Toss with your hands to coat the squash with the oil.
4. Roast, stirring once or twice, until the squash is lightly browned and tender, about 40 minutes. Sprinkle the squash with the herb and adjust the seasonings. Serve immediately.

Baked Squash Casserole with Indian Flavors

I sometimes turn this squash casserole into a vegetarian winter meal. Add some rice (preferably basmati) and a salad and everyone will be satisfied. You can also serve smaller portions as a side dish with roast chicken or fish.

SERVES 4 AS A MAIN COURSE OR 6 TO 8 AS A SIDE DISH

1 large butternut squash (about 2½ pounds)
2 tablespoons canola or other tasteless oil
2 medium onions, halved and sliced thin
2 medium garlic cloves, minced
1 teaspoon curry powder
2 tablespoons minced fresh cilantro leaves
  Salt
1 cup coconut milk

1. Preheat the oven to 400 degrees.
2. Halve the squash lengthwise. Use a spoon to scoop out and discard the strings and seeds. Cut the squash into pieces about the size of your hand. Remove the skin and a layer or two of flesh (you want to remove any whitish or green flesh right beneath the skin) with a vegetable peeler or paring knife. Cut the peeled squash into 2-inch chunks.
3. Heat the oil in a large skillet. Add the onions and sauté over medium heat until golden, about 8 minutes. Add the garlic and curry powder and sauté until fragrant, about 1 minute. Add the squash pieces and toss just long enough to coat with the onions and curry. Season with the cilantro and salt to taste. Scrape the mixture into a 13 by 9-inch baking dish. Drizzle the coconut milk over the squash.
4. Bake until the squash is tender and lightly browned, about 1 hour. Let settle for several minutes and then serve.

Spaghetti Squash with Parmesan and Sage

I like to highlight the sweet, nutty flavor of this squash with a little browned butter, sage, and Parmesan. Make sure to puncture the squash as directed in step 2 to prevent it from exploding in the oven. In order to prevent the butter from burning, cook it in a light-colored or shiny skillet; dark finishes make it hard to judge the color of the butter.

SERVES 6 AS A SIDE DISH

1 medium spaghetti squash (about 3 pounds)
3 tablespoons unsalted butter
1 tablespoon minced fresh sage leaves
⅓ cup grated Parmesan cheese
  Salt
  Freshly ground black pepper

1. Preheat the oven to 400 degrees.
2. Use a paring knife to make several slits in the squash so steam can escape as the squash cooks. Place the squash on a baking sheet and bake until a skewer glides easily through the flesh, about 1¼

hours. Remove the squash from the oven and set aside briefly.

3. Melt the butter in a small, light-colored or shiny skillet over medium heat. When the butter stops foaming, add the sage leaves and cook until they release their flavor into the butter and the butter has turned golden brown, about 1 minute. Remove the skillet from the heat.

4. Slice the squash in half lengthwise. Scrape out and discard the seeds with a spoon. Drag a fork through the flesh to pull the strands of squash away from the skin. Place the squash strands in a large bowl. Toss with the sage butter and cheese. Add salt and pepper to taste and serve immediately.

Individual Baked Pumpkins

Those tiny pumpkins sold in some supermarkets make an excellent single-serving squash. Just make sure to buy pumpkins that have not been covered with shellac. Mini pumpkins make an excellent addition to a holiday meal. The recipe can be doubled and the pumpkins share the plate nicely with turkey, stuffing, gravy, cranberry sauce, and Brussels sprouts or another green vegetable.

SERVES 6 AS A SIDE DISH

6 miniature pumpkins
3 tablespoons unsalted butter
1 tablespoon minced fresh sage leaves
    Salt

Freshly ground black pepper
Nonstick cooking spray

1. Preheat the oven to 375 degrees.
2. Slice the top off of each pumpkin, about ½ inch below the stem, and reserve. With a spoon remove the seeds and strings from inside the pumpkin and the bottom of the stem piece and discard.
3. Place ½ tablespoon butter and ½ teaspoon sage inside each pumpkin. Sprinkle the inside of each pumpkin with salt and pepper to taste.
4. Place the tops back on the pumpkins. Lightly coat a small baking sheet with cooking spray. Set the pumpkins on the greased baking sheet. Bake until the flesh is soft (test this by opening one of the pumpkins and piercing the inside with a skewer), about 45 minutes. Serve immediately.

Butternut Squash Soup with Cider and Cardamom

This pureed soup combines Indian and American flavors for a refreshing change. Fresh ginger and ground cardamom, an aromatic spice used in curries as well as in many Scandinavian breads and desserts, are sautéed briefly in oil to intensify their flavors. The aromatic oil is then used to coat cubes of butternut squash, potatoes, and Granny Smith apple. The liquid in the soup is a combination of apple cider and water.

1 large butternut squash (about 2½ pounds)

3 tablespoons extra-virgin olive oil

1 tablespoon minced fresh gingerroot

2 teaspoons ground cardamom

2 medium russet potatoes (about 1 pound), peeled and cut into 1-inch cubes

1 large Granny Smith apple, peeled, quartered, cored, and cut into ½-inch chunks

1½ cups apple cider

3½ cups water

  Salt

  Toasted walnut halves and/or snipped fresh chives

1. Halve the squash lengthwise. Use a spoon to scoop out and discard the strings and seeds. Cut the squash into pieces about the size of your hand. Remove the skin and a layer or two of any whitish or green flesh right beneath the skin with a vegetable peeler or paring knife. Cut the peeled squash into 1-inch cubes.

2. Heat the oil in a large soup kettle or stockpot. Add the ginger and cardamom and sauté over medium heat until fragrant, about 2 minutes.

3. Add the squash, potatoes, and apple to the pot. Stir to coat the vegetable and apple pieces with the spiced oil. Sauté the mixture, stirring occasionally, for about 5 minutes.

4. Add the cider, water, and a generous amount of salt to the pot. Bring the soup to a boil and cook briskly until the vegetables are quite tender, about 35 minutes.

5. Puree the soup in batches in a blender. Return the pureed soup to a clean pot and reheat briefly. If necessary, add a little water to thin the soup to the desired consistency. Adjust the seasonings. Ladle the soup into individual bowls and garnish with the toasted walnuts and/or snipped chives. Serve immediately.

Yams

What we call yams in the United States are actually a variety of sweet potato with bright orange flesh. True yams, one of the most important tubers in tropical regions around the world, bear no relation to the vegetable we top with marshmallows at Thanksgiving.

A true yam is an especially hearty, starchy tuber that is never orange and not at all sweet. There are countless varieties of yams grown in the Caribbean, Africa, and Asia. Yams are a main source of calories and nutrition for millions of people around the globe.

Several sources mention yams weighing several hundred pounds being hauled out of the ground. The yams I have seen in American markets generally weigh a couple of pounds. They are shaped like logs and are covered with a thick, dark brown skin that looks like tree bark.

Given its external appearance, it's no wonder that American cooks have no idea that the yam is actually a foodstuff. However, once the bark-like skin has been removed, the flesh is easy to prepare. The flesh is usually white but can be yellow, depending on the variety.

Yams are fairly bland and quite floury and starchy. They are denser than potatoes. The phrase "stick to your ribs" certainly applies to yams.

Yams have an incredible ability to absorb liquids. Boiled chunks will soak up an unbelievable amount of dressing and thus become especially flavorful.

Frying (after boiling) is another good option. It seems that the hot oil creates a protective seal around the pieces of boiled yam, so that the interior remains ungreasy and even a bit dry while the exterior becomes crisp and golden brown. This is probably the most appealing way to prepare yams.

In most of the world, chunks of yam are added to stews to give them heft. Yams are often paired with other tropical tubers in these recipes. The dishes that follow keep the emphasis on the yams.

OTHER COMMON NAMES: Igname and ñame.

AVAILABILITY: Year-round, in Latino markets.

SELECTION: Choose yams that are firm and show no signs of mold. If cut, examine the flesh, too. It should be firm and moist-looking. Avoid yams with spongy flesh or soft spots.

STORAGE: An uncut piece of yam will keep for weeks at a cool room temperature. The ends may start to look a bit dry and even moldy, but they can be cut away and the interior portion will still be moist and firm.

BASIC PREPARATION: A 2- or 3-pound chunk of yam can be daunting to look at. Many yam novices wonder if the log would work better in the fireplace. Despite their appearance, yams are fairly easy to prepare.

Start by cutting the yam crosswise into manageable-sized rounds or chunks you can hold in your hand. Use a paring knife to remove the brown skin and outer ⅛ inch of flesh. The flesh will be white or yellow, depending on the variety.

Once cut, yam flesh can discolor, so drop the peeled yam pieces into a bowl of cold water. Repeat the peeling process with the remaining chunks of yam. Yams exude a sticky substance when cut. Dropping them in cold water washes away some of this sticky material. You will also want to wash your hands a couple of times as you work with a yam. Holding a knife in your slicked hands will become dangerous. In addition, the sticky substance can irritate your skin.

BEST COOKING METHODS: Boiling (and then dressing with a vinaigrette or pan-frying) or frying in fritters.

Pan-Browned Yam

Boiled chunks of yam can be thoroughly dried and then pan-fried until golden brown. The contrast between the crisp outer flesh and the moist, firm interior is delicious. Serve with pork, chicken, fish, or even with eggs for a hearty breakfast. Make sure not to boil the yam too much. It needs to be tender inside but still firm and must hold its shape in order to be pan-fried.

SERVES 6 AS A SIDE DISH

One 2-pound yam
Salt
About 1 cup peanut or vegetable oil for frying

1. Bring several quarts of water to a boil in a large saucepan. Cut the yam crosswise into 1-inch rounds or chunks. Use a paring knife to remove the brown skin and outer ⅛ inch of flesh. The flesh will be white or yellow, depending on the variety. Drop the peeled yam piece into a bowl of cold water. Repeat the peeling process with the remaining rounds of yam. When finished peeling all of the yam, remove the pieces from the cold water and cut them into 2 by 1-inch chunks.

2. Add the yam chunks and salt to taste to the boiling water. Cook over medium heat until the pieces are almost tender but are still holding their shape quite, about 20 minutes. Drain well, cool slightly, and then blot thoroughly dry on paper towels.

3. Heat about ¼ inch oil in a large skillet until shimmering. Add half of the yam pieces and pan-fry, turning each piece several times with a pair of tongs, until golden brown and crisp, 5 to 6 minutes. Transfer the yam pieces to a platter lined with paper towels and sprinkle with salt to taste. Serve hot. Fry the remaining yam pieces.

Yam Fritters with Garlic, Chile, and Cilantro

Boiled and riced yam makes an especially dry, fluffy fritter. Make sure to serve with plenty of lime wedges to moisten them. The fritters are also delicious with tomato salsa or Garlic Mayonnaise (page 8)

SERVES 6 TO 8 AS AN APPETIZER

One 1-pound yam
Salt
4 medium garlic cloves, minced
1 medium jalapeño chile, stemmed, seeded, and minced
3 tablespoons minced fresh cilantro leaves
2 large eggs, lightly beaten
About 1 cup peanut or vegetable oil for frying
Lime wedges

1. Bring several quarts of water to a boil in a large saucepan. Cut the yam crosswise into 1-inch rounds or chunks. Use a paring knife to remove the brown skin and outer ⅛ inch of flesh. The flesh will be white or yellow, depending on the variety. Drop the peeled yam piece into a bowl of cold water. Repeat the peeling process with the remaining rounds of yam. When finished peeling all of the yam, remove the pieces from the cold water and cut them into large chunks.

2. Add the yam chunks and salt to taste to the boiling water. Cook over medium heat until the chunks are very tender, about 30 minutes. Drain well and cool slightly.

3. Put the yam chunks, one a time, through a ricer, pressing the small bits of yam into a large bowl. Add the garlic, chile, cilantro, eggs, and 1 teaspoon salt. Mix well with your hands. Take 2 tablespoons of this mixture and shape it into a fairly flat patty that measures about 2½ inches across. Repeat with the remaining yam mixture.

4. Heat about ¼ inch oil in a large skillet until shimmering. Add half the fritters to the hot oil. Fry, turning once, until the fritters are golden brown and crisp, about 3 minutes. Transfer to a platter lined with paper towels and sprinkle with salt to taste. Serve immediately with lime wedges. Fry the remaining fritters.

Yuca

Yuca is one of the most important crops in the tropics. This elongated tuber is covered by brown skin that is often waxed. The flesh is crisp and bright and has a mild, buttery flavor. Yuca is very starchy but has a waxy texture, like a red potato. Yuca, the vegetable, is not to be confused with yucca, the green (and inedible) plant.

Yuca is boiled, fried, or simmered in soups and stews. However, the starch is also processed and made into tapioca as well as cassava flour.

OTHER COMMON NAMES: Cassava and manioc.

AVAILABILITY: Year-round, especially in Latino markets.

SELECTION: The skin should be completely intact and firm. Many markets slice open this long, spindle-shaped tuber. The flesh should be pure white.

STORAGE: Yuca does best out of the refrigerator, in a cool, well-ventilated spot. It should keep for a week or so.

BASIC PREPARATION: Like other tropical root vegetables, yuca has a tough outer skin that must be removed with a paring knife. In addition, yuca often has a spongy core. Cut the yuca into manageable pieces. Use a paring knife to remove the brown skin and outer ¼-inch layer of flesh. Next quarter the yuca lengthwise and cut out the spongy, stringy piece of the core attached to each quarter. The yuca can then be cut as desired.

BEST COOKING METHODS: Boiling and frying.

Cuban-Style Yuca with Citrus-Garlic Sauce

This sauce, which is called mojo criollo, *or Creole sauce, is usually made with sour oranges, which rarely make it to markets in the United States. A blend of fresh-squeezed orange and lime juices is a good approximation. This sauce is used not only with boiled tubers, but with chicken or fish.*

SERVES 4 TO 6 AS A SIDE DISH

2 pounds yuca
Salt
2 tablespoons extra-virgin olive oil
1 medium red onion, halved and sliced thin
4 medium garlic cloves, minced
1 tablespoon minced fresh parsley leaves
1 teaspoon minced fresh oregano leaves
1 cup orange juice
½ cup lime juice

1. Cut the yuca into manageable chunks. Use a paring knife to remove the brown skin and outer ¼-inch layer of flesh. Quarter the peeled yuca lengthwise and then remove the spongy, stringy piece of the core attached to each quarter. Cut the peeled, cored yuca into 2-inch lengths.

2. Place the yuca pieces in a large saucepan. Add enough water to cover by several inches as well as salt to taste. Set the pan over high heat and bring to a boil. Reduce the heat and simmer until the yuca is tender but not falling apart (test with a skewer), 20 to 25 minutes.

3. While the yuca is cooking, heat the oil in a medium skillet. Add the onion and sauté over medium heat until softened, about 4 minutes. Stir in the garlic, parsley, and oregano and cook until fragrant, about 1 minute. Add the juices and simmer until the flavors blend, about 3 minutes. Add salt to taste.

4. When the yuca is tender, drain and transfer it to a large serving platter. Pour the sauce over the yuca and serve hot or warm.

Garlicky Yuca Fritters

I first had these chewy, garlicky fritters, called arepitas, *about fifteen years ago in the Dominican Republic. Thank you to Dulce Maria de Castro and Mayra Altagracia Rodriguez for sharing with me the secrets of grating raw yuca for fritters. Serve these delicious, anise-flavored fritters with cold beers.*

SERVES 6 TO 8 AS AN APPETIZER

1½ pounds yuca
2 large eggs, lightly beaten
4 medium garlic cloves, minced
1¼ teaspoons salt
1 teaspoon anise seed
2 to 3 cups peanut or vegetable oil for frying
Lime wedges

1. Cut the yuca into manageable chunks. Use a paring knife to remove the brown skin and outer

¼-inch layer of flesh. Quarter the peeled yuca lengthwise and then remove the spongy, stringy piece of the core attached to each quarter. Cut the peeled, cored yuca into small chunks. Place half the chunks in the work bowl of a food processor fitted with a metal blade. Process until finely grated. Scrape the grated yuca into a large bowl and repeat with the remaining yuca pieces.

2. Add the eggs, garlic, salt, and anise seed to the bowl with the yuca. Stir until the batter is smooth.

3. Heat ½ inch of oil in a large skillet over medium-high heat. When the oil is quite hot (the batter should sizzle when added), carefully drop the batter into the pan by the rounded tablespoon. Add as much batter as can comfortably fit in the pan. Fry, turning once, until the fritters are well browned, 3 to 4 minutes. Use a slotted spoon to transfer the fritters to a platter lined with paper towels. Serve the fritters hot with the lime wedges. Repeat with the remaining batter.

Garlicky Yuca Fries

Boiled yuca can be cut into thick steak fries and then deep-fried in hot oil until crisp and golden. These fries are especially light and crisp with the underlying buttery flavor of yuca. Because the yuca has been first boiled, it puffs when fried, producing fries that look somewhat craggy and irregular. However, when served as a side dish with a Latin meal (and plenty of cold beers), they are every bit as delicious as fries made from potatoes, with an especially crisp texture.

You will need to fry the yuca in batches. You can keep the first batches warm on a baking sheet in a 300-degree oven for 10 minutes if you like. In my house, the smell of the garlicky oil draws everyone into the kitchen and the fries get eaten as soon as they come out of the hot oil.

SERVES 4 AS A SIDE DISH

1½ pounds yuca
    Salt
    About 4 cups peanut or vegetable oil for frying
4 large garlic cloves, peeled and lightly crushed

1. Cut the yuca into manageable chunks. Use a paring knife to remove the brown skin and outer ¼-inch layer of flesh. Quarter the peeled yuca lengthwise and then remove the spongy, stringy piece of the core attached to each quarter. Cut the peeled, cored yuca into 2-inch lengths.

2. Place the yuca pieces in a large saucepan. Add enough water to cover by several inches as well as salt to taste. Set the pan over high heat and bring to a boil. Reduce the heat and simmer until the yuca is just tender (test with a skewer), about 20 minutes. Drain the yuca and transfer it to a bowl of ice water. When cool, drain the yuca and cut it into strips that measure about 3 inches long and ½ inch thick. Pat the yuca thoroughly dry with paper towels.

3. Place 1½ inches of oil and the garlic cloves in a 4-quart saucepan. Turn the heat to high and heat until the garlic turns golden brown. Use a slotted spoon to remove and discard the garlic.

Add about one third of the yuca, making sure not to crowd the pan, and fry at 360 degrees until golden brown, 5 to 6 minutes. Use a slotted spoon to transfer the yuca fries to a platter lined with paper towels. Sprinkle the fries with salt and serve hot. Repeat with the remaining yuca.

Creamy Yuca Soup •

Potatoes and leeks are a classic combination in European soups. Yuca can be used in pretty much the same fashion as the potatoes to create a thick, smooth soup. Whole milk works fine here, but you can use half-and-half for added richness. I usually serve this soup hot (it makes a nice winter lunch), but it can be served chilled. To do so, simply whisk the milk into the pureed soup and don't bother to reheat the mixture as directed in step 4. The chilled soup can be refrigerated for a day before serving.

SERVES 6 TO 8 AS A FIRST COURSE

2 pounds yuca
2 tablespoons extra-virgin olive oil
3 medium leeks, white and light green parts, sliced thin
5 cups chicken stock
Pinch grated nutmeg
Salt
1 cup whole milk or half-and-half, or more as needed
Minced fresh chives for garnish

1. Cut the yuca into manageable chunks. Use a paring knife to remove the brown skin and outer ¼-inch layer of flesh. Quarter the peeled yuca lengthwise, and then remove the spongy, stringy piece of the core attached to each quarter. Cut the peeled, cored yuca into 1-inch lengths. Set aside.

2. Heat the oil in a large saucepan. Add the leeks and sauté over medium heat until softened, about 8 minutes.

3. Add the yuca, stock, nutmeg, and salt to taste. Bring to a boil, reduce the heat, and simmer until the yuca is quite tender, about 40 minutes.

4. Puree the soup, in batches if necessary, in a blender until smooth. Return the soup to a clean pot and turn the heat to medium-low. Whisk in enough milk to create a thick but smooth consistency. (You will need about 1 cup, perhaps a bit more.) Adjust the seasonings. Once the soup is hot, ladle portions into individual bowls and garnish with chives. Serve immediately.

Zucchini and Other Summer Squash

Bright green zucchini is the best-known summer squash in this country. Like all summer squash, zucchini have thin, edible skins and tender flesh. Zucchini are about 95 percent water—among vegetables, only lettuce contains more water—and have a mild, pleasant flavor. I find that zucchini benefit from dry-heating cooking methods, such as grilling and sautéing, which will drive off excess moisture and concentrate their flavor.

There are numerous kinds of summer squash grown in this country. Here are the most common varieties:

ZUCCHINI: This green squash has a firm texture and mild flavor. Most zucchini are elongated, although one variety grows in small balls the size of an orange or grapefruit.

YELLOW SQUASH: Crookneck is the most famous of the yellow squash. The skin on this variety is pale yellow and the shape of the fruit is cylindrical, like zucchini, except that the squash narrows at one end to form a curved neck. Personally, I find that zucchini has a better flavor and firmer texture than crookneck squash, which can be loaded with seeds. I like crookneck squash in soup, but it is my second choice for quick side dishes.

Another yellow squash variety is shaped like zucchini but has a vibrant yellow skin; some markets call it yellow or golden zucchini. I find that this yellow squash tastes and cooks just like green zucchini.

PATTYPAN SQUASH: Also called scallop squash, pattypan looks like squat flying saucers with scalloped edges. The skin can be various shades of yellow, green, and white and the flesh is particularly firm and sweet.

SQUASH BLOSSOMS: Bright orange blossoms, usually from zucchini but not always, are a summer delicacy. Gardeners are best able to appreciate this treat since blossoms must be cooked the day they are harvested. However, many farm stands sell squash blossoms. One near my home takes orders 24 hours in advance, picking as many as you need on a particular day. Squash blossoms are easy to prepare and delicious.

AVAILABILITY: Zucchini is available year-round, although the prime season for zucchini and other summer squash is summer through early fall. Squash blossoms cannot be shipped so they are found only when the local squash crop is in season.

SELECTION: Size and firmness are the most important factors when purchasing zucchini and summer squash. I find that smaller zucchini and yellow squash are more flavorful and less watery than larger specimens. Smaller squash also have fewer seeds. Look for squash that weigh less than 8 ounces, and ideally less than 6 ounces. Mammoth squash may be fine as boats for a vegetable stuffing, but they are not my first choice for quick side dishes. All squash no matter their size should be firm with no soft spots.

Pattypan should be firm like other squash with unblemished skin. I prefer small pattypan since they usually have fewer seeds.

When buying blossoms, make sure they are fully open and without bruises or blemishes. Wilted blossoms should not be purchased. Some stores stand blossoms in water (they are flowers after all) and I find that blossoms handled this way are generally in better shape when you get them home. When buying squash blossoms, ask when they were harvested. If it wasn't that morning, don't bother with the blossoms. If you garden, harvest squash blossoms just minutes before cooking.

Sometimes you will see blossoms attached to tiny zucchini, no bigger than your finger. See the recipe on page 376 for a suggestion about cooking the zucchini and their blossoms together.

STORAGE: Zucchini, yellow squash, and pattypan squash can be refrigerated in a loosely sealed plastic bag for several days. Don't try to store squash blossoms. They should be cooked the day they are harvested.

BASIC PREPARATION: Because summer squash grow close along the ground, tiny bits of dirt and sand can be embedded in their skin. Rinse all squash and then run your hand up and down the length of each one. If you feel any bumps, soak the squash in a bowl of cold water for 5 or 10 minutes to flush out these tiny granules of sand.

Once zucchini have been rinsed, they are ready to be cut. For sautéing, I generally slice them crosswise into thin circles and then salt the rounds to draw out some of the moisture. After an hour or so, the zucchini can be rinsed well to wash away the salt and then blotted dry. The other option when sautéing zucchini is to shred it in a food processor or on a box grater and then wring out the excess moisture in a towel.

Zucchini destined for the grill should be sliced from end to end so that you have large strips that won't fall through the grill rack. The intense heat of the grill will evaporate excess liquid in the zucchini. In addition, an open rack ensures that the liquid drops onto the coals, as opposed to sitting with the zucchini in a skillet.

Blossoms should be rinsed briefly to flush out any dirt or bugs. Shake gently to remove excess water and then blot dry if adding blossoms directly to hot oil without battering.

BEST COOKING METHODS: Broiling, grilling, and sautéing (either after shredding or salting). Very small squash can be thinly sliced and used raw in salads. Blossoms are best deep-fried, pan-fried, or poached.

OTHER RECIPES WITH ZUCCHINI:
Ratatouille (page 141)
Smoky Potato and Zucchini Stew (page 275)

Shredded Zucchini with Garlic and Herbs

This simple shredding and drying technique is the best choice when you are pressed for time and want to cook zucchini indoors. Use any fresh herb on hand, varying the amount depending on its intensity.

SERVES 4 AS A SIDE DISH

4 medium zucchini (about 1½ pounds)
3 tablespoons extra-virgin olive oil
2 medium garlic cloves, minced
1 to 2 tablespoons minced fresh herb leaves
   (see Headnote)
   Salt
   Freshly ground black pepper

1. Trim the ends from the zucchini. Shred the zucchini using the large holes on a box grater or the shredding disk of a food processor. Wrap the shredded zucchini in several layers of paper towels or in a kitchen towel and squeeze gently. Continue squeezing, using new towels if necessary, until the zucchini is fairly dry.
2. Heat the oil in a large skillet set over medium-high heat. Add the zucchini and garlic and cook, stirring occasionally, until the zucchini is tender, about 8 minutes. Stir in the herb and salt and pepper to taste. Serve immediately.

VARIATIONS: SHREDDED ZUCCHINI AND CARROT WITH GARLIC AND HERBS

A shredded carrot adds color and sweetness to this dish.

Reduce the number of zucchini to three and add 1 large carrot, peeled and shredded, to the pan along with the zucchini.

SHREDDED ZUCCHINI WITH CREAM AND HERBS

A richer variation that works especially well with fish.

Replace the olive oil with 2 tablespoons butter and 1 tablespoon vegetable oil. Omit the garlic. Add ¼ cup heavy cream along with the herb and briefly simmer until the cream is absorbed.

Sautéed Zucchini with Lemon and Parsley

Salting is necessary if you wish to sauté sliced zucchini. A thickness of ¼ inch is the best size. Thinner slices will fall apart during cooking, while thicker slices require longer salting in order to shed enough water before cooking.

SERVES 4 AS A SIDE DISH

4 medium zucchini (about 1½ pounds)
2 teaspoons kosher salt, plus more to taste
3 tablespoons extra-virgin olive oil

1 small onion or 2 large shallots, minced
½ teaspoon grated lemon zest
1 tablespoon lemon juice
2 tablespoons minced fresh parsley leaves
   Freshly ground black pepper

1. Slice the zucchini into ¼-inch-thick rounds. Place the zucchini in a colander and sprinkle with 2 teaspoons salt. Set the colander in a sink or over a plate for 30 minutes. Rinse and thoroughly dry the zucchini.

2. Heat the oil in a large skillet. Add the onion and sauté over medium heat until softened, about 3 minutes. Add the zucchini. Raise the heat to medium-high and cook, stirring occasionally, until the zucchini is golden brown, about 10 minutes.

3. Stir the lemon zest and juice, parsley, and pepper to taste into the pan. Toss the ingredients and heat through for another minute. Adjust the seasonings and serve immediately.

VARIATIONS: SAUTÉED ZUCCHINI WITH WALNUTS

Walnuts add a rich, slightly bitter flavor to this dish.

Omit the lemon zest and juice and add 2 tablespoons toasted and chopped walnuts along with the parsley.

SAUTÉED ZUCCHINI WITH OLIVES AND LEMON

This variation works well with grilled fish or chicken.

Add ¼ cup chopped pitted Kalamata olives along with the lemon zest and juice and replace the parsley with 1 to 2 teaspoons minced fresh thyme or oregano leaves.

SAUTÉED ZUCCHINI WITH PANCETTA

Use regular American bacon if you want to add a smoky note.

Cook 2 ounces chopped pancetta along with the onion and omit the lemon zest and juice.

Grilled Zucchini

This is one of the easiest and most delicious summer side dishes you can make. The zucchini can be served with beef, pork, chicken, or fish, and take very little preparation. Grilled zucchini are delicious at room temperature, so grill them first, then the main course. Serve as is or drizzle with a little balsamic vinegar once the zucchini comes off the grill.

SERVES 4 AS A SIDE DISH

4 medium zucchini (about 1½ pounds), cut lengthwise into ½-inch-thick strips
2 tablespoons extra-virgin olive oil
   Salt
   Freshly ground black pepper
   Balsamic vinegar, optional

1. Light the grill.

2. Lay the zucchini on a large baking sheet and brush both sides with the oil. Sprinkle generously with salt and pepper to taste.

3. Remove the zucchini from the baking sheet and put them on the grill when the fire is medium-hot. Grill them, turning once, until dark grill marks are visible on both sides, about 10 minutes. Transfer the zucchini to a platter. Drizzle with a little vinegar if desired. Serve hot, warm, or at room temperature.

Zucchini Fritters

These fritters are more like savory pancakes than conventional fritters, which are usually fried. The batter is pan-fried in a film of olive oil just until the exterior of the fritters becomes crisp. The interior remains soft and a bit creamy. I sometimes serve these fritters (one to a person) as a plated first course over some baby greens. The fritters can also be served as a side dish with chicken or fish. Or, serve two fritters per person as a light summer dinner, perhaps accompanied by a tomato salad.

SERVES 6 TO 8 AS A SIDE DISH OR FIRST COURSE OR 4 AS A LIGHT MAIN COURSE

1 pound zucchini

1 large garlic clove, minced

¾ teaspoon salt

¼ teaspoon ground black pepper

1 large egg

½ cup all-purpose flour

4 tablespoons extra-virgin olive oil

1 lemon, cut into wedges

1. Trim the ends from the zucchini. Shred the zucchini using the large holes on a box grater or the shredding disk of a food processor. Wrap the shredded zucchini in several layers of paper towels or in a kitchen towel and squeeze gently. Continue squeezing, using new towels if necessary, until the zucchini is dry.

2. Place the shredded and squeezed zucchini in a large bowl. Add the garlic, salt, pepper, and egg and mix well. Stir in the flour.

3. Heat 2 tablespoons of the oil in a medium nonstick skillet over medium heat. Fill a ¼-cup measure with the zucchini batter. Turn the batter into the hot pan and use the back of the spoon to shape the batter into a 2- to 3-inch patty. (Much like pancake batter, it will spread, but since the batter is quite thick, it's best to help it along.) Quickly repeat until the pan is full but not crowded. Sauté until the fritters are nicely browned on the bottom, 2 to 3 minutes. Turn the fritters and continue to cook until they are nicely browned on the second side, 2 to 3 minutes longer. Transfer the fritters to a platter lined with a paper towel to drain. Keep hot.

4. Briefly heat the remaining 2 tablespoons of oil in the empty skillet. Add the remaining batter as directed in step 3 to make more fritters. Cook the fritters until browned on both sides. Drain on paper towels. Serve the fritters hot with the lemon wedges.

Zucchini and Tomato Gratin with Pesto

Grilled strips of zucchini are layered with sliced tomatoes and pesto to create a lasagne-like dish, minus the pasta. Grilling the zucchini may seem like an extra step, but it's the only way to rid the zucchini of excess water that would otherwise make this dish soggy. As a vegetarian main course, serve with a leafy salad. As a side dish, pair this gratin with fish, chicken, or beef.

SERVES 6 AS A MAIN COURSE OR 8 TO 10 AS A SIDE DISH

8 medium zucchini (about 3 pounds), cut lengthwise into ½-inch-thick pieces

2 tablespoons extra-virgin olive oil

Salt

Freshly ground black pepper

4 medium ripe tomatoes (about 2 pounds), cored and sliced crosswise into ¼-inch-thick rounds

⅔ cup pesto

½ cup grated Parmesan cheese

1. Light the grill.

2. Lay the zucchini on two large baking sheets and brush both sides very lightly with the oil. Sprinkle generously with salt and pepper to taste. Remove the zucchini from the baking pan. Grill, turning once, over a medium-hot fire until dark grill marks are visible on both sides, about 10 minutes total. Cool slightly.

3. Preheat the oven to 400 degrees.

4. While waiting for the zucchini to cool, place the tomato slices in a single layer over a double layer of paper towels. Sprinkle lightly with salt and cover with another double layer of paper towels. Set aside for 10 minutes. Press lightly on the tomatoes so that the towels absorb the excess moisture.

5. Smear a generous tablespoon of pesto across the bottom of an 11 by 7-inch baking dish. Cover the bottom of the dish with a layer of grilled zucchini. Smear a generous tablespoon of pesto across the zucchini. Top with a layer of tomatoes. Smear another generous tablespoon of pesto across the top of the tomatoes. Repeat the layering of the zucchini, pesto, tomatoes, and pesto two more times, spreading any remaining pesto over the third (and last) layer of tomatoes. Sprinkle the cheese over the top.

6. Bake until the gratin is bubbling and the top is brown in spots, about 40 minutes. Let the gratin settle for 10 minutes. Serve hot or warm.

Zucchini "Carpaccio" with Parmesan and Parsley

Tender, young zucchini can be sliced very thin—the way cured beef is for the Italian dish known as carpaccio—and then served as an appetizer before a summer meal. I find this salad just as refreshing after dinner in place of a cheese course. Note that the quality of the ingredients in this dish is paramount. Use extra-virgin olive oil, the freshest parsley, Parmigiano-Reggiano (no substitutes), and, of course, just-picked zucchini without too many seeds. If you like, slice the zucchini on a mandoline. I find that a food processor slicing blade does a good job, too. Most cooks (myself included) won't be able to cut the zucchini thin enough using a chef's knife.

SERVES 4 TO 6 AS AN APPETIZER OR AFTER THE MAIN COURSE

3 small zucchini (about ¾ pound)
¼ cup packed fresh parsley leaves
2 tablespoons extra-virgin olive oil
  Salt
  Freshly ground black pepper
1 small hunk Parmesan cheese

1. Trim the ends from the zucchini. Using the slicing disk of a food processor, slice the zucchini into very thin rounds, no more than ⅛ inch thick and preferably much thinner. Arrange the zucchini rounds on a platter. Sprinkle with the parsley, then the oil, then salt and pepper to taste.
2. Using a vegetable peeler, remove thin shavings of cheese from the hunk of Parmesan. Shower several dozen cheese curls directly over the zucchini. (You will use about an ounce of cheese.) Serve immediately.

Parmesan-Crusted Zucchini

This unusual but simple recipe produces zucchini that is almost as crisp as fried zucchini. The combination of textures, not to mention the strong cheesy flavor, is unbeatable.

SERVES 4 TO 6 AS A SIDE DISH

4 large zucchini (about 2 pounds), cut lengthwise into ½-inch-thick strips
  Salt
2 tablespoons unsalted butter, melted
⅔ cup grated Parmesan cheese

1. Bring several quarts of water to a boil in a large saucepan. Add the zucchini and salt to taste. Cook until the zucchini is almost tender, about 5 minutes. Drain and place the zucchini in bowl of ice water. Drain again and pat thoroughly dry.
2. Adjust the top oven rack so it is 6 inches from the broiling element and preheat the broiler.
3. Place the zucchini on a large rimmed baking sheet. Brush the tops of the zucchini pieces with the butter and then sprinkle carefully with the cheese.
4. Broil the zucchini, watching carefully to prevent burning, until the tops (zucchini is not turned) are deeply browned and crisp, for about 12 to 15 minutes. (You don't want the zucchini to burn, but you do want it to brown as much as possible for the best flavor and texture.) Serve immediately.

Zucchini, Corn, and Red Pepper Sauté

Versions of this summer sauté are made throughout Mexico. I find that just 2 tablespoons of cream brings all the flavors together and gives the sauce a lovely consistency. The cream can be omitted if you don't mind a slightly less refined flavor and looser sauce.

SERVES 4 TO 6 AS A SIDE DISH

- 2 tablespoons extra-virgin olive oil
- 1 medium onion, chopped fine
- 1 medium red bell pepper, cored, seeded, and cut into ½-inch dice
- 1 medium jalapeño chile, stemmed, seeded, and minced
- 4 medium zucchini (about 1½ pounds), cut into ½-inch dice
  Salt
- 2 medium ears corn, husks and silks removed and discarded; kernels cut away from the cobs with a knife (about 1½ cups)
- ¾ cup chicken or vegetable stock
- 2 tablespoons heavy cream
- 2 tablespoons minced fresh cilantro leaves

1. Heat the oil in a large sauté pan. Add the onion, bell pepper, and chile and sauté over medium heat until the vegetables soften, about 6 minutes. Add the zucchini and raise the heat to medium-high. Sauté until the zucchini begin to brown, about 7 minutes. Season with salt to taste.

2. Add the corn and stock. Bring to a boil, cover, reduce the heat, and simmer until the corn is tender, about 5 minutes. Stir in the cream and cilantro and simmer just until the liquid in the pan thickens, about 2 minutes. Adjust the seasonings and serve immediately.

Slow-Sautéed Pattypan Squash with Onion and Parsley

Small pattypan squash, each the size of a golf ball, can be halved and sautéed very slowly to make them especially sweet-tasting. Because of their small size and high skin-to-flesh ratio, they hold their shape better than other squash and are my first choice for this preparation. However, small zucchini cut into ¾-inch-thick rounds could be handled the same way.

SERVES 4 AS A SIDE DISH

- 2 tablespoons extra-virgin olive oil
- 1 medium onion, minced
- 1½ pounds small pattypan squash (each the size of a golf ball), halved
  Salt
- 2 tablespoons minced fresh parsley leaves

1. Heat the oil in a large skillet. Add the onion and sauté over medium heat until softened, about 3 minutes. Add the squash and stir to coat well

with the oil and onion. Sprinkle generously with salt. Reduce the heat to medium-low.

2. Cook, stirring occasionally, until the squash is tender and golden brown in spots, 20 to 30 minutes. Stir in the parsley and adjust the seasonings. Serve immediately.

Beer-Batter Fried Squash Blossoms

Perhaps this is my favorite way to prepare squash blossoms because the effort is minimal and the results so addictive. Make sure to have everyone gathered in the kitchen ready to snack on the hot blossoms. Wait even 5 minutes and the blossoms will be soggy.

SERVES 4 AS AN APPETIZER OR SNACK

  1 cup beer
  ⅔ cup flour
 12 large squash blossoms
    About 4 cups peanut or vegetable oil for frying
    Coarse salt

1. Pour the beer in a medium bowl and let stand until flat, about 1 hour. Place the flour in a small mesh strainer. Sieve the flour over the bowl of beer, whisking constantly to incorporate the flour. When all the flour has been added, the batter will have the consistency of heavy cream.

2. Rinse the squash blossoms and inspect them for insects.

3. Heat 1½ inches of oil in a deep 4-quart pot to a temperature of 375 degrees.

4. Working with three or four blossoms at a time, dip them into the batter and let the excess drip back into the bowl. Add the batter-coated blossoms to the hot oil and fry, turning once, until golden brown and crisp, 3 to 4 minutes.

5. Use a slotted spoon to transfer the fried blossoms to a platter lined with paper towels. (The blossoms can hold on to oil, so try to tip the spoon slightly to pour as much oil back in the pot as possible.) Sprinkle the blossoms generously with salt and serve immediately. Repeat the process with the remaining blossoms.

Pan-Fried Squash Blossoms with Cheese Filling

The cheese filling makes this blossom dish more substantial and appropriate as the first course of an elegant summer meal. Pan-frying is less turbulent than deep-frying, so the filling won't leak quite as much. Try to twist the ends of the blossoms shut just as they go into the pan so they seal in the filling. If you have blossoms with tiny (no larger than a pinkie) zucchini attached, you can cook the zucchini with the blossoms. Although the blossoms are best served straight from the pan, the first batch can be kept warm for several minutes in a 250-degree oven while you cook the remaining blossoms.

SERVES 6 AS A FIRST COURSE

1 cup ricotta cheese
¼ cup grated Parmesan cheese
1 tablespoon minced fresh basil or tarragon leaves
  Salt
  Freshly ground black pepper
12 large squash blossoms
2 large eggs
2 tablespoons water
1 cup cornmeal
1 cup extra-virgin olive oil
  Lemon wedges

1. Combine the cheeses, basil, and salt and pepper to taste in a small bowl.

2. Rinse the squash blossoms and inspect them for insects. Blot the blossoms dry on a paper towels.

3. Gently spoon a heaping tablespoon of the filling into each blossom. Press the ends of each blossom shut to enclose the filling. Beat the eggs in a shallow bowl with the water. Measure the cornmeal into another shallow bowl.

4. Heat the oil in a large skillet over medium-high heat. While the oil is heating, dip half the blossoms in the egg mixture then roll them in the cornmeal. When the oil is shimmering, add the cornmeal-coated blossoms, twisting the ends of each blossom shut just before it goes into the pan. Fry, turning occasionally, until golden brown and crisp on all sides, 4 to 5 minutes.

5. Use a slotted spoon to transfer the blossoms to a platter lined with paper towels. Sprinkle with salt to taste and serve with the lemon wedges. Repeat the battering and frying process with the remaining blossoms.

Index

red wine:
   leeks braised in, 197
   portobello mushrooms with
      oregano and, 217
rice and pea soup, Italian, 246
risi e bisi, 246
risotto with radicchio, pancetta, and
   onion, 280–81
roasted, roasting, xiv
   artichokes and new potatoes, 4–5
   asparagus salad with blood orange
      vinaigrette, 17
   asparagus with olive oil and salt,
      16
   asparagus with peanut sauce,
      16–17
   asparagus with rosemary and
      garlic, 16
   beet salad with lemon and olives,
      29–30
   beet salad with sherry vinegar,
      29
   beet salad with walnuts and goat
      cheese, 30
   carrots and turnips, 83
   chicken breasts with duxelles,
      219
   endive with Gruyère, 145
   fennel and red onions, 164
   garlic and potato soup, 167–68
   green beans with garlic and gin-
      ger, 174–75
   Jerusalem artichokes with garlic
      and mixed herbs, 180
   kohlrabi with whole garlic cloves,
      191
   onions with balsamic vinegar and
      rosemary, 231–32
   parsnips with balsamic vinegar
      and rosemary, 238–39
   potatoes with rosemary and
      garlic, 271–72
   potato salad with mustard-
      balsamic vinaigrette, 272
   radishes with soy and sesame
      seeds, 284
   shallots with vinegar, 298

squash pieces with fresh herbs,
   355
sweet potato "fries," 318
tomatillo salsa with ancho chiles,
   326
roasted peppers, 252–53
   with onion, 256
   with sherry vinegar, green olives,
      and capers, 255
   simple uses for, 252
roasted red pepper:
   and mozzarella sandwiches with
      basil, 254
   sauce for pasta, 255
   soup with basil cream, 256–57
   spread with goat cheese and
      herbs, 253
   spread with Near Eastern flavors,
      253
romaine lettuce, 200
rosemary:
   broiled boniato with rum-brown
      sugar sauce and, 40
   and garlic mashed potatoes,
      265
   pan-cooked new potatoes with
      garlic and, 274–75
   roasted asparagus with garlic and,
      16
   roasted onions with balsamic
      vinegar and, 231–32
   roasted parsnips with balsamic
      vinegar and, 238–39
   roasted potatoes with garlic and,
      271–72
rum-brown sugar sauce, broiled
   boniato with rosemary and,
   40
rutabaga(s), 288–91
   about, 288
   "fries" with warm spices, 290
   mashed, and apples with sautéed
      onions, 289–90
   mashed, with orange and ginger,
      289
   stewed, with chard and garlic,
      290–91

sage, spaghetti squash with Parmesan
   and, 356–57
salad:
   arugula, see arugula salad
   avocado, orange and radish, with
      lime-chile dressing, 24–25
   avocado and shrimp, with
      grapefruit dressing, 25
   baby spinach, broiled or grilled
      portobellos and, 217
   beet, roasted, with lemon and
      olives, 29–30
   beet, roasted, with sherry vinegar,
      29
   beet, roasted, with walnuts and
      goat cheese, 30
   Caesar, 204–5
   Caesar, grilled chicken, 205
   calabaza, steamed, with sour
      orange-chile vinaigrette, 74
   carrot, bistro, 84
   celery, apple, and walnut, 95
   celery heart, with pears and
      Parmesan, 96
   celery root and apple, with
      creamy mustard dressing, 99
   chayote and tomato, with lime
      and allspice, 109–10
   corn, grilled, tomato, and red
      onion, 118
   cucumber, Asian, with sesame,
      126
   cucumber, spicy, with peanuts,
      127
   cucumber, with yogurt and dill,
      126
   daikon, shredded, with sesame
      seeds, 287
   eggplant, grilled, with Thai
      flavors, 136–37
   endive, watercress, and pear,
      147–48
   endive and apple, tart, 148
   escarole and orange, with sherry
      vinaigrette, 151–52
   fennel and apple, 160
   fennel and orange, Italian, 161